PRAISE FOR MI MOTO FIDEL:

"Baker's kiss-and-tell account of his romps across Fidel's island offers a bittersweet glimpse of life inside the last Marxist utopia."
     —**Jon Lee Anderson,** author of *Che Guevara: A Revolutionary Life*

"Chris Baker's chaotic pilgrimage—by turns sharp-eyed, lustful, poetic, feverish, and joyful—brings a tropical nation of 10 million to vivid, pulsating life. The motorcycle proves itself, once again, a brilliant, ice-breaking instrument of true travel."
     —**Ted Simon,** author of
     Jupiter's Travels: Four Years Around the World on a Triumph

"*Mi Moto Fidel* should be in the briefcase of every man in midlife. The erotically charged adventure through the forbidden island by a man on a motorcycle in his 40s is a fantastic fantasy realized.... It captures a whole receding time and place with prickly cinematic takes."
     —**Richard Bangs,** Editor-in-Chief, Expedia.com

"Baker's intriguing account of his romp through Cuba on a fire-engine-red motorcycle is perhaps the most thorough portrait of this faded Communist country to date. Baker effectively captures the essence of the Cuban people—primarily their generosity and resilient spirit.... After reading *Mi Moto Fidel,* you'll no doubt be inspired to hit the road."
     —**Jill Fergus,** Amazon.com

"Baker's efforts to reconcile [preconceived] visions of the country as a socialist and sensual Shangri-la with the reality of life drive this energetic street-by-street examination of contemporary Cuba."
     —**Kevin Baxter,** *Miami Herald*

"Baker is a terrific writer... adept at both deeply scored portraits of the people he met and penetrating analysis of the wacko politics and economics of the Castro regime. And throughout, his enthusiasm for Cuba and its people leap off the page."
     —**Douglas J. Johnson,** *Winnipeg Free Press*

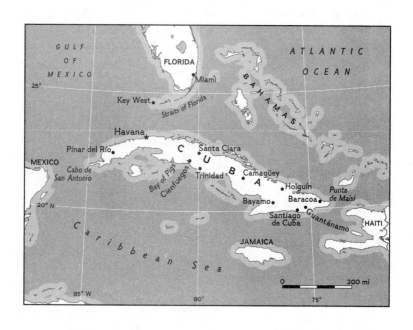

MI MOTO FIDEL

Also by Christopher P. Baker

National Geographic Traveler: Costa Rica
Costa Rica Handbook
Cuba Handbook
Havana Handbook

MI MOTO FIDEL

Motorcycling through Castro's Cuba

Christopher P. Baker

NATIONAL GEOGRAPHIC
ADVENTURE PRESS

WASHINGTON, D.C.

Published by the National Geographic Society
1145 17th Street NW, Washington, D.C. 20036

First Printing February 2001
First Paperback Edition 2002

Interior design by Melissa Farris
Printed and bound by R. R. Donnelley & Sons, Crawfordsville, Indiana

Library of Congress Cataloging-in-Publication Data

Baker, Christopher P., 1955-
  Mi moto Fidel : motorcycling through Castro's Cuba / Christopher P. Baker.
    p. cm.
  ISBN 0-7922-6422-3 (paperback) ISBN 0-7922-7961-1 (hardcover)
  1. Cuba--Description and travel. 2. Cuba--Social conditions--1959- 3. Cuba--Economic
conditions--1990- 4. Motorcycling--Cuba. 5. Baker, Christopher P.,
1955---Journeys--Cuba. I. Title.

F1765.3 .B34 2000   917.29104'64--dc21   00-052684

One of the world's largest nonprofit scientific and educational organizations, the National Geographic Society was founded in 1888 "for the increase and diffusion of geographic knowledge." Fulfilling this mission,
the Society educates and inspires millions every day through its magazines, books, television programs,
videos, maps and atlases, research grants, the National Geographic Bee, teacher workshops, and innovative
classroom materials. The Society is supported through membership dues, charitable gifts, and income from
the sale of its educational products. This support is vital to National Geographic's mission to increase global
understanding and promote conservation of our planet through exploration, research, and education.

For more information, please call
1-800-NGS LINE (647-5463)
or write to the following address:

National Geographic Society
1145 17th Street N.W.
Washington, D.C. 20036-4688 U.S.A.

Visit the Society's Web site at www.nationalgeographic.com.

CONTENTS

MI MOTO FIDEL

PREFACE

I n January 1994 I signed a contract to write a guidebook on Cuba. I had three years to complete the project, but I immediately became excited about writing a narrative of my experiences as well. Two travelogues on Cuba had been published within the past decade. In each, the authors had traveled by car. I wanted something different, something sexy—something like a motorcycle.

Touring Cuba by *moto* made sense: A motorcycle would be more versatile than a car, taking me places a car might not be able to reach. Above all, I liked the panache; the bike would turn my travels into adventures, and Cuba seemed like a great place to ride. I saw myself as a latter-day Ernesto "Che" Guevara, who had set out from Buenos Aires in November 1952 to explore South America on an ancient Norton motorcycle. His *Motorcycle Diaries*, published posthumously in 1995, provide a lively account of what might have been the adventure of Che's lifetime, had he not hooked up with Fidel Castro and turned his existence into an even more fantastic adventure. Che fills his book with moving examples of his idealism, hinting at an evolving tilt toward communism that found its full blossoming when he became Cuba's Minister of Finance and Industry following the "triumph of the Revolution." Philosophically Che and I started at a similar reference point; ultimately, by contrast, my own Cuban journey tilted me the other way. But that would come later.

I figured the project would be costly. The guidebook publisher was paying royalties only, so I would not see any return until after the guidebook's appearance. I needed a major infusion of cash. Hence, in November 1994 I signed a contract with another publisher to write a guidebook on Jamaica, with a plump payment up front. I could hammer out the book in a little over a year, I figured, reading up on Cuba all the while. Jamaica would also make a superb springboard for preliminary forays to the forbidden island.

As a full-time professional journalist, I could travel to Cuba and spend money there under a "general license" without requesting official permission from the U.S. Treasury Department. The biggest stumbling block would be transporting a motorcycle. I had two options: air or sea. Either way, direct traffic from the United States seemed out of the question. Under provisions of the U.S. embargo, no commercial transportation is allowed between the United States and Cuba. Worse yet, in 1992 the Torricelli (Cuban Democracy) Act had closed U.S. ports and airports to any foreign vessel that had called in Cuba or carried Cuban goods or nationals during the previous six months. My only options seemed to be to freight the bike via Mexico, Canada, or a Caribbean island.

I made my first reconnaissance trip from Jamaica in September 1994, returned to Cuba in October, and followed up with several visits to Havana in 1995. In February 1996, after two years' preparation, I shipped my motorcycle to Cuba and toured the island from end to end, logging 7,008 miles. It was a fascinating time to be there. Cuban MiGs had just shot down two private planes operated by a Cuban-American organization, Brothers to the Rescue, over the Straits of Florida. Washington was at the boiling point, and the understandably edgy Cubans had heightened their internal security.

Cuba was also just beginning to recover from the worst traumas of the "Special Period"— the draconian conditions imposed when the Cuban economy imploded after the Soviet bloc collapsed. The hardships had ruptured the nation's ethics and social fabric, making my travels there both disheartening and uplifting. I saw Cuba sweet and sour. The mainstream media were full of grim stories about Cuba's desperation, and the finger of blame was pointed squarely at Fidel Castro and the communist system. My own inclinations, fed by a youthful flirtation with socialism, were to blame the U.S. embargo initiated in 1961 by President John F. Kennedy, a ban that still hung over Cuba like an ax. As I explored the island and attempted to make sense of the Cuban enigma, I would experience a radical shift of sympathies.

In October 1994, I had met a wonderful 18-year-old *habanera* named Daisy. Over the next two years, she filled my time in Havana with incredible joy. By the time I arrived with my BMW motorcycle, however, our time together had run its course, and during my ensuing journey through Cuba I had intimate encounters with several other women. Those experiences are a part of this book because they illustrate an overriding Cuban quality: its eroticism.

I have used the voices of Cubans I met along the way to explain how my experiences reshaped my perceptions of the country. Only one person asked me to change his or her identity to guard against reprisals. Nonetheless, I have opted to mask real names on several other occasions, and have chosen to relocate at least one individual. The characters and conversations themselves, however, remain quite real.

—Christopher P. Baker
December 2000

≈

CHAPTER ONE

CROSSING OVER

I cruised to Cuba at night like the smuggled human freight in Ernest Hemingway's *To Have and Have Not*. The boat yawled drunkenly as gunmetal waves smashed violently against the bow. I hung on grimly.

"Don't vorry, your bike vill be in Havana," Rolf Runerberg said unconvincingly, his voice rising and dipping like the great swelling sea. The Finnish skipper gripped his bottle of rum. "I hit a rock and ve sunk last year, but I got her patched up okay."

The *Kalevala*, a 58-foot cruiser, was in decrepit shape. Bits of superstructure were scattered about the boat. My BMW motorcycle was wedged between two 55-gallon fuel drums to keep it from rolling overboard. But the pounding and heaving was tossing the motorcycle around, and the rear rail to which it was tethered was missing most of the screws that secured the rail to the hull. In my mind's eye I saw the rail collapse and a great splash as my Beemer hit the ocean, a gift to King Neptune. Bile—from anxiety, not the sea—rose in my stomach.

Three hours out of Key West, I watched the shadows thicken into the blackness of the tropical night. In the dark the seas grew ever larger, the screaming wind slicing off streaks of foam. We were being pummeled by waves 15 feet high. The *Kalevala* was smashing the bottom of huge troughs as though she had fallen off a cliff top. It was a dangerous business. Despite what Rolf said, beads of sweat beetled his brow. *I should have flown.* Only a madman would sail to Cuba on a night like this.

With images of disaster fevering my mind, I decided to tether the bike more securely. The deck rolled beneath me as I slithered across it on my butt. I braced myself between the fuel drums and tied ropes around the motorbike's frame and wheels, then looped them around the stanchions that held up the roof, figuring that would help stop the bike from falling overboard if the rear rail gave way. The wind had ripped the nylon cover off the bike, which was being lashed by salt spray and waves. I recalled my friend Ted Simon's words of wisdom: "If the bike's going to be on deck, be sure to cover it with a tarpaulin and a thick coating of grease."

As I crab-crawled my way back to the cockpit, the boat heeled sharply, spinning me around on my back and hurtling me across the slick deck—which was falling from beneath me. I grabbed desperately for a stanchion and felt a searing pain in my shoulder as the sudden jolt twirled me onto my stomach. I hung on grimly with my feet dangling over the pitch-black void. One of my panniers—the one containing my laptop computer—whizzed past my head. Miraculously, I caught it with my free hand. I scrambled back to the forecastle and, feeling fortunate to be alive, took a hearty swig from Rolf's bottle of rum.

It was a hell of a start for my journey, but I had been given ample warning: "Brother," wrote Ernest Hemingway, "don't let anybody tell you there isn't plenty of water between Key West and Havana!"

At 1 a.m., Rolf announced he was going below for a nap.

"You take the vheel. But listen. The compass vos fitted only two day ago. It hasn't been calibrated. I figure it is reading ten degrees off true," he said dolefully. "But you haf no problem. The electronic navigation system tells you the course deviation and distance."

He showed me how to read the electronic instrument panel, which glowed luminously in the dark and displayed our position relative to Havana, pinpointed by satellite. An arrow showed the direction to steer. All I had to do was keep the arrow pointed to 12 o'clock.

I sat in the wooden captain's chair, which swiveled like a lopsided bar stool, tipping first to port, then to starboard as the swells passed beneath us. The seas muscling up through the wooden wheel as waves slammed against the port bow. A moment's relaxation and the bow would swing around, sending the waves crashing into us broadside.

The sky was a canvas of India ink. Stars sparkled brilliantly and the lustrous moon cast the heaving swells in high relief, edging the taluses in opalescence and sinking the depths in dark shadow. The play of light and shadow gave me fair warning of massive rogue waves bearing down with frightening force. The ocean—a giant whale rising beneath us—heaved the *Kalevala* skyward. We hung in midair momentarily, then came a vacant sensation in my stomach as we fell. I braced myself against the shuddering impact as we plunged down into the troughs. The vessel quaked and made gut-wrenching groans, and the wheel stuttered like a Gatling gun in my hand.

Suddenly the lights of the navigation system went out. *Uh-oh!* I wondered whether or not to wake Rolf, but decided against it; I would steer by the compass instead. It bobbed in a sea of oil inside a large glass globe, like a crystal ball glowing red from within.

I found myself thinking of the crisis in U.S.-Cuba relations that had erupted six days earlier, when Cuban MiGs shot down two private planes piloted by members of Brothers to the Rescue—a Miami-based Cuban-American group founded by José Basulto, an anti-Castro Cuban exile and Bay of Pigs veteran. Since 1991, the group had been flying over the Straits of Florida looking for *balseros*— people fleeing Cuba on homemade rafts. The flow of balseros had effectively stopped following immigration accords between the U.S. and Cuba in September 1995, so the group began buzzing Havana to drop leaflets inciting Cubans to overthrow Castro. On February 24, when two Brothers to the Rescue Cessnas made a beeline for Havana, the Castro regime blasted them out of the sky ten miles north of Cuban waters.

I had watched TV newscasts flash pictures of F-15s and F-16s bristling on alert as 18 civilian planes piloted by Cuban exiles lifted into the wet sky aiming for the spot 21 miles northwest of Havana where their brethren had gone down. Then the screen filled with dramatic scenes of a flotilla of 35 vessels carrying angry Cuban exiles churning through storm-tossed seas. The small craft had put out from Key West to drop red roses at the fatal site. Eleven Coast Guard vessels tagged along to keep a lid on things, but the Coast Guard eventually called a halt and turned the flotilla around because of the tempestuous seas.

Then, with tensions mounting, President Clinton placed a moratorium on sea traffic to Cuba. I had hoped to slip into Cuba quietly, but tonight the Coast Guard was out in force. Three U.S. warships were cruising the straits, and

AWACs—Air Force radar-tracking planes—circled above, keeping tabs on all sea and air traffic.

It seemed a portentous moment to be heading to Cuba.

We were ten hours out from Key West, and the loveliness of the sea had eclipsed my deep sense of danger and isolation. I was instinctively responding to the roll and pitch of the ocean, playing the slack and tension in the wheel the way a fisherman feeds and reels the line of a sporting gamefish. My alertness, sharpened by fear, soon gave way to familiarity and fatigue. The rhythmic rolling had a calming quality, like the rocking of a crib. Drowsiness washed over me. My eyelids grew heavy, then closed.

BOOM!

A massive wave crashed over the bow, startling me awake. The *Kalevala* heeled acutely, and for a heart-stopping moment I thought it was over. I was thrown to the floor as the wave burst over the deck. Water poured into the cabin. As we swung broadside on the wind, another huge wave smashed into us, tearing the roof from the metal stanchion to which I had tethered the bike. I struggled to my feet and fought to get the ship hove-to. As we swung slowly into the wind, the *Kalevala* began to push forward once more, like an acrobat feeling for his footing after a near disaster. I looked over my shoulder. The motorbike was still there.

"*Vot the hell happen?*" cried Rolf, clawing his way up the stairwell. "I thought ve capsize!"

"Just testing to see if you were awake," I answered meekly. Below, cupboards had been flung open and their contents scattered across the floor. Broken glass was washing about the galley floor. How on earth had he managed to sleep anyway?

"The lights on the satellite positioning screen went out a couple of hours ago. I've been steering by the compass," I added.

Rolf touched a button and the digital panel came back to life. He peered at the tiny screen and did a double-take. His brow tightened.

"*Vot course haf you been steering?*"

"Er, 240 degrees west, like you told me," I replied.

"The compass is wrong. You haf to compensate ten degrees. *I told you zis!*"

"But I have been."

"Then you haf been steering the wrong way. For God's sake, ve are heading for Cozumel."

"Would you like to take the wheel, captain?" I replied abjectly.

Rolf swung the *Kalevala* around, directly perpendicular to the waves, which smashed into us head-on, making a thunderous clap that shook the boat like a jackhammer. The motorbike was being lifted from the deck with each fall. The roof, no longer secured to its stanchion, was flapping wildly up and down. A sudden squall would tear it clean off.

I'm not a believer, but that night, for the first time in years, I hedged my bets and offered a silent prayer. In response, the right engine quit.

"Blocked fuel lines," said Rolf, trying not to seem worried. His cheek twitched as if snagged on a fishhook. He disappeared below. Five minutes later he emerged, looking alarmed and sweating as if he had just stepped from a sauna.

"I need your help. Come! Come!" he cried. To leave the helm in these seas seemed like madness, but with trepidation I followed him down to the engine room.

The *Kalevala* was a stinking little den below the waterline, reeking of diesel and bilge. The one working General Electric diesel engine was clattering like an iron foundry gone mad, producing not only noise but tremendous heat. The stench of fuel and fumes tore at my stomach. I hung back as far in the companionway as possible, holding a light while Rolf lay on his side in the sloshing water, prying and hammering and swearing in the glare. I couldn't hear a word over the deafening *thwunk-thwunk* of the second engine, but I could tell he was swearing profusely as he scuffed his knuckles and banged his head on hot metal.

The boat was rolling untended in the ocean swells, but below the waterline the motion wasn't too bad. If not for the heat and stench, I might have ridden out the storm below. Thankfully the engine kicked back to life.

The seas died down abruptly about six that morning. The stars faded and the sun rose like a benediction, splashing Cuba with blazing orange and mauve. We scudded before the wind under shafts of amber light. I was at the helm, steering due south for Havana hovering faintly on the horizon.

I leaned against the wheel with the wind whipping my hair and took in the astonishing view. To the west, the Sierra de Rosario reared up like a crocodile-backed sea beast, its peaks smothered in purpling cloud; to the east, an elevated plateau slanted gradually to thread-thin beaches silvered in twilight. Havana emerged from the cobalt sea. An imposing castle loomed over the harbor entrance, guarding the waters where Spanish treasure fleets once marshaled for the return voyage to Europe.

The rising sun washed the ancient city in gold. Old Havana unfolded like an abandoned stage set, its gilded castles and churches and columned mansions rising above narrow, deep-shadowed streets that radiated toward the harbor like a fan. I felt a jumbled welling of emotions, as if in crossing the Straits of Florida I had just traveled to the far ends of the world.

Key West to Havana—90 miles of shimmering ocean that had been churned into a watery no-man's-land by political bile. I had just crossed the widest, deepest moat in the world.

Winston Churchill had felt "delirious yet tumultuous" as he approached Havana by sea in 1895. "I felt as if I sailed with Long John Silver and first gazed on Treasure Island. Here was a place where anything might happen. Here was a place where something would certainly happen. Here I might leave my bones."

As the *Kalevala* slipped into the harbor channel of Marina Hemingway, I too felt that intangible yet irresistible aura of adventure and promise.

CHAPTER TWO

HAVANA HIGH LIFE

H*avana!* I can't wipe the grin off my face.

After three hours of methodical officialdom oiled by charitable dispensations of cigarettes and beer, I coax the immigration officials into helping manhandle the BMW onto the dock. Cubans gather reverentially. One volunteers to hose down the bike, and I take him up on it for a few dollars. Then I get to work with elbow grease and metal cleaner, removing the rust that has already started to show on the disc brake and chrome. Standing back to admire my Teutonic marvel shimmering in the magnesium light like a muscular horse, I break out my camera to prove I am here.

I had imagined it would take all day to clear the Beemer through Customs, but in no time at all I'm issued a permit that grants me seven days to register with the police and receive a *chapa* (license plate). Four hours after arriving in Cuba, I wheel through the gates of Marina Hemingway and turn east for downtown Havana.

First I call on my friend Sandra Levinson, director of the New York-based Center for Cuban Studies, at her apartment on Avenida Primera in the leafy Miramar district.

"Sandra isn't here!" A middle-aged lady peers down from a third-floor window. "She's in New York," she continues in Spanish, eying me with avid curiosity. Am I a friend of Sandra's? Yes, I tell her—I've just arrived and am seeking an apartment.

"Oh, I have one," she exclaims, lighting up. "Come!"

We agree on a nightly fee of $20, and I haul my bags up the narrow stairs. Then, unable to contain my excitement any longer, I fire up and roar off to find Daisy, my Cuban girlfriend.

Cruising along the Malecón, the boulevard that follows Havana's dramatic shoreline, I feel trapped in a 1950s time warp. Relics from the heyday of Detroit are everywhere: Chrome-laden Chryslers, corpulent Cadillacs, and other voluptuous dowagers conjure up the gaudy excess that marked halcyon Havana. They putter along beside modern Japanese taxis, sober Russian-made Ladas, and 650cc Ural motorcycles belching out smoke. Bicyclists are everywhere, too, wobbling through the streets with a leisurely disdain for traffic. Havana has all the sunwashed sadness and sultry spontaneity of Naples and New Orleans.

I curl along Zapata past the flamboyant mausoleums of Cementerio de Colón, roar down Paseo toward the sprawling Plaza de la Revolución, turn right past the labyrinthine government palace where Castro and the Council of Ministers hatch their perplexing policies of state, sweep south down palm-shaded Avenida de la Independencia, and veer left on Calzada del Cerro.

Calzada del Cerro—or Monte, as locals prefer to call it—invokes a deep melancholy. During the last century, wealthy families built summer homes in classical style on the cool hill, or *cerro*, south of Habana Vieja (Old Havana) to escape the torrid heat. By the 1930s the rich families had begun moving out to newer, more fashionable suburbs. Ruin set in, hastened after Castro took power when his government parceled out the former homes of the white upper and middle classes to others who couldn't afford the upkeep. In later years the mansions were subdivided into smaller and smaller apartments, and the ruin accelerated. Many of the houses transcend sordid; they should have faced the bulldozer's maw ages ago. It is a blight I will see throughout Cuba.

I steered past an obstacle course of potholes and rubble and wooden braces propping up teetering buildings, then turned onto San Cristóbal and cut the engine. Three young boys stopped chasing hoops. Others materialized as if from thin air. They stood at a respectful distance, staring wide-mouthed as I dismounted and locked the front wheel. Old men in grubby singlets and flip-flops sat listlessly beneath crumbling colonial cornices and laundry-laced balconies, thinking of who knows what faded dreams.

The stairs to Daisy's apartment were so dilapidated I was afraid to step onto them. Makeshift wiring festooned the tenement.

Ten families shared the building, which had been subdivided and a new floor added to create extra rooms called *barbacoas*, originally meaning "houses on stilts." Daisy lived with her mother, Alicia, in a single room, about 12 feet by 18, with a small tiled sink and gas stove at the rear and a rustic stone-floored shower and toilet tucked in one corner. A tall armoire and a chest of drawers stood against one wall. Two small metal-frame beds abutted another wall, leaving room for a couple of rockers from which to watch their Russian-made Zenith TV. Daisy's grandmother and aunt lived in a neighboring barbacoa. A cousin lived alone in a third.

Each of the family members had applied for passports and exit permits. Because Castro does not appreciate Cubans who disdain the Revolution, the Cuban government had turned its back on them. The quintet clung tenaciously to family life behind crumbling, unpainted walls mildewed by tropical mire.

I peered in through the half-open door. Daisy, Alicia, and the cousin sat on the stone floor, playing cards.

"¡Hola!"

"¡Cristóbal!"

Daisy leaped to her feet and engulfed me in her embrace. I held her head to my chest while she squeezed. Alicia stepped forward and kissed me. The cousin clasped me fondly.

"And your *moto?*" Daisy asked softly.

"Yes, yes, it's downstairs. Come and look."

I squired them down the rickety stairs and into the street. The trio oohed and aahed at the magnificent moto.

"Never did I think you would bring it," said Daisy, leaning her head against me. "Cristóbal, where are you living?"

"Remember Sandra? I have an apartment with one of her neighbors," I replied. "Come on. Let's go for a ride."

I set off briskly with Daisy clinging tightly behind.

"Do you like it?" I asked.

"Sí...Sí...¡Es magnífico!" she replied, reaching forward and gently pinching my cheek. I loved it when she did that.

We swept down Monte past crumbling colonnaded mansions that James Michener had perceived as "marching backward into the past." I threaded between the freewheeling bicyclists spilling through Parque de la Fraternidad, turned left past the Hotel Inglaterra with its tourists sipping beers on the patio, and merged into the courtly boulevard colloquially known as the Prado, which flows gracefully downhill to the Malecón and the harbor channel. Schoolchildren in prim uniforms sat in neat circles in the shade of Spanish laurel trees on the raised pedestrian median, listening attentively to lessons presented alfresco while old men and women gossiped on ornate marble benches.

Passing the Castillo de San Salvador, I could make out the SAU-100 tank that Castro had commanded at the Bay of Pigs. The vehicle squatted in front of the Palacio de la Revolución, the presidential palace from which dictator Fulgencio Batista had spun a web of corruption that turned Havana into a tropical buffet of sin. Assassins and conspirators still lurk in the shadows; the whiff of liaison and adventure is still in the air.

I sense that I am living in a romantic thriller, riding through Havana with the wind in my hair and the woman I love gripping my waist. Everyone is staring at the Brobdingnagian Beemer with its rider in leather pants and a stunning *negrita* in a flame-red skirt slit to the thigh.

Daisy is exhilarated too. Our craving needs no words. So, west along the Malecón. Under the tunnel of the Río Almendares. Right onto Avenida Primera. Soon we are in my apartment, and she is stripping in front of me.

"Cristóbal," she croons, "I have longed for this moment. Make love to me like before."

We make love while a fan stirs the hot, languid air.

"I like look you in your *ojos azules*," she says later, staring deeply into my eyes. "When you kiss me is living in one dream. For this, never stop of kiss me," she says. But I know it cannot be. I sense this is the last time we will share ourselves fully. The woman I have loved for two years is now married to another man, and soon she will leave Cuba forever.

I had briefly been the luckiest man in the world, and my anguish is amplified by the knowledge that it was I who had tossed aside the opportunity to marry this precious jewel. Months before, Daisy had confessed to me that she also had an Italian lover; a regular visitor to Cuba, he was in ardent pursuit.

Whether he had entered her life before or after I met her I did not know—nor did I care, for it changed not a bit how I felt toward her (nor she toward me).

Daisy was a pragmatist. Like scores of other young Cubans, she dreamed of escaping a dismal life. She had picked me up in the Plaza de Armas by placing herself in my line of vision and tendering a priceless smile. But Daisy would have laughed to be called a *jinetera* (literally "jockey," from *jineta*, or horse-woman), a woman who forms an intimate relationship with a tourist for financial gain. She wanted more than a generous suitor who could wine and dine her, buy her fashionable clothes, pay her way into fancy discos, and grant her a stipend—assuredly more in one night than she could otherwise earn in a month—as a charitable afterthought for a romantic encounter. Life held no hope for her here. She wanted a foreign boyfriend who would marry her and take her away. With the Italian, Daisy was hedging her bets against me. A wise move: In September, he had proposed.

"He is *dulce* [sweet], but I don't want make my life with the Italiano. This I do for you because I don't want another man. I want you," she beseeched me. *"Tu iluminas mi vida. Estoy enamorada de ti. Te extraño mucho.* You illuminate my life. I love you. I yearn for you. *Quiero hacerte llegar al cielo y ver las estrellas.* I want to make you arrive at the heavens and see the stars," she said poetically.

Daisy's letters, too, were filled with adoration and anguish.

"Cristóbal, I must know how you feel toward me," she implored. "I fear that you will forget me."

When I was with her I bubbled over with radiant joy. I felt alive, enraptured, carefree, as if I had slept with Aphrodite, the Greek goddess of love and beauty. According to Greek legend, premature old age is the penalty paid by mortals who dare to sleep with a goddess. But my Cuban nymphet filled me with sensations of youthful immortality. I loved her as one might love an angel.

Yet fear struck me and roiled my vision. She was only 19, and I was 41. Did I dread opprobrium and ridicule? Or was I paralyzed by fear that my life, my career, my commitment to my goals would be eclipsed by the responsibilities of nurturing this flower in bloom? Perhaps I believed that Daisy would always be there for me—mine to have and hold on a whim.

Months went by and still I resisted.

"Maybe you think I have all the time in the world because I have only 19 years," Daisy pleaded, "but is no truth. I can't wait forever." She had delivered an ultimatum, but I could not make the commitment she was seeking. So, three weeks before I set out from Key West, Daisy had married her Italian suitor at Havana's Palacio de Matrimonio in a civil ceremony at which her 34-year-old mother had also wed her new son-in-law's closest friend. The Italians had then returned to Milan to await their brides.

Lying in Daisy's arms, sadness floods through me. Daisy gently wipes away my tears.

"I feeling empty," she says softly. "When you go, my gloominess so big." Her words tear at my heart.

"Eres la luz de mi alma," she whispers. "You are the light of my spirit. You are inside me, part of my body, part of my being. *Siempre te llevaré conmigo.* I will always carry you with me."

I clasp her tightly, enfolding her in a desperate embrace.

"I remember always the time we spent together was fantastic," she continues in Spanish. "Walking hand in hand. Looking deep into your eyes. Breathing the air that you breathe. That was all I ever needed at those moments. Neither distance nor time can ever make me forget the beautiful history of our relationship."

I had fancied myself riding through Cuba with Che Guevara's son Ernestico. Like his father, Ernestico was an avid motorcyclist and a *harlista*—Havana's proudly fanatical owners of antique Harleys who gather on Friday nights in the parking lot of the Habana Riviera Hotel to cruise the streets on their archaic hogs.

When it came to choosing a motorcycle for touring Cuba, what better than a Harley-Davidson? With its voluptuous, chrome-gilded, teardrop tank and deep-throated rumble, it hinted at all the fantasy, gaudiness, sex, and excessive wealth of prerevolutionary Cuba.

Sure, a Harley had the perfect cachet for touring Cuba, but Harleys were also expensive, overweight gas-guzzlers. Even the Heritage Softtail—a 710-pound whopper with a 4.7-gallon fuel tank—would get me barely 150 miles in Cuba, which was in the midst of a gasoline crisis. In some areas, gas stations were few and far between. Many no longer had gas to sell; of those that did, electricity blackouts often rendered the pumps inactive. I figured I needed a bike with a range of at least 250 miles.

I set my hopes on a BMW, a brand synonymous with ruggedness and reliability. The moto-minded wizards of Munich had just announced a stunning new adventure touring enduro that had stolen my heart: The R1100GS, with a price tag of $15,000, hovered between the impossible and the inevitable. Perhaps BMW would be philanthropic. I called Robert Mitchell, Director of Marketing for BMW North America. He sounded interested—could I send a proposal?

In the meantime, I had to get my travel plans approved by the Cuban government. Permission for a journalist seeking to travel willy-nilly through Cuba is not granted automatically. Nor swiftly. Sure, journalists are often admitted for a few weeks, but longer visits must be authorized by an agency of the Cuban government; because only one or two individuals usually have the power to issue an approval, this can take forever.

Securing the support of key Cuban officials seemed essential. To put Cuba's creaky bureaucratic machinery in motion, I contacted the Cuban Ministry of Foreign Relations (MINREX), housed in a Soviet-inspired carbuncle at the bottom of Paseo in Havana's Vedado district. In September 1994, I flew to Havana and presented a copy of my proposal to Raul Colominas, MINREX's amiable press relations officer in charge of handling U.S. journalists.

About this time I was developing a friendship with Sandra Levinson. She would later prove to be an invaluable contact—a human Rolodex acquainted with powerful figures throughout the Cuban political and intellectual pantheon. Sandra invited me to join her in Cuba, so I returned to Havana the following February.

"Christopher, I want you to meet Marta Rojas," Sandra said, welcoming me into her apartment on Avenida Primera. An attractive woman in late middle age rose from the sofa and extended her hand. As a young reporter for the Cuban magazine *Bohemia*, Rojas had been one of six journalists permitted to witness Fidel Castro's trial (famous for his "History Will Absolve Me" speech) following the attack by 122 revolutionaries that he led on July 26, 1953, against the Moncada Barracks in Santiago. It was Rojas who had smuggled out the film, hidden in her bra, that showed the bodies of captured rebels who had been tortured to death; when published, the pictures shocked the nation and unleashed a wave of sympathy for Castro. Rojas had since risen to a position of some influence and was highly placed in UNEAC, the powerful Cuban Writers' and Artists' Union.

Rojas listened with growing interest as I outlined my plans for a motorbike journey. I expressed my fears that my proposal would be rejected or become bogged down in the MINREX bureaucracy. She beamed, placed her fingertips atop my hand, and promised to pass a copy of my proposal to "the appropriate people."

"Marta is the most famous journalist in Cuba," Sandra told me after Rojas left. "If she says yes to your proposal, then it is certain."

Things were looking rosy as I strutted through the front doors of MINREX and presented Raul Colominas with half a dozen press clippings of my travel stories on Cuba.

"Has my proposal been approved?" I asked expectantly. Six months had passed since I had last seen Colominas.

"Please be patient," he replied. "These things take time."

Three months later I was back in Cuba, this time to attend the 15th annual Cuban Tourism Convention, at Havana's Palacio de Convenciones. Colominas had been assigned to "support" me throughout the convention. I asked for a progress report. He echoed his previous reply and offered a token smile.

The next day—May 21—Cuban ministers of state and leading tourism figures assembled for a major press conference in the vast convention hall. Every seat was taken. During question time I identified myself as a U.S. journalist, then directed a question to Edmundo Rodríquez, Cuba's Minister of Economic Planning and Development. Rodríquez sidestepped the query and took a jab at the U.S. media. A brown-nosed reporter from Argentina then rose.

"We are not interested in the comments of U.S. journalists," he began spitefully.

I was still chagrined during the final press conference the next day, when another barb was fired my way. I leaped to my feet and raised my hand high above my head—an unmistakable sign that I wanted the microphone—yet the emcee ignored me. Spurned and frustrated, I started waving my arm. A buzz spread through the hall. Heads turned. Eyes stared.

"Give him the microphone!" someone called.

A little red light blinked atop my desk, indicating that my microphone was live.

I began cautiously.

"I have a question for the minister of tourism, but first I wish to make a statement...."

The emcee's voice interrupted. "Identify yourself, please."

"My name is Christopher Baker. I'm a journalist from the USA, but a citizen of the United Kingdom. To the delegate that has just criticized U.S. journalists—and I take his comment as a stiletto aimed at my heart—and to all the other delegates assembled here today, you should know that you have no understanding of my feelings toward Cuba, nor of those of tens of thousands of American citizens."

The hall fell deathly silent. I leaned toward the microphone. Buoyed by sudden confidence, my voice took on what I like to think of as a Churchillian cadence.

"Countless numbers of U.S. citizens respect Cuba...admire Cuba...honor Cuba...," I continued, pausing between each phrase, "and I believe that I speak for all these individuals, as I do for myself, when I say that they *love* Cuba."

The translators were miming behind their glass screens.

"Yes, it is true that Cuba is misrepresented by much of the media," I added, warming to the rapt attention. "But that is only half of the story. You have many friends in the United States, even among those who do not agree with much of your politics, and you should know that many tens and hundreds of thousands of U.S. citizens are dedicating their time and their energy to end the embargo in the hope that more rational policies and a future based on respect and common cause will prevail. I believe that there is a new movement afoot in the media, conscious or otherwise, to represent Cuba in a more balanced light. Many of my own stories on Cuba have been published in recent months, and I take this as a sign that more and more travel editors are willing to promote Cuba as a tourist destination."

I prattled on a while longer, sounding much like a fellow traveler, and closed by saying that I was writing a guidebook that would be distinguished by its fairness to Cuba.

My comments had come from the heart; little did I guess the resounding effect they would have. When the session ended, the emcee pushed through the crowd and intercepted me as I emerged from the hall. Ramón Perdomo thrust a business card into my hand identifying him as the Principal Executive of Marketing for Publicitur, the state agency in charge of tourism promotion. "Your comments were appreciated," he said. "Be sure you attend the banquet," referring to the guests-only gala reception being held that evening.

I arrived in a white linen suit of the kind fashionable in Havana before the Revolution. The foyer was thronged but Perdomo was there to greet me, his Falstaffian figure filling the door.

"I'm glad you could make it," he said, grabbing my elbow and ushering me away from the crowd and through a blood-red velvet curtain into a brightly lit anteroom.

Two security agents stepped forward to frisk me, then waved me in. A banquet table had been laid out with victuals that most Cubans can only dream of: shrimp cocktails, pâtés, rolled hams, and caviar. I noticed familiar faces—those of Cuba's elite of the ruling elite. State security agents wearing earphones and bulging suits milled about the doors and driveway at the rear, where Fidel's Mercedes limousines were expected to draw up at any moment.

I was going to be introduced to Fidel!

Perdomo took my elbow and guided me toward Osmany Cienfuegos Gorriarán, Minister of Tourism, who greeted me with cool civility. I launched enthusiastically into my plans for a motorbike journey. The minister listened without comment. "Of course," I continued unfazed, "I rely upon the support of the Cuban government, and it is with this hope that I wish to reassure you of my warm feelings toward Cuba." I repeated what I had said in the convention hall.

Cienfuegos , the most powerful figure in Cuba after Fidel and Raúl Castro, stared down at me without speaking or smiling, his sentiments hidden behind thick spectacles and a granitic countenance. Vice-president of the Council of Ministers and secretary of the Executive Committee that administers Cuba on a day-to-day basis, the old revolutionary is one of Cuba's least-known political figures. The archcommunist, an architect by training, is the elder brother of Camilo Cienfuegos—the revolutionary hero and Chief of Staff of Fidel's Rebel Army, who died in a mysterious plane crash in 1959. Osmany sat out the war in Mexico as a member of a hard-line communist cell and was later instrumental in Cuba's military involvement in Africa.

"You have our support," Cienguegos finally replied, though without visible thaw. "Perdomo will set it up for you. Now, if you will excuse me...." He dismissed me with a headmasterly air and turned away.

Although Fidel never showed, I had reached as far up the ranks as necessary. Perdomo moved quickly. He called the next morning to report that Juan Pardo, Publicitur's press executive, would await me in the lobby of the Hotel Cohiba around two o'clock. Pardo was a lanky, white-haired mulatto—the epitome of the gracious Cuban bureaucrat—and I liked him immediately. There was a soft serenity in his warm hazel eyes. I felt we could be friends. I told Pardo that I had delivered a proposal to Raúl Colominas of MINREX. Yes, he replied, he knew. And to Marta Rojas. Pardo knew that too. Foreign journalists hold few secrets in Cuba.

Six months passed, and in September I returned to Havana. At Pardo's office on Calle 19 in the leafy, formerly tony suburb of Vedado, he beckoned me into a high-ceilinged room dripping with stucco. Light from *mediopuntos* (arched windows of stained glass) diffused the sunlight and saturated the room with shifting color. I sank into a sumptuous sofa and admired the glistening mahogany panels and 18th-century furnishings while Pardo went to fetch coffee; when it arrived, it was dark as molasses and syrupy sweet, served in Wedgewood china on an ornate silver platter.

"Your proposal looks excellent," Pardo smiled. "We have accepted it. However," he added coolly, "your title does not seem appropriate. We suggest a change."

I had anticipated that my proposed book title—*Mi Moto Fidel*—might cause ripples. The name, suggested by my friend Ciaran McGowan, refers only obliquely to the bearded one, and is a play on the Spanish word *"fidelidad."* Hence, loosely, "my faithful motorcycle." But in Cuba, no one takes Fidel's name in vain.

Pardo likewise balked at my request to travel unrestricted: "We want to ensure that a representative meets you each day. It is in your own interests. You're in for a surprise if you think a Yankee on a flashy motorbike can breeze through Cuba unannounced and unnoticed," he declared ominously.

"I prefer to be flexible," I replied. "I need to be able to adjust my itinerary on a day-by-day basis."

"It would be better not to change your itinerary," Pardo sternly parried. Then, more lightly: "We'll take care of your hotels and have a representative waiting for you when you arrive."

I didn't like the sound of it. "A representative?"

"Someone who can ensure that you get to see everything," he added. "You understand? There are many things we would not want you to miss. No, it is better if we make your arrangements."

I understood. I was going to be policed. Where I traveled, where I stayed, and, presumably, whom I talked to would all be officially sanctioned. I stepped out into the daylight, breathed deeply, and returned home shadowed by doubt.

Upon returning to the States in October, I learned that BMW of North America would not offer its support. I therefore decided it was time to go shopping.

I drove over the San Rafael-Richmond Bridge to check out my options at BMW & Ducati of Marin. In the showroom, salesman Doug Shaw was showing a customer my dream machine—the BMW R1100GS. I sauntered over. The customer had owned several Beemers, and I felt out of my depth as I listened to his sapient probing. Doug, however, calmly answered every question about bucket-type tappets, sintered-steel cams, and the model's closed-loop three-way catalytic converter.

"How well will it run on leaded fuel?" I asked meekly.

"It'll run okay, but eventually you'll burn out the catalytic converter," Doug replied. "That's no worry these days, anyway. Where are you going to find leaded gas—Mexico?"

"I'm taking a motorbike to Cuba," I ventured.

"What the hell are you looking at this for?" said the customer. "*That's* the bike you want!" I followed his finger toward a white-and-red monster with a gas tank the size of the *Hindenburg*. It was a R100GS/PD—a 1,000cc all-terrain model acknowledged as the king of enduro motorbikes. It was huge and at first sight ungainly, but its rugged constitution impressed me.

"You can't go wrong with one of these," the fellow continued, taking over Doug's job. "I've had one, trust me. They're as reliable as any bike on the road. You can put anything short of piss in the tank and it'll run."

"It also boasts outstanding touring features and operating economy," added Doug, sounding more like a salesman. "How will you get it to Cuba?"

"Don't ask," I replied.

When BMW introduced the 800cc GS in 1980, it was the first of its kind: A large-engine enduro with heaps of power, it blended ruggedness with supreme ride comfort; the modified Paralever rear suspension permitted exceptional travel. In 1981 a specially equipped GS won the Paris-Dakar Rally, the world's toughest race, and the GS legend was born. The PD (for Paris-Dakar) appeared in 1990 with a built-in crash frame and metal headlamp grill, Bilstein rear shock absorber, a fairing and heavy-duty bash plate to protect the engine, and a mammoth 9.25-gallon gas tank containing a built-in, lockable storage compartment. It was a Rolls Royce and Range Rover merged into one.

I straddled the PD. Although my toes barely reached the floor, it had a made-to-measure comfort and, even under the worst conditions, an impressive 300-mile minimum range. The price tag—$8,500, roughly half that of the R1100GS—was attractive. It was a 1994 model with 8,927 miles on the odometer—another advantage, meaning it had been broken in. It also sported a few after-market bells and whistles that I considered essential: rear panniers, an expandable tank bag, a touring windshield, and a Corbin touring seat that Doug assured me would stave off hemorrhoids.

I bought it without even riding it around the block.

I sent a fax to Juan Pardo of Publicitur in Cuba, informing him that I had purchased a bike. Would Pardo take care of the official documentation? Could I be certain that the Cuban government would not change its mind? What documents did I need? Could Pardo arrange transportation for the bike aboard a Cuban freighter from Mexico? And, again, would he provide a letter authorizing me to travel wherever I wanted?

I heard nothing. Whenever I called, Pardo was unavailable. I left messages to which he never replied.

After several more attempts to raise the dead, I decided to go it alone.

My own efforts to arrange transport for *mi moto fidel*, meanwhile, were hitting nothing but roadblocks. Fortunately I had made a new acquaintance, Ben Treuhaft, a Berkeley piano tuner and the son of muckraking journalist Jessica Mitford. Treuhaft was making a name for himself shipping pianos to Cuba. Maybe he could offer some advice.

"Forget the bullshit," Ben said in typically contrarian family fashion. "Just hire a private yacht in Florida. Lots of skippers make the journey."

Three months later, I had things arranged.

Rolf Runerberg, the *Kalevala's* captain, was tall and stocky, with a large, well-squared head and a well-rounded, beer-nourished paunch. His hair was thinning and silvered and slicked down with gel. Every few minutes he lifted up his skipper's cap to firm down his hair. His face was sun-bronzed and loving and in it shone jade-green eyes, scintillating as glacial ice.

"The Coast Guard gif me hell," Rolf said, purpling at their indignities. "I vos caught in bad weather coming down from Fort Myers. Some goddam idiot called the Coast Guard to report me missing and told them I vos going to Cuba. They didn't like that. It's this fucking Brothers to the Rescue business, I tell you. But I haf all the paperwork to show them that I am carrying humanitarian aid," he added. He pointed to a battered old saxophone, two time-worn guitars, and a rusty Würlitzer accordion. One of the guitars had no strings.

"Still zey try to stop me leaving. Bastards! Zey harassed me last time, too. Zis time I call the Customs headquarters in Washington. Zey give me clearance. I should haf been gone hours ago," he said, still simmering.

"Okay, ve go now," he added, calming down.

Rolf tossed me two thick bungee cords to lash the bike to the rail. "Be quick. Ve go!" Rolf was already easing away from the dock. I was still tethering the bike as we slipped past the Coast Guard station. Rolf had already been cleared for departure, and he was justifiably nervous; if the Coast Guard saw us loading the motorbike, he'd be in trouble. "Get out of sight!" he cried. *"Get below, for God's sake!"*

Beyond the harbor mouth, the Gulf Stream was in tormented flood. The *Kalevala* began to pitch and roll wildly.

On my first morning in Havana I rode down to the Customs office in the Terminal Sierra Maestra on the harbor's inner shore. The office faced Plaza de San Francisco, dominated by the cathedral of Saint Francis of Assisi, initiated in 1719 in honey-hued limestone and recently restored to grandeur. Children splashed about in the Fountain of the Lions.

Carlitos—a slender, poker-faced man with a bushy mustache—came forward. He studied my papers issued at Marina Hemingway, then asked for my *pasaporte*. Carlitos returned to his old metal desk, pulled out two sheets of coarse brown paper, slipped a much-used carbon paper between them, loaded them into a typewriter of World War II vintage, and began hitting the keys. The place looked like it hadn't seen a coat of paint since the fall of Batista. The ocher walls were stained a deep tannin. The marble countertop looked as if someone had gone at it with a sledgehammer.

A measured buzz filled the office. Loyal functionaries in olive-green uniforms with red epaulettes were shuffling through piles of dog-eared papers and weathered ledgers tied with string, lending a Dickensian air to the dark setting. Most of the women wore body-hugging outfits. Cuba has probably done as much for women's rights as any nation on Earth, with equality guaranteed by the Family Code. But the Revolution has made little headway against coquetry and the Cuban female's preference for minimal, tight-fitting clothes. Even the most ardent revolutionaries shorten and take in their uniforms to better show off their legs or outline their backsides—to heighten the *femme fatale* effect. How on Earth could Carlitos concentrate? He never smiled—the textbook image of bureaucratic indifference.

Carlitos handed me a form to take to the *tránsitos*, the traffic police. Fortunately, the inspection office was only two blocks from my apartment. I arrived the next day bright and early and parked in a special area for foreigners between a shiny new Volvo sedan and a Ford Bronco sporting a logo for a Canadian mining company. A wild norther had swept down from the United Sates, lacing the morning air with a cold sting. Pewter-colored clouds slid slowly across the leaden sky, blown by the icy wind tearing in off the sea. Waves crashed over the seawall along Avenida Primera, adding salt spray to the stop-and-go showers that drove the inspector—a tall Afro-Cuban man dressed in a smoke-gray frock—to seek shelter, leaving the rest of us standing outside in the rain.

A black Mazda Miata sports car tore into the parking lot. From it stepped a deeply tanned young male with stylishly close-cropped blond hair. He was dressed in sharply pressed black pants and a black camel-hair jacket worn loose on his shoulders with a charcoal velvet waistcoat and collarless white dress shirt beneath. Had he fallen from the pages of *GQ* magazine? He lolled against his car in an effete pose.

As the inspector turned toward me, a bystander—a *tramitador*, or someone employed by another to stand in line on his behalf—grabbed his arm and ushered him toward the Miata.

"¡Soy el próximo!" I protested feebly. I'm next. The inspector halted. The blond shot me a steely look. But a crowd had gathered around his expensive import, and their gravitational pull drew the inspector irresistibly forward. I decided that it was a minor matter.

I turned to the blond: "Where are you from?"

"Montréal...Québec," he replied, tacking on the province as an afterthought, as if I was a geographic ignoramus. He owned a business supplying restaurant equipment to the Cuban government. Puffed up with self-importance, he showed no interest in my adventure. I returned to the bike, sat on the saddle, and watched the Canadian getting off on the Cubans adoring his car. I was envious.

Finally the inspector approached, made multiple rubbings of the BMW's registration numbers etched into the frame and engine, and handed me a scrap of paper—proof of ownership, I guessed, in case the motorbike was stolen. I joined the crowd milling inside the tránsito office. Signs read "No smoking." The Cubans smoked anyway. A ceiling fan whined, shuddered, and groaned. A time-faded visage of Fidel looked down from one wall.

Margarita Martínez beckoned me into her compact office. She smiled—the first official who had done so—and motioned for me to sit *"por favor!"* The negrita was pretty and slender yet buxom, and her robust breasts so strained her blouse that one of the buttons had failed, revealing a tantalizing cleavage. The furnishings predated the Revolution and the metal filing cabinets were much banged about. Martínez hammered away on a rusty old Royal typewriter. I had neglected to bring a special 15-peso stamp, however, and she was unable to issue my license. Martínez therefore directed me to a nearby post office, where I handed the postal clerk a dollar bill. The clerk shook her head: *"Moneda nacional!"* she said, pointing across the street to a booth run by Cadeca, an acronym for *casa de cambio* (literally, "house of change").

After the collapse of the Soviet Union, the cash-strapped Cuban government urgently needed to get hold of the dollars floating freely in the underground economy. Economics minister Carlos Lage had estimated that up to $300 million in U.S. currency enters Cuba each year as aid from relatives abroad or as tips from foreign tourists; current estimates put the figure at $1 billion. In 1993 the Castro regime legalized possession of that paramount capitalist tool, the yanqui dollar, and opened up "foreign exchange recovery stores" where every item imaginable—from toothpaste to TVs—was made available for dollars. Suddenly Cubans could buy everyday items they had never hoped to find in state stores. Prices, however, were kept high as a "tax" on Cubans privileged to have hard currency. The result was an immediate increase in black-market dollar transactions. The value of the peso, officially set by the government at parity with the U.S. dollar, plunged to 150 to the dollar. Cadeca was created in 1995 to exchange dollars for pesos at the black-market rate. The peso had recovered and stabilized at about 25 to 1. The bureau was soaking up dollars from the local economy.

Martínez smiled as I handed her my hard-won stamp. She puffed out her chest (was she flirting?), attacked her typewriter, and handed me a *licencia de circulación*, a yellow vehicle-registration card containing details of the bike and valid for 30 days from my arrival. Martínez then opened a file drawer and extracted a bright yellow *chapa*—a metal license plate about five inches by seven. I was now officially *moto particular* (private motorcycle) HK529 (H for Havana, K for foreign vehicle). My chapa had set me back 60 cents.

David Wardle has flown in from London and is staying at the Hotel Sevilla, the setting for the comical intrigues of Wormold in Graham Greene's *Our Man in Havana*. A mutual friend, Roger Oyama, will join us tomorrow. I have promised David a tour of Havana. I pull up, put the bike on the stand, and bound through the Gaudiesque arched doorway.

It's like entering a Moroccan *medina*. The lofty lobby is a graceful marvel of Moorish imagination and artistry. A gilded ceiling sculpted in lace-like relief is supported by fluted columns, twirled like candy sticks, that auger up from a cool gray marble floor. Carved motifs dance across walls of vivid sea-blue *azulejos*, glazed tiles decorated with breathtaking geometrics and plaited strapwork softened by flowers that repeat themselves in delicate patterns of arabesque. The lobby is suffused in luminous light. The soft ripple of an indoor fountain conjures images of a cool oasis. A vision from *A Thousand and One Nights*.

In my mesmerized state, I hardly notice David. He has no trouble spotting me, however: I'm wearing shiny leather pants and motorcycle boots.

"*Old chap!*" says David, beaming with boyish delight. "Pleased to meet you." Very English. Skin like porcelain, rose-tinted cheeks—a dead ringer for the young Michael Palin. Our rapport is immediate.

"Right, you old fart, I'm ready," he says, drawing up the collar of his gaberdine raincoat.

David mounts behind and we're off through the puddle-strewn streets. I nip down the Prado and lean into the spiraling curve that drops under the harbor tunnel. No motorcycles are allowed. A policeman spots me and blows his whistle. *Phweeet! Phweeet!* He is running down the bank to intercept me. I twist the throttle and we shoot past and into the tube. Unfortunately, he radios ahead and two cops grimly flag me down at the tollbooth on the other side—the first of dozens of times I will be pulled over in Cuba. I play the remorseful Brit: *Terribly sorry, officer. You should put up a sign?* It works.

We skirt the ghostly Morro castle guarding the rocky point at the entrance to Havana's deep, flask-shaped harbor. A gale is tearing in from the north and the Morro is no place to linger, so we drop down to the shore, where we sip warming rum at a bodega-style bar hanging over waters the color and consistency of olive oil. The sky is the color of steel and the clouds the color of cold steel when it has been fired and the gray becomes filmy with lilacs and blues like the thin wash of a watercolorist's chiaroscuro. The rain falls like muslin. Through the veil I watch ferries bobbing lazily across the harbor while cargo ships cut between them. As I stare across the forlorn harbor, I imagine the silhouettes of great galleons slipping out, laden with treasure en route to Spain.

Should I return by the harbor tunnel? The only alternative requires a 15-mile detour. I'm in no mood for that. Thankfully the cops seem preoccupied. I take the far lane, slow coming up to the tollbooth, then at the last moment roar away, whipping the bike up through the gears, and we fly through the tunnel like a log down a flume.

"Bloody good show!" yells David. He really does talk like that.

Great waves are crashing over the Malecón so I cut west through Centro and motor up La Rampa, the wide, tree-lined boulevard that climbs sharply to the heart of Vedado, past faded awnings and dirt-stained neon signs bearing the names of famous nightclubs from the heyday of sin. Gone are the pimps and the porn-palace fiefdoms. But Communist Cuba is still carnal. As I pull up to the stoplight outside the Hotel Habana Libre, we are accosted by two dark-eyed *mulatas* in heels trolling for loose foreign males.

"*Ssst! Ssssst!*" They hiss like serpents. One puts her hand on David's crotch.

I let the clutch fly as the light turns green.

Beyond Vedado we swoop south to Plaza de la Revolución, a vast tarred piazza laid out for the masses to gather so that Fidel can hold them spellbound with his brilliant oratory. On those occasions the mood is as charged as thick Cuban coffee, but today it has all the thrill of an abandoned lot. Dour post-Stalinist carbuncles rise on three sides, including the windowless Ministerio de Interior, whose grim facade boasts a four-story-high visage of Che

Guevara in his trademark beret. To the west is the glass-fronted Teatro Nacional, still waiting for the curtain to rise.

Sentries eye us icily as I pull up and put the bike on its stand.

"Watch this!" I say to David, pulling my camera from a pocket at the bottom of the tank bag. I point it at the Monumento José Martí, a huge statue of the national hero sitting in a contemplative pose reminiscent of Rodin's *Thinker*. The granite edifice looks north over the square from atop a vast pedestal crowned by a soaring 109-meter-tall marble tower that bristles with antennas. Vultures wheel and slide overhead, adding to the somber scene.

A soldier on the platform waves his arms in the universal gesture that says "No!" Two others appear and hurry toward us.

"Er, is this okay?" David asks limply.

"Just keeping 'em on their toes," I reply, firing up and cruising off before they can do any harm.

That night I hopped in a taxi and headed out to Cerro to pick up "the girls." I had invited Daisy and her mother to join David and me for dinner. Alicia looked smashing in a skin-tight black cat-suit with a silver-studded black belt pulled tight at the waist to accentuate her Sonia Bragaesque figure. She had anointed herself with fragrant oils, and her rich chestnut skin had the sheen of a well-worn saddle. The soft down on her cheeks sparkled like a cobweb gilded with dew. David, I knew, would be pleased.

"*Ah, ¡La mamá!*" he exclaimed, holding his stomach with one hand and bowing deeply, as if he were Sir Walter Raleigh greeting the queen. "*Mon plaisir!*" he added, switching to French. Alicia beamed. She had studied French at a Havana branch of l'Alliance Française, the Paris-based institution dedicated to promoting French culture abroad. She gave David a warm *abrazo*, then kissed his cheek.

"*Ooh la la!*" he stammered, pretending to swoon. Alicia howled. Daisy looked at her mother and winked.

We dined at the Sevilla's resplendent Roof Garden Restaurant. Through the wide-open windows, the city lights smoldered in the drizzly mist. A hook-nosed pianist was tickling the ivories of a Russian Tchaika grand piano. Kemal Kairus, a Lebanese Cuban, resembled a circus figure in his toupee, the color of varnished mahogany whorled in Harpo Marx flowing curls. His faded tuxedo was two sizes too small and the arms had ridden up to his elbows, making it seem as if he was wearing stretched seaweed. His music, however, was heavenly: He roamed between classical pieces and romantic ballads with mellifluous ease.

A government minister and his entourage arrived and were seated ceremoniously at a banquet table in the middle of the marble floor. We were the only other diners. They were talkative, and the bedlam of their voices and the piano melodies soon struck dissonant notes. The communist bigwig ordered silence. Kairus looked crestfallen. His brow furrowed as the group's shouts and laughter mingled with the muted hum of traffic passing along the Prado below. As the minutes ticked by, he looked toward us, rolled his eyes, and flicked his tongue up and down to suggest they were yakking too much. I coaxed him to play again. He sneaked a glance toward the minister's table, then cautiously began. He gradually grew more brazen as his chutzpah went unchallenged, until his rich bass voice pealed a victory song through the cathedral-like room.

The cubanas wanted to dance, so we headed to Ipanema disco at the Hotel Copacabana on Avenida Primera. It had the grim decor and appeal of a student union. The rock-pop music was not to my taste, but Daisy eased me onto the dance floor, where a Rolling Stones number was playing. David was stalking her mother in a salacious tango. Alicia, stumbling to keep up with his long gliding steps, seemed captivated. But later, incautiously...

"¿Pero conocen los italianos como bailar el tango?" David asked, his crisp Castilian blurred by a surfeit of rum. *But do the Italians know how to tango?*

"Como estuvo el juego de pelota?" Alicia replied curtly. Literally, it means "How was the ball game?" It was her way—the Cuban way—of changing the subject. Her hand slipped onto his thigh. Alicia was putting the moves on David.

Roger flew in from San Francisco the next day and joined David at the Sevilla. I agreed to meet them in the hotel's lobby bar. First, I rode out to the office of Esen, the state-run insurance agency, on Calle 18 in Miramar. Maritza Naranjo peered at me over half-glasses, her flame-red hair curled up like a bell in 1960s fashion. She looked like Wilma Flintstone. I valued the bike at $8,000 and opted for a three-month package covering theft, fire, accident, and medical expenses. The premium cost $228.

My pals were two *mojitos* ahead of me. The drinks were weak and the mood insipid. I suggested we head to El Bodeguita del Medio.

We turned onto Agramonte and followed the cool shade of a long arcade past Sloppy Joe's, "a high-ceilinged, bottle-encrusted, tile-floored oasis" for partying tourists in Batista days. "No Havana resident ever went to Sloppy Joe's," wrote Graham Greene in *Our Man in Havana*, "because it was the rendezvous of tourists; but tourists were sadly reduced in number, for the President's regime was creaking dangerously toward its end." It was shuttered, its innards a dusty ruin awaiting the restoration now sweeping Habana Vieja.

The clouds briefly parted, illuminating Havana in phosphorescent light that gleamed on the chrome of prerevolutionary American cars and silvered the Malecón sinuously fronting the Atlantic shoreline, where a band of indigo marked the edge of the Gulf Stream that Hemingway called his "Great Deep Blue River." Hemingway first set out from Key West to wrestle marlin in the teeming currents off the Cuban coast in April 1932. Yearly the blue waters drew him closer until eventually, "succumbing to the other charms of Cuba, different from and more difficult to explain than the big fish in September," he settled on this island of tropical charms.

Hemingway's ghost haunted us everywhere we walked in Havana. At the top of Calle Obispo we passed El Floridita, Hemingway's favorite watering hole, which he immortalized in his novels. His bronze bust looked down from its pedestal beside the dark mahogany bar where Constante Ribailagua, the barman, had once served Hemingway and such illustrious guests as Ava Gardner, Tennessee Williams, Marlene Dietrich, and Jean-Paul Sartre. The sugarless frozen daiquiris that Constante made, wrote Hemingway, "had no taste of alcohol and felt, as you drank them, the way downhill glacier skiing feels running through powder snow and, after the sixth and eighth, felt like downhill glacier skiing feels when you are running unroped."

The place had been spruced up for tourist consumption with a 1930s art deco polish. Waiters hovered in vermilion tux jackets and bow ties. I expected Papa Hemingway to stroll in as he would every day when he lived in Havana and drank with Honest Lil, the Worst Politician, and other real-life characters from his novels.

We decided to leave the Floridita for another day.

"Jesus! It wouldn't have surprised me if Desi Arnaz had appeared conducting his jazz band," said Roger as we stepped back into the pearly light.

I was, to say the least, dramatically overdressed. My oversize leather pants bulged in the rear like a baby's diaper, and the thick knee pads had given me a bad case of water-on-the-knees. As we walked down Calle Obispo, the main thoroughfare sloping gradually eastward to the heart of Habana Vieja, I looked like a ridiculous figure from a *Mad Max* movie.

Obispo resembled an operatic stage. Children in colorful uniforms were streaming homeward from school. Adolescents in shorts and T-shirts, their baseball caps worn stylishly back to front, lolled against car hoods and fenders touched up with housepaint. Old men in neatly pressed *guayaberas* and tight-fitting, slightly flared trousers cycled by on Chinese-made *bicis,* tinkling their bells as they weaved through the crowd. Bare-chested *compañeros* dressed in shorts and flip-flops sat on chipped doorsteps and dank marble stairwells, chatting with female counterparts in halter-top dresses, body-hugging boob tubes, and butt-hugging Lycra shorts. Young or old, it made no difference: Even grandmothers with doughy figures can't resist the desire to be noticed, to show off their *nalgas cubanas*—the Cuban ass.

A middle-aged mulata sashayed by. She was dressed in a backless white swimsuit and lime-green spandex shorts, and as she walked her spheroidal, double-D buttocks pumped up and down in piston rhythm. Male eyes followed every rise and fall of her well-rounded rump. Would-be suitors began hissing like snakes. *Ssst! Ssssst!*

"Goodness," said David. "Listen to that."

"*Look* at that!" exclaimed Roger.

We howled in unison. David's comment reminded me of a scene in *Our Man in Havana,* when Wormold, the tepid Englishman, is told by his Cuban assistant, "You are not a Cuban. For you the shape of a girl's bottom is less important than a certain gentleness of behaviour."

"Don't women mind?" an American magazine writer once asked his female Cuban guide.

"Oh, no!" she replied. "In Cuba the women love to hear that they've been noticed....You mustn't be too thin, of course, especially in the back."

The mulata was now working the crowd.

"Without asses in motion," says Cuban therapist Ana Fernández, "we would never achieve the degree of feeling that we have here."

Calle Obispo was steeped in Latin rhythms. Twangy guitar music and the measured clacking of *claves* mingled with the chirp of bicycle bells, the tinny beating of tinker's hammers, and the creak of decrepit jalousies swinging on rusty hinges in the brusque wind eddying in off the sea. Petty hawkers had set up their stalls on the sidewalks, selling peanuts, home-baked confections, small limes, and pomegranates shriveled like raisins. Every block had its puncture repairman (*"se reparan ponchera"*) and those eking out a living refilling cigarette lighters (*"se llena fosforera"*). They were part of Cuba's new army of small-time entrepreneurs, legalized in the summer of 1993 to save the country's rust-bucket economy from collapse. They touted their trade beneath timeworn buildings held up by nothing more than makeshift wooden braces.

We passed a 650cc Norton Commando from the 1960s parked on the sidewalk. True to form, it was dripping oil. A big-boned '57 Studebaker with a voluptuousness tailor-made for pre-Castro Cuba forged its way through the narrow street like a square-rigged galleon. It was followed by a Russian Gaz jeep full of military figures in olive-green uniforms beeping a path through the crowd. Battered, high-finned relics of 1950s ostentation littered the side streets. Because of the gasoline shortage, many had been left to decay in the tropical heat and rain. They seemed a metaphor for the state of much of Habana Vieja, a 350-acre repository of castles and churches and columned mansions dating back centuries and boasting a spectacular amalgam of styles. The academic classicism of aristocratic 18th-century Spanish homes blended with 19th-century French rococo, while art deco and art nouveau exteriors from the 1920s fused into the cool, columned arcades of ancient palaces in Mujedar style. Havana ached with pathos and penury.

Fortunately, the heart of Habana Vieja—proclaimed a UNESCO World Heritage Site in 1982—was in the midst of a complete restoration. At the bottom of Obispo, we passed by the Hotel Ambos Mundos, where Hemingway laid his head in Room 511 during the 1930s. Here the plot of *For Whom the Bell Tolls* filled his mind. After the Revolution the hotel was turned into a hostelry for employees of the Ministry of Education. Hemingway's room, however, was preserved down to the old Spanish edition of *Don Quixote* on the night table. We paused to read a plaque on the exterior wall: *"En este edificio Hotel Ambos Mundos vivío durante la decada del 1930 el novelista Ernest Hemingway."* The word *"edificio"* was missing. Plaster and broken glass and fallen beams lay against the wall in great dusty piles. Workmen scurried in and out through the tall doorway, carrying tradesman's paraphernalia meant to give the Ambos Mundos a new lease on life.

I noted how Havana's city fathers have leased Papa's spirit and are polishing up his favorite haunts.

"That's jolly clever marketing," noted David.

"Yeah, but the cult of Hemingway is very real," I replied.

"Really! How so?"

"Well, for example, his works are required reading in Cuban schools. His books are best-sellers," I answered. "Daisy once told me, 'We admire Hemingway because he understood the Cuban people; he sympathized with us.' The Cubans believe his novels support the socialist tenet that humans are fulfilled only when they act for a moral purpose. When you think of it, most of his novels deal with economic and political injustice, or the underdog fighting against impossible circumstances. That's how Cubans see their contemporary history. Fidel has even claimed that Hemingway's works 'are a defense of human rights.'"

Castro knows Papa's novels well; he once claimed that *For Whom the Bell Tolls*, Hemingway's fictional account of the Spanish Civil War, had inspired his guerrilla tactics. Fidel, whose own exploits have been remarkable, has said that he admires Hemingway for the adventures he had. He holds Hemingway to his chest as one complex man to another. The two headstrong fellows met only once, during the Tenth Annual Ernest Hemingway Billfish Tournament in May 1960. As the competition's patron, Hemingway invited Cuba's youthful new leader to be his guest of honor. Fidel was to present the winner's trophy, but instead he hooked the biggest marlin and won the prize himself. A black-and-white photograph shows Hemingway surrendering the trophy to a beaming Fidel.

We emerged in Plaza de Armas, ground zero in Havana's antiquity, lorded over by the somber Palacio de los Capitanes Generales. Fronting the palace was a cool loggia supported by a facade of Ionic columns, in whose penumbra a life-size statue of Fernando VII holds a scrolled parchment; when viewed in profile, the document takes on a priapic angle.

"Looks like he's massaging a hard-on," said Roger, noting the resemblance that has long been the source of bawdy jokes among Cubans.

We strolled north to the more intimate yet imposing Plaza de la Catedral, dominated by a decadently baroque cathedral completed in 1777. Its scalloped facade, adorned with clinging columns, seemed to ripple like chords in a fugue. "Music turned to stone," wrote Cuban novelist Alejo Carpentier. On either side are asymmetrical towers containing two bells supposedly cast with a dash of gold that accounts for their musical tone.

Sunlight briefly gilded the plaza, sending dusty streams between the thick columns, and the time-mellowed mansions trimmed in Monet pastels smoldered gold in the lyrical light. A sensuous mambo number wafted evocatively over the plaza. Quintessential Havana.

A Chinese man emerged from the shadows. With his droopy mustache and peridot silk robe crawling with golden dragons, he resembled Fu Manchu. Roger, a Japanese-American, looked astounded.

"¿Eres chino? You're Chinese?"

"Chino rojo; Cubano rojo," croaked the gaunt man. Red chinese; red Cuban. Chinese mixed with black and white blood, resulting in a mahogany complexion. He handed us a flyer advertising a Chinese restaurant called the Torre de Marfil, then turned and vanished as enigmatically as he had appeared.

Two flirty negritas moved into the vacuum, preening and posing for my camera. They wore traditional flounced cotton dresses, blithe shawls and sashes, and colored beads representing individual gods from the African pantheon. The first blew David a kiss. The other brushed my arm with her breast, then ran her eyes over Roger: "Hey, chinito guapo. Show us your little chopstick!"

We pushed through the saloon-style swing doors of La Bodeguita del Medio, Hemingway's favorite watering hole half a block from Havana's antique cathedral. The inn's earthy walls looked like a swarm of preschoolers had been let loose with crayons. One tippler, inspired by mojitos and micro-bikinis, had scrawled: "Me gusta el tango, pero más me gusta la tanga" (The tango's a feast when dress is the least). Errol Flynn thought it "a great place to get drunk." The most famous graffito is credited to Papa: "Mi mojito en la Bodeguita, mi daiquirí en el Floridita," he supposedly scrawled on the sky-blue walls. In reality, as Tom Miller points out in his 1992 book Trading with the Enemy: A Yankee Travels through Castro's Cuba, it was a marketing scam concocted by tourism officials.

Troubadors moved among the thirsty turistas as we savored the proletarian fusion of dialectics and rum. Seduction, however, kept creeping in. We sipped mojitos, the rum mint julep that Hemingway had rescued from obscurity. The mojitos were strong, and as a sultry cubana at the bar stared into my eyes, I felt a glimmer of the "other charms" to which Hemingway had succumbed.

A willowy down-and-outer peered in through the rejas, the lathe-turned wooden grill fronting the street. He whispered a plaintive cry and stuck his cupped hand through the bars. Roger poured sunflower seeds into the man's outstretched palm, which withdrew. The beggar peered at them quizzically. *"La comida para los pájaros!"* he cried. *Birdseed!* He poured the seeds back into the bag and departed.

My friends ordered another round. I decided to call it quits.

Stepping from La Bodeguita with rum in my veins, I felt an exhilarating sensation, as if Hemingway himself was walking beside me through the cobbled streets of this most literary of Havana's terrain. Walking back up Obispo, I could feel his presence. In a way, Papa never left Cuba. It was easy to imagine the sunbronzed novelist strolling along the cobbled street, white mane and beard haloed in tropical light, chest showing beneath khaki shirt, en route to a sugarless double daiquiri with his friends.

We regrouped that night at the Cabaret Parisienne at the Hotel Nacional. On stage, a trio in creased formal wear were sitting stiffly in straight wooden chairs, scratching out classical pieces and old crooner favorites on a cello, violin, and accordion. We got there early and sought refuge in a bottle of rum. A morose, middle-aged man arrived in a black leather jacket. He looked as if he had been chiseled from a block of cement. Russian. We nicknamed him Boris. He was accompanied by an equally stone-faced babushka, who sat with her arms folded and glowered at the musicians. They never smiled. Boris looked like he was contemplating a murder.

"Probably hers," suggested Roger.

"Perhaps he's KGB. Ah'll go ask him," said David, his words steeped in seven-year-old rum. I put a hand on his shoulder.

The music droned on uncertainly. Boris sunk his head in his palms. Then the violinist wandered over to their table and launched into a Slavic number. Their Russian stoicism crumbled. The babushka started crying. She wiped her tears with the tablecloth.

Finally the louche cabaret. Rumbling drums. Trilling trumpets. Whirling spotlights. A troupe of long-legged showgirls and besequined males rush onto the stage in a high-kicking flurry of flesh and feathers. The sexually charged show consists of creative song-and-dance routines and a rotating parade of tall mulatas gyrating their glistening copper-colored bodies into an erotic frenzy. They rush offstage, giggling, only to reappear in sexy outfits from a Frederick's of Hollywood catalog: tasseled thongs with ruffled tails, skin-tight bustiers with pull-ring zippers, silk chokers, elbow-length gloves, and fanciful feathered headgear more ostentatious than peacocks.

One of the beauties sashays down from the stage and begins shimmying in front of our table. In her fishnet tights, spiked heels, silver G-string, and coiled-wire bra tipped by fake rubies that fail to hide her dark nipples, she is a feminist's nightmare. She begins swimming in place, quivering her bum like a jellyfish about two feet from David's face. He sucks in his cheeks and moans. His lips quiver.

The dancer moves away, but the devil is in David. He gets up from his seat and begins hopping around on his haunches like a cossack. With his flapping elbows and gangly strides, he is an idiotically prancing drunken stick insect. The crowd seems not to notice, but Roger and I double over laughing.

I ride back to Miramar through rain-soaked streets full of unseen potholes. I am blinded by the lights of oncoming traffic, which refract in weird explosions like the spiked bursts of a paparazzi's flashbulb. In dim-lit Havana my halogen headlamp is barely sufficient. I need my twin Piaa spotlights, which have been draining the battery. I don't have the wiring diagram to figure things out, so I've disconnected them.

Sandra Levinson of the Center for Cuban Studies has returned from New York. The lights of her apartment glow wanly. She beckons me in, and I settle with my feet tucked up in a rocker while she unpacks a large carton of medicines that she has brought to distribute to local clinics.

"I wouldn't be surprised if my editors delete my text on Cuba's cabarets," I confide.

"That's ridiculous," Sandra replies. "Cuban cabarets aren't sexist. They're part of Cuban tradition. Cabarets are integral to Cuban culture."

I muse on how remarkable it is that Havana's old sauciness lingers on. Kicking out the Mafia and closing the strip clubs, casinos, and brothels had been one of the revolutionary government's first moves. "It is as if the Amish had taken over Las Vegas," lamented Kenneth Tynan in *Holiday* magazine. Not quite! Cuba is, after all, a Caribbean nation, and Latin at that.

I recalled an earlier visit to the Tropicana, the most famous of Cuba's pre-revolutionary open-air extravaganzas—*girls! girls! girls!*—now in its sixth decade of Vegas-style paganism. I had watched, mesmerized, as rainbow-hued searchlights swept over hordes of voluptuous showgirls, and gaudily feathered mocha-skinned mulatas paraded 20 feet up among floodlit palm trees, quivering beseechingly like tropical birds. After the show a striking *modelo* came and sat down beside me. The young beauty smiled wistfully, then screwed up her nose, which I took to mean, "I like you, you like me, what are you going to do about it?" I admired her boldness, so characteristic of Cuban women. "Dark-eyed Stellas light their feller's panatellas," Irving Berlin, the American songwriter, once wrote of Havana.

The dancer invited me to a Cuban soirée hosted by Dulce María, an ebullient and gifted Afro-Cuban composer and singer. Climbing a rickety staircase to the top of a dilapidated four-story building, we emerged on a rooftop overlooking the Plaza de la Catedral. Hands were extended. I was hugged warmly by Cubans I did not know. Dulce's band, Son de Cuba, was gearing up with a rumba. The rhythms of the marimba, the *tres*, and the bongo pulsed across the rooftops of Habana Vieja. Rum and beer were passed around, and soon we were clapping and laughing beneath a star-filled sky while Dulce belted out traditional Cuban compositions, her hips swaying undulantly. The narcotic rhythms lured us to dance. It was like the plague. You could only flee or succumb.

It is hard to believe that the U.S. government's Trading with the Enemy Act is directed at these people. My new friends never stopped smiling. I teared up, almost cried, dancing as it were with the enemy.

"I want to see the stars. They're so beautiful," said my Tropicana nightingale, leading me by the hand toward the Malecón. Couples were necking openly. The air was languid, and we were seized by desire as we strolled. My paramour's white skirt glowed luminously in the moonlight as we made love on the rough limestone seawall. Our furtive passion must have made great street theater for onlookers. Then the beam of a floodlight from the Morro castle swept over us.

I laughed nervously. She asked me why.

"This is a ridiculous situation," I said.

"Everything in Cuba is ridiculous," she replied, as if being caught in flagrante delicto was the most normal thing in the world.

Indeed, life here seemed a paradox. The ironies were many. Caribbean communism. Socialism and sensuality. Cuba was proving much like I had been told it would be, yet none of those things. Thirty-odd years of negative made-in-the-USA images have led North American visitors to expect the worst: a "fossilized, sclerotic society," "worm-eaten from within," with a sullen population "toppling toward starvation," their "lips glued by fear." It was easy to enumerate the Kafkaesque elements. But it was easy, too, to find beguiling reservoirs of delight amid the decay and dishevelment.

I remark to Sandra that virtually every North American I know who has been to Cuba has come home enchanted.

"If Cuba really is so horrible," Sandra replies, "why not let Americans visit? Surely they'll come back and say horrible things. No, the U.S. government knows that people come back and rave."

Perhaps she was right. I could remember only one exception—a New Yorker I had met at the Havana airport in 1994. When I asked him what he thought of Havana, he replied, "In three words: It's a slum!" I was stunned. What had Pico Iyer written? "Every time I go to Cuba I come back sounding like a tourist brochure. I bore my friends by counting the ways I love this improbable idyll."

"People who've met each other in Cuba know that they have a special connection," Sandra adds. "They've taken a stand against the rest of the world."

True enough. But in the end, I felt, it did not come down to politics. I had begun to realize that what sends visitors into flights of ecstasy is their sensation of having stumbled upon a bewitchingly otherworldly domain. Sure, I was only 90 miles from the neon-lit malls and McDonalds of Florida, but I had transported my BMW across an arcane threshold to discover an unexpectedly haunting realm full of eccentricity, eroticism, and enigma.

CHAPTER THREE

∼

TO THE TIP OF CUBA

I tank up, record that my odometer reads 10,998 miles, then set out along the Autopista La Habana-Mariel that leads west from Havana, skirting forlorn fishing villages and cattle-grazed pastures as closely cropped as golf links. Beyond Marael, I cross into Pinar del Río province along the well-tarred Carretera Norte, a gentle roller coaster pitching in great sweeping curves past sugarcane fields undulating like a vast swelling sea. The fields are shaded by clumps of Royal palms rising like silver-sheathed Corinthian columns. The sea glows an impossibly pavonine blue.

Just 20 miles west of Havana, I am already amid quintessential Cuban land-scapes. Stilt-legged egrets move through the cane fields, jabbing at exposed bugs. *Pick! Pick! Pick!* The air is choked by the sweet cloying odor of molasses ema-nating from *centrales*—sugar mills—belching out billowy plumes of black smoke. There is no traffic save for a few tractors and trucks and creaky wooden carts pulled by sturdy oxen, dropping long stalks of cane as they go.

Workers, *macheteros,* in coarse linen work clothes and straw hats are slash-ing the cane with short, blunt-nosed machetes. They stand stock-still and stare as I zoom by. I wave cheerily. They raise their machetes, which glint in the sun.

Even at 60 miles an hour, the wind is warm and the sun massages my back. I take off my jacket and tuck it beneath the bungee cords that secure the duffel. I'm thirsty, but there's not a store, café, or roadside stand for miles. Nowhere to buy even a soda. In the countryside, Castro has put Coke on ice.

To my left the Sierra del Rosario rise in the distance, plump and rounded and mauve. I turn south and begin to climb into the contoured foothills along a switchback so twisty it makes me feel dizzy. The bike and I cant as one, arcing gracefully through the curves with the shadowed foliage almost brushing my shoulders. White *yagruma* and fiery *popili* grow wild by the road, and the thickly forested slopes blaze with bright red *flamboyanes* and the yellow chrysanthemum-like blossoms of *palo babo*. The air grows cooler and takes on a piny crispness. I am glad for my leather jacket.

At Soroa, billed by the Cuban government as an eco-retreat in the heart of the mountains, I park the bike and follow a concrete path down through fragrant woodlands. I emerge at the base of the El Salto cascades, spilling their sulfurous water into natural pools—*baños romanos*—good for bathing. The sun's rays dapple the water and create a misty rainbow that holds me spellbound. The faint buzz of dragonflies and chattering birdsong mingles with the lulling hum of the breeze through the trees. It is congenial among the cool shadows, so I sit on a rock and listen to the falling water metamorphose into music.

I had been this way two years before while exploring Pinar del Río with Sandra Levinson and travel photographer Jan Butchofsky-Houser. We had roamed in Sandra's creaky Russian Lada, which wheezed along like a broken donkey, gasped up the hills, and finally sputtered to a stop on the road to Soroa. A *guajiro*, a peasant farmer, sunbaked like an iguana, had appeared and, poking his nose under the hood, revived both our car and our flagging spirits. We had arrived famished, appeasing our appetites with omelets and chicken creole at the restaurant of the Villa Turística Soroa, a motel-style resort with handsome stone *cabinas* shaded by trees on the slopes overlooking an Olympic-size pool.

Today the hotel is full. A movie—Tomás Gutiérrez Alea's *Guantanamera*—is being filmed, and cast and crew have taken over the property. I retreat to the Castillo de las Nubes, a Spanish-style restaurant hailed by some as the finest in Pinar del Río. Its menu trumpets the restaurant's "chicken gordon blue." Alas, since the onset of the Special Period, the "Castle in the Clouds" has lost its luster, and all it can offer me is a *bocadito*, or Spam sandwich.

I have better luck at La Moka, perched amid eucalyptus and smooth-barked *almácigo* trees on a hillside overlooking a showcase village called Las Terrazas. My room boasts a steeped wood-beamed ceiling and tasteful decor. Furniture of glossy hardwoods. Cowhide chairs. Bronze-gilt paddle ceiling fans. Shuttered windows with wooden *rejas*. A cool, ceramic-tile floor with a matching tile headboard runs the length of one wall. I pull off my leathers and soak in a bathtub that offers a picture-perfect view through a floor-to-ceiling glass window down through the trees to a lake.

In the dining room, Chris Mattison introduces himself with a cheery "'ello!" He is from Sheffield, in northern England—a fellow Yorkshireman. His business card shows two lizards peering bug-eyed into his camera. Chris has written several books on reptiles and amphibians; he and his wife, Gretchen, are here to photograph local fauna.

"T' staff laughed when they saw me chasing lizards across t' lawn," Chris says in his soupy dialect. "Don't be alarmed if ah jump over t' railing onto yer balcony."

The couple are going to spend the evening hunting for snakes. Rain falls as we speak.

"What a pity. I guess you won't be going out tonight."

"*Au contraire.* It's just the job. T' rain 'll drive t' snakes out o' their 'oles," he replies.

Gretchen gets to hold the flashlight. She also catches the snakes, which the couple put in boxes kept in their room so Chris can photograph them by daylight. Any reptiles they catch by day are put in an ice cooler in the trunk of their rental car.

"We've not lost any snakes yet," Chris adds, "though Gretchen thought she'd killed a pygmy boa when she sat on it, di'n't yer, luv?"

They've been in Cuba ten days and have caught only three snakes. Gretchen has managed to catch a huge toad, but *Sminthilus limbatus*, the smallest frog in the world, is proving elusive. Chris expounds on the local ecology.

"T' Yanks introduced white-tailed deer to t' island some time earlier this century. It were an eco-disaster," he says. "Yer see, they graze on saplings. Most of Cuba's forest were cut down in t' 19th century for sugarcane. T' local primary forest dun't 'ave time to regenerate 'cause t' deer nibble on t' saplings."

These mountains were heavily logged for coffee plantings in the 1800s by French settlers who had fled Haiti in 1792. As time passed, erosion and infertility led to the land's abandonment. The slopes were further denuded in the 19th century by impoverished peasants who, living amid mountain terrain ill-suited to farming, attempted to eke out a living as charcoal burners. In 1967 the government initiated a reforestation project, employing the impoverished *campesinos* and providing them with housing in a model village designed by Osmany Cienfuegos, the communist patriarch and architect I met at the tourism convention in Havana. Las Terrazas is named for its terraces of teak, cedar, mahogany, and pine; the trees are planted two at a time, side by side, so that of each pair one will die in the struggle for life, providing a source of charcoal and lumber.

Las Terrazas, tucked into a narrow valley above the shores of Lago San Juan, is unlike any other village I will see in Cuba. The red-tile-roofed, prefab concrete apartment homes rise on stilts and are aligned in sinuous rows on grassy slopes cascading down to the lake, proving that Communists can harmoniously blend humanity with nature when they try. The houses have been spruced up with whitewash and fresh coats of paint—orange for the doors, blue for the shutters. Renowned as an artisans' center, the community features pottery and serigraphy workshops, as well as a cooperative where women conjure hats, baskets, and other items from banana leaves and straw.

I knock at a door in Unit 4 and Lester Campa answers. The 27-year-old artist doesn't recognize me: I have cut my hair and traded my contact lenses for glasses since I last saw him two years ago. When I mention that I am a friend of Sandra Levinson's, however, Campa instantly recalls my visit. He ushers me into his tiny apartment studio, cluttered with canvases. An easel stands in the center. Paintbrushes and tubes of watercolors are scattered about.

Campa—short and impish, with long dark hair tied up in a ponytail and a neatly trimmed beard—is one of Cuba's foremost young artists. He is known for his tropical primitivist landscapes, in which fantastic forests and surreal formations stand in halftones against foreboding backgrounds. They are etched with the painstaking love of a Persian miniaturist.

Campa tells me that a show of his works, arranged through Sandra's Center for Cuban Studies, is to be held in New York; he is hopeful that the U.S. State Department will grant him a visa to attend the opening. It was later denied, possibly because Campa—insufficiently anti-Castro for Uncle Sam— feels that he has been well served by the Cuban state.

Cuba has 21 art schools, organized regionally with at least one per province. Budding talent is identified at an early age, and the most gifted children are boarded at these special schools. Campa studied at Havana's Escuela Superior de Arte, Cuba's preeminent art school, reserved for *la crema de la crema*. After graduating he chose to return to his village in Pinar del Río.

I ask what his training was like.

Campa explains that formal schools in Cuba emphasize fundamental classical techniques in still life, figure form, and landscape. This accounts for his delicate precision and technical finish.

"When students have mastered these skills," Campa informs me, "they are challenged to explore and develop their personal styles as their individual imagination permits."

"Then you weren't intimidated into an ideological straitjacket?"

"No, we were given encouragement. You cannot institutionalize art. It is a living thing that sparks in spite of dogma. But there are limits," he replies, shrugging his shoulders. "Most artists working today are true to what they perceive their social obligations to be. But they're moving. They're not bound to one way of working. We're walking a path between worlds."

Campa's themes dwell on deforestation. It is socially engaged art, reflecting Castro's 1961 maxim: "Think more of the message than the aesthetic."

"What about money? Does the state employ you?"

"That used to be the case for most artists. But since 1992 the government has acknowledged that the artist has a right to his works. They are sold through state institutions, which retain a percentage. Sandra sells my works in the United States. It's incredible! I owe a lot to her."

Theoretically, artists receive up to 85 percent of earnings from their works licensed or sold abroad. Artex—a self-financing, profit-oriented government agency—represents Cuban artists and markets their works on a contractual basis. I cannot believe that Campa receives his full share, though he says so. In North America, his works sell for hundreds of dollars—far more than the Cuban government, with its fixation on socialist equality and communist purity, allows individual citizens to earn. The government occasionally purges entrepreneurs it considers too prosperous by seizing their possessions bought with "excess profits."

The scenery continued to build with tropical intensity. The towns thinned out and the coast highway began to deteriorate; deep potholes stole my eyes from the topaz bays and bottle-green mountains. Occasionally I passed thatched rural homesteads—*bohíos*—and oxen working the palm-studded fields. Beach-rimmed cays hovered tantalizingly on the horizon of a teal blue sea.

West of Bahía Honda, I was lured from the highway by a sensuously rounded peak, the color of a bruise and shown on my map as Pan de Guajaibón. The road curled upward between billowing hillocks. It was hedged by fence posts cut from the *piñon* tree, which grows from a stick in the ground and bursts into efflorescent pink blossom in season. Soon I was edging along beneath sheer-faced mountains. The rust-red soil had been planted with coffee bushes, dark green and shiny-leafed and aligned in neat rows. Bundles of burlap and cotton lay in pools of shade on the ground. As I roared by they stirred, rolled over, and turned into people—field hands snoozing under Royal palms. They held up their hands and made strange hand signals, as if they were handling glove puppets, with all four fingers extended and the thumb beneath, opening and closing like a duck's beak. *Quack, quack!*

I waved back.

The road fizzled out at the hamlet of Rancho Canelo, where a half-dozen rusty metal cutouts of pint-size military tanks and planes had been propped up in a field overgrown with scrub and grasses. There were metal GI Joes, too, like giant-size cookie-tin figures. Real-life soldiers began to appear, emerging from a brick-walled compound riddled with weeds. They were dressed in a motley assortment of tatterdemalion fatigues.

The past decade has seen a dramatic fall in military spending—from $2.24 billion in 1988 to $701 million in 1996, according to the CIA—that has forced the 180,000-strong Fuerzas Armadas Revolucionarias (FAR) to earn its way by what it produces. In recent years it has returned to the model of the "civil soldier" who assists in construction and agriculture. These young conscripts were singing for their supper in the coffee fields. In scuffed boots and patched pants, they did not inspire much confidence in Cuba's ability to repel a U.S. invasion. I knew otherwise.

"If they come," warns Fidel. "they'll experience another Vietnam."

Cuba boasts a formidable military commanded by Fidel's younger brother, Raúl. Its ranks are filled with battle-tested soldiers: About 377,000 Cuban troops were rotated through Angola and Ethiopia between 1975 and 1991, when the last soldiers came home. In addition, Cuba has several hundred thousand reservists and territorial militias. The key to defense, however, is the *Guerra de Todo el Pueblo* (War of All the People); the words are written on the back of the 10-peso bill. In the event of an attack, the *entire* population of Cuba will be called into action. To this end, regular defense exercises are conducted for all segments of the civilian population one Sunday, called *Día de la Defensa,* each month. The island is saturated with weapons, and virtually every adult knows how to use them.

At a dusty hamlet called Las Pozas, in a restaurant called El Mambí—the first I had seen in two days—I quaffed a *refresco* of deliciously sweet fresh-squeezed orange juice scooped from an earthenware vat resembling an Etruscan amphora. Seven pesos (30 cents) bought me a salad of pickled cucumber and a plate of fatty roast pork with black beans and rice. La Palma, farther west, had the first shops I had seen since Havana. Nor had I seen any billboards, no advertisements imploring me to buy, buy, buy. There was a distinct lack of hype.

I was riding in a tank top with the hot sun on my shoulders and the wind rippling the hair on my arms. I felt engaged. Now I understood the glory of motorcycling. I could never have gotten as close to this beauty inside a car. The soft texture of Cuba and the sizzling microwave heat got to me. It felt intoxicating. Just me and the bike purring steadily along a wide-open road.

Valle de Viñales took my breath away. Great *mogotes*—sheer, freestanding knolls the size of skyscrapers—loomed over a broad valley suffused with the sunlit softness of Pisarro. The mogotes had gotten their start during the Jurassic era about 160 million years ago, when a great limestone plateau rose from the sea. Over the eons, rainfall dissolved pockets in the limestone mass, forming underground caverns. Eventually these collapsed, leaving jungle-smothered mogotes towering over a broad valley and separated by canyons called *hoyos*. Loamy soil the color of ripe tomatoes was being tilled by ox-drawn plows tended by guajiros, or Cuban peasants—always mustachioed, dressed in straw hats and white linens or army fatigues, machetes at their sides.

I dismounted and strolled into a *vega*, a tobacco field, where a sun-bronzed, middle-aged *veguero* stood chest high amid the crop he was harvesting.

"¿Me permite, señor?"

"Sí, claro. Venga, amigo!"

Alejandro Alejo snicked the leaves swiftly yet gently with a tiny sickle, then bundled them up into *planchas*, or hands, which he laid out on long *cujes*, or poles. He fussed over the leaves as if he were, in the words of José Martí, handling the "gracious plant...as though each plant were a delicate lady."

Eager to understand why Cuban cigars are the best in the world, I asked Alejandro how tobacco is grown.

"First we must plant the seeds," he began. "This we do beneath beds of straw or cloth toward the end of October when the rains are over. Once the seeds germinate, the cover is removed and the baby plants are nurtured like little children, until they are large enough to be introduced to the fields perhaps one month later."

He swept his arm over his vegas.

"It takes four months or so to mature, after which it is ready to harvest. But you must have patience, and care for each plant as you would a child. It is *precioso* and requires daily attention. You must love it, for everything about its nurturing is rewarding."

I followed Alejandro into a windowless log structure with a steep-pitched thatched roof. Here the tobacco is cured in the cool shade on cujes until the green chlorophyll turns to brown carotene, giving the leaves the look of smoked kippers. I breathed in the heady sweetness of sour tobacco. The hut was aligned east to west, Alejandro explained, so that the sun would heat one end in the morning and the other in the afternoon. The doors are opened and closed, too, to help maintain the desired temperature and humidity.

After two months or so in the sheds, the leaves are taken down and bundled into wooden cases. These are taken to the *escogida*, the sorting house, where they are separated, dampened, aired, flattened out, and tied again in bundles, then stacked in piles for up to three months. During that time they ferment like compost heaps to release ammonia and other impurities. Whenever the temperature reaches about 110°F, the pile is turned to ensure even fermentation. The leaves are graded according to color, size, and quality, then stripped of their midribs and flattened, moistened with water, covered with burlap, and fermented again before being reclassified, packed up in bales, and shipped off to factories. There the leaves will be stored and matured for up to four years before they are ready to be rolled into cigars.

Alejandro owns the land he tills, as do many of Viñales' vegueros (the average vega is 25 hectares; the maximum permissible holding is 150 hectares), although he must sell his crop to the government at a fixed rate. His home is his, too—a simple one-story wooden structure with a red-tile roof, linoleum floor, and glassless windows. Ampara, his wife, took my two hands disarmingly and drew me inside. The cozy dwelling was spotlessly clean. There were plastic flowers in a bowl on the table, antimacassars draped over the sofa. A framed photo of Che Guevara stared down from atop a huge Russian refrigerator in the hallway.

I asked how things were. Had the Special Period been hard for them?

"For us, the people of Viñales, things are good," Alejandro answered. "We are simple people. We are not rich like you *norteamericanos*. But we grow all the food we need. And we have our health. The Revolution has been kind to us."

"Why does your government not like us?" Amparo asked. "They are too hard on us Cubans." As I left, she kissed my cheeks and thrust half a dozen tomatoes into my hand.

I cruised slowly down the tree-lined main street of Viñales, a charming village edged with turn-of-the-century, red-tile-roofed cottages shaded by columned arcades called *portales*. Heads turned as I continued down Calle Salvador Cisneros. Cubans gawked at the yanqui in his black leathers astride his ostentatious capitalist toy.

There were those hand-signals again. *Quack, quack!* The sign seemed like a secret code, a freemason's greeting. I replied with a thumbs-up. People stopped what they were doing to watch me pass. Another arm went up. *Quack!* I waved. Then another. *Quack, quack!* Still no response. A third. *Quack, quack, quack!*

"*Lalooshendi!*" one of the rubberneckers screamed. *What?*

A *tráfico*—a motorcycle cop—stepped into the road and pulled me over. He saluted, glanced at my *licencia* and driver's license, then launched into a barrage of questions: "*¿Que marca? ¿Cúantas ce-ce? ¿Qué velocidad?*" What make of motorbike? What size engine? How fast will it go? Then "*Pheeew...hombre!*"

A crowd had gathered around us, and onlookers were probing the BMW's organs. No one seemed incredulous that I had traveled from California. Cubans rarely betray astonishment. Their lives are so topsy-turvy that not much can surprise them any more. But the motorbike's gargantuan size and its gaudy lipstick-red paint job held them spellbound. With its tubular-steel crash frame and armor plating designed to go one-on-one with a charging rhino, the Paris-Dakar was unlike anything these Cubans had ever seen. You'd have thought I'd landed in a flying saucer.

One of the onlookers had a Ural with sidecar, and he invited me to give it a try. It was no Swiss watch. I pulled on the clutch. It didn't budge. Greater determination was needed. *Ker-LUNK!* The gear dropped into place like the lock of a safe snapping shut. I let out the clutch and leaned down on the throttle, and the funky slab of retro iron eased away like a snail. The overhead-valve, opposed-twin, four-stroke 649cc engine was as responsive as a Mexican burro. It had the solidity of a T-34 tank and a fittingly deep, phlegmy sound—a gruff conveyance forged for the bland steppes of Russia.

The Ural dates from 1939, when the Soviets bought five sample BMWs from the Germans in the days of the Hitler-Stalin nonaggression pact. Russian engineers then duplicated the no-nonsense machine for the Soviet military. Their job was made easier in 1945, when the Russians captured Munich. They dismantled the city's BMW factory, loaded up the tools and dies, and shipped them east to their factory at Irbit near the base of the Ural mountains. The factory has been churning them out ever since. After the Cuban Revolution, the World War II workhorse—a version of the 1938 R75 BMW—invaded Cuba along with the Soviets. In the ensuing years, the design has hardly changed at all.

I took a room at La Ermita, another au courant hotel. This one hinted architecturally at ancient Crete; it nestled atop the valley's southern scarp, giving dramatic views over the village and quilted fields where white oxen combed the cinnamon soils into furrows. From on high, Viñales looked as if it had fallen from its own postcard. Everything still seemed sharp in the evening light. Egrets were winging across the tobacco fields, while buzzards wheeled overhead on the thermals. The crowing of cockerels and the muffled clip-clop of hooves on cobbles echoed up from the valley below. I heard the *thwump-thwump-thwump* of a helicopter, imagining myself for a second in a scene from *Apocalypse Now*. Then I realized the noise came from an old American car puttering along far below. The valley was a gargantuan soundbox.

I sat in an Adirondack chair on my patio, sipping chilled Hatuey beer and watching the setting sun gild the mountains and fire the billowy clouds luminescent within. Then the sun slid from view below a molten sky turned to flaming orange and carnal plum purple. The barman had been playing a Van Morrison tape. He turned it off for the sunset, and together we watched the shadows thicken and the mogotes fade into darkness in silence. Pinpricks of light—bohíos lit by the warm glow of lanterns and wan lamps tracing the village streets—began twinkling across the valley.

I sat in the dark and pursued the fireflies of my day's recollections as real fireflies flitted by and the geckos called from the eaves.

The blacktop had disappeared long ago, and I paralleled the north coast on piste so jarring that at times I rode standing on the footpegs.

The sun blazed. The air shimmered. By 11 o'clock, the heat was ferocious. Sweat trickled down from inside my helmet. Even my hands were sweating inside my mitten gloves, which in time became encrusted with a fine film of salt. I passed cattle lying doggo-style and guajiros standing shell-shocked in the shade of Cuban pines.

Outside a pretty village called Dimas, I spotted a gleaming 1953 Oldsmobile Super 88. It was a foppish metallic peacock blue, so gorgeous it would have fooled any peahen, and as shiny as the day it rolled from the factory floor. I pulled over and cut the motor.

The Olds was a blunt-nosed behemoth with a broad, grinning grill—the automotive equivalent of Jack Palance. It had a symbol of a rocket next to the "88," a chrome rocket for a hood handle, and glinting chrome stars down the side. Amazingly, there was not a single dent in the bodywork. A museum piece.

The burly owner, Aramís Santana Cosme, emerged from beneath the hood and extended an oil-blackened hand.

"*Mire, señor,*" he said, proudly inviting me to admire the original leather and trimmings. A small fan had been wired to the battery and screwed to the dashboard. Strings of red and black beads dangled from the mirror, invoking the protection of Elegguá, the Yoruban *orisha,* or god, of destiny and the guardian of roads in the Cuban *Santería* religion. Aramís wanted to take me for *una paseíto,* a little rumba down the road, but "*desgraciadamente, señor,*" his mechanical dinosaur had run out of gas.

In Cuba you can drive for two hours or more and not see a car. How many cars had I passed today—half a dozen? They were all yanqui classics evoking 1950s nostalgia. Pride-in-America pathos is reason enough to visit Cuba.

American cars had flooded Cuba for 50 years culminating in the Batista era, when no other country in the world imported so many Cadillacs and Studebakers and DeSotos. Most numerous were staid Buick Centurys, Chrysler New Yorkers, and Ford Customlines. According to the 1960 *United Nations Statistical Yearbook*, in 1959 Cuba possessed more privately owned passenger cars per inhabitant than did Spain, and almost as many as Italy. Then Castro & Co. made a beautiful revolution but spun off into Soviet orbit, invoking the U.S. trade embargo that had cast a time-warp spell over Cuba.

It's a tribute both to Detroit and to Cuban ingenuity that the antique rolling stock heroically soldiers on. Lacking proper tools and replacement parts, Cubans adeptly coax along their dilapidated hulks, their reconstituted engines monuments to mechanical wizardry. Decades of underhood guile and improvised alchemy have melded parts from Detroit and Moscow. Carburetors are held together with homemade nuts and bolts; vital organs are replaced with parts cannibalized from other cars.

The Cuban government is well aware that the island is a four-wheeled museum to sockhop-era American capitalism. During the 1980s it attempted to redeem this aging asset by selling the cars to foreign collectors. For a while, old yanqui clunkers could legally be turned over only to Cubalse, a state agency, which offered only worthless pesos or a dowdy Soviet Lada (everyone agreed they were lemons) in return. Cubalse then sold the vintage autos for dollars to foreign buyers. Throughout the island, government lots were turned into acres of ancient chrome. In 1989, having discovered that officials were diverting cash into their own pockets, the government ended the program. Quixotically, the Trading with the Enemy Act prevents U.S. citizens from buying a Cuban *cacharro;* whatever their color, the cars are apparently a little too red.

I set off again with the mercury well above 100°. Before long I was broiling. Even the livestock was having a hard time: Near Mantua I passed a horse lying by the side of the road, done in by heat exhaustion. Four guajiros were trying to rally it to its feet with poles while a dog snapped at the horse's nose, drawing blood.

After three days' riding, my back had stiffened and my left shoulder felt like it had been pierced by a hot poker. I leaned forward and rode with my chest on the tank bag, but that fatigued the muscles in my forearms. I had anticipated a numb butt at the end of a long day of motorcycling, but the Corbin seat was well scooped out and wide enough to provide plenty of inner-thigh support; even after a full day in the saddle, I never got sore.

I had traveled 226 miles since last tanking up, but I wasn't worried. The Paris-Dakar's refrigerator-size gas tank holds enough fuel to qualify for OPEC membership. I could cruise all day, but never had to. Cupet, the state petroleum agency formed in 1990 as a joint Cuban-Mexican venture, had been busy opening up state-of-the-art gasoline stations all over Cuba. A liter of gas cost 90 cents (about $3.40 a gallon)—greenbacks only, *por favor.*

Whenever I found a hotel or restaurant, I stopped and checked it out for my guidebook. My map showed a motel called Las Cuevas on the outskirts of Isabel Rubio. A faded plastic sign pointed the way. The motel was tucked off the main road in a bowl surrounded by cliffs pocked with caves containing stalagmites and stalactites resembling silken curtains. A young woman dressed in clinical whites peered up at me from behind the reception desk.

"Buenos días, compañera," I said, trying out the term coined in the Revolution to replace the more bourgeois *señor* and *señora,* with their intimations of status and class. I liked the word: It rolled off the tongue and seemed to resonate, as someone had suggested, with a revolutionary sense of *egalité.*

"Do you accept foreigners?" I asked in Spanish.

She looked perplexed. "Are you alone, *compañero?"*

"Excuse me?"

"Where is your partner?"

"My partner? Yes, I'm alone. If you accept foreigners, I'd appreciate it if you could give me a few moments of your time. It won't take long. I only need five minutes," I continued.

Perhaps my Spanish was off. The woman's jaw dropped slightly. She frowned and seemed abashed. *"Those* days ended with the *triunfo de la revolución,"* she replied enigmatically. "You must bring your own partner."

Those days? What did she mean?

"I'm sorry, I don't understand," I replied, feeling like Alice talking to the March Hare.

"Then you should say what you mean," the March Hare went on.

"I do," Alice hastily replied: *"at least—at least I mean what I say—that's the same thing, you know."*

"Not the same thing a bit!" said the Hatter. "Why, you might just as well say that 'I see what I eat is the same thing as I eat what I see.'"

A tall black man appeared. He too wore a white smock. She whispered into his ear, and his eyebrows furrowed.

"I'm writing a travel guidebook about Cuba," I explained. "I'd appreciate the opportunity to take a look at your hotel."

"Ah!" he exclaimed, breaking into a hearty guffaw. "This is a *posada, señor,* not a hotel. The *compañera* misunderstood you and, I am sorry to say, believed that you wished to purchase her services along with a room."

Now I understood: The motel was a 24-hour "love hotel," operated by the state to provide relief for Cubans seeking a place of coital convenience. Most towns have at least one. They're usually discreetly hidden—proof that the Cuban government is sensitive to all basic human needs. The facility charged five pesos for three hours in a wooden *cabina*, with the state thoughtfully providing a bottle of rum by the bed.

"We used to provide condoms also," the woman added matter-of-factly, "but they are now in short supply."

I asked who supplied them. They were Kohinoors, the heavy-duty Cuban condoms that islanders call *el quitasensaciones* (the killjoy) and which, in all senses of the word, are hard to come by. I tried to explain the double entendre, but it didn't survive the translation.

I get lost trying to find Laguna Grande, a lagoon that boasts a hunting and fishing resort, and end up beside a starkly functional Bauhaus structure where the road peters out amid weed-infested farmland. The two-story prefab concrete structure is identical to dozens of uniformly ugly Bulgarian carbuncles that I will see throughout Cuba doing duty as hospitals, hotels, and housing. Most were built by unskilled volunteer labor; as a student, Daisy had a hand in such projects. Faceless bureaucrats had dictated that she study civil construction.

"I hate it," she once told me.

"But if you hate it, why do you study it?" I had naively asked. "Can't you tell them you want to study something else?"

"Are you crazy?" she replied, stroking her chin, a silent reference to *el barbudo*—the bearded one. Few Cubans utter Fidel's name aloud. The reference is usually communicated by the gesture of a hand stroking an imaginary beard.

It was her way of suggesting that survival requires complicity to the Revolution. Daisy showed me her *cédula*—a little blue book that every adult Cuban must carry at all times, containing the person's family details and residential and employment history.

"What's this space here for?" I asked, pointing to a blank section.

"*Noticias.* I have to be a good revolutionary. If I cut class they'll record it here. *No integrado.* Everyone has to pretend to be loyal to get by."

It wasn't just the *cédulas*, Daisy explained. The Ministry of the Interior (MININT) maintains a file on every adult—a dossier that follows him or her from home to home and job to job. Daisy had studied diligently until the state pulled the plug on her as punishment for marrying a foreigner and applying for an exit permit. To Fidel Castro you are either for the Revolution or against it. There is no middle ground.

"What happens to those students who flunk their studies?" I asked.

"Oh, they're sent to work on construction projects."

No wonder this structure, a rural boarding school, looks jury-rigged. It is stained black by tropical mire and utterly melancholy. Rubble litters the forecourt. Teenagers mill about dressed in uniform. White shirts and red neckerchiefs; ocher yellow long pants for the boys and, for the girls, indecently short miniskirts worn all the way up to their...12th grade.

Other students, dressed in civvies, are out in the fields. The school is part of Cuba's Schools in the Countryside program, begun in 1971 as part of the Revolution's effort to build the New Man—an individual selflessly motivated to building a new society. The program was also a handy way to bring in the harvest. Although the legal minimum working age in Cuba is 17, the Labor Code exempts 15- and 16-year-olds to allow them to fill labor shortages. Thus, secondary schoolchildren spend a part of each year at rural boarding schools attached to plots of arable land, where time is equally divided between study and labor. The kids are fulfilling José Martí's dictum: "In the morning the pen, but in the afternoon the plow."

Very little work gets done in the fields. Students spend much of the day in dalliance, often carnal, until it is time to go home. A recent issue of the weekly *Juventud Rebelde* accused the city-raised youngsters of engaging in orgies, "a collective exhibition of the most crude coitus," and went on to warn youths against "excessive fornication."

Was this true? I asked Daisy.

"Yes, it's true," she replied, dropping her eyes. "We spent a lot of time fooling around."

At La Bajada, the road dips to the shore. A chain has been stretched across the road at waist height. A soldier appears. His face is pinched like a turtle's, and he carries an AK-47 in his hands. My lighthearted "Hi!" leaves him cold. Behind him a huge bay—Bahía de Corrientes—curls around like a shepherd's crook, fringed by a narrow sliver of talcum-white sand dissolving into a coruscating sea the color of melted peridots. These waters are famed for superlative diving, and the Cuban government promotes the deep-sea treasures to scuba divers.

My back is burning; I pull up at Villa María la Gorda with huge relief. I dismount, make two trips to my room with saddlebags, tank bag, and duffel, then pull off my leathers and collapse on the bed. My arms are so tired I can hardly bend them. My bungalow—lumpy mattress and all—is as spartan as the land I've just passed through. The only other furniture is a utility-style table and chair, an empty refrigerator, and a Russian television from the days of Sputnik. Gecko droppings are piled on the windowsill. The room costs 15 dollars.

The parking-lot attendant appears at my door and recommends that I put my bike inside the games room, so I fire up and ride it down the beach to the bar, where I get a good grip on the handlebars and give it some throttle to bounce the front wheel over the sill and between the glass doors.

Out in the bay a yacht flying the Stars and Stripes is attempting to anchor. American accents echo across a sea as calm and as warm as bedtime milk. I watch a blond bombshell in a pink bikini hauling on the anchor line while the setting sun turns the Caribbean to copper.

The dining room resembles a workers' canteen. The patrons—two German guys, a young French couple, a family of Cubans, and four Cuban dive masters—keep to themselves. Photos of Neptune's larder festoon the walls: Giant grouper and other tasty treats stare eye to eye with divers and otherwise ham it up for the camera. On the buffet table, by contrast, not a semblance of fish can be seen. It's like a potluck party where most of the guests failed to contribute. I make do with pickled cucumber, sliced ham and cheese, a chicken leg, and boiled potatoes speckled by hard black nodules like grapeshot. Another 15 dollars.

Russell Haertl, the Yankee skipper, introduces himself in the bar. He describes his yacht, the *Endeavor,* as a "pocket cruiser." He's six weeks out of Galveston. This is his first ocean voyage. We sip frosty Hatueys and watch the Cuban staff play pool. One guy keeps grabbing his balls before each shot, giving a new meaning to the term pocket billiards. The BMW stands in the center of the dance floor.

"Any problems getting it into Cuba?" Russell asks me.

"Nah. It was surprisingly easy. How about you?"

"Nope. Except they held us up for two days in Havana after those two Brothers to the Rescue planes were shot down. No boats were allowed in or out," he replied. "So what do you think that affair is all about?"

Cuban news reports had been giving the incident prime coverage and were bubbling with indignation over the incendiary reaction in Washington. The shooting had happened at the peak of the Florida primaries, and Republican presidential hopefuls were leaping over one another trying to win the Cuban-American vote. Senator Jesse Helms, Chairman of the Senate Foreign Relations Committee, had harnessed the anti-Castro momentum to push his stalled Cuban Liberty and Democratic Solidarity Act through Congress.

President Clinton had threatened to veto the legislation, more commonly known as the Helms-Burton Bill, but then got sucked into the political vortex. The act had shredded Clinton's carefully calibrated policy of encouraging democratic change within Cuba, forcing him to make a sharp right turn. He had just promised to sign the legislation, which would add draconian elements to the existing embargo and hand the reins on Cuba policy to Helms, an unrepentant Cold Warrior who had threatened to take Castro out "in either a horizontal or vertical position." Details of the law were being widely publicized in Cuba, accompanied by cartoons depicting Helms as Hitler and the Devil. Meanwhile the Castro regime was still claiming that the two paramilitary planes had been shot down inside Cuban airspace; the MiG pilots, it claimed, had been defending national sovereignty.

Without access to international news reports, it was difficult to determine the truth.

"I don't know, Russell," I reply. "But when the fog lifts, I bet you the whole thing will look like it was written by a conspiracy theorist."

On the bar's television, Ricardo Alarcón, the National Assembly president and Cuba's top emissary in dealings with the U.S., is denouncing Clinton for allowing himself to be manipulated by the Cuban-American lobby.

Russell wisely changes the subject. "How'd this place get its name?"

María la Gorda. *Fat Mary.* I hadn't thought about it. We ask the barman.

"María era una puta," he replies.

"A prostitute?"

"Sí, she very big. *Muy gorda,"* he says, tracing his hands around her imagined voluptuous contours. "She come from Venezuela with pirates who make her slave. They live here. Bahía de Corrientes have many pirates."

Later, it seems, María gained her freedom, leased her ample flesh to passing sailors, and prospered. Her venue became known as *Casa de las Tetas de María la Gorda*...House of Fat Mary's Tits.

Next day, the turtle-faced soldier was still nursing his AK-47. I showed him my handwritten permit to travel along the Península de Guanahacabíbes, a rugged, uninhabited witch's finger that juts out into the Strait of Yucatán. He scrutinized my papers, then raised the barrier and waved me on. Immediately the road became a jarring piste of sharp coral blazing so bright that my sunglasses couldn't cut the glare. It was white-hot, like burning magnesium. I needed welder's glasses.

Patches of loose sand and scree lay in irregular windrows that shook my bones till they rattled. I gave the Beemer more gas, thinking I could speed up and stay on top of the teeth-chattering washboard. I hauled along in third gear, but the bouncing and beating sounded like a monkey going ape-shit with a hammer and anvil. I couldn't stand beating my bike that hard, so I slowed to a snail's pace. The bike, for its part, was feeling no pain; this was just the kind of abuse the brutish Paris-Dakar had been built to withstand.

The Paris-Dakar is neither small nor light. A full tank of gas adds 60 pounds. Fully laden with luggage and the tank topped up, I figured the bike was edging up to the 800-pound figure with me astride the saddle. That's heavy. Soft sand is no fun with a third of a ton to control. At slow speeds, the weight was too much to wade through the sandy pools that made the bike mush and waver so that the front wheel augered in, threatening to spill me into the cactus. I tightened my hold on the grips and felt my body tense in anticipation of falling.

Then I almost collided with a Gaz jeep careering madly toward me. I hit the front brake. The wheel lost traction, and it was only by judicious footwork that I didn't go down. *Gotta remember to use the rear brake in loose gravel*, I told myself. The jeep was teeming with Cuban troops, including a military bigwig who demanded to see my passport and permit. Then he noticed my California license plate. His face knotted. *Where was I going? Where had I been? Why was I here?* He studied me gravely, then waved me on. These military figures were ever vigilant for foreign subversion, and they took their business seriously. I understood; 90 miles away stood the most powerful nation on earth, bent on destroying the Cuban government. It was a scenario guaranteed to create paranoia.

After 35 miles of tortuous piste it was a relief to arrive at Cabo San Antonio, where I fished out my camera to prove I had reached the westernmost tip of Cuba, capped by a lighthouse and a military camp. A soldier rushed up and warned me not to take any photos, but my tongue turned the tables: He wound up snapping a shot of me in front of the lighthouse, beaming proudly alongside *mi moto Fidel.*

CHAPTER FOUR

A SEDUCTIVE ISLE

I was famished. In the small fishing town of Cortés I located two state-run *merenderos*, or snack counters. One was closed and the other had nothing to sell. *"¡No hay!"* was all I heard. *There is none!* Where was McDonald's when I needed it? Or 7-Eleven? Come to think of it, there weren't *any* groceries— at least none worth the name. The state-run *puesto* could offer only a small stock of potatoes, onions, and some overripe plantains as black as garden slugs. I had passed row upon row of citrus trees. Why was it impossible to find an orange for sale? A woman behind the counter pointed me to the state-run Tienda Panamericana, or "foreign exchange recovery store," stocked with imported goods sold for dollars and hidden behind silvered windows. It was closed. A small crowd had gathered outside. No one was sure when it might open. They waited anyway. I joined the *cola*, the line.

No tourists ever came through Cortes. Where on earth were these folks getting greenbacks?

"The lucky ones have family abroad," said a middle-aged woman with her hair in curlers. "Me, I have a son in Spain."

"We all get by on *fé*," said another; she had a towel stylishly tied up on her head.

"¿Fé?"

"Sí. *La familia extranjera*," she replied, referring to families abroad but alluding to an acronym that is a subtle play on the Spanish word for "faith."

A few years ago, the peso had some value. Today it is virtually worthless. Life has become organized around a mad scramble for dollars. About 25 percent of the population has regular access to greenbacks, Cuban economists reckon. Those without *fé* must rely on their ingenuity. The majority have to simply *buscar la forma*—find a way.

The 1990s were calamitous for a population used to a far higher standard of living. On the eve of the collapse of the Soviet Union, 84 percent of Cuba's trade was with the Soviet bloc, on which Cuba relied for virtually every item imaginable (the Soviet Union also sustained the Cuban economy with an aid package averaging $3 billion a year). In 1989, the Berlin Wall collapsed and the communist dominoes came tumbling down. That same year General Noriega was ousted from Panama, Cuba's main conduit for Western goods. Then, on August 18, 1991—the last day of the highly successful Pan-American Games in Havana (Cuba won with 140 gold medals)—the Soviet Union began its dizzying unraveling. Cuba was cast adrift, a lone socialist island in a capitalist sea. When Castro announced that the country was entering a "special period in a time of peace," he was warning that it was about to experience a level of austerity normally seen only in war.

By 1992, trade with Cuba's former communist partners had shriveled to seven percent of its former value. People accustomed to a government-subsidized food basket that guaranteed at least two meals a day suddenly faced acute shortages of every staple. When East German powdered milk ceased to arrive, Cuba eliminated butter; when Czechoslovakian malt no longer arrived, Cuban beer disappeared. Soaps, detergents, deodorants, toilet paper, clothing—*everything* vanished. Even cigarettes were limited to three packs a month. The scarcities were manifest in long lines for rationed goods, a phenomenon that had nearly disappeared by the mid-1980s. People had to stand in line, sometimes all day, for everything.

After the last Soviet tanker departed in June 1992, the economy slipped into a coma. Without oil or gasoline, tractors and harvesters lay idle, replaced by mules and oxen. There was no fuel for transportation. Harvests rotted in the fields, undermining Castro's bedrock promise that all Cubans would have enough to eat. A country that had eliminated hunger began to suffer malnutrition. I had heard tales of hamburgers made from banana peels and steaks made from grapefruit rinds. *Buzos*—people who forage in garbage bins—had returned for the first time since the Revolution. Cubans began rearing jutías, the ratlike native rodents. The most desperate resorted to rats.

Only in 1995 had things begun to improve. Making dollars legally available had eased life for those Cubans with access to greenbacks; the *mercados agropecuarios* (farmers' markets) and *paladares*—restaurants in private homes— had improved matters for those without. But Cortés was an indication that Cuba's decrepit economy was still in shambles. A melancholic stillness lay upon the forlorn streets lined by sun-blitzed houses that hadn't seen a coat of paint in almost four decades.

Growing tired of waiting for the *tienda* to open, I opted for a snack from roadside food stalls that displayed their meager offerings in glass cases: *galletas* or sweet biscuits, deep-fried donut rings called *churizo*, and Spam *bocaditos*. I bought a bocadito for 50 centavos. It tasted loathsome: It was *picadillo*, a "meat-some mass"—the official term—of second-grade ground meat mixed with soybean. Much of the food supplied by the state and provided for in the *libreta* you would not feed to your cat. Not that there are many of those anyway; most of their forebears having wound up in cooking pots in the early 1990s, cats are only now making a comeback. Horribly dry, my bread metamorphosed into a sticky mass in my mouth.

I couldn't blame the Revolution for the bread. It had always been that way. Even Che Guevara, stoic among stoics, arriving in Cuba in 1956 complained: "Why can't the Cubans make decent bread?" I dislodged the gooey blob and washed away the evil Spam taste with a delicious *refresco* of fresh-squeezed sugarcane juice to which the fruit of the baobab had been added to lend it a pétillant fizz.

The Hotel Pinar del Río is not the Cinderella portrayed in its brochure; despite a recent facelift, the establishment has yet to meet the standards of a two-star hotel. My room has bright red plastic chairs, a sagging bed, and chipped furnishings. When I pull back the curtains for the view, I am dismayed to find frosted windows. A cockroach scuttles for cover. I pull off my boots, wriggle my toes to get the blood back, and fall onto the bed, done in by heat and fatigue.

When I come to, I throw on denims and go down to the bar, swilling a *mojito* while mosquitoes nibble my ankles. They are breeding in the stagnant lily pond in the center of the lobby. Then the lights go out. An *apagón*—a power blackout intended to save electricity. So I fire up the bike and cruise into town in the dark, savoring the rich, moist, warm Cuban air smelling sweetly of mimosa and mildew. Fortunately the town center has power. I head down Calle Gerardo Medina, where the town's youths are gathered outside Coppelia, Cuba's answer to Baskin-Robbins. The youngsters are dolled up in the latest fashions, as far as their paltry budgets permit. The girls flaunt flared jeans, miniskirts, halter tops, diaphanous blouses, and thick-soled shoes. Many wear modish little rucksacks on their backs. The young men follow suit in loose jeans, sneakers, T-shirts, and baseball caps emblazoned with slogans for Reebok and Nike. Several of the males sport earrings and long hair worn stylishly loose or tied back in ponytails. Black and white mingle with ease.

They are jiving in the street to a brassy salsa tune played on bassy speakers tethered to telegraph poles, moving sinuously to Latin rhythms under bare light bulbs that cast shadows on crumbling stucco and cinder-block walls. Fast and infectious, the music is hot enough to melt the ice cream. Girls are being whirled sensuously just a little closer than groin to groin. I am amazed the birth rate isn't higher.

Everywhere I go I am surrounded by sexy rhythms. Norman Mailer once scolded President Kennedy for the Bay of Pigs defeat, says author Tom Miller: "Wasn't there anyone around to give you the lecture on Cuba? Don't you sense the enormity of your mistake—you invade a country without understanding its music."

Farther up the street I pass a gorgeous *negrita* with an hourglass figure and slinky legs. She is wearing the tightest hot pants I've ever seen, and she displays her ample attractions with mischievous wiggles. Two young suitors are trailing her, calling out *piropos,* hoping to reel in a catch. But it is she who has cast the baited hook.

I can't resist. I snatch the brakes and stop too abruptly. The bike and I almost fall over. She smiles and raises her eyebrows. I inflate my qualifications as a potential lover by puffing up my chest, then tell her she is beautiful and provocative.

"Ochún es muy provocativa," she enigmatically replies, referring to the sensuous black goddess or *orisha* of love in *Santería.* The ubiquitous Cuban saint worship—a fusion of Catholicism and the Lucumí religion of the African Yoruba tribes—has been firmly established in Cuba for 300 years. In Santería, Catholic saints are schizoid avatars of the Yoruba orishas, who let down their

hair and are downright salacious. Santería is perfectly suited to Cuba's climate. The orishas let adherents have a good time.

"Are you a goddess?"

"Perhaps. I'm a *bailarina*. When I dance I feel like Ochún. She overwhelms me completely."

Her name is Yudenia. She tells me she is a dancer at the Rumayor Cabaret. "Come see the show this evening." I tell her I'll be there.

At Rumayor, a huge log-and-thatch structure a mile north of town, I pay five dollars and pass through an entryway decorated with African drums, cowhide shields, and fearsome masks. In the open-air courtyard beyond, the seats are all taken—the crowd is entirely Cuban, mostly young couples who have paid 20 pesos—so I stand at the rear and listen to a willowy, coal-black crooner belt out love songs in a white sequined suit. Then stiletto-heeled *mulatas* in riotous feathers and sequined bikinis bounce into the arena, accompanied by a frenzied melee of horns, drums, and maracas, and by male dancers in tight neon spandex. They are followed by a juggling act. Next, drums pound out a *tun q'tu q'tu q'tun* rhythm that builds to a narcotic crescendo; the near-naked girls reappear, adorned as representations of orishas. There is Yudenia, laden with jangling silver jewelry and white and yellow beads of Ochún. She is flailing wildly in the grip of a collective orgy of dance full of sinister and sexual content.

Suddenly the dancers rush into the audience. I am dazzled by spotlights. Yudenia grabs my arm and I am whisked onto the dance floor to make a fool of myself doing a white boy's sclerotic version of the rumba while she shimmies up against me like Jell-O in an earthquake. The crowd roars its approval. Yudenia turns her behind toward me, draws me onto her writhing buttocks, and pulls me across the stage in mock sexual union.

After the show, Yudenia seeks me out. With an easy smile, she calmly says, "Let's go."

"Where to?"

"Your hotel."

Cuban youths discover sex at an early age. In a country where everything else is rationed, they make the most of it. Fortunately, I too am a glutton for what the Spanish term *amante de los placéres*—love of pleasures—which in my case is best enjoyed langorously with a bottle of rum at the side of the bed.

"You taste like chocolate," I say, kissing the nape of her neck. With a flick of her slender foot, Yudenia sends her vermilion panties sailing over my head.

Afterward, I get out of bed to open the window slats. Although the tile floor feels pleasantly cool underfoot, Yudenia tells me to put my shoes on.

"Why?"

"You should always wear shoes after making love."

"Why?" I ask again, even more puzzled.

"You'll catch gonorrhea."

Surely she means the *nigua*, a microscopic mite that burrows into the feet?

"No," she replies. *"Enfermadedes sexuales.* Don't you know that sexual diseases are caught through the soles of your feet after making love?"

For all their intellectual voracity, Cubans constantly astound me with their naiveté.

A pleasing cosmopolitan feel pervades the town of Pinar del Río in the daylight, but it is hardly the "Paradise of the West" touted by the tourist literature. I wander the streets, up one *calle* and down the next, taking stock of the place.

At the bottom of Máximo Gómez I pass horse-drawn *coches*, or canopied wooden carts that serve as taxis. They are tethered behind withered mules that stoically bear the crushing intensity of the sun. I'm standing in the shade of a doorway sketching a map in my notebook when a young Cuban comes up and sticks his nose in my face. He is twenty-something, with almond eyes and an epicene face, and wears a light-blue *guayabera*—the quintessentially Cuban double-pleated, four-pocketed, short-sleeved tropical shirt that is an unofficial uniform of government bureaucrats. Because most younger males wouldn't be caught dead in one, I guess he is employed by MININT.

"Why are you drawing maps?" he asks imperiously. He is six inches shorter than me and has a pugnaciousness rare to Cubans. His tone is all wrong.

"I'm sketching a line from here to there to see how far it is."

"Who gave you permission?"

"Actually, *el jefe* asked me to check." I stroke my chin in an unmistakable gesture.

He grows sterner and deepens his tone. "Are you attempting to find things wrong with the official map?"

Apparently he is convinced that the foreigner is up to no good. I would be happy to explain what I'm up to, but he continues to rub me the wrong way. More important, I fear that to succumb to his questioning will render me accountable to whatever power he may possess. Determined to maintain the upper hand, I ignore his officious quizzing.

"Who gave you permission?" he asks volubly.

I hope to emasculate him with my silence. I stare beyond him and continue sketching. He repeats his question. He stands rooted in front of me, glowering, until I tire of his presence and walk off with a breezy *"Adiós!"*

A *tráfico* waves me down as I roar out of town the next day—could this be related to the map incident? I pull over and cut the engine 100 yards beyond where he stands in the cool penumbra of a spreading jagüey. I stay put, unsure of the protocol, until he eventually emerges from the shade and saunters over.

"Buenos días, señor," I say as he salutes me.

He doesn't even ask for my papers.

"¿Qué marca?" he asks softly. I point to the BMW logo on the gas tank. He reads aloud: *"¿Bay...em-me...doble vay? ¿De dónde?"* He asks where it's from.

"West Germany...And yours? A Moto Guzzi?"

"No. Jawa."

"Ah, Czechoslovakia."

He has never heard of BMW. He wishes me a pleasant journey and gives me another salute.

The Carretera Central wound along the foothills of the sierras and led me to San Diego de los Baños, a small but once-important spa town born in the 17th century—supposedly when a leprous slave was miraculously cured by bathing in the bubbling waters of the Temblado spring. German scholar and explorer Baron Alexander von Humboldt praised the waters, spurring European socialites to flock here. In time the resort was promoted in the United States as the Saratoga of the tropics. After the Revolution, the leisured class fled the island and thermalism found a new clientele from Eastern Europe.

I had hoped for the embalmed grandeur of caryatids and Pompeiian-style frescoed walls—a place to soak up the decadent past—but it was gone, washed away (if ever it existed) by communist asceticism. Still, there was enough mosaic tilework to give a Roman emperor raptures, though the glistening turquoise medium bore none of the fleshy voluptuaries depicted in the great spas of Europe. Worst of all, no sexy Amazons could be found staffing the steam room.

My guide recommended that I imbibe the waters as a stirring tonic. The warm water tasted like sewer-tainted Alka-Seltzer, and I rode the few miles west to Parque Nacional La Güira feeling queasy.

La Güira preserves 54,000 acres of sylvan wilderness rising to pine forests on the upper slopes of the Sierra de los Organos. The road grew steeper with every bend. It was exhilarating opening the throttle on the straights, then dropping into second and cruising effortlessly through the curves. The engine's drone deepened as I wound into the hairpin bends. The cycle thrummed happily as the road swung upward through the dark forest, sunlight flitting through the trees like a strobe.

The road dropped between towering *mogotes* and ended at a riverside *campismo*—a basic holiday camp for Cubans with concrete bungalows, concrete barbecue pits, and a concrete playground. It was easy to imagine the place ringing with children's laughter, but the Special Period had rung the death knell for homegrown tourism, and vegetation was reclaiming the camp.

A short, middle-aged man appeared. He wore a red-and-white-checked shirt, khaki pants, and an impish smile. He shook my hand firmly. Gilberto Cruz was the epitome of Cuban goodwill and good humor. He led me along a stone walkway that sloped gently downhill to the river and opened to a wide platform beneath a great tunnel that the Río Caiguanabo had carved through the mountain.

One side of the arch had been scalloped by the eddying waters to form a deep recess, and a cave entrance was tucked in its fold. Steps led up to a wooden walkway along the slender defile. Gilberto ushered me through the portal. I was astonished to find myself inside an enormous cavern—a vast, vaulted cathedral with tall stalagmites and stalactites forming an organ on one wall. At one end, the cave sloped gently upward to a tubular entrance; at the other, a broader egress opened over a great bend in the river, where a fantasia of philodendrons and figs vibrated with birdsong. The cave was as cool and as damp as a well.

Che Guevara had selected the cave as a perfect spot to set up his staff headquarters during the 1962 Cuban Missile Crisis, when he commanded the Western Army. Castro had entrusted Che with the final negotiations in Moscow in August that approved the delivery of Soviet missiles, many of which were positioned at San Diego de los Baños. Che dreamed of a continental guerrilla struggle against Yankee imperialism. According to Jon Lee Anderson in *Che Guevara: A Revolutionary Life*, Che fervently hoped that the crisis would lead to superpower war; once the missiles were in place, he yearned for a preemptive strike against the U.S.

Fidel—always the gambler—was equally reckless. According to Carlos Franqui, editor of *Revolución* at the time, on October 27 Fidel "drove to one of the Russian rocket bases, where the Soviet generals took him on a tour....At that moment, an American U-2 appeared on a radar screen, flying low over the island....The Russians showed him the ground-to-air missiles and said that with the push of a button, the plane would be blown out of the sky."

"Which button?" Fidel reportedly asked.

"This one," a general replied.

At that, says Franqui, "Fidel pushed it and the rocket brought down the U-2. Major Rudolf Anderson, the American pilot, was the only casualty in that war. The Russians were flabbergasted, but Fidel simply said, 'Well, now we'll see if there's a war or not.'"

Castro has vigorously denied that he (or any Cuban) shot down the U-2. "It is still a mystery how it happened," he claims. However, Soviet ambassador Alexander Alexeev had cabled Moscow on October 25, warning that Castro wanted "to shoot down one or two piratic American planes over Cuban territory." The next day, claiming that an American invasion was imminent, Castro urged the Soviets to launch a preemptive nuclear strike on the U.S.: "However difficult and horrifying this decision may be," he wrote, "there is, I believe, no other recourse." He and the Cuban people, Castro assured Soviet premier Nikita Khrushchev, were "ready to die fighting."

Castro was "in the throes of a military ecstasy of Napoleonic calibrations," thought Castro biographer Georgie Anne Geyer. "The world of the Superpowers was at his feet...he had entered the Game of Nations as vainglorious croupier." The next day, Castro learned that the Kremlin had signed a deal with Kennedy behind his back: The missiles would be removed. Fidel and Che were both furious.

Che was still fuming a few weeks later when Sam Russell, a correspondent for the British socialist *Daily Worker*, interviewed him: "Alternately puffing a cigar and taking blasts on his asthma inhaler," records Jon Lee Anderson, "Guevara told Russell that if the missiles had been under Cuban control, they would have fired them off." Russell deemed Che "a man of great intelligence, though I thought he was crackers from the way he went on about the missiles."

Gilberto Cruz pointed out the table where Che and his men had dined, as well as Che's office—made of concrete blocks and containing the original table and chairs—abutting the cave's rear wall.

"This is where *el comandante* slept," said Gilberto, pointing to an opening that led into a secondary cave, where Che's iron-frame bed stood on a floor of rough-hewn boards. Gilberto spoke simply yet reverentially, as if the restless revolutionary leader's ghost were still present.

"We loved that man, you know," he added.

I asked what it was about Che that made most Cubans regard him with awe.

"We saw in Che what we ourselves would wish to be," replied Gilberto, smiling beatifically. "He was ideologically pure—a model for honest people who wish to improve the world. He was incorruptible and selfless in his revolutionary virtue, and he had unsurpassable faith and determination. Building a revolution requires personal sacrifice. He was our guide and teacher. We admired him because he demanded more of himself than of others and because he gave himself completely to the Cuban people."

Gilberto's reply reminded me of Jean-Paul Sartre's remarkable comment that Guevara was "the most complete human being of our age."

"What were his faults?" I asked, curious to know whether Cubans acknowledged that the perfect revolutionary was flawed.

"Perhaps he was *too* rigid, too dedicated to revolutionary purity. Maybe he was too romantic also. He was a complicated man. Who knows? Things would undoubtedly have turned out very differently without him," Gilberto responded. He was referring to the early days of the Revolution, when the improbable Marxist guerrilla leader had been appointed Cuba's Minister of Finance. In 1961, Che became Minister of Industry and promptly devoted his energies to replacing "market anarchy" with a socialist system based on collective spartanism.

I asked Gilberto if he had heard of *The Motorcycle Diaries,* Che's account of his six-month odyssey through South America in 1952 on a vintage 500cc Norton motorbike nicknamed *La Ponderosa.* He had not.

"It's obvious that Che's idealism was awakened during his journey," I said. "I think the heartlessness of the poverty he saw spawned his affinity with the poor and exploited. It fired his latent Marxism."

Many times during his journey, which took him from Argentina to Venezuela, the young bourgeois student-doctor had earned his keep by tending the sick. In Valparaíso, where his "dilated nostrils" inhaled "the poverty with sadistic intensity," he attended an old servant woman "in an awful state, breathing the smell of stale sweat and dirty feet" in a room where she lay dying from chronic asthma and a feeble heart. Her family resented her illness with "barely disguised acrimony." All Guevara could do was give her a few Dramamine tablets. Deeply affected, he railed at "the profound tragedy which circumscribes the life of the proletariat the world over. In these dying eyes there is a humble appeal for forgiveness and also, often, a desperate plea for solace which is lost in the void....How long this present order, based on an absurd idea of caste, will last I can't say, but it's time governments spent less time publicizing their own virtues and more money, much more money, funding socially useful projects."

But Che was often far from politically correct back then. I told Gilberto so. I had just read the diaries, published only in 1995, and was struck by how different in outlook and behavior the philandering Argentinian had been from the man who later earned worldwide renown as a righteous upholder of virtue. Perhaps this was why the book's publication had been delayed for so long.

"He spent much of the six-month journey stealing food, bumming beds, and seducing women, sometimes forcibly, until his welcome ran out," I explained. "He wrote rather proudly of his audacity and conniving."

"All men mature," Gilberto replied philosophically.

He refused my tip. It had nothing to do with my comments. Gilberto was happy to share his time. He waved cheerily as I rode away.

I descended to the plains of southern Pinar del Río, as flat as a billiard table and emerald green with sugarcane. Tractors tilled patches of land, releasing moist tropical odors from the freshly turned earth. I headed for the coast at a sign for Los Palacios, a neat agricultural town that sprawled alongside a rusting railway line that ran down the main street. A farm worker's canteen stood amid the roseate fields. Appropriately, it was called El Tornado—the wind was ferocious. The small restaurant was surrounded by tall walls, copper colored against the cloudless sky, reminding me of a Moroccan citadel of mud clay sunhardened like a baked biscuit. I drove the bike over the threshold and parked in the center of the courtyard, where I watched it while I ate a freshwater fish called *tenca* that resembled a giant pilchard, served with heaps of boiled potatoes and well-salted tomatoes. The kitchen staff peered at me through the half-open door, giving me their best "Aren't you hot in that there getup?" stare.

The rivers that flow down from the Sierra del Guaniguanico slow almost to a standstill and meander across the plains of Pinar, losing themselves amid swampy marshlands drained by watery sloughs that transform the lowlands into a patchwork of rice paddies. Brawny humpbacked cattle grazed knee-deep in the flooded meadows.

The road south of Los Palacios was a scrambler trail with deep-gouged ruts brimming over with a bouillabaisse of blood-red mud. My slalom riding was a little tentative, but the Paris-Dakar took it all in stride; its uncanny balance helped me power through the slippery troughs. The bike's high-impact plastic shroud, designed to protect the header pipes and cylinders from being bashed on rocks, was useless against the explosions of mud. My leather pants were spattered as if by a bloodletting. The heat of the exhaust pipes soon baked the sludge to a ceramic-tough crust. More than 15,000 miles later, I'm still riding around with that glaze of red mud; dynamite would be needed to remove it.

The farmland gave way to lagoons and tan carpets of sturdy sedge and copses of stunted woodland that floated like rafts on the water. The air was full of blue-winged teal, snipes, and shoveler ducks settling and taking off.

Almost two hours later, I came to a sign pointing the way to Club Maspotón, a hunting-and-fishing reserve that I wanted to check out. The lodge was described in tourist literature as having "comfortable, air-conditioned bungalows," and by Carlo Gébler, in *Driving Through Cuba*, as "like a garrison town with rows of ugly cabins." The concrete huts overlooked a small swimming pool that seemed better suited to reptilian reproduction than swimming. The place had the forlorn air of a working-class holiday camp five years after the last guest departed.

No one answered my calls. The mosquitoes, however, had eyed my arrival greedily. The minute I dismounted, they launched a vicious blitzkrieg. I peered in through the screened windows, made some notes, and moved on.

Southern Havana province seemed relatively prosperous. The area is the breadbasket of the capital city, and its fertile soils abound in tomatoes, cabbages, and bananas. Modest bungalows had been splashed with fresh coats of paint and stood in counterpoint to the rustic *bohíos* of Pinar del Río. They had garages, too, from which Yankee jalopies poked their curvaceous rear ends.

In Caimito, a dusty provincial town spanning the old Carretera Central, I stopped beside a dramatic political mural writ large on a gabled wall in front of a dun-colored church. This bureaucratic attempt at brightening up a bruised and battered town featured an imperious bald eagle voraciously attacking a grim-faced Cuban peasant and Indian, shown defiantly defending themselves with machetes. For simpletons who might miss the point, the bird wore the Stars and Stripes across its chest. It was muscular agitprop art of a style I would see throughout Cuba.

As I raised my camera, a middle-aged woman stirred and hurried away.

Caimito's colonnaded main street was graciously timeworn, lined with arches supported by rounded columns linked by a balustrade upon which an old man with a bushy silver mustache rested his elbows. His eyes glowed warmly beneath the shade of a wide-brimmed straw hat, while the late-afternoon sunlight spilled across his face, burnishing his skin. He was smoking a robust cigar. As I passed, he stared down at me and offered a disarming smile.

To his right, a young boy dressed in a snow-white school shirt and red kerchief echoed the old man's posture and consolatory smile. They waved in unison. The duo—well nourished, well shod and clothed, and beaming benignly—embodied the innocence of a people who can still take simple pleasure in leaning on a veranda and watching a stranger go by. It seemed a strange juxtaposition: the rousing mural offset by two generations of Cubans sending reassuring gestures to a Yankee.

Smooth pavement seeped down to the sea.

I had expected more of Guanimar, marked on my map by an umbrella denoting a *playa*—a beach resort. Perhaps it was the cartographer's idea of a joke. The narrow beach was a ghastly gray, the Caribbean the color of an old, yellowing bruise. A scummy froth washed up on shore. Marshland pressed in on Guanimar with murky closeness. A motley assemblage of wooden shacks tilting at drunken angles passed for the hamlet; the sole street was littered with empty cans and broken glass. Menfolk sat on their porches in soiled shorts and worn flip-flops and watched impassively as I passed. Four rusting trawlers were berthed alongside an oil-stained wharf, from which an old man was untying a rowboat of beaten tin and polystyrene held together by corroded wire. It seemed remarkable that such desolation could exist within a few miles of Cuba's most prosperous region.

If Guanimar was depressing, Surgidero de Batabanó was worse. Not only that, but I had missed the ferry to Isla de la Juventud and would have to overnight in this pathetic port. The town's only hotel was a sordid hovel. The acrid smell of urine in the lobby sent me reeling. The receptionist led me up a dingy stairway to the rooms. The punched-out walls, broken beds, and soiled mattresses told me that drunken sailors favored it for fighting and fornicating. Even the price tag—50 cents—couldn't tempt me.

"Welcome to the flight for Nueva Gerona," the pock-faced attendant said as we settled into the hydrofoil's recliner seats. His shiny black hair was shellacked back like the wings on Mercury's helmet. He wore his spectacles stylishly atop his head and his shirt was unbuttoned, revealing a chest whorled with tufted hair.

The attendant's safety drill lasted all of five seconds. "Take your life jacket," he began. (*What* life jacket? I couldn't see any.) He pointed toward the ocean, placed his outstretched palms together as if he were about to dive into the water, and made a noise like the carbonated hiss of soda water. "Pssht!"

Cockroaches scattered as a female attendant moved down the aisle, handing out Spam bocaditos and tiny cartons of fresh-squeezed orange juice.

We taxied out through the harbor, the pale, bottle-green waters yielding respectfully to the *kometa's* bow. Then came an awesome surge as the pilot throttled up. The vessel rose on its hydroplanes, and we glided atop the water at a rollicking speed. The Russian-built hydrofoil, incongruously dubbed the *Delta Queen 1*, roared across the Golfo de Batabanó like a sleek space machine from a Flash Gordon movie.

Soon enough, Isla de la Juventud came into view. Flat, barren, and fringed by mangrove-covered cays, it hardly looked like an island paradise. We sliced up the Río Las Casas past a row of decrepit factories and berthed at the ferry terminal.

I emerged into incandescent light and felt the heat rising in waves off the asphalt. A *coche*—a mule taxi—waited outside. The simple contraption had been nailed together from salvaged lumber and metal; for running gear, four thick bicycle wheels had been welded onto two axles. The carriage had narrow wooden seats along each side, and sacking had been thrown over the metal framework to protect passengers from sunstroke. The mangy mule was a dilapidated and half-starved Rocinante; like Don Quixote's own scrawny steed, it "had more quarters than there are pence in a groat." Slung under its tail was a *manta*—a bag to collect droppings.

"Something for your garden?" I asked the driver as the mule clip-clopped desultorily down the street.

"*¡Coño!* It's required by law," he replied, flicking the nag's bony rear end with a leather whip. "I forgot the bag one time, so they fined me and made me clean up the mess."

He stopped outside the Hotel La Cubana. The lobby looked like it had hosted a skinheads' convention. Someone had punched holes in the thin chipboard walls. A shirtless youth slouched on the couch.

"*¿Qué busca?*" he asked without looking up.

I told him I wanted a room.

"*¡No hay!*" he replied. The hotel was full. I was relieved. The boy grudgingly stirred and pointed the way to a *casa particular*, a private house that rents rooms. I slung my duffel bag over my shoulder, trudged down the hot, dusty lane, and turned into a narrow alley that led to a high-walled compound; from it stepped a middle-aged man as big as a Buddha. He swung open a barred metal gate and beckoned me into the courtyard, its glimmering whitewashed walls a glorious counterpoint to exorbitant fuchsias as crimson as succulent plums.

"*¿Cómo anda?*" Juan Polanco Rivera asked in a rich bass voice. His giant hand gripped my own. He was wearing a singlet, knee-length pink shorts, and a baseball cap emblazoned with the logo of the New York Giants. His hair was sheep's wool and his calves were cured hams.

Juan ushered me into his home through floral screens made of painted sacking; hung in lieu of doors, they allowed fresh air to flow through the house. A dachshund barked a greeting. Tiny flies hovered over the dog, following its every move like a gloomy cartoon cloud.

Juan showed me to a small room at the rear. When I sat on the bed, the mattress sank like a deflating soufflé. Plastic wall hangings and other 1950s kitsch festooned the wooden walls, a large Sony television sat atop a china closet, and an old Russian refrigerator—empty but for a bottle of mineral water—stood in one corner.

"Do you know what we call a refrigerator here in Cuba?" Juan asked. "A *coco!* Know why? Because it has a hard shell on the outside and nothing but water inside." He laughed uproariously. "You know, my wife thinks she's going blind. When she opens the refrigerator, she doesn't see anything."

Later, I joined Juan and his wife in the courtyard. Elisa was comely, with teak-colored eyes, dimpled cheeks, and a rococo exuberance of raven hair cascading over her shoulders. The couple were poring over heaps of rice, picking out the bad grains and dirt under the wan light of a low-wattage bulb. Two cockerels scratched at their feet.

"We work together. *Una buena esposa y un buen esposo, ¿verdad?*" said Elisa, smiling serenely. Juan took her hand. The couple seemed deliriously happy. They teased each other constantly. I asked if I could help sift the rice.

"*Gracias, puro.*"

Elisa was a *peluquera,* or hairdresser. Juan was officially unemployed, a victim of Cuba's hard times. But Cubans are nothing if not self-reliant. Juan had learned to *resolver,* he explained.

"*El cubano inventa, chico,*" he said, nodding toward a small shed made of adobe.

The shed was cool and dark, like an underground cavern. I heard scuffling to my right, then piercing squeals and nasal grunts. Something large was moving unseen on my left. The smell of feces assaulted my nostrils.

My eyes began to adjust, and the obscure scene came to life. A small pig emerged, staring up at me from a sty no bigger than a chest of drawers. Its testicles were the size of grapefruits. Its penis was proportional, said Juan with schoolboy enthusiasm, and he leaned into the pen to perform some strategic tickling in the hope of exciting a demonstration. The only thing that straightened out was the pig's tail.

"Tickle my balls," I said, "and my tail would straighten out too."

Elisa laughed. "*¡Es lógico!*"

There were hens, too, in wire cages racked end to end. Juan reached in and collected the eggs, worth one peso apiece on the *bolsa* (literally, the exchange) or black market, the cut corner where much of Cuba's economy operates.

That evening Elisa produced a prodigious meal of delicious black bean soup followed by lobster served with boiled potatoes and rice, sweet fried plantains called *maduros,* and a salad of blood-red tomatoes and crisp cucumber that we washed down with *miel,* the sweet honey wine unique to Isla de la Juventud. Afterward, Juan leaned back and laced his hands over his stomach.

"His *neumático,*" said Elisa, reaching over and patting her husband's paunch.

We settled on metal rockers in the courtyard and bobbed slowly back and forth beneath a jet-black sky spangled with pointillist dots that winked and danced in the heavens. The Milky Way hung like a gossamer veil across the sky, luminous as St. Elmo's fire. A soothing breeze stirred the balmy air, bringing with it faint aromas of jasmine salted by hints of the open sea. I clasped my hands behind my head, closed my eyes, and savored the felicitous silence interspersed with the occasional sounds of the little pig snuffling and grunting.

"You're an intelligent man," said Elisa, breaking the spell. "What do you make of our situation?"

"I'm not sure," I began, measuring my words. "So many of my assumptions have been challenged. Cuba resembles a jigsaw puzzle, and I feel like I've been given only a few pieces."

"That's a good analogy, a *rompecabezas!*" Juan exclaimed. "I'll tell you, you'll never understand Cuba."

In truth, I wasn't quite sure how I felt.

I had been raised during Britain's leftist heyday in a coal-mining community in northern England, where socialist sentiments ran deep and class distinctions had meaning. I had experienced firsthand the subjugation and debilitating hardship of working-class life. I grew up greatly influenced by my paternal grandfather—a dour, hardworking achiever who taught me in the lugubrious Yorkshire tongue that "t' working class are t' salt o' t' earth" and that poverty and inequality are wicked consequences of a competitive social order in which money was the root of all evil. In a world where only the poor go hungry, this seemed to make sense.

It was the beginning of a passionate, bitter journey. I took my class-conscious critique of capitalism with me to college, where I read for a geography degree and majored in Third World issues, became a New Left internationalist, and came to understand that the standard liberal solutions for the Third World—population control and the "Green Revolution"—were palliatives that papered over what the world's hungry needed: justice, which in turn demanded a revolutionary change in the social order. My journey was lit by torches held aloft by Fidel and Che, whose implacably resolute face—the famous poster image shot by Alberto Korda showing Guevara in trademark black beret—adorned my lapel and the wall of my dorm room. I deemed myself a revolutionary, or at least a supporter of revolutionaries, a believer in Che's conviction that "Revolution cleanses men."

In 1980 I moved to California, my moral commitment to the lumpen proletariat part of my baggage. The failed examples of Eastern Europe and the Soviet Union, however, deflated my hope in the Marxist model. Furthermore, Marxism was a historical treatise that has failed to foresee the extent to which capitalism was capable of reform and goodness. Slowly the pendulum swung. I adopted North American ideals of liberalism. Still, I remained aware that as a middle-class ideology of developed nations, liberalism was a Milquetoast model for tackling the problems faced by the Third World's impoverished. I harbored a muted conviction that Castro's revolution had reached further than any other modern society in attaining the utopian dream. Although time had tempered my faith in socialism, I arrived in Cuba with my leftism far from exhausted.

I said all this to Juan and Elisa—but not in so many words—as I grappled to understand where I stood. I spilled out a diatribe against the embargo, but I sensed in my heart that the source of Cuba's problems lay somewhere else, somewhere closer to home.

"¡Mira chico! Forget *el bloqueo,"* replied Juan, using the Cuban term for the embargo. "With him in charge—bah!—we can't even breathe. We're like trained seals in a circus. He's a *chismoso,"* Juan continued, using the term for a busybody.

"Do you know what the three biggest failures of the Revolution are?"

"Er, no."

"Breakfast, lunch, and dinner!"

Juan's swollen belly rippled as he leaned back in his chair and laughed heartily.

"We're a country of slogans. *¡Coño!* I'm supposed to think like my neighbors. *¿Me entiendes?* You understand? It's a *capricho*—a stupid notion. It undermines our desire to fight for the future, mine or anyone else's," said Juan, rocking vacantly like a zombie. An automaton. I got the point.

"¡Está loco!" said Elisa. Did she mean her husband or Fidel?

"Es un capricho," her husband repeated, running his thumb and forefinger down his chin.

"You mean Fidel?" I whispered.

"Sí, el caprichudo. The stubborn one," said Juan, edging forward on his seat. He raised himself slightly as he talked, in the manner of Fidel talking into a TV camera.

"Want to know why *el barbudo* always sits forward when he's talking?" Elisa asked. "We Cubans say it's because he has hemorrhoids." She chortled at her own joke.

She asked if I was married. I replied not.

"*¡Ay, chico!* You need to find a beautiful *pinera* to marry."

Their home was like Grand Central Station. Friends and neighbors slipped in and out. Two men entered and slumped onto the couch in the lounge. They nodded. I nodded back. One was conservatively dressed and fat, and sweat hung in beads on his brow. His partner was slender yet muscular and handsome. Basques from northern Spain, Elisa explained.

A third man—a Cuban—appeared and sat beside them. He was black and incorporeally thin, with etiolated eyes and gangly arms like a Rwandan refugee.

"Is he their guide?" I asked.

Elisa smiled. "Well, yes and no," she whispered. She slipped her tongue out slightly and raised her eyebrows to hint at a carnal taboo.

Juan leaned close. I could feel his moist breathe in my ear. "*¡Son homosexuales!*"

"Last night," said Elisa, lowering her voice conspiratorially, "the good-looker slipped into the *sala* to make love to the *negro*." She nodded toward the scene of the crime, a rust-red divan.

"*¡Coño!*" Juan exclaimed, winking in affirmation.

I said I wanted to explore the town after dark to discover the best bars and night spots.

"Don't go out at night," Elisa exclaimed. "*¡Es muy peligroso!*"

Dangerous?

"*Sí, hay robos.*"

Robbers?

"You're a foreigner. You have to beware of the *jineteras,*" Elisa continued, speaking of the young prostitutes who come to the island to pick up foreign students.

"What's so dangerous about jineteras?" I asked.

"Many of them are *robos.* They'll say to the men, 'Come to my *casa.*' Then they'll tempt you with drugged wine or beer. When you wake up she'll have gone, like a butterfly. It's a big problem in Nueva Gerona. There are very few police."

Juan was nodding in agreement. "And you need to be careful with the African women. *¡Mucha enfermedad!*" he said.

Illness?

"*Sí, enfermedades sexuales.*"

"It is best if you go with a friend," suggested Elisa. "I know just the person."

"Only if she's beautiful," I joked, balking at the notion of a chaperone.
I needn't have worried.

Teresa arrived after dinner. She was six inches shorter than me, a tad Rubenesque but undeniably cute, with full lips and cloying jeans that did little to conceal her curves. Two blocks from the house, Teresa took my hand in hers. No equivocation. No distance. Totally self-assured. We strolled down the street at a languid pace. Had I been blessed with a curly tail, I would have wagged it.

Teresa led me down Calle Martí, the main artery of Nueva Gerona, lined with congenial colonial buildings in mid-restoration. The town had a well-heeled, cosmopolitan air, thanks in part to the marble hewn from humpbacked mountains, lustrous with reflected moonlight, that rose west of town. It was everywhere, gleaming underfoot and along the countertops of cafeterias and bars. Even the streets sparkled with marble gravel that glistened like diamond dust.

We arrived at Cabaret El Patio, where the burly doorman asked a cover charge of five pesos each and seated us directly in front of the stage. I ordered two beers. The waitress returned with two bottles of *clara*, the government-issued brew, half-flat and bitter.

"Yours will be one dollar, and four pesos for the *muchacha*," said the waitress. The difference in price was a factor of six. Teresa protested. The waitress shrugged her shoulders and left. Moments later, the doorman appeared.

"You are a foreigner. You will have to pay dollars," he said softly.

"That's unfair. Why should he pay more? It's the same shitty beer," Teresa replied.

"Look, *mulata!* I don't make the rules."

He turned and walked away.

I had no problem with paying in dollars—why should the Cuban state subsidize me?—but Teresa wouldn't have it. She disappeared and returned with the waitress, who handed me back the 10 pesos I had paid at the door. Things hadn't gone the way Teresa planned.

"She says you also have to pay a five-dollar cover charge," said Teresa disgustedly.

"Let's play for time. Maybe they'll let it drop," I replied.

"No! The *portero* says you have to pay dollars."

"Okay. It's no big deal."

I proferred a five-dollar bill to the *portero,* the doorman, but he smiled and waved me away.

"I think he said to forget it," I told her. I was utterly confused. Cuba always did its damnedest to confound me.

But Teresa wouldn't leave well enough alone. She went over to speak to the doorman, who now looked as puzzled as me.

"The portero wants five dollars," she said, looking down at me sympathetically. "But I told him you don't have dollars. Pretend you only have pesos."

"But I just waved a five-dollar bill in his face."

"Oh!"

Five minutes later, the doorman returned and asked for the five dollars. I felt trapped in a Kafka novel. I paid up. Teresa began to scold him.

"Forget it," I said. "It's *no problema.*"

And it wasn't. The waitress kept piling beers on our table.

We watched an *espectáculo*—more stiletto-heeled *mulatas* whirling their boas and behinds—followed by a local band called La Tumbita Criolla, which played a carefree, countrified salsa. Their riffs harmonized with the sound of feet shuffling to the infectious rhythm—*Sucusúcu, Sucusúcu*—after which the sensuous homegrown music, born here early last century and deeply rooted in the island culture, was named. Teresa whisked me onto the dance floor and showed me the moves. *Sucusúcu, Sucusúcu.* My English feet seemed weighted down by the clay soils of Yorkshire. I felt like a pinniped practicing the waltz.

Teresa led me home with decidedly un-Cuban haste. I lay on the bed and watched the shafts of light streaming through cracks in the door silhouette her voluptuous body. Her fingers unbuttoned her blouse, then reached behind her. I heard a faint click and saw her breasts shift as the clasp parted. She peeled away each cup with tantalizing deliberation, and leaned over to claim me hungrily with her lush lips. Soon, she had me banging my head on the headboard.

Through the thin walls, I could hear Juan and Elisa laughing.

Juan took me down to the commercial dock north of town the next morning to meet the flatbed barge bringing my motorcycle from Batabanó. Three *kometas*—*hidrodeslizadores,* officially—had been hauled onto the dock and raised on wooden blocks, exposing their silvery scutums and long, leglike foils.

They resembled giant locusts. A rusty tugboat had also been hauled out. The propeller and drive shaft lay on the ground, and an elderly man was reaming the bore with an oversize rasp like a ramrod priming a cannon.

The barge appeared, moving with the excruciating deliberateness of a tai chi master. It pulled alongside, and claimants moved forward to retrieve their vehicles.

Back at Juan's, I rinsed *mi moto Fidel* with fresh water to remove any salt, then set out to explore Cuba's largest offshore isle with Teresa clinging behind.

Isla de la Juventud (Isle of Youth) is a special municipality, a 1,180-square-mile inverted comma slung beneath the belly of mainland Cuba. It claims an anomalous history of socially transforming experiments, beginning in the 19th century when the Spanish used the remote island they called Isle of Pines as a prison for Cuban nationalists, including José Martí, shipped here to labor in the pine-studded marmoreal hills for the crime of sedition. The Spanish also billeted military recruits on the island to escape the tropical diseases that plagued them on the mainland; those already ill were sent here to regain their health at the mineral springs at Santa Fe. After the Santa Rita Hotel was built in 1860, tourists from North America began to arrive.

Following the War of Independence, the 1898 Treaty of Paris left the island in legal limbo: Although the U.S. government recognized Cuba's claim on the island, it forbade any settlement by Cubans; only in 1925 did the island officially become part of the national territory. Yankee speculators poured into the vacuum, bought up much of the land, and sold it to gullible Midwestern farmers suckered by tales of an agricultural paradise. The farmers planted the citrus groves that have since become the mainstay of the island economy. In the 1960s, Castro launched a settlement campaign and vastly expanded the citrus groves, which were tended by youths from around the world. At the height of Cuba's internationalist phase in 1977, the first of 53 schools was established for foreign students—known as international work brigades and hailing primarily from Africa, Nicaragua, Yemen, and North Korea—to learn the Cuban way of work-study. The Cuban government paid the bill. In exchange, the foreign students joined Cuban students shipped to the island in September for the citrus harvest. Together, the youths helped turn the island into a major producer of grapefruit. To honor them, Isle of Pines was renamed the Isle of Youth in 1978.

The Special Period had dealt the international schools a killer blow. The number of foreign students dwindled rapidly, and most of the schools were abandoned. When I arrived, the last foreign students were finishing their terms. It seemed tragic that this noble experiment—in which 11,262 foreign students had been trained in practical sciences and had returned home with invaluable knowledge—was over. Cuba's gift to the impoverished world was incalculable.

I rode out to the Presidio Modelo, the Model Prison built between 1926 and 1931 by General Machado and designed—after the model penitentiary at Joliet, Illinois—on a panopticon plan, with four circular cell blocks each centered on a watchtower that kept prisoners under constant surveillance. The prison did duty until 1967, when its doors were slammed shut by its most illustrious erstwhile occupant, Fidel Castro (he and 24 fellow revolutionaries had been incarcerated here after their failed attack on the Moncada Barracks in July 1953). The decayed structures resembled topless mushrooms studding the dun-colored earth. They were gutted, and only their graffiti-strewn walls and the ghosts of murderers, miscreants, and maltreated innocents remained to tell of their horror and hopelessness. A perimeter road looped around the panopticon and deposited me outside the old hospital block, which had been converted to isolate Castro and his companions from the other prisoners. Safer, I suppose, to have infectious minds in a hospital. The squat structure had been restored as a museum.

A guide led the way.

The walls of one wing were lined with metal frame beds, each with a pillow and a single neatly pressed sheet, as if patients were still expected. Above each, its former occupant mugged for the camera. There was a youthful Fidel—prisoner RN3859—staring at me from above the third bed from the left, facing the door, his steely eyes flashing self-assured indignation. He was beardless and puffin-faced, with a clipped moustache and a double chin that accounts in Cuban folklore for why Fidel, with his monumental vanity, never shaves. The room was otherwise bare except for Fidel's battered suitcase encased in glass in one corner.

Sunlight drew us into the courtyard, where three long wooden tables and a blackboard were cordoned off along one wall in the cool penumbra beneath the eaves. Incredibly, Fidel had turned the edifice into a place of edification by gaining permission to set up a school—the Abel Santamaría Ideological Academy—where the group boned up on radical theories and tactics. This honeymoon period ended in February 1954 when Batista visited the prison and Fidel—never able to resist a challenge—taunted the dictator by leading his group in revolutionary songs. He was promptly placed in solitary, as he no doubt had planned.

We entered his cell.

The pastel-blue room was immodestly large, with a lofty ceiling trimmed by stucco and a bathroom of *pinero* marble boasting a capacious shower lined with white tiles. The windows, though narrow and far up the wall, admitted Cuba's incandescent light, which sparkled the tilework and *mármol*. Fidel had received kid-glove treatment. I perused the bookcase. Fidel had spent his time brushing up on the complete works of Marx, Engels, and Lenin.

The media gave wide coverage to Castro during his incarceration. His lustrous stature was magnified when the Cuban courts accepted his lawsuit, initiated in prison, that charged Batista with treasonous crimes. A nationwide campaign was launched to secure his release. In November 1954, Batista won the presidential election; the elections were rigged, but Harry Truman quickly embraced the "constitutional regime." Six months later, bowing to public pressure, Batista signed an amnesty bill passed by the Cuban congress that freed Castro and his cohorts. Castro immediately undertook an anti-Batista campaign that forced him to move constantly for his own safety. On July 7, 1955, he boarded a flight to Mexico. "From trips such as these," he stated, "one does not return or one returns with the tyranny beheaded at one's feet." Three and a half years later, he had Batista's job.

A concrete two-lane road led south through the center of the island. It was deserted, with long straights where I could cane the bike in top gear before settling back to savor the sweet smell of jasmine that hovered over the citrus groves. Small reservoirs stippled the valley bottoms. The heat was intense. I rode shirtless, with Teresa running her hands over my chest.

I whizzed past a pea-green Studebaker Silver Hawk, circa 1958, parked beside the road. Its hood was propped open while two men peered into the engine. A third lay half-hidden beneath the car. They were still there, frozen like museum pieces, when we zoomed by in the other direction two hours later.

They quacked me as I flew by. Most Cubans did.

The number of Cubans who gave me the sign varied. In small towns it averaged about one in every six people, regardless of age or gender; on country roads it averaged about one in three. Frequently the "quacking" signal was accompanied by a *grito*, a shout— *"¡La luz encendida!"*—uttered as if I were committing a heinous sin. The words mean "Your lights are on," but the Cubans ejaculated them in an incomprehensible porridge: *"Lalooshendi!"* I had no idea what they were saying until one day it dawned on me: Only emergency vehicles are permitted to use their lights during the day. Even under a dark, roiling sky, with the rain pouring down in sheets, Cuban cars rolled along without lights.

A flock of parrots, green as emeralds, shot across my path in tight formation like jet fighters on a low-level raid. Stubby palms exploded above the mangroves like flak bursts, and between them I caught a glimpse of tempting white sand bracketed by bottle green scrub. Beyond it beckoned the glassy waters of the Bay of Siguanea.

The road flowed down to the Hotel Colony, a two-story concrete structure lauded in guidebooks as a lively resort and scuba-diving center. The place was dead except for six middle-aged Germans seated by the pool. With their blubbery bellies, they looked like sunburned walruses hauled out at an *uglit*. They puffed on cigars between quaffs of Tecate beer and made leering remarks at Teresa. Their gruff guffaws reverberated around the concrete courtyard and eventually drove us down to the beach.

Sea grass pushed up through the sand. Two elderly women were sitting on deck chairs, staring glumly out to sea through rheumy eyes. They seemed shell-shocked. Who could blame them? It must have seemed like a cruel joke, being sentenced to a week-long vacation with a bunch of loutish Germans.

"Good afternoon, ladies!" I intoned, curious to know their nationality.

They turned. Meek smiles.

"Bonjour!"

French Canadians.

The southern half of Isla de la Juventud is a military zone with glorious beaches, a turtle farm, and a cave known for its Indian petroglyphs. I needed a permit to visit. The MININT officer eyed me with furrowed brows, then stared at my bike.

"Is that your moto?

"Yes."

"And you plan to travel to the military zone on your moto?"

"Well, yes."

"Why do you wish to visit the military zone?"

I explained that I was researching a guidebook and that I needed to see the tourist attractions for myself. He seemed suspicious.

"And you intend to travel alone?" he inquired.

"Yes."

"That is not possible," he replied sternly. I could, however, hire a guide for 15 dollars and ride two-up, he suggested, in which case he could issue me a permit. "Otherwise you may go only as far south as the *creadora,*" he added, referring to the crocodile farm mantled in mangroves near the military checkpoint at Cayo Piedra.

The farm lay at the end of a dusty dirt road in the heart of the Lanier swamp. Oneldi Flores, the director, gave me a tour when I got there.

"We have about 2,000 youngsters," explained Oneldi, "plus about 500 juveniles and adults. Crocodiles are cannibalistic, so we divide them by age." We peered into small enclosures with concrete pools in which great clumps of babies were crawling over one another and piping squeakily for their mothers.

A path led through the sedge wetlands and paperbark swamps, which had been cordoned into lagoons rimmed with wire fences. I could hear larger reptiles plopping into the water as we approached. Scores of plump olive-green crocs were sunning themselves on the mudbanks, motionless as logs.

The endemic *Crocodylus rhombifer,* hunted to near extinction during four centuries of colonial rule, is today found only in the Zapata peninsula (on the Cuban mainland) and the Lanier swamp. Following the Revolution, Castro ordered the remaining crocodiles to be rounded up for breeding and reintroduction into the wild: "When we have millions of them, then we'll have an industry." There are about a dozen *criaderos* throughout Cuba. The program has been successful. In 1995 the Convention on International Trade in Endangered Species granted Cuba the right to market the skins worldwide to be turned into shoes and handbags.

We stumbled upon a six-footer sprawled across the path, still as death, jaws agape in a toothy leer. Vultures were hunched in the treetops like a conclave of hopeful undertakers.

"No closer!" warned Oneldi as I crouched low and raised my camera. "The *Lagarto criollo* isn't like your timid American crocodile. This species is much more aggressive." Apparently the endemic crocodile is genetically coded to strike at anything that moves, and when he does he's as quick as lightning.

"We're beginning to see six-meter animals again," Oneldi continued, "the ones that used to terrify the *campesinos* and eat their dogs." He guided me toward the safety of a wooden stockade. Peering over the chin-high stakes, I found myself eye to eye with a pugnacious croc the size of a Peterbilt truck. Chunks of hacked-up cattle had just been tossed into the enclosure, and the monstrous, evil-eyed male was lumbering out of the water for lunch. I watched him tear off a chunk of thigh, bone and all: Snap, tear, swallow. The mean-looking sexagenarian—five meters of saurian splendor—guarded his harem jealously; Oneldi pointed toward a smaller male that the vindictive giant had chewed up and nearly killed the day before.

Oneldi reached for a pole with which to prod the bad-tempered monster. The animal exploded in fury, teeth bared in rage. A momentary glimpse down the gullet of the huge crocodile sent adrenaline coursing through my veins.

I shipped the BMW on the evening ferry to Batabanó. The next morning, I said goodbye to Juan and Elisa and walked to the ferry terminal to catch the kometa.

A crowd was pushing up against the ticket booth as if this were the last boat to flee a beleaguered island. Cubans were frantically waving carnets like buyers at the Chicago commodities exchange. Arms extended beseechingly toward the half-moon window. The glass was cracked; behind it sat a female factotum whose frozen countenance could have been chipped from *pinero* marble.

I joined the melee. "A ticket for the kometa, please," I said, finally reaching the window.

"It's full," the woman replied without bothering to look up. A blob of bubble gum appeared between puckered lips. I reminded her that five seats were supposedly reserved for foreigners. She shook her head adamantly, then gazed up at me with vacant eyes.

"Yes, but you're supposed to have special seats for foreigners," I persisted. "Look, it says so right here." I pointed out a notice pinned to the wall.

She was unmoved. *"¡Lleno!"*

"Full!" My voice rose an octave. "I don't see any other foreigners. You're asking me to pay 15 dollars, and you can't give me a seat?"

She repeated her mantra.

"Okay, look: If you can't guarantee me a seat, let me pay in pesos, the same as a Cuban."

"Take it up with the *ministerio*," she said, staring over my shoulder toward the scrum, which had stopped jostling and was following the proceedings intently.

"What about the next hydrofoil? Are there tickets for that?"

Yes, she replied. A kometa was scheduled to leave at one o'clock.

"Okay, I'll take a ticket for this afternoon, please."

She glowered. "The ticket office isn't open." Was I having a bad dream?

"Excuse me. I've been in line almost an hour. I've seen you selling tickets. And what are all these people trying to buy?" I swept my arm dramatically to embrace the now quiescent throng. In Cuba, rantings are usually answered by quizzical looks and raised shoulders. She merely shrugged, then called the next customer.

"Listen, if you don't want to help, then please get the ministerio." I stood my ground.

The beetle-browed ministerio explained that the kometa was full.

"What about the five seats supposedly reserved for foreigners?"

"They're taken."

"Where are the foreigners? There are no other foreigners. If there are no seats, then I should be charged in pesos."

The ministerio rolled his eyes. "You can buy a ticket for the next kometa," he said.

"She won't sell me a ticket," I replied, pointing accusingly at the *boletera*, who had taken her gum from her mouth and was kneading it between her fingers and thumb, drawing it back and forth until each finger was webbed by a disgusting, unruly mess.

"The ticket office doesn't begin selling tickets for the afternoon kometa until ten," he said, explaining that the boletera was selling tickets for the overnight ferry. I felt like a jerk.

"I'm sorry. I misunderstood. Wouldn't it be easiest for her to simply sell me the ticket now?"

The ministerio pondered a moment, then nodded affirmatively to the boletera. The woman scowled as I passed a 20-dollar bill through the window.

"I can't change that!"

An old man dressed in a guayabera and straw hat pushed forward like a benediction; with a saintly gesture, he passed me a well-sugared mint tea in a glass bottle with a wide lip. It was his gift to a yanqui. It seemed so innately Cuban—the considerate expression of a people uncommonly gracious and generous to a fault.

I felt boorish by comparison. Cuba was showing me my own insensitivity.

CHAPTER FIVE

RETURN TO THE BAY OF PIGS

The Autopista Nacional, Cuba's only freeway, is a concrete eight-laner—colloquially called the Ocho Vías—that runs through open countryside east of Havana for 350 miles. Flat as a carpenter's level, it has only a few potholes and the occasional mule-drawn cart or stray cow in the road to contend with. I had the highway virtually to myself as I ran east at 75 miles per hour past green swaths of sugarcane.

Cruising down an empty road with the rush of warm air caressing my skin stirred sensations of self-reliance and freedom. It was exhilarating to be riding alone, a million light years from anything familiar. Just me and *mi moto Fidel.* I couldn't remember when I had last been so happy.

I was traveling with my duffel farther forward for back support. My shoulders no longer ached. I felt perfectly poised, my ass snug and secure in the saddle as if human and bike had become one. I was in a kind of highway heaven where heightened awareness merged with the exhilaration of absolute freedom.

I'm a cautious rider, not fast, but that morning I felt the urge to twist the throttle, to thrill to the bike's awesome power and hear the steady beat of the big twin in its glory. I cranked the bike open until the handlebars were quivering.

Then—*BLAM!* I hit a railway track running across the freeway, hidden deep in the shadowy pool of an overpass. The bike shuddered and we flew through the air like Evel Knievel, smashing down 20 feet farther along the highway. The springs bottomed out; my helmet crashed down on the windshield. I had come down perfectly square, however, and roared forward with my heart racing.

The simultaneous fright and relief made me laugh out loud. Bloody hell! The Paris-Dakar had taken the impact in stride, but I slowed to 50 to regain my composure.

Ahead the gelid sky was turning to pewter, and a storm was gathering in great roiling clouds. There was steel in the wind now buffeting me from the north. Soon the first raindrops began to splatter the windshield. The road gave off moist odors. I stopped and pulled out my rain gear. There was no sign of shelter for miles, so I continued with my head and body bowed low to avoid the pellets that stung my face. Then it really began hammering down. I carried on at a crawl, the rain invading the cuffs of my poncho and creeping up my arms in cold rivulets. Water trickled down into my waterproof boots. At least they were warmed by the heat from the cylinders.

An open-bed truck passed. It was laden with passengers huddled shoulder to shoulder against the driving rain like penned-in cattle, so crowded together and wearing such looks of misery that I could not imagine a more disconsolate-looking bunch. Cuba was forever putting my sense of hardship in perspective.

Near Jagüey Grande the rain let up as quickly as it had begun. Sunlight poured down through gaps in the clouds and steam rose off the highway. I turned into town to dry off and tank up on gas. I passed a *parque de diversiones* where children whirled giddily on mechanical rides. Their gleeful faces lifted my spirits.

Jagüey is an agricultural town, railhead, and crossroads whose junction is a major *botella* (literally "bottle"), the colloquial Cuban term for a post where Cubans gather in droves to hitch rides. Virtually the entire Cuban population relies on the bus system for travel between cities, but demand so exceeds supply—Cuba's bus stations have been called "citadels of desperation"—that there is often a waiting list in excess of one month for the most popular long-distance routes. The gasoline shortage had so worsened things that hitchhiking had become a way of life, and the government had formed a state agency, Inspección Estatal, with officials strategically placed at botellas to flag down passing vehicles and fill empty seats democratically. Recognizable by their mustard-colored uniforms, the officials were called *coges amarillos*—yellow jackets.

Hitchhikers waved beseechingly as I pulled up to inspect a tourist attraction called Finca Fiesta Campesina, with a zoo, a traditional *trapiche* (sugarcane press), and a souvenir shop selling deliciously dulcet Cuban coffee, thick and rich as molasses. A dirt road led into a field behind the *finca*, where a little village of rustic log-and-thatch cottages had been opened as a homespun "hotel" called Bohío Don Pedro, named for the patriarch around whose farmstead the affair had been built. I parked the bike in gear, on the kickstand, and walked up to the farmhouse. I liked it immediately and decided to stay. The manager, Danilo Canizo, welcomed me warmly, then led me to one of the cozy huts. Randy roosters were chasing chickens around the grounds.

"The parking lot is secure," suggested Danilo in fluent English, "but if you want you can pull your moto onto your veranda."

I did so, but not from paranoia. I wanted my bike where I could see it. I was beat, worn down by the rain and the wind, so I spent the afternoon sprawled in a hammock and stared at my BMW enameled in the late afternoon sunlight, contemplating it as if it were my lover. I even dropped to the floor and moved around it to admire its muscular curves from a different angle.

A sweet perfume drifted on the warm air, and the only sounds were the thrumming of bees, the steady cadence of the cicadas, and the rustling of palm fronds from the breeze. A chestnut gelding grazed nearby, adding to the bucolic enchantment. Pigs were grunting and scrapping over slop that Don Pedro was pouring from a rusty bucket. The old farmer was bare-chested and bronzed, dressed in straw hat and torn trousers, and he chomped on an unlit cigar.

I pulled on a pair of jeans and a denim shirt and joined Danilo. We rocked on the porch outside the kitchen, where Don Pedro's wife, Hildeliza, was preparing a dinner that smelled strongly of garlic. Together we watched the farm animals feasting while the setting sun gilded the leaves of the alum and mango trees like shimmering foil. With dusk the cockerels scattered the leaves as they chased the recalcitrant females.

The scene reminded me of a famous anecdote, apparently true, regarding ex-president Calvin Coolidge and his wife—who, it is said, shared a lackluster love life. Danilo asked to hear it.

"Well, it appears that the president and his wife visited a farm and were given separate tours. Mrs. Coolidge asked the guide if the rooster copulated more than once a day. 'Dozens of times,' she was told. 'Tell that to the president,' she replied. When Coolidge was told, he inquired if it was with the same hen every time. 'Oh, no, a different hen every time.' came the answer. 'Tell that to Mrs. Coolidge,' he replied."

Danilo laughed heartily. I heard Hildeliza chuckling in the kitchen.

"It is beautiful when the chickens and little birds are here at this hour," said Hildeliza, peering out from her workplace. Gaily colored songbirds had gathered to drink from the dripping faucet.

I asked Danilo where most of the guests come from.

"The majority are Canadian, but we get plenty of anglers from the United States come to fish in Laguna Salinas."

"They molest the chickens," Hildeliza added. I thought she was still speaking of the cockerels, but she meant the yanqui fishermen, who can't stand the crowing in the morning and throw stones at the *gallos* to chase them away.

Laguna Salinas is part of the vast Zapata swamp, which extends south from Jagüey Grande and smothers the shoe-shaped Zapata peninsula, forming a 4,230-square-kilometer morass—the largest wetland ecosystem in the Caribbean—that is Cuba's foremost wildlife reserve. Zapata envelops the deep, finger-like Bay of Pigs. The area is considered a sensitive region for more than ecological reasons, and the Cuban government has traditionally kept a tight rein on foreign visitation. But things were easing up, said Danilo, and fishermen were now making a beeline.

"The fish are so numerous here, the waters boil like a kettle," Danilo claimed matter-of-factly. "There are places where you can catch them with your bare hands, the way the Indians did. I've seen it myself. Bonefish here will swim between your legs and not scatter." He disappeared and returned with a brochure for a U.S. company that brings fishermen on prepaid, all-inclusive tours.

We dined in a *bohío* lit by the warm glow of kerosene lamps. Bats wheeled in and out, swerving like intergalactic warships from a battle scene in *Star Wars*.

I complimented Hildeliza on her cooking.

"But I make the bread!" chimed in Don Pedro.

"It's the best bread in Cuba," his wife added proudly. She asked how I liked Cuba. Her smile broadened when I told her "very much."

An Israeli drip-irrigation expert called Shlomo sat on my right. He was working on a 115,000-acre citrus project nearby. The enterprise was being run by an Israeli company that hoped to increase the quality of the notoriously poor Cuban citrus (most of which previously supplied the Soviet bloc or found its way into juices) to compete on world markets.

"How long before Cuba begins producing fruit as good as Florida's?" I asked.

"They already are," Shlomo replied. "The quantity is small as yet, but they're now producing grapefruits equal in quality to those of Israel. Only about one percent of their total production is export quality. The Cubans claim that it's far higher, but you can't trust any of the official figures. The decimal points gets 'accidentally' moved in their annual reports so that managers can show that they've met their production quotas. Once the mistake is made, it becomes fixed. I've challenged the figures several times, but the answer is always the same. 'It must be correct. See, it says 12 percent here!'

"I once saw a report showing X number of boxes with 500 kilos of fruit. I knew it was wrong. A box holds 400 kilos. It was impossible to get that much fruit in a box. Know what they said? Cuban citrus are heavier!" He laughed. "They claim that they make a profit. No one knows whether they make a profit or not. Indirect costs aren't taken into account."

I related a joke told by Andrés Oppenheimer in *Castro's Final Hour* explaining why it was impossible to find pork, the traditional Cuban staple, on supermarket shelves:

"Fidel visits a pig farm and stops to admire a pregnant pig. 'Beautiful specimen,' says Fidel, 'I bet it will produce at least ten piglets.' Everyone applauds and nods in agreement. Fidel leaves. Two weeks later, the pig gives birth but delivers only six piglets. The farm's administrative office is beside itself with panic. The farm manager fears Fidel will be furious at the lower-than-expected production, so he records in his report that the pig delivered seven piglets. His supervisor, the regional farm director, raises the number to eight and passes his report to the national farm director, who changes the figure to nine. *His* boss, the minister of agriculture, adds one more piglet and submits the report personally to Castro. 'Fabulous! Ten piglets!' says Fidel, delighted that his prediction has come true. 'We'll use 60 percent of the pigs for export, and 40 percent for domestic consumption.'"

The trio had already heard it. They laughed anyway.

Two Spanish tourists—husband and wife—were watching a video replay of their visit to the Bay of Pigs. They passed the camera around the table.

On the tape, crabs the size of dinner plates crawled up the banks and went click-clacking across the road. The wife pinned one with a big stick, picked it up from behind, and held it up to the camera. Fearsome claws waved defiantly in my face.

"Every mid-March the crabs begin gathering in the mangroves for vast orgies and egg-laying parties," said Danilo. "First come the really big ones on their way to lay eggs. At the end, the newborn crabs make their way to the sea. Hence, we say it's a smaller problem in April. There are probably 100,000 *cangrejos* crossing the road as we speak. You're going to have problems with the moto," he added ominously. "It's crazy to go in a motorcar. Think what it's like on a motorcycle. I can put all the money in the world on the table you'll not make it."

"True? Or are you kidding?"

"True!"

I studied the video again. The road was littered with broken shells and upturned pincers. My mind turned to punctures. I thought for a moment about skipping the Bay of Pigs and continuing east along the Autopista, but that seemed like touring Paris without visiting the Eiffel Tower.

"If you hit a log, just keep going," said Don Pedro, smirking gleefully. "It could be a crocodile!" He gripped my hand and hugged me before wishing me *"¡Buenos sueños!"* Sweet dreams!

I lay awake for a while, listening to a gallimaufry of tooting whistles and clanking engines and carriages drifting across the cane fields from the local *central*, where sugarcane was being unloaded around the clock.

The road ran south like a plumb line past endless miles of dark-green saw grass and reeds swaying in the wind. I arrived at Playa Larga, a small fishing village tucked into the head of the 20-kilometer-long bay where 1,297 heavily armed CIA-trained Cuban exiles had come ashore in April 1961 to establish a beachhead and incite a counterrevolution that would topple the Castro regime. Concrete monuments lined the roadside. Each one marked the site where a member of the Cuban militia—161 in all—had fallen defending *la revolución* during the three-day battle. I passed a youth camp and through the corner of my eye caught the unflinching gaze of a young communist pioneer peering down from his watchtower.

Farther south came the crabs. The gravel road was strewn with crustaceans squashed flat by vehicles, like giant M&Ms crushed underfoot. Their black carapaces littered the path ahead, and my route was patterned in pointillist dots. I dodged around them, avoiding the margins where the razor-sharp shards and pincers of partially crushed crabs stuck up like broken bottles. The air stank of fetid crabmeat. Vultures hopped about, drawn greedily to the prodigal banquet.

I passed my first live crab scurrying toward the sea. Bright orange. A newborn. Then a large black crab with terrifying red pincers ran across my path, the forerunner of a lethal invasion heading the other way. Suddenly I was surrounded by a battalion of armored, surly crustaceans that turned to snap at my tires. I slalomed between them as they rose in the road with menacing claws held high. Then I hit one square on. *POOF!* It sounded like bubble wrap exploding.

Finally I arrived at the climactic spot where socialism and capitalism had squared off. Cuban families and Canadian package tourists slathered with suntan oil splashed about in the shallows before trim bungalows. My black leathers and boots must have looked absurd. I gave one of the Cubans my camera and asked him to snap a shot of me straddling the bike in front of a huge billboard reading "PLAYA GIRÓN—THE FIRST ROUT OF IMPERIALISM IN LATIN AMERICA." It was difficult with the sun beating down on a beach as silvery as mountain snow to imagine that blood and bullets had mingled with the sand and the surf here 35 years before. In the bay, pelicans were diving for fish inside a concrete barrier that had been erected offshore to guard against a second invasion.

The barrier seemed symbolic. The real barrier was the coral farther out. In photos of Playa Girón taken by U-2 spy planes, the CIA's photo interpreter identified seaweed offshore. "They're coral heads," said Dr. Juan Sordo, a member of the invasion brigade. "I know them, and I have seen them." Another brigade member agreed. But the CIA wouldn't listen. At 1:15 a.m. on April 17, the landing craft came roaring in. About 140 meters offshore, they hit the coral reefs that the CIA had dismissed as seaweed. The landing craft faltered and the brigade had to wade ashore with most of its heavy armaments stranded offshore.

The CIA also failed to evaluate the mood of the local people. On the eve of the Revolution, about 8,000 impoverished *cenagueros*—"swamp people"—had inhabited the Zapata region. They lived without roads, schools, or electricity, eking out an austere living as *carboneros*, or charcoal burners. The Revolution had changed their lives. Castro had an affinity for the area (the youthful Cuban leader often flew down to Zapata to fish, hunt, and swim), and shortly after taking power he had highways of hard-packed limestone built into the swamps. He also established the first schools (more than 200 teachers from the national literacy campaign arrived in 1960) and even a hospital.

While experts who had visited Cuba were reporting on the Cuban population's general support of Castro, the CIA fed President Kennedy a delusional story: "A great percentage of the [army] officers are believed ready to rebel against the government at a given moment, taking their troops with them," Richard Bissell, Deputy Director of the CIA, told Kennedy in an appallingly incorrect assessment. Despite the CIA's predictions, the local people—some armed only with shotguns or old British Enfields—defended their homeland until the first battalion of Cuban regulars arrived.

The yanqui spooks also discounted reports that Castro—who was familiar with every path—knew the area intimately. In November 1960, while inspecting one of his pet projects at Girón, Castro turned to a Cuban journalist and said, "You know, this is a great place for a landing....We should place a .50-caliber heavy machine gun here, just in case." Two weeks later, that machinegun fired the first shots at the invaders. Castro had also installed tall, extremely bright lights on the beach. "It looked like Coney Island," recalled Gray Lynch, the CIA point man who ended up directing the invasion. The brigade had also been told that "no communications existed within 20 miles of the beach." In fact, there was a radio station only 100 meters inland. By the time the brigade stormed it, Castro had been alerted.

I learned more details at the Playa Girón Museum. The entire story of the invasion was shown in maps tracing the evolution of the 72-hour battle that Cubans call *La Victoria*. There were gory photographs of civilians caught in the preinvasion air strikes, and of all the martyrs—the "Héroes de Girón"—killed in the fighting. The youngest, Nelson Fernández Éstevez, was only 16. The oldest, Juan Ruíz Serna, was 60. A frieze portrayed the invaders as rich reactionaries bent on reclaiming what had been dispensed to the poor.

The Bay of Pigs fiasco had incalculable consequences for Cuba and, ultimately, the rest of the world. It fired nationalist passions that Castro—nationalist redeemer—would use to turn his rhetoric into reality. Castro used the funeral for the seven Cubans killed in air strikes on the eve of the invasion as a stirring call for revolutionary defiance: "What the imperialists cannot forgive us for....is that we have made a socialist revolution under the nose of the

United States." It was his first public characterization of the Revolution as socialist. The debacle thus created the conditions by which socialism became acceptable to a nation facing invasion during a period when many Cubans felt about *La Revolución* the way U.S. citizens would have felt in the euphoric days of 1776. An infectious dynamism seeped through the masses, inspiring them with the notion of building a socialist utopia. "The horizons were open," an aging revolutionary named Martha told reporter Lynn Darling. "We had a world to conquer, a world to give to our grandchildren." The white elites and others opposed to this desideratum facilitated the process by decamping for Florida, while those who stayed either adapted or were tossed in jail.

I continued east. The coastal track of crushed coral was blindingly white; the dancing candescence of the sun hurt my eyes. In the absence of shadow it was impossible to tell patches of soft sand from hard coral on the road ahead. In front of me appeared a tractor pulling a great wooden cart kicking up a cloud of talcum-fine dust that made it even harder to see the road. As soon as it seemed feasible to overtake the rig, I took a deep breath and charged through the fog. As I throttled past, the bike hit a sandy patch. The front wheel burrowed down like a corkscrew, sending a violent yawing back through the bike. The Beemer careened to a shuddering halt, catapulting me over the handlebars. I landed on my left side amid the coral rocks. Amen for my leather pants!

The bike was on its side. Gas was pouring from the carbs into the sand. I turned off the fuel cocks, ripped off the duffel, and crouched down to hoist up the bike. Picking it up was no fun. I heaved and grunted but only sank deeper into the sand.

The sun beat down as hard as a nail, and soon I was perspiring like a pig. Sweat poured into my eyes. Fortunately, the mosquitoes supplied the necessary motivation, and I was finally able to lug the beast upright. The bike had gone down heavily, and I feared that the left cylinder might have cracked on the rocks, but the steel-tube crash bar had absorbed the impact. As I pulled my leathered leg across the saddle, however, I felt a gnawing pain in my thigh. Although it proved to be no more than a bruise, it bothered me for a week. The spill was the only time the bike went down in Cuba.

Farther east, the main track veered inland to a small gate; beyond it, the coastal trail narrowed down. It looked prohibitive, but a desire for adventure lured me on. The trail was convex in the middle and overgrown with tall grasses. It was difficult to ride the ridge, forcing me to ride in the ruts made by the few vehicles that had come this way before. In patches the path turned to bone-rattling rocks or gnawed through gulleys that I had to climb and descend like a mountain goat—a true enduro trail. The PD loved it, and so did I. Thorny scrub brushed against me. Thank God for handguards!

Serendipity was kind that day. In the midst of this no-man's-land, I happened upon the fuselage of a B-26 bomber from the Bay of Pigs invasion lying alongside the path. Although the years had barely weathered it, the plane was riddled with bullet holes, and its flanks were deeply gored where it had come to earth and torn along the ground like an antelope brought down by lions.

I felt strangely elated. Had any other foreigner gazed upon this monument to futility buried deep in the brush? I dismounted, wedged my camera in the crook of some branches, and stationed myself in a reverential pose beside the fuselage to capture a shot for posterity.

For the next 20 miles I passed not a soul. Then a watchtower loomed over the scrub, with the obligatory sentry recording my passage. I felt a kind of adulterous excitement in following that lonesome track, as if I was riding behind enemy lines.

The track spilled me out near a vast bubble floating over a plateau that rose above Bahía de Cienfuegos. The great orb gleamed softly in the evening sunlight, as if the globe was in meltdown. I had sneaked up on Cuba's nuclear citadel—the Juragua reactor—by the back route. The place was deserted. Amazingly, there weren't even sentries. Acres of rusting metal girders and abandoned trucks lay like dinosaur carcasses among the weeds. A group of tilting cranes guarded the massive dome. The fields surrounding the nuclear reactor were being plowed with oxen by farmers awaiting the day when the hum of energy overhead will turn the lights back on in Cuba.

It could be a long wait. Construction of the reactor began in 1983, when Soviet aid was flowing freely. Assembly of one of the two planned 417,000-kilowatt reactors was almost complete when the plant was mothballed in September 1992, after Cuba announced that it couldn't meet the financial terms set by the new Russian government. A review by the International Atomic Energy Commission (IAEC) in 1995 gave the green light for construction to resume. In October 1995, Cuba signed an agreement with Russia's Atomic Energy Ministry to complete the plant, despite threats from the U.S. Congress to sever aid to Russia. The Russians, who had sunk more than a billion dollars into Juragua, agreed to provide a further $350 million of the $800 million needed for completion.

Cuba has suggested creating an international consortium to conclude construction and operate the plant, and it has invited the United States to participate. Rather than jumping in to secure the safety of Juragua, however, the U.S. government seems determined to kill it. Congress held hearings dominated by anti-Castro lobbyists, who claimed that the plant would pose a serious threat to the safety of the southeastern United States, overlooking the fact that Florida has nuclear plants of its own. Washington spinmeisters also portrayed Juragua as similar to Chernobyl, the Ukrainian reactor that exploded in April 1986. Nonetheless, in 1993 the Pentagon commissioned its own study: Juragua, it found, is a VVER-440 reactor similar to the world's most advanced reactor—the Russian-built VVER in Finland—yet wholly different in design from Chernobyl's outdated graphite technology.

Let's hope so. The Soviet-built structures I had seen in Cuba so far had inspired little confidence.

I continued up the hill to Ciudad Nuclear, the spartan "Nuclear City" built in the 1980s to house the Juragua workers. Its dreary high-rise apartment blocks had been assembled from mass-produced prefabricated concrete modules shipped in from Russia. This building style, known as the Soviet *gran panel*, was introduced to Cuba in 1963, where it joined with the Yugoslavian IMS, which relied on precast columns and slabs post-tensioned during installation. The move to centralized industrial planning under the Ministry of Construction had eclipsed independent architects, replacing them with a utilitarian doctrine that defaced the entire island with concrete buildings made of these mass-produced modules. Everyone agreed that they were failures, but their construction continued until the Soviet Union itself collapsed.

Cyrillic writing was visible above the dank doorways on the mildewed facades. Refuse littered the potholed roadsides, and the roadside parks were untended. Juraguans were drowning out the melancholy in the middle of the street, which quaked to the hissy bass of megawatt speakers. They offered me lemonade and begged me to join them. One girl blew a saucy kiss—another reminder that Cuba's material impoverishment hasn't stifled the passions of this generous culture.

Came finally Cienfuegos. I dropped onto a bed in the Hotel Jagua, greatly satisfied at the end of an exhausting but exhilarating day.

"My friend. Hey, friend!"

The Malecón was a gantlet.

Jineteros—petty hustlers—shadowed my every step along the waterfront boulevard that led into town. "Friend" was always a prelude to being pestered by touts and hawkers—young men in shiny new Reeboks and denims. Their uniforms gave them away. I ignored them.

Cienfuegos was pleasant, its streets lined by trees. Its plaza, Parque Martí, was surrounded by stately mansions of the *belle époque* era. The old town core was in the midst of restoration. Many colonial buildings had been gutted and reborn as restaurants or classy boutiques. There was even a store selling electronic equipment, including—my God!—computers, though ordinary Cubans weren't permitted to buy them. Who on earth were they selling to? Gawking Cubans pressed up against the window.

"Without dollars," said a young woman, "all you can do is look."

Most storefronts were eerily empty.

An emaciated Great Dane shuffled through the square, dragging his bones inside a scrawny hide. His days were numbered. Since the onset of the Special Period, many Cubans, unable to feed their pets, had turned their dogs out onto the streets. I had seen dozens of mangy curs ravenously combing through piles of garbage.

I watched two adolescents wearing boxing gloves and protective headgear scrapping in a ring on the bust-lined promenade called the Prado, the city's social center, bustling with gossipy life. Bootblacks were shining shoes beneath the pink colonnades, just as Wormold had reported to his sister in *Our Man in Havana*. Lively music wafted from sidewalk cafés.

As I strolled, a young beauty in skintight shorts and a halter top brushed past me and flicked me a coquettish smile. She looked 14. She had glossy brown hair and hazel eyes and already a lovely figure. This apparition of virginal beauty sashayed across the street. Our eyes met, but she feigned insouciance, then glanced back to gauge my reaction. A young lad who had been trailing me in the hope of hitting me up for money suddenly changed his tune. *"¿Quieres una chica?"* he asked. Want a girl?

I retraced my steps to my hotel, near the tip of a peninsula called Punta Gorda, a once-exclusive residential district recalling 1950s North American suburbia, with Detroit classics still parked in the driveways of art deco bungalows.

I stopped en route at a Caribbean-style wooden home called Casa Caribeña, where I could dine with a view of the bay through lathe-turned wooden *rejas*. Blobs of glutinous tar floated atop harbor waters filmy with pumpings from the oil tankers berthed in the bay. Locals were trolling for shellfish in rough-hewn coracles made from polystyrene lashed between planks. I made a note not to order shrimp off the menu.

Casa Caribeña was exquisite, with a warm ambience enhanced by the Trio del Caribeño playing lilting *guajiras*—Cuban folk songs. The *criollo* menu, alas, was uninspired. The tasteful decor suggested that this was a *paladar*, a private home-restaurant legalized since September 1994; that impression was bolstered by the gracious attention of the manager, Miguel Ángel Chivandi. But no, it was run by Rumbos, one of Cuba's state-owned tourism agencies. The other diners were all well-dressed Cubans.

Miguel was middle-aged, short, and handsome, with a *copete*—a curly tuft of hair touching the forehead, like a quail's coiffure—and a thick mat of chest hair peeking out from the open collar of his gaily colored Hawaiian shirt. He unfurled my napkin across my lap and rearranged the place settings with courtly care.

I started recording my impressions in my notebook. Miguel peered over my shoulder.

"To whom are you writing, *amigo?*"

"I'm writing a note to *el jefe* telling him what a fine job you are doing," I replied, smiling.

His Cuban humor shone through. "Then I hope you will send him my regards," he replied, not missing a beat. He asked my name, and where I was from, and "Are you staying long in Cienfuegos?"

I told him my mission and that I was from San Francisco.

"Ah! The motorbike, it's yours? Everyone's speaking about this. *Muy grande. Muy fuerte.* Very big. Very strong." Then, more questionably: "You too are *un carácter muy fuerte*, I believe." Apparently my bike was the talk of the town. I was glad it was securely under wraps in the hotel forecourt.

Miguel set a small crystal bottle of vinegar and another of oil on the table, then tipped each upside down to fill the hollow bottle tops that doubled as dispensers. He trembled, and drops stained the tablecloth. He seemed tense and nervous. His fastidiousness had turned to fawning. Miguel, I guessed, was aiming at a *confianza*—a confidence—that displayed more than professional interest. Had he interpreted my mention of San Francisco as a suggestion that I was gay? His hand hovered over me, then settled on my shoulder. I felt a squeeze. I turned my head and looked disdainfully at his hand. He got the hint. His sweet face contorted, and the hand sharply withdrew.

There is irony in the fact that the capital of the homosexual world is San Francisco's Castro Street. It is surely not named in Fidel's honor; Cuban gays were systematically persecuted after the Revolution. Castro supposedly told U.S. journalist Lee Lockwood that a homosexual could never "embody the conditions and requirements of...a true revolutionary." Thus, homosexuals were among the groups identified as "undesirable."

Castro, who denies the comment, says that such prejudices were a product not of the Revolution but of the existing social milieu. "We inherited male chauvinism and many other bad habits from the *conquistadores*," he told Tomás Borge in *Face to Face with Fidel Castro*. "That historical legacy...influenced our attitude toward homosexuality." Thus gays and lesbians suffered "homophobic repression and rejection" just as they did in the States. The gay rights movement had not yet been born in the U.S., and the same prejudices that the revolutionaries inherited about homosexuals prevailed elsewhere in the world.

In Cuba, however, the repression was more widespread and brutal.

The pogrom began in earnest in 1965. Homosexuals were arrested and sent to agricultural work and reeducation camps—UMAP (Units for Military Help to Agricultural Production)—that gay filmmaker Néstor Almendros revealed in his documentaries *Improper Conduct* and *Nobody Listened*. Echoing Auschwitz, the gate of one camp in Camagüey bore the reproach "WORK MAKES YOU MEN." Many intellectuals lost their jobs because they were gay, or because they had been denunciated anonymously. Homosexuality was also considered an aberration of nature that could weaken the family structure. Hence homosexuals were not allowed to teach, become doctors, or occupy positions from which they could "pervert" Cuban youth.

Although UMAP camps closed in 1968 (later, those who had lost their jobs were reinstated and given back pay), periodic purges occurred throughout the 1970s and early 80s. By the mid-1980s, Cuba began to respond to the gay rights movement that had already gained momentum worldwide. Officially, the new position is that homosexuality and bisexuality are no less natural and healthy than heterosexuality. In 1987, a directive was issued to police to stop harassment. An official atonement was made through the release at the 1993 Havana Film Festival of *Vidas Paralelas (Parallel Lives)* and *La Bella del Alhambra (The Beauty at the Alhambra)*, and the 1994 hit movie *Fresa y Chocolate (Strawberry and Chocolate)*, which dealt with the persecution of gays in Cuba and the government's use of informers. The films were officially approved by Cuba's Film Institute, headed by Alfredo Guevara, a homosexual and a close confidant of Castro's, offering proof that the government is attempting to exorcise the ghost of a shameful past.

I retired to my hotel, showered, snoozed a while, and stepped across the street for dinner at the Palacio del Valle, the town's architectural pride and joy. Erected in the late 1800s as the home of a merchant, Celestino Cáceres, it later passed out of his hands and was given in 1912 as a wedding present to one Aciclio Valle, who flaunted his wealth by adding to the mansion in virile Mughal style. Moroccan craftsmen were imported to grace it with delicate arabesques, bulbous cupolas, and cupped arches. The Castro government having turned it into a restaurant, I dined in a room dripping with carved ornamentation.

Carmen Iznaga, a niece of acclaimed Cuban poet Nicolás Guillén, greeted me with a lingering handshake. She had a wild shock of white hair and sensual, soul-melting eyes. After seating me, she settled at a Steinway piano and hammered out a medley of classical and popular pieces, stopping only once to greet two elderly Spanish tourists and their pretty young paramours.

The cubanas were dressed in high heels and miniskirts, and they were well perfumed. One was a slender brunette with glistening raven hair; the other was a busty redhead in a blood-red dress that fit her body like a second skin. All four clearly relished their respective good luck, though I couldn't help feeling jealously that it was the males—each was old enough to have fought in the civil war—who had hit the jackpot. The only other patron was a 20-something German tourist with a *negrita*. He was having trouble communicating in Spanish and kept referring to his pocket-sized dictionary. No worries. Sex is an international language.

My lobster arrived on chinaware. It was huge. Ten bucks, including beer.

As I left, I tipped Carmen a dollar bill, adding to the two arranged conspicuously in a fishbowl atop the piano. Carmen stood, took my hand, and kissed it.

~

CHAPTER SIX

TRINIDAD

East of Cienfuegos, the saw-toothed Escambray Mountains soar ridge upon ridge to the north. The massif forms a rain shadow, and with it comes an abrupt change in the landscape: Sugarcane fades to parched golden grasslands grazed by hardy humped cattle, ash-colored and well muscled, standing fixedly in the magnesium light like bovine figures on a spotlit Cretan urn. Rounded hillocks pimple the plain. Each is tipped by a few palms in whose scant shade stand simple adobe *bohíos*. Deciduous trees speckle the scene in Monet colors: yellow corteza amarilla, scarlet poró, and bright orange Spathodea— the "African tulip tree"—locally called the Jesús Cristo tree because it blooms blood-red at Easter.

The heat builds infernally, drawing a searing wind across the plains. It is as if I've passed into a new continent in the space of a few miles. I hum along at 70 miles an hour, the twin cylinders singing a symphonic serenade to the livestock.

A dirt road spins me south, snaking downhill to Playa Inglés, where I edge up to the lonesome beach and cut the motor. Old fishing boats draped with nets are keeled on their sides, providing cover for a family of snoozing pigs. Roosters trot across the hot sand. A small group of fishermen eyes me impassively from beneath the shady eave of a tumbledown shack as I scribble notes in the cool penumbra of a nearby tree. The calm sea is inviting and I am tempted to strip off my leathers and dash down the sands but am dissuaded by the chilling scrutiny of a soldier peering at me through binoculars from a watchtower a short distance away. Military camps are everywhere. I fire up and retreat to the highway.

Farther east, the ragged Escambray crowd dramatically down to the shore. Tumbling rivers have gnawed deep ravines spanned by thin bridges above the river mouths that during dry season form little beaches on the shoals. I speed down the empty road, the warm rays of the afternoon sun and the mellow wind caressing my face. The Beemer is purring. My happy thoughts roll in synchronized rhythm with the drone of the engine and the blur of the unfurling highway.

Beyond the Río Yaguanabo I pass into Sancti Spíritus province and power up the hill upon which Trinidad, the crown jewel of Cuba's colonial cities, is poised.

Trinidad, the fourth of the seven cities established by colonizing governor Diego Velásquez, was founded in 1514 on a site already settled by Taino Indians, whom the Spanish conquistadors found panning for gold in the rivers. The gold-hungry arrivistes established a lucrative if short-lived gold mine that lent vigor to the young township and the wharves at nearby Casilda. Hernán Cortés set out from here in 1518 to conquer the Aztec empire for Spain. Fleets bearing the spoils of Mexico soon gathered in Casilda, eclipsing Trinidad's meager mines but filling its vaults as down payment on a glittering future. Trinidad's position on Cuba's underbelly was also perfect as an entrepôt for the Caribbean slave trade. Many slaves were put to work locally, stimulating the sugar trade. Trinidad prospered greatly; the 18th century was its golden age.

By the early 19th century the growth of nearby Cienfuegos, with its vastly superior harbor, began to surpass Casilda, which was then silting up. Trinidad sank into a steady decline, hastened by tumult in the slave trade and competition from more advanced sugar estates elsewhere in Cuba. Isolated from the Cuban mainstream, Trinidad floundered. By the turn of the 20th century the wealth had vanished, and only the beauty of the baroque churches and neoclassical mansions remained.

In the 1950s, when Batista declared Trinidad a "jewel of colonial architecture," a preservation law was passed prohibiting development. The construction of the Carretera Central, on the north side of the Escambray Mountains, had already stolen the through traffic, ensuring that Trinidad would be preserved in the past—a shadowy, lived-in museum. Today, this aging and romantic beauty is a UNESCO World Heritage site.

I cruised up Calle Ciro Guinart and lost my way in the heart of the old city, befuddled by a warren of cobbled streets. Some ended at T-junctions; others curled or bifurcated, with one street leading uphill while the other dropped sharply to another fork or odd-angled bend. Before long I began to wonder if I'd been that way before.

The streets were designed this way to thwart pirates. The layout reminded me of mazes built into the floors of 12th-century English cathedrals in the belief that the devil, who couldn't resist the challenge of a maze, would follow the path to the center and then out again, thus leading him back to the cathedral door. The illogical puzzlement and confusion of the bending, doubling-back, surreal world of Trinidad's labyrinth seemed a perfect metaphor for the tangled skein of Cubans' lives.

I pulled over and studied the road map, mounted in a clear plastic pocket atop the tank bag. Instantly a crowd gathered. Women never took more than a passing interest in the BMW, but men flocked to run their hands reverentially across the paintwork or go down on their haunches to study the mechanical minutiae.

"You want a room?" a wiry youth inquired in Spanish while his friends crowded in. His face was pocked and pimply, and his sinewy body was tensed like a panther's.

"No, thanks. I want my bearings."

"A *casa particular* is cheap."

"No, thank you. I'm staying at the hotel."

"Yes, but a casa particular is much cheaper."

"Maybe some other time," I replied. "What's the name of this street here, please?" I asked, indicating the narrow *calle* that ran off to left and right. He called it Lirío, which was shown on the map as Abel Santamaría. I was confused.

"And what's the name of the church, there?"

"Santa Ana."

"Ah, now I see where I am. Many thanks," I said, putting the bike in gear and feathering the clutch to clear the crowd, which separated as if I were Moses parting the Sea of Galilee.

"Hotel no good. I know casa particular. Very clean. Very cheap," said the youth, stepping into the void in front of the bike.

"Listen, I'm not interested, okay?"

I eased forward. He stood his ground.

"Excuse me!"

He didn't move.

I tweaked the throttle and let the clutch fly. He leaped nimbly aside.

I emerged onto Plaza Mayor, the compact main square lorded over by the simple Catedral Santísima and five exquisite colonial mansions painted in fresh, vibrant pastels: burnished ocher, rose-pink, flame-orange, morning-sky blue, and daffodil yellow. At its heart was a small park with Royal palms, framed by wrought-iron fences draped with hibiscus bowers tumbling onto the cobbled streets. A young girl with her hair bobbed like the ears of Minnie Mouse sat atop one of two bronze greyhounds that belonged in a Landseer painting. She was smiling serenely, a picture of artfully delicate innocence. The plaza was saturated in a warm roseate glow. Everything looked so nostalgic. I put the bike on the kickstand, dug out my camera, and stepped back to capture the mellow scene.

A cocoa-dark cubana appeared in the viewfinder. She paused by the Beemer, then looked toward me, smiled, and threw back her tousled hair. A large pearly orb hung from each ear. I lowered the camera. She was tall and svelte, with dusky skin silvered like satin, and she wore a sensual moue. Her name was Osmara. I asked her to pose by the *moto*.

"*¡Ay, senor! ¿Cómo está su moto?*"

It was the pock-faced youth. He had followed me on a bicycle and was puffing from the exertion of the uphill pursuit. I studied him closely, registered predatory eyes.

I was feeling ungracious. "Get lost!"

"You no want to talk to me?" he replied, switching to faltering English.

"That's right. I don't want a casa particular."

"I no talk about house," he said. "You bring *tapa* but no have now." *Tapa?* What was he talking about?

"I think you lose something, eh?"

"Lose something?"

"*Sí, señor.* You no have thing here no more," he said, pointing toward the back of the bike.

Sonofabitch! He was right. The nylon cover was missing. I had secured the *tapa*, or cover, inside its bag under an elasticized net beneath the duffel. It must have been stolen when I stopped to ask directions. I figured the youth had distracted me while his pals lifted the net and made off with it. The duffel had blocked my view in the mirrors and prevented me from seeing the cover being filched.

"You no want to listen to me. Now it gone," the scurrilous urchin intoned. "I try to tell you, but you no have interest."

"Where is it now?" I asked. He threw back his head and nodded toward the sky. "Only God knows," he said disdainfully. I wanted to hit him.

"I'm willing to pay a reward. If you find it, you know where to find me," I said, comprehending the scam and handing him the cue he wanted to hear. I said goodbye to Osmara and rode off to check into the Motel Las Cuevas on the bluff above town. As I rode up the hill, the red oil light flickered on. I cut the engine and pulled the bike onto the center stand. The frame was scorching hot. Freaked out, I let the bike cool for a few minutes, then checked the oil level. Bone dry.

I hadn't thought to check the oil since setting out from Florida. After all, I'd racked up barely 2,000 miles. I had no experience with motorbikes. My Porsche 944 could go to the moon and back without an appreciable dip in the oil level, and I assumed a quality motorbike would do the same. I felt like John Sutherland, the character in *Zen and the Art of Motorcycle Maintenance* to whom the author, Robert M. Pirsig, could "preach the practical value and worth of motorcycle maintenance till hoarse and it would make not a dent in him." Like Sutherland, I prefer to let a competent mechanic take care of things. But this potentially catastrophic error was due entirely to my negligence. I was lucky that the oil-cooled engine hadn't seized.

Osmara called. The youth had contacted her and asked her to call me.

"He says he has found the cover, but it will cost you."

She asked me to be at her house on Calle Jesús Menéndez at nine o'clock.

We set out together through the darkened labyrinth. A rake-thin boy of eight or nine led the way. Mysterious voices called from the shadows: "Sssst! *Amigo*. Where is your moto?" People I had never seen knew me instantly as the foreigner with the motorbike.

Osmara seemed to know everyone. Even ten or fifteen blocks from her home, we were still among people calling out greetings. She had a six-year-old son, she told me, who lived with her parents. We passed by their house. Osmara's mother had pulled her rocking chair onto the elevated sidewalk and was sitting in her grubby shift, staring listlessly ahead. She looked like she had been there a century, waiting for something to happen. The woman gave me a warm *abrazo*—a hug. Through the wide-open windows I could see her father rocking gently, shirtless in Cuban fashion, illumined by the glow of a flickering TV. Seeing me, he stepped onto the porch and clasped my hand tightly.

Farther down the cobbled street, we passed her son playing hoop. It was a cool encounter. Osmara pointed him out as one might indicate a specimen in a zoo: "And this here is a lesser macaque." She never acknowledged him. Nor he, her. He looked ashamed, or embarrassed.

Then Osmara's brother appeared. "Hey, *amigo! ¿Su moto?*"

He asked a few questions about the BMW, then changed the subject. "You like her?" he inquired, indicating his sister. Yes, I replied.

"She make love good, I hear. Many men tell me this." He turned to Osmara and translated what he had told me. She smiled, then lowered her eyes. *"Es bueno. Is good thing," he said, reassuringly. "¡Las cubanas son caliente!"*

I agreed, more to end the conversation than anything, but it was true. I had never met such hot-blooded women. "Love, marriage, home, that means nothing to them," a Cuban intellectual told author Arnold Samuelson half a century ago; "they love you today, and tomorrow they love somebody else.... It is in their blood."

I once asked Daisy if that was true. Were Cubans promiscuous?

"Of course," she replied, as if it were a stupid question. "Don't you know? Sex is the only thing Castro can't ration." It was meant as a *chiste,* a joke, but it went much deeper than that. Everywhere I traveled, Cubans seemed to thrive on physical contact. Men and women alike spoke of sex as a human imperative, like daily bread. As Argentinian journalist Jacobo Timerman wrote, "Eros is amply gratified in Cuba and needs no stimulation." Seduction seemed like a national pastime pursued by both sexes—the free expression, as Timerman put it, of a "high-spirited people confined in an authoritarian world."

The island was peopled by sensualists impermeable to the puritanical communist doctrine that had turned the Soviet bloc into a frigid convent. The Cuban revolutionaries weren't prudish. They have treated sex as both natural and healthy. "It would be a revolution with *buchango* (pizzazz)," said Che Guevara. Teenagers become sexually active at an astonishingly early age: the girls at 13 on average, and boys at 15, according to Cuba's National Center for Sex Education, which dispenses sex counseling (along with condoms and birth-control pills) to youths. Hence it is not unusual for a schoolgirl to announce she won't be coming to class next day because she's going to have an *interrupción*—an abortion. As the director of Baracoa's family-planning clinic once told the editors of *Colors* magazine, "Here you have girls who at 13 are already experts in sex."

After an interminable number of lefts and rights, the three of us arrived at a house on Calle Conrado Benítez. The boy pushed open a tall, weathered door and beckoned us in. Plastic ducks in freeze-frame flight had been hung on the canary-yellow walls. An old woman and her daughter stared at me from their seats in front of the TV. They were watching *Te Odio, Mi Amor,* an immensely popular Brazilian *telenovela* dubbed into Spanish.

Osmara explained who I was.

"So, this is the man with the moto, eh?" the crone declared, piercing me with dark eyes rimmed by mascara. Her pouty lips were smeared with red lipstick, her cheeks were circled by rouge, like *sindur,* and her thinning hair was dyed with henna that had stained her forehead like a scummy brown bathtub ring.

"Then this is the one who dropped his tapa—the one who rushed away on his motorbike when my grandson tried to tell him he had *dropped* it?" She stressed the word "dropped" for effect. Ah-ha! The tapa had *fallen* off the bike. I was tempted to tell her it had been lashed down good and tight, but decided to go along with her story.

"How much do you want?" I asked, speeding things along.

"Whatever you wish to give," she replied, shrugging her shoulders in mock indifference, as if pecuniary gain were the last thing on her mind. It would be almost impossible to buy another cover in Cuba, and I was prepared to pay whatever sum she demanded. I had anticipated a lively negotiation, but she had just made a tactical error. The advantage was mine.

"*Bueno.* Then first I'd like to see the cover," I said. The *abuela* said something to the youngster, who darted out into the night. He reappeared moments later bearing the tapa. "Check it. Make sure that it is all there," said the grandmother, taking the cover and handing it to me. It was still in its bag.

My anger abated. I was tempted to walk out, but magnanimity got the upper hand. I slipped two dollar bills to Osmara and asked her to dispense my philanthropy. She knew she was holding a trifle, but she was loath to invoke my anger by suggesting a more substantial reward. She handed a greenback to the boy, who plucked it swiftly and melted into the dark like one of Fagin's urchins.

"And the other for the grandmother," I said, stepping back into the street. The old woman shot me a look of disgust. Her grandson, the thief, had gotten nothing.

"¿Te gusto?" Osmara inquired as we strolled back uphill. *Do you like me?* I said that I did. She took my hand and whispered solicitous words. As we crossed Independencia, Osmara tugged my arm and steered me down a narrow and forbidding side street whose roofed balconies deepened the shadows cast by 40-watt street lamps.

"Where are we going?" I asked. She explained that my hotel didn't allow Cuban women to accompany foreign men to their rooms. Osmara, it seems, had decided upon her daily bread.

We stepped through dark streets full of potholes and seeping water. At night cool air blows downhill, and doors and full-length glassless windows remain open to admit the breeze. Trinitarios, like all Cubans, live their home life in full view of passersby. Even the shutters of the Hogar Materno, the local maternity home, were open to the street, tempting me to peer in through the *rejas*—intricate, wood-turned spindles—the way one is irresistibly drawn to sneak a glance when, the neighbors leave their drapes open at night back home. Pregnant women in cotton nightgowns lounged on their beds or rocked together, nursing their swollen bellies while paddle fans stirred the torpid air. I felt like a voyeur on the set of a Fellini movie.

We zigzagged some more, then stopped outside a house on the edge of the old city. The town was eerily silent but for the barking of dogs and muffled television staccato. Osmara's knock reverberated down the dim-lit cobbled street. The door cracked open. Words were exchanged and the door opened wide. A middle-aged man motioned us in. He was unshaven and disheveled and dressed in an unbuttoned shirt, soiled shorts, and flip-flops, and we had clearly aroused him from slumber. He rubbed his eyes. He was *muy gordo*—very fat—with a huge winesack belly. At first I didn't fathom it, but Osmara had led me to a private *posada*—a room or house rented by the hour for love. I hesitated, unsure of my situation. Osmara gave me a gentle shove in the back.

Our host pushed aside lace curtains with the back of his arm to reveal a small boudoir. The room was the essence of kitsch. It overflowed with whimsical Woolworth's art. Cheap *muñequitas* (dolls). Plastic flowers and animals. Old perfume bottles. Two inflatable Day-Glo yellow elephants the size of French poodles adopted sit-up-and-beg postures on the couch. Photographs of a young girl and other family members were pinned on the dresser. The host's daughter was probably at college; this, I guessed, was her room.

A transaction was negotiated and dollar bills—mine—changed hands. *El gordo* disappeared and returned moments later with some fresh-laundered sheets. My mood was sinking fast. I had been happy to stroll the streets with Osmara, toward whom I felt a warming yet platonic affection. She was comely but not beautiful, and my ardor had yet to rise. In other circumstances, I might have enjoyed making love to her. But *el gordo* had now departed and Osmara was stripping with avaricious speed, and I couldn't help feeling that the only bulge in my pocket that excited her was that of my wallet. The clinical nature of the proceedings cheapened the situation. At least soft candlelight hinted reassuringly, albeit vaguely, at romance. I resigned myself to the fait accompli.

Trinidad enjoys a setting of great natural beauty, astride a hill where it catches the breezes and gazes out over the Caribbean, with green mountains—the Topes de Collantes—edging skyward behind. The views from the Motel Las Cuevas were splendid, but I felt removed and disconnected from a red-tile-roofed town that had sidestepped the currents of time. The breakfast buffet was dismal—fatty ham, tasteless cheese, bone-dry biscuits, half-frozen papaya, fried eggs swimming in grease—yet I felt guilty when the waitress removed my plate. Her family would have been glad for the leftovers.

I checked out and rode into town, searching for a casa particular. A matronly woman said she knew just the place. I followed, idling along in first gear, as she led me down cobbled streets to a timeworn house on Calle Juan Manuel Márquez, a block north of Plaza Mayor, the central plaza. A youth was sitting on the front step, strumming a guitar and humming softly. My guide called out loudly in Cuban fashion, producing a tall, red-haired woman who sallied down the dark hallway and into the lyrical sunlight. She had a tomboy's voice and spoke with self-confident grace.

Isabel's well-preserved one-story home was a capacious charmer entered through massive wooden doors studded with rosehead nails. Like most Trinidadian structures, it was designed in the classical Mudéjar style fashionable in Cuba in the 18th century, with an open-air patio at the back and a hierarchy of rooms of graduated size and ceiling heights for different functions befitting the social requirements of wealthy sugar merchants of the day. Cool stone floors and thick walls of porous brick covered with whitewashed stucco kept out the heat. The main quarters—Isabela's—were to the right of the soaring hallway.

Isabel pushed aside tall *mampársas*—double-swing half-doors that serve as room dividers—and ushered me into my more humble abode. The front room, or *sala*, had a large double bed sagging in the middle, a Zenith television, and a smattering of simple furniture adorned with family portraits and homey vases and trinkets. A faded painting of Jesus in a baroque gilded frame looked down from one wall. Light poured in through a tall, shuttered window barred with *rejas* and looking onto the street. I stepped up into a second bedroom, open to the first. This also contained a bed and television; crowning the TV like a museum speicmen was a rotary-dial telephone—an antediluvian piece of "fraternal Hungarian equipment," in Castro's words. To the rear was a large kitchen with a stone sink and, high up near the aged cedar roof beams, a large paneless window letting air flow down through two generously proportioned, lofty-ceilinged *aposentos*, or bedrooms. The place was cool and inviting. I loved it. Isabel was asking ten dollars.

"The municipal authorities inspect the rooms and determine the rental value," she explained. "They also charge me a hefty monthly license."

"How much do they take?"

"*¡Demasiado!*" Too much!

She reached for a *libreta*, a notebook, and recorded my passport details and the terms of my stay.

I gunned the bike up over the stairwell, squeezed it gingerly between the narrow doorjambs, then rolled down the hallway and into my *sala*, where it remained on the stand, dripping fresh oil onto the gray sandstone floor.

The shower worked most of the time; not so the electric heater. When I pulled the cord on the ceiling fan—ZAP!—a jolt like a million bee stings tore up my arm. The shock from the short-circuited wiring had been magnified because I was standing barefoot in a puddle of water.

Two days I spent roaming streets cobbled with upturned river stones called *chinas pelonas* ("bald stones"), worn through the centuries to a dark gloss like turtle shells packed end to end. The streets sloped in a slight V with gutters in the center—so designed, I was told, because the city's first governor had a right leg shorter than the left and could thereby always walk level. The unfathomable composition both beguiled and confused; I felt like I was stumbling through a Daedalian artifice. Then, with a grateful sigh, I plunged unexpectedly from the labyrinth onto palm-garnished plazas surrounded by beautifully restored colonial homes and quaint churches.

White light sheathed the town in a celestial glow, adding gleam to a recent restoration that made the living past seem cinematic. A tour group crawled through the streets like invading army ants. Two sunburned French women adorned in silk scarves and gaudy sunglasses scurried past, as if they had been given only ten minutes in a Walt Disney theme park. They were perspiring and panting from the heat. *"Mon dieu!"* exclaimed one, raising her camera toward a toothless old Cuban and his graying mule, whose pointy ears stuck through holes in a straw hat like a cartoon postcard. Thank God there were no souvenir shops, billboards, or other tourist concessions.

In Havana I had sensed anxiety and tension. Here I could sense a deep ease.

"Amigo."

Amigo. It was a respectful greeting in passing. No one ever disdainfully called me a gringo or a yanqui, nor even an American. "We, too, are Americans," one Cuban told me. I was an amigo, a welcome friend to a stranger. My greeter, an old black man with skin like an Egyptian mummy's, was coaxing a simple *guajira* (country folk song) from a penny whistle made of bamboo. He was sitting on the steps of his home and being serenaded in turn by twittering show birds in a bamboo cage—a Trinidadian tradition—on the wall.

I waved and returned the greeting. When I asked him if he had made the whistle, he said yes. They, too, were a local tradition.

Where could I buy one?

His dark soulful eyes widened with pleasure. He smiled angelically, then reached out his bony hand and dropped the whistle in my palm. I was exultant. Digging into my pocket, I drew out a five-dollar bill, which he declined.

"We may be poor," he replied, "but we Cubans have not forgotten how to give gladly."

At that moment a young boy tugged at my singlet; in a frail, uncertain voice, like Oliver in the Dickensian poorhouse, he asked me for *"chiclet"*—chewing gum. He stared fixedly and repeated the mantra: *"Chiclet...Chiclet!"* For good measure, he held out a tiny, upturned palm. The old man shooed him away. He looked pained and said he felt ashamed that Cuban youth were resorting to begging. He began to expound on Cuba's woes, stating that there was nothing wrong with the system. It was the economy that was to blame. I heard the refrain throughout Cuba, suggesting a serious disconnection with reality.

Weren't they one and the same? The old man parried my reference.

"Listen, how many other nations are as self-reliant as Cuba, eh? We have had to learn to make do, to rely on no one," he explained proudly. "We have our dignity, and no other nation can take that away. We built socialism with our own hands, do you understand? No one had to ask us to sacrifice, because we did it willingly to build a better society.

"Look at me. I am black. Do you know what life was like for people like me before *el triunfo?*" he asked, using the Cuban term for the triumph of the Revolution. "Few people spoke of our racial problems, as if they never existed. But let me tell you, the wealthy people, the landowners—they were almost all white. They used to treat us like animals. Not all were this way, you understand, but in general, to have African blood in your veins, well...to many people that made you worse than a donkey. Why do you think Batista had to pay a million dollars to join the Havana Yacht Club? He was too *negro.*"

In elitist prerevolutionary Cuba, even a president, if mulatto, was mere hoi polloi.

"I don't think they ever let in him, did they?" I replied. "I gather that when he arrived, the members turned the lights out."

The story of racism in prerevolutionary Cuba wasn't quite so black-and-white. To be sure, slavery gave republican Cuba a triple-tiered social structure, with pure-blooded blacks at the base. In the middle were the mixed bloods; at the top, the whites and near-whites. But these lines were "never so tightly drawn as in the other islands of the Caribbean," thought Langston Hughes, a black writer who visited Cuba in 1930. "The British islands are the worst in this respect. The Latin islands are more careless concerning racial matters."

Hughes found Havana's color line to be "much more flexible than that of the United States, and much more subtle. There are no Jim Crow cars in Cuba, and at official state gatherings and less official carnivals and celebrations, citizens of all colors meet and mingle." Nonetheless crashing through social divisions required that a person have wealth and celebrity status in proportion to the duskiness of his skin.

Hughes visited Cuba at a time when tourism was booming. When the island's first scheduled airline service began in 1931, socialites and the working class alike hopped planes for Havana to sidestep propriety and class barriers and nourish their human frailties. Havana, wrote Juliet Barclay, filled with "milk-shakes and mafiosi, hot dogs and whores. Yanqui Doodle had come to town and was having martini-drinking competitions in the Sevilla Bar."

To court the favor of bigoted Yankees, hotels that "were formerly lax in their application of color lines began to discourage even mulatto Cubans," recorded Hughes. And the Biltmore club, which had taken over the city's only wide, clean stretch of beach, charged a dollar for the privilege of its use (no small sum in those days) and introduced a color bar as well, although mulatto plutocrats and policemen still mingled.

"I don't know how it is in your country," the old man continued, "but I know this: The Revolution has been kind to us. Can you name me another country where blacks are treated as equals? Here we are human beings. Without Fidel this would never have happened."

I had to concur. Cuba seemed color-blind. Prejudice is still subtly woven through the social fabric, but the remarkable changes wrought in the past four decades have resulted in the abolition of lily-white scenes. Everywhere I had traveled, black and white mingled with unself-conscious, self-assured ease.

Slavery had shackled countries throughout the Americas with racial problems; for all I could see, however, Cuba has gone further than any other to root out the evil. In trademark heroic fashion, Fidel Castro had cut the Gordian knot with a stroke: "We have to straighten out what history has twisted," Castro declared shortly after winning power. He swiftly outlawed institutionalized discrimination and applied his bulldozing determination to enforce laws to bring about racial and social equality—part and parcel of a systematic effort to forge a new society of selflessly motivated people in which everyone would take pride not in class or color but in being Cuban.

"*Los gusanos* forget that Cuban culture has African roots," the old-timer added. He was speaking of "the worms"—the upper- and middle-class exiles, 98 percent of them white, who fled Cuba after the Revolution, carrying their prejudice with them. Officially, 66 percent of Cuba's population is "white," but this is misleading; even the fair-skinned ones often carry at least a trace of African blood.

Not surprisingly, Afro-Cubans—the greatest beneficiaries of the Revolution—are, on the whole, more loyal to Castro than whites. Today, Cuba's blacks are better educated, far healthier, and more confident than blacks anywhere else in the Americas, including the United States. Black Cubans raised during the Revolution no longer see themselves as a separate class. Nor, as novelist Alice Walker has pointed out, "do they appear able to feel, viscerally, what racism is." Instead, Cubans of every shade feel their *cubanidad*—a Cuban-ness they all have in common.

With darkness, Trinidad became more beguiling still. Breezes that once filled the sails of galleons carried on their warm breath the sweet aromas of tropical scents and the hint of salt air from the sea. In the Restaurant Las Begonias—an elegant seafood eatery lent a Parisian feel by awnings striped blue and white—the tables had been set with elegant porcelain and silverware, as if royalty were expected. I was the only diner. Trinidad has a fistful of atmospheric restaurants, but that night they lay fallow. Bored waiters in ill-fitting tuxedos milled around expectantly for guests who would never arrive, giving me a sense that I was the only non-Cuban in town. After an interminable wait, my red snapper arrived, teeth bared grimly and a mint sprig sticking up from its spotted belly like a cocktail umbrella.

By eleven, Trinidad had bedded down. The ancient doors were locked tight and the town was still as death. I lay on my bed and savored the welcome silence, broken only by the snuffling of a pig next door and the *cock-a-doodle-doo* of an insomniac cockerel crowing up the moon. Then a clap of techno thunder exploded from the building across the street. The roof having long ago collapsed on the old red-brick structure, Trinidad's communist city fathers had conjured the roofless carcass into the Discoteca Escalina, which was now pumping boom-box madness to the masses so that only the dead could sleep. They should put a lid on it—literally.

Trinidad's beach, Playa Ancón, was a ribbon of silver lamé unspooling along a clawlike peninsula enclosing the lagoon of Casilda. Its waters were thick with mangroves riding atop spidery interlocking stilt roots that made the trees appear as if walking on water. Homespun fishing craft with crudely stitched sacking for sails threaded unsteadily through the channels. A handful of enterprising Cubans had set up stalls on the sand and were hawking seashells and trinkets to pale-skinned, lotion-basted tourists from the Hotel Ancón. In the lobby, a salsa band tried to bring the necrotic tourists to life.

I felt like an extra from *The Road Warrior* plodding along the sand in my padded leather pants. My feet were scorching inside my metal-lined boots, so I took them off and felt the sand soothe my toes. I whipped off my shirt, fell back, and let the rustling palms lull me to sleep. I dreamed that Daisy was riding my motorcycle through the streets of Havana. I waved from the sidewalk, but she passed me by.

"*Ssst!*"

A sibilant whisper roused me from sumptuous slumber.

"*Sssst!*"

I felt fingers caress my shoulder. Opening my right eye slowly, I saw a jet-black face haloed by glaring incandescence. Second eye open. Incandescence faded to eggshell blue. Black face smiled, revealing slight gaps between pearly teeth. The woman was caressing me with her eyes, telling me she would relish a taste of a foreigner.

"My name is Yuri. What is yours?"

"Er, Cristóbal," I replied groggily, still drunk on sunshine. Her hot-pink bikini was no more than two dots and a dash.

She trailed a pointy fingernail down my chest. "Why are you wearing such strange pants?" she asked, her fingers edging indiscreetly down past my navel. She pulled on the elastic waistband and let go. *Twang!*

In my notebook she wrote: "Yuri. Discoteca Escalina. Ten o'clock." With that, she puckered her lips saucily and sauntered off to join her friends playing volleyball farther down the beach. Her body was firm and lissome, all muscle and mellifluous curves, like a jungle cat patrolling the beach.

On the way back to Trinidad I passed a billboard reading: THE ENEMY SHALL NOT PASS OUR FRONTIER.

I have been reading about a spa hotel at Topes de Collantes, high in the Escambray Mountains. The road curves steeply. I am tensed with concentration. I don't want to misjudge a corner and plow a furrow in the Cuban hillside. Small branches and damp pine needles litter the road; gravel washed down by torrential rains has gathered in troughs gouged in the tarmac by heavy trucks braking hard on hairpin turns. The sudden sharp dips test my nerves. Twice I am spooked as the rear wheel spins loose. Otherwise the BMW takes the climb in stride, and I knife in and out of dark morning shadows in the crisp April air.

The Beemer is dripping oil steadily from the sump gasket and pushrod tube seal. I've been too flippant and have scared myself. Kicking myself for letting the machine run out of oil, I am now acutely attuned to every sound, listening closely for telltale rattles or other mechanical problems. The bike is running as smooth as before, however, and I try unsuccessfully to reassure myself that nothing is wrong.

Every so often I steal a glance at the breathtaking landscapes flitting through gaps in the dense forest. Wispy bamboo waves over the road, and air-plants weigh heavily on the moss-laden boughs; Cubans call these antediluvian tree ferns *rabo de mono* (monkey tail), an allusion to the young fronds uncurling like the fiddleheads of giant cellos. Silver light seems to pour from the clouds. The beauty of it all makes me laugh out loud.

Then the gargantuan Kurhotel comes into view, towering in blunt-faced tiers like a Stalinist ziggurat and approached via a stone staircase on a Siberian scale. It is topped by a monstrous TV transmitter. The edifice was erected in 1936 as a sanatorium for victims of tuberculosis. After the Revolution the disease was eradicated in Cuba, and the structure was turned into a spa resort for specialized treatments and postoperative rehabilitation. Today, as part of the "sun and surgery" program for foreigners run by Servimed (a division of the state-run tour agency, Cubanacán), the Kurhotel offers health packages featuring everything from massage and physiotherapy to herbal mud wraps. Shafts of sunlight gild its face, and for a moment I am awed by the glowing monument to good health. Then the clouds close above, veiling the bone-gray hotel in melancholy.

The receptionist, a slender woman with large hazel eyes and golden hair, offers to show me around. The elevator takes an eternity to arrive. I tell her that I can feel the stubble growing on my chin. "True?" she replies, taking me at my word. "It's a joke, no?" The elevator arrives. A middle-aged man in a turquoise jogging suit occupies the center. He has Brezhnev eyebrows and a tubercular look. Romanian, I figure. The elevator shudders but refuses to rise.

"You must stand in the middle," says the receptionist, pointing at the center of the floor. I do so. She pushes the button for the top floor. The elevator groans. Still no movement. My fellow passengers edge closer. Nothing. We shuffle around until all three of us are dead center, squeezed shoulder to shoulder with our arms stiffly at our sides. Now perfectly balanced, the contraption vibrates madly and we make our torpid ascent like Siamese triplets.

Slavic accents echo in the hallways. Everyone is wearing identical turquoise sweats. Have I stepped into a skit from *Monty Python*?

The sun has disappeared behind bruise-colored clouds. Before long, icy raindrops slicken the muddy road that descends north to Lake Habanilla. I pull over and slip on my raingear. As I drop gingerly to Habanilla, a young woman appears like a wraith and steps out in front of me. I brake sharply, almost losing control on the slick surface. She has hair of flax and wears a tight, knee-length skirt. Without even a *"Buenos días"* she hoists herself sidesaddle onto the pillion, as if I am Jeeves and have just pulled up in the Bentley. *"¡Adelante!"* she cries, flicking one hand peremptorily to indicate *Go!*

The road rolls and twists as the long, hard grade coils down through narrow valleys carpeted in rows of dark coffee bushes like undulating folds of green silk. Approaching a hairpin, I drop into second and the rear wheel spins out briefly. *Don't tense up!* Taut muscles make a rider unresponsive. I am fearful that my passenger will destabilize me. Yet she is poised with perfect composure like a caged bird on a swing. At Manicaragua she hops down and disappears without a word.

I encircle the foothills of the Escambray through tidy agricultural communities with neat, whitewashed curbs. The sun reappears between scudding clouds, suffusing sepia-toned bohíos and orange groves in golden light. There is barely any traffic on the road, and I race my shadow along the pavement at 60 miles an hour. Lost in contemplation, I return to Trinidad and hit the sack with my mind still in the Sierra Escambray.

Even the noise from Discoteca Escalina doesn't disturb me. Not until the next day does it hit me: I've forgotten all about my date with the sultry beach girl named Yuri.

CHAPTER SEVEN

HUNGER IN THE HEARTLAND

Sancti Spíritus province was a gently undulating sea of chartreuse. The landscape grew larger, like a Hollywood drama, as I dropped into the Valle de los Indigenes, roared past rippling fields of *azúcar*, and swung rising and dipping up through the Alturas de Banao, whose wild, barren, whisky-brown crags seemed to belong in the Scottish Highlands.

My eyes were being poached in molten light. The intensity of the sun had sent the mercury soaring, and the fiery heat of the day combined with that of the cylinders to stoke the temperature of my steel-reinforced upper soles. My feet sizzled inside my boots. I pulled up alongside the Carretera Central, eased off my boots, rested my feet on the crash bars, and savored the orgasmic relief.

I spotted two elderly peasants in straw hats cycling insouciantly toward me down the middle of the road, trailed by two plodding oxen hauling a cart piled high with sugarcane. A tractor brought up the rear. Then an ambulance—an aging Lada station wagon—appeared in the distance, flying along in the oncoming lane. Its rising drone *weee!...Weee!!... WEEE!!!*—lifted a confetti shower of cattle egrets from the cane fields. I glanced in my mirror. A Russian army truck was bearing down from the other direction.

I watched as the ambulance gained upon the tractor, and the tractor upon the cart. The two pulled into my lane together at the same moment the truck

driver swung out to overtake me. Bug-eyed, the ambulance driver raced frantically to regain the other lane.

I heard squealing brakes and smelled burning rubber as the olive-green
truck slithered to a stop inches from my rear tire. I felt the wind whip, saw the
terrified face of the passenger, as the ambulance sprang back into the oncoming lane, slicing between the truck and the cyclists with millimeters to spare,
like a shot expertly placed by a pool player. A jeep that had been whipping along
behind the truck flew past me on the grassy shoulder and narrowly avoided
sailing into the cane field. The cyclist nearest the center line teetered over,
knocking the other old codger off his bike. Fortunately, no one was hurt.

I had planned to spend the night at the Hotel Zaza, a hunting-and-fishing
lodge on the shores of Presa Zaza, a man-made lake surrounded by wetlands a
few miles east of the city of Sancti Spíritus. The communist architects had
unaccountably ignored the stunning views over the cobalt lake, where marsh
birds were winging in and taking off. The rush of their wings made a muffled
roar like distant jet aircraft. Zaza also bubbles with fish, notably trout and large-
mouth bass in such numbers that they jostle for space. An angler's nirvana.

Amazingly, there was no fish on the hotel restaurant's menu. I ordered the
mixed salad. The waitress returned with a plate of canned vegetables. I was flabbergasted. I had just passed through mile after mile of arable land, indecently
fertile, tilled with vegetables. My growling stomach dictated a change of plan.
I declined a room, fired up the engine, and rode into Sancti Spíritus.

"I'm sorry, there are no rooms available," said the desk clerk at the Hotel
Plaza, a restored colonial edifice gracing Plaza Sánchez in the center of town.
The hotel was run by Islazul, a state agency that looks after national tourism
but whose peso properties—usually the bottom rung on the star-rated lodg-
ing ladder—also accept foreigners with dollars.

"Are you sure you don't have anything? I'm really tired."

"Nothing. You should try the Rancho Hatuey."

"I have. It's full."

"Then you should stay at the Hotel Zaza."

"There are no rooms there either." The receptionist frowned at my transparent lie.

Outside, a crowd had gathered around the BMW. Centripetal force had
struck Sancti Spíritus, the horde drawing more and more men into its vortex

until they were craning over one another's shoulders. Young men ran across the square, while those already in the outer ring circled like a slowly revolving galaxy merging slowly into the core. The clogged street had descended to Neapolitan chaos. Taxis were honking their horns, and the drivers of horse-drawn *coches* were whipping their scrawny charges, urging them to move through the crowd. I felt strangely guilty.

In the hotel lobby, a father and his two sons were watching cartoons on a flickering Russian-made TV. I saw a gorilla dressed as Uncle Sam beating its chest while two young communist pioneers tried to teach it good manners. Then Fidel appeared, gesticulating colorfully in black and white.

I smiled at the desk clerk, a handsome young man whose good looks were marred by a hair's-breadth mustache that might have been drawn with mascara.

"Can you look again? Maybe you missed a spare room," I said, fingering my wallet to hint that a commission could be paid.

He drew his finger slowly down the register. Magically, a vacancy appeared.

"You're correct," he replied, feigning astonishment. "We do have a room available." He emerged from behind the counter to show me up a cramped flight of stairs lined with colonial tiles. Seven bucks for a high-ceilinged cubicle with a lumpy bed so narrow I would be afraid to turn over in it. Mosquitoes eyed my arrival greedily. At least the room was clean.

I tipped the desk clerk. He said I could park the bike in the hotel kitchen, so I did, gunning it up onto the sidewalk and edging it through the narrow doors of the delivery entrance. I leaned it up against a metal bread trolley and secured it with chains.

I took a nap and awoke groggy, mauled by mosquitoes, and touchy as a boil. I stumbled downstairs to the restaurant. The menu listed five entrées, including fish for four dollars and "tendriloin stakes" for six. No fish was available. Remarkably, neither was chicken, Cuba's staple. The waitress assured me I would like the steak, which was all that the kitchen could offer, *desgracidamente, señor*. She arrived bearing a dumpling separating two lumps of braised beef. The meat was resilient, like a marinated army boot. I slept hungry—not for the first time, or the last.

Breakfast was a cruel joke. I asked for scrambled eggs.

"*¡No hay!*" replied the waitress. *There are none.*

"An omelet, then."

"*¡No hay!*"

What was the point in handing me a menu?

"What *do* you have?" I pleaded.

"*Solamente bocaditos,*" she replied indifferently. Spam sandwiches! I groaned despairingly. The Spam looked like something a dog had fetched up. It was served in stale crusty bread that turned to glue in my mouth as if the flour had been adulterated with plaster.

I asked for milk for my coffee.

"*No hay.*"

"Is there orange juice?" I inquired.

"*Sí, señor,*" she replied, hustling away. The glass was the size of an egg cup. I felt guilty asking for more.

"There is no more, *señor,*" she replied.

"*No hay*" was beginning to sound like a mantra. Sancti Spíritus felt like a town picked clean by looters. The stainless-steel shelves in a nearby *merendero*— a state-run lunch counter—were as bare as Mother Hubbard's. The gloomy grocery, or *puesto*, next door could muster only two items: a pile of potatoes and a dozen or so metal tins stacked in a row, without labels. I asked the store clerk what was in them.

"Boiled potatoes," she replied.

A Cuban flag hung limply above the counter, adding color to an anemic scene.

I didn't get it. Cuba has indecently fertile soil. Traveling across the island, I was continually awed by the rich red earth and the vast potential that had inspired René Dumont, the French socialist agronomist, to say, "With proper management, Cuba could adequately feed five times its current population." Fidel himself, in his famous 1953 "History Will Absolve Me" speech, had stated that "Cuba can support splendidly a population three times larger than it now has…. The market should be flooded with produce, pantries should be full."

What had gone wrong?

I spent hours caught in perplexed rumination as I rode along. By now I had become habituated to long days in the saddle, and stretches that had seemed unending in Pinar del Río now seemed a breeze. I was floating as if suspended in time. I couldn't remember when I had last felt so clear-headed. It was obvious, thrumming through the Cuban countryside, that communist management of agriculture had been dumbfoundingly inept. Dumont, who always wanted to believe in Castro's self-grown brand of socialism, eventually stopped visiting Cuba, disillusioned by its mismanagement, waste, and pursuit of pseudo- science. The thought pained me.

Earlier that day I had flashed past a billboard that screamed "RAGE AGAINST THE BLOCKADE." It is stock leftist cant that the U.S. embargo is to blame for Cuba's shortfalls—a position I had adopted at an early stage. But the billboard cast a shadow over fecund fields as florid as the plump tomatoes that grew there, heaped by invisible field hands into yawning crates and destined for God knows where. Certainly not the hotels of Sancti Spíritus, or the merenderos or craven *puestos*. Probably nowhere. The cultivated fields were untended, the ripe fruit left to blister beneath a fearsome sun. Daily throughout my journey I had passed vast acres of arable land lying fallow, ravaged by weeds, while produce was left to rot in the fields.

Before the Revolution, Cuba couldn't feed itself: The overwhelming majority of arable land was planted in sugarcane for export. The U.S. government had maintained a preferential quota for Cuban sugar—40 percent of sugarcane fields were owned by U.S. interests—in exchange for a guarantee of tariff concessions for U.S. goods; this tied Cuba to a one-commodity economy and bound it to U.S. foodstuffs and manufactures, which made up 80 percent of Cuban imports.

Alas, the Castro government sacrificed thoughts of self-sufficiency to feed sugar to the Soviet bear. A mere 12 percent of Cuba's cultivated land was planted in food crops; the rest was dedicated to pasture and export crops, almost exclusively sugarcane—Cuba's "bittersweet calvary," in the words of Guillermo Cabrera Infante. The cane was supplied to the Soviet bloc in exchange for rice, grains, and other staples, turning Cuba into a dependent state for four long decades of socialism.

With the Soviets as their benefactor, thought political satirist P. J. O'Rourke, "The Cubans got the luxury of running their economy along the lines of a Berkeley commune, and like California hippies wheedling their parents for cash, someone else paid the tab." The result was a freewheeling license for chaos. Dandy revolutionaries they may have been, but the iconoclastic duo of Castro and Che Guevara—who following *el triunfo de la revolución* was named head of the National Bank of Cuba and Minister of Finance and, in 1961,

Minister of Industry—lacked the acumen and temperament necessary to run an efficient economy, which they had swiftly nationalized. Che loved to tell a well-known Cuban *chiste* about how he got the job, revealing a penetrating sensitivity for the absurd:

At an early meeting of his cabinet, Castro asks who among them is an economist. Che raises his hand and he is sworn in as Minister of Finance. Afterward, Castro says: "Che, I didn't know you were an economist."

Che replies: "I'm not!"

Fidel asks: "Then why did you raise your hand when I said I needed an economist?"

"An economist?" exclaims Che. "I thought you asked for a Communist!"

Following the 1960 Agrarian Reform Law, private farmland was seized and organized in a system of centralized, inefficient state farms dedicated to perpetuating what the World Bank, in 1956, had called "the diabetic dangers of the dominance of sugar in [Cuba's] economic bloodstream."

Skilled managers had been replaced by loyal communist cadres with diddly economic experience. Monetary work incentives had been replaced by "moral" inducements. And the state, which set artificially low prices and got diminishing supplies in return, had taken over all distribution. The revolutionaries had bucked the law of supply and demand, explaining why tomatoes were left rotting in the fields.

The gasoline shortage didn't help matters. How otherwise can you move goods to market? But seeing the menus in the Hotel Zaza and the Hotel Plaza made me realize that hotel menus throughout the island were all the same, dictated by Havana bureaucrats, who run the distribution system, known as *Acopio*, that prevents hotel managers from purchasing local items to meet shortfalls.

"Where the food goes is a mystery," said the waitress at the Hotel Plaza, when I pressed her to explain the *Acopio*. She shrugged her shoulders. "Cubans learned long ago not to rely on the state."

Priority is given to hospitals, schools, and work canteens, along with the better tourist hotels, but very little reaches the state groceries or the restaurants—or Islazul hotels—out in the countryside. By one account, almost 40 percent of produce in the Acopio is filched for the home kitchen or for the black market upon which Cubans rely. Another 20 percent simply perishes in limbo-like transit. Castro had briefly flirted with free farmers' markets in the mid-1980s, prompting the reappearance of garlic and other items that had vanished from kitchen tables long ago. But the experiment proved so successful that Castro swiftly closed the markets, railing infamously against "millionaire garlic growers."

A synapse fired this realization: Cogent economic decisions had been forfeited for revolutionary canons designed to subjugate private initiative to the power of the state. The U.S. embargo was really a sideshow. It wouldn't have surprised me to learn that Fidel himself had dictated the hotel menus. After all, reported Maurice Halperin, it was Castro who had decreed that Cuban nurses should wear trousers, not skirts; a nurse in a skirt leaning over a patient, Fidel impishly suggested, might cause a man lying in the next bed to have a heart attack.

Almost a month had passed. I needed to return to Havana to extend my visa and Customs permit. I turned west and followed the Carretera Central through dusty towns where trees threw great pools of shade on wide streets; the sidewalks had old-fashioned hitching racks for horses ridden by dark-skinned *vaqueros* sporting lassos and wide-brimmed hats. Oxcarts lumbered along the streets, lending timeless grace.

I tanked up in Placetas at a ServiCupet station—Cupet for Cuba Petroleum—selling snack foods, sodas, a motley assemblage of spare car parts, tires, and Castrol oil. A canary-yellow Jaguar sedan from the 1950s puttered past.

"Few cars," I remarked to the leathery pump attendant. "Little gas," came the reply. In reality he meant "not many dollars." There is gas for those with the means to pay.

As I roared off, a *tránsito* tore up alongside and waved me over. He flicked his leather-gloved hand forcefully toward the side of the road as if he were swatting a fly.

"*¡Documentos!*" he boomed. His face was small and tight, with piggy eyes sunk in purpled hollows, like a Neanderthal. He spoke monosyllabically, with a contemptuous, Gestapo air. I handed him my international driver's license and the *licencia* issued by the Ministerio del Interior.

"Foreigner!" he exclaimed, surprised and dismayed. His haughtiness vaporized. He handed me back my papers, attempted a desultory salute, and gestured toward the horizon. "Go!"

Barely a day had gone by in which I wasn't stopped by tránsitos, but this surly cop was a first. I wondered what my fate would have been if I'd been Cuban. He had the air of a thug itching to dust someone up in a jail.

Santa Clara is a sprawling city, gateway to the eastern provinces, and as such was a plum in Cuba's wars of independence and revolution. On December 29 of 1958, Che Guevara's Rebel Army attacked the town and derailed a troop train carrying reinforcements and armaments for Batista's troops in Oriente. Two days later, the Rebel Army captured the city. By three o'clock in the predawn darkness of the New Year, Batista was winging his way to exile. As Minister of Industry, Che developed a soft spot for the city. Today it is an industrial town. On the outskirts, I passed a billboard reminding citizens that "HARD WORK IS A DUTY TO THE FATHERLAND." The factories looked dead beat.

Farther in, Santa Clara had a mellow provincial feel with pockets of charm at its center. I parked outside the Hotel Santa Clara Libre, a somber high-rise glass-and-cement edifice facing Parque Vidal; the large paved square was ablaze with pink *guasima* trees full of sparrows and Cuban blackbirds caterwauling, honking, and chirping. A young black girl in white shoes and frilly bobby socks and a crinoline dress was being pulled around the square in a canopied cart towed by a goat wearing full harness.

"Hey, my friend!" *Jineteros* hustled me for dollars in exchange for guarding the bike.

I bought a single-scoop ice cream at Coppelia on Calle Colón. A young cubana standing in line tugged my arm. Pointy breasts like cocoa pods pushed against her see-through blouse. She asked if I wished for her company. I said not.

"Why not?" said her friend. "You can have both of us, if you wish." The friend endorsed the invitation by flicking her tongue out lasciviously like a lizard, a manifest sexual signal offered freely by immodest cubanas. I declined.

A calliope of Cuban sounds assaulted my senses: the clomping of horse-drawn taxis, puny mopeds buzzing past, the crunching of worn gears from overworked buses, the deafening racket of exhausted trucks rumbling down potholed streets, the backfiring of Yankee *cacharros* whose weary engines must have had beer cans for pistons. And always the irresistible, syncopated blaring of Cuban music—the pulsing undercurrent of Cuban life—piping from hidden speakers or a sidewalk ensemble.

After exploring the center, I roared off down Independencia to see the remains of the *tren blindado,* the armored troop train whose demise had sealed Batista's fate. Preserved were four rust-colored carriages cantilevered in suspended animation as they came to rest at a railroad crossing four decades ago, derailed in a sensational cataclysm of twisted metal. It was easy, under the searing Cuban sun, to imagine the carnage, to hear the screams of Batista's men burned alive in their upturned metal ovens by a volley of Molotov cocktails.

On Santa Clara's western outskirts I emerged onto a sprawling hilltop piazza—the Plaza de la Revolución—dominated by a granite monument supporting a gargantuan bronze statue of Che Guevara toting a rifle silhouetted against a symphonic sunset. Wagnerian was the blood-red orchestration, its proportion appropriate to the scale of the monument. Gun-toting sentries moved out of camera range as I leaned the bike on the side stand, maneuvered for the perfect angle, and shot a few frames of the national hero.

The Hotel Los Caneyes resembled a make-believe Indian village. Thatched wooden bungalows surrounded a swimming pool in a landscaped garden with bougainvilleas and shade trees and palms overhead like tattered umbrellas. Tourists with an English company called Bike Tours were unloading shiny capitalist cycles from a truck in the parking lot. They sported fanny packs and streamlined crash helmets. I recognized them as English by their otherwise dolorous dress, including black Adidas sneakers worn with dark dress socks.

I checked in, took a snooze on a sagging bed, and headed for the dining room, where the air conditioning had been slammed into overdrive. The buffet smorgasbord was a veritable potlatch of privilege. A trio of German males were complaining volubly that it wasn't up to European standards. A quartet of Italians, presumably more discerning in the culinary arts, seemed quite content. A voluptuous Italian woman got up. She had squeezed her ample bosom and hindquarters into a body-fitting black top and even tighter zebra-striped pants, and she sashayed to the buffet table with the hauteur of a catwalk diva. Two overweight slobs from New Jersey with white Cuban consorts one-third their age occupied an adjacent table. "Nyoy, buddy! Yo American?" they called at me through their noses.

The bicyclists, a pasty lot, filed in by ones and twos and looked about them like lost sheep.

"Bloody 'ell!" said one, shivering as he stepped through the door.

"Yer right, luv, it's freezin,'" said his wife. "A hot cuppa tea will put us right, though." She was dressed in black exercise tights, well-worn bicycle shoes, a denim shirt with the collar stylishly turned up, and a bright red scarf around her neck.

"Tea? You'll be lucky," her husband lamented, his back tensed against the cold. "Use yer noggin. Coffee, that's what yer'll get. With lots o' sugar. Me? Ah want a stiff shot o' rum."

Sprigs of gray hair curled up from the sides of his sunburned cranium. He was dressed in a pea-green, short-sleeve dress shirt, obscenely snug-fitting red-and-white-check shorts, and black Adidas sneakers with brown dress socks.

"Enjoying yourself?" I asked, intercepting the husband as he headed for the buffet.

"Absolutely champion," he piped in an emphatic northern brogue. Goose bumps covered his arms.

"Lovely, thanks," chimed the wife, rubbing her arms.

"Are you from Yorkshire?"

"Aye, lad," he replied. "How'd yer know?"

"I'm from Yorkshire too."

"Eeee! Really. Yer'd never know. Where from?" he asked. I told him. "Me name's 'arry. Wife's name's Ethel," he replied, seating himself beside me. "We've toured Europe and the like by bicycle. We thought we'd see wot t' Caribbean were like."

Cuba, I told him, was unlike any other Caribbean island he was likely to visit. "Certainly not any of the English-speaking islands."

"How'd yer mean?" he asked.

I explained that the Caribbean was a potpourri of cultures, and terrains too, as varied as they are numerous, strewn like isles within isles. "But the English-speaking isles lack the profundity of Cuba. It's more developed culturally," I replied, offering my own interpretation of Cuba's enigmatically ethereal moods. Our hearty repast turned the talk toward food.

"What 'bout starvation?" asked Harry. "Ah'v been readin' 'bout how things are so bad, some folk are makin' pizzas with—pardon me—condoms and pretendin' its cheese. It's cruel, poverty!"

I replied that poverty is a relative concept and a much-misused word. I'd traveled almost 3,000 miles and had seen little of the heart-rending poverty prevalent on neighboring islands.

"There are still pockets of poverty here, no doubt about it," I answered, "but it was plenty more ubiquitous 40 years ago. Most Cubans today are materially poor, at least by Western standards. I guess most folks now live in a state of paucity. But if you want to see poverty in Cuba, real poverty, then get on a plane in Havana and fly to Jamaica or Haiti. Anyway, as a rule the people here don't measure their lives by a person's acquisitions or level of consumption. The real success of the Revolution has to do with its nurturing of the human soul. The Cubans are inordinately rich in human spirit."

Cubans seemed the most generous people in the world, despite their material dearth. A sense of egalitarianism has seeped into the Cuban persona, embodying the New Man ideal that has sought to draw together and nurture the strands of compassion and connectivity that bond all people in common. Cubans had spread their spirit through the Third World, helping the poor and the miserable. Castro deserves full credit for this exemplary gift to Cuba and the rest of the world.

I mentioned all this, explaining that the country is such an emotional tangle of metaphors that it leaves no one indifferent.

"Tragically, we're seeing Cuba when she's still down on her knees," I continued. "The same awful burdens that caused such despair in the past have resurfaced. Ten years ago you would never have seen the petty thieves and jineteras, or the children who now beg for Chiclets."

The New Man—perhaps the greatest gift of the Revolution—seemed to be slowly dying. "The world is poorer for the loss of that intangible, optimistic, altruistic spirit," thought writer and film producer Saul Landau. Indeed it is. It didn't help that the Helms-Burton legislation, expanding the embrago, had just been signed into law. It struck me as a unique piece of right-wing sickness.

"It's all politics, innit?" said Harold. "Ah'm not a Communist, but ah'll tell yer this. I admire Castro for pokin' 'is snook at t' Yanks."

He reached inside his shorts and pulled out a handkerchief. He blew his "snook," admired his snot for a moment, then stashed the precious treasure back inside his shorts. The English, I mused, are the only race you can rely on to always have a hankie at hand.

The decrepit Dodge truck wheezed lethargically along the Carretera Central like a geriatric turtle. It was piled high with furniture, atop which a family perched precariously, like a balancing act from a Chinese circus. Seeing it lumbering along reminded me of a poem by the Peruvian, José Juan Tablada:

> *"Aunque jamás se muda*
> *a tumbos, como un carro de mudanzas*
> *va por la senda la tortuga.*
>
> Although never changing houses,
> in lurches, like a moving van
> the turtle goes along the road."

A punishing wind threatened to sweep the family from its tenuous aerie. I throttled up and swept past. Six heads turned in unison. One of the mustachioed men showered my overmuscled machine with kisses blown from the palm of his hand.

"Beautiful!" he screamed, romancing *mi moto Fidel.*

Their adolescent daughter followed suit, but her kisses were for me.

Colón, a dusty town named for Columbus, had a sense of history arrested. Its colonnaded streets were littered with crippled cacharros—Chevrolet Stylelines, Buick Roadmasters, Dodge Coronets, even a '54 Cadillac Fleetwood—and lined with tumbledown neoclassical facades. Old gents sat on porches, steeped in the ebony shadows of streets that shimmered with microwave heat. The geezers were folded up, inert as reptiles; with their heads down and their hands in their laps, they could have been attending mass. The warm wind stirred the dust at their feet. When I waved, they sat upright and waved back cheerily, full of dignity.

All the town's color had long ago faded, bleached by the sun and by time. Colón hadn't seen a can of paint in more than three decades. Even the most diligent search turned up nothing more interesting than a life-size bronze statue to the town's namesake hero erected in Parque de la Libertad, the main square. His patinaed visage looked down as I passed. Guarding Columbus were four lions, one on each corner, hewn in limestone and looking sad, noble, and poised with fearsome energy, as if ready to leap from the harsh glare of the sun.

I wanted to breathe life into them and watch the gold run along their white backs like flame creeping along the edge of a paper as their stone folds rippled into sinewy flesh. But their roars never came. They were as lifeless as Colón itself.

Beyond Matanzas, I climbed the eastern flanks of the Alturas de la Habana-Matanzas. The tachometer needle rose and fell as I trod up through the gearbox. As I eased the BMW around the sharp bend at the top of the hill, the world seemed to fall away. The road spiraled down into a vast valley rimmed by a meniscus of sheer-faced *mogotes*. Below, the gray scar of road threaded broad swaths of sugarcane and disappeared from view beneath a brooding twilit fusion of valley and sky. I edged down the haunches in second. Hit the valley in third with daylight swiftly fading. Powered up into fourth. With a merest feathering of the throttle and clutch, I slipped up into top, nailed the throttle, and reveled in the induction roar. Enraptured, I cooked down the highway, the bike purring sexily as it ate up the hardtop in a sensuous intertwining of glorious harmonics and warm, perfumed air.

I called it quits at a colonial-style villa, now the Casa del Valle Motel, built in 1936 atop a sulfurous mineral pool smelling vaguely of clogged sewers. Four young Cuban couples in swimwear were dancing on the sundeck by the outdoor swimming pool, moving in a soft frenzy, hips swinging to a scratchy radio cranked full bore. My room in the honey-hued mansion had patrician airs, including an antique four-poster bed and deep claw-foot bathtub in which I could recline with hot water up to my nose. At 32 dollars, it was a bargain.

The custodian picked open a large rusty lock and swung open aluminum-framed glass doors, revealing a ten-pin bowling alley where my bike spent the night as if displayed in a showroom, dripping oil onto cardboard atop the linoleum floor.

I shared the dining room with a triumvirate of middle-aged Englishmen. We exchanged no greetings—English reserve, I suppose. Lord, how we English cherish our privacy! They talked in conspiratorial whispers, as if plotting a coup against Castro. Snippets of conversation drifted across the room with the aromas of Cuban cooking. They were dissecting southern Africa with an eye for arcana—the vagaries of the Zimbabwean constitution and the state of the roads in Okavango. I thought they might be servants of

Her Britannic Majesty's government or workers for a British aid organization. They finished their meal and filed out, acknowledging me each in turn with aloof nods.

Next morning when I arrived for breakfast, the trio had already gathered outside the dining room. The door was locked. They were miffed that the staff hadn't opened up exactly on the half-hour. I looked at my watch: 7:34.

"Nothing runs to schedule," complained the first man through a thick, graying beard. Graybeard was stocky, with a splendid paunch that drooped over his shorts like a large sack of flour. "It'd be a poor bloody show if British Rail operated like this."

"Ha! Cuba'd be in an even worse state if British Rail were in charge," the second exclaimed with a cynicism that only the English can muster. He had a quintessential civil servant look: ruddy skin, wire-rim glasses, and a balding pate that gleamed in the morning sunlight. Necrotic legs with varicose veins dangled from beneath Baldpate's khaki shorts. He was wearing black Adidas sneakers with brown dress socks.

The third, a portly chap, asked where I had come from. Matanzas, I replied. "Ah, the Athens of Cuba," he said.

"You mean fadin' facades and crumblin' ruins," Baldpate responded.

"I was trying to figure out the connection," said Graybeard. "I think you just hit on it."

"What would Jean-Paul Sartre have made of it all?" Portly added quixotically, parodying the squawky notes of the woman's voice in the famous Monty Python skit.

They were train spotters on their third foray together through Cuba in pursuit of the sensual hiss of steam. China, southern Africa—the Three Musketeers had been there, spotted that. That explained their conversation of the previous evening; Cuba had about 200 steam trains still in operation. Only China had more.

"Lots of train spotters come to Cuba," said Graybeard. "You know the British built the first railway in Cuba in 1837, don't you?"

I replied, "No."

Graybeard looked dismayed. "The youngest trains here date from the 1920s, but many narrow-gauge locomotives are more than a century old. Some were running around when Custer was being attacked at Little Big Horn."

I asked why so many in tiny Cuba.

"It's all thanks to sugar," Baldpate explained. "They manage to keep the trains going because the sugar mills operate only four or five months a year, during the *zafra*," he added thickly, using the Cuban term for the sugar harvest. "After that, the engineers can crawl around inside the boilers and tinker around for the rest of the year. Keeps 'em 'ealthy. The trains, I mean, not the engineers. Don't suppose there's anything 'ealthy in squirmin' around inside a train's boiler. Ha ha ha!"

The first began to scroll through a litany of nearby sugar mills with active steam trains.

"Do you know the Hershey Train?" I asked. "I just heard that it's been converted to carry tourists, with special trips for railroad enthusiasts."

I was referring to the famous electric railway that runs lazily between Matanzas and Havana through the Yumurí Valley. The train has its origin in a chocolate bar. In its heyday, before the Revolution, much of the lush cane fields hereabouts had belonged to Pennsylvania-based Hershey Chocolate Company, which owned a 69-square-mile estate centered on a modern sugar-factory town and *central,* now called Camilo Cienfuegos, laid out in 1916. At its peak the estate had 19 steam locomotives. Operating on coal and oil, they were expensive and their sparks constituted a serious fire hazard, so the trains were replaced by seven 60-ton electric locomotives built especially for the Hershey-Cuban Railroad. The so-called Hershey Train—which, operating by electricity, had an advantage in these days of oil shortage—was the sole working survivor, providing three-car passenger train service between Havana and Matanzas thrice daily.

The Hershey properties had been nationalized after the Revolution. Graybeard thought this unfair.

"The bloody Yanks have got nothing to complain about. Batista nationalized the British assets in 1952," he said, bubbling with indignation. "The railway were built in 1898 by a British company called the United Railways of Havana. The trouble was, it had no liquidity. It went bankrupt because the Cuban government, which was the company's biggest debtor, wouldn't pay its bills. So the cheeky buggers, the ones that owed the money, had the nerve to nationalize it and sell it for a bloody great discount. The Yanks got it by default. They were in cahoots with the government, you can bet your bottom sock on it!"

I had taken a trip on the Hershey train the year before. It was a sugar of a journey—a combination of the picturesque and the prosaic—despite the lack of steam rising sibilantly between giant piston rods. The diminutive orange locomotive (Ferrocarril de Cuba #20803) looked like it could have fallen from the pages of a story about Thomas the Tank Engine. The gold-leaf lettering on the two maroon carriages had long since faded, as had the maroon itself, and the hard wooden seats were guaranteed to turn the most inured ass to stone.

The conductor had tooted the horn two minutes before departure and a mad rush ensued. Soon we were winding in and out among the palm-studded hills of the Yumurí Valley, with the pantographs singing merrily overhead and the rhythmic rattling of the rails beneath. *Clickety clack, clackety click, clackety clack.* The doors remained wide open, providing plenty of breeze. Two hours into the journey, we arrived at the eggshell blue station of Central Camilo Cien-fuegos, still bearing the Hershey sign on one wall. We were in the heart of the old Hershey sugar factory, where the train paused just long enough for me to get down and snap a shot for posterity.

Portly asked if I had explored the railroad barn.

"No," I replied, "but the journey provided some poignant moments that I still cherish."

I recalled how we had stopped in the midst of the valley in front of a sim-ple thatch-and-adobe *bohío* framed by flame-red bougainvillea and shaded by a single palm tree. A young woman stepped down from the train clutching a newborn child swaddled in blankets, while a sun-baked *guajiro* in tattered straw hat and faded Army fatigues strode forward from beneath the shady eave and moved slowly toward her, arms outspread as if to embrace all the world. The whole train looked on as he bent down to kiss his daughter. She, in turn, reached down to kiss her young brother, who had come hauling up the dusty lane as fast as his long flying legs could carry him. Then the beaming elder reached out and tenderly took the cocooned baby in his arms, his laborer's hands cradling the bairn like a precious diamond. Tears fell as he took his first look at his grandchild.

"Quite touching," said Baldpate. Then he turned the conversation right back to trains.

I speed along the coast, within sight of the deep blue Atlantic. A cooling breeze blows in off the ocean like a benediction. Bay after scalloped bay loops toward the horizon.

From afar, the Puente Bacunayagua is peppered with camera-toting tourists like a storm of no-see-ums. They swarm the 112-meter-high bridge, scaling the steps to the lookout, gawking and gasping at the vast views down into the gorge and south across the valley, which unfolds dramatically, palm-tufted, framed in the hazy distance by mauvish mogotes squashed flat by the great weight of blue sky. I pull over, park between two Mercedes tour buses, and shoot six frames of the canyon and the Yumurí Valley spreading out like a Chinese fan.

I am back in Havana province.

Beyond Santa Cruz—a ramshackle industrial town steeped in rum and sulfurous petrochemical fumes—I whiz past oil derricks pumping atop the coral shore. Camouflaged military bunkers face the Florida Straits, with sentries scanning the waters.

Ever mindful of researching my guidebook, I make forays to a series of pencil-thin beaches lined with basic *campismos*, ensembles of gimcrack concrete bungalows that prior to the Special Period were popular holiday spots for Cuban families and children on sponsored school outings. I seek out El Abra, promoted to foreign tourists as an eco-camp by the sea. Weeds inch up through cracks in the concrete paving. The pool is empty. The door to the restaurant is padlocked. I am the only visitor. As I ride away, I pass a Cuban woman wearily dragging a battered suitcase along the road that slopes down to El Abra. Her young daughter skips alongside. Vacationing in the Special Period, Cuban fashion. I hope she's brought food.

On the outskirts of Havana, I pass through Playas del Este, popular with *habaneros* for its four-mile-long beach of pulverized sugar. The beach action is concentrated in front of the Hotel Tropicoco, where tourists (predominantly Italian and male) and Cubans (predominantly young and female) gather lemming-like to tan their bodies, play volleyball, and flirt under the *palapas* and palms. Italians flashing gold chains and silvery smiles have turned a section of *playa* into a virtual colony—a ritual temple of narcissism drawing lissome Lolitas from all over Cuba. Lasses like perfectly shaped figure eights parade along the sands in next-to-nothing swimwear, sticking out their tongues at the *italianos* to indicate sexual interest. The males, it seems, are easily seduced by the siren call of tall and tan and young and lovely dripping with brine from the sea.

Daisy and I had spent a weekend here two years before, buzzing down from Havana on a Yamaha scooter to sun ourselves and swim in the surf conjured by the breeze from the warm turquoise sea. Thoughts of her draw me magnetically along the wide coastal highway. A tingling excitement tells me that she hasn't yet left for Milan. *She's here. I can sense it!* I can't wait to hold her, to feel her hand in mine one last time.

I coax the bike through the bends, fast...faster...as if the hot air fanning my face will cool the fire inside me.

~

HAVANA NOON

arta was delighted to see me. Fresh sheets had been laid on my bed, as if my unannounced arrival in Havana had been expected. She made me a fresh cup of thick coffee, a *cafecito*, sweet as treacle, black and strong like espresso.

"Thanks. It's delicious," I said ingenuously.

"Bah! It's *mezclado*," Marta replied, meaning that it was adulterated, probably with chicory, like most domestic coffee sold in Cuba these days. The good stuff is vacuum-packed and exported for precious dollars. I made a note to buy her some quality coffee at the Diplotienda, the dollars-only supermarket stocked with Western goods.

Marta kept her third-story apartment squeaky clean and was forever mopping around my feet. The furnishings included wicker-backed rockers and dowdy, well-worn remnants from the 1950s, and the metronomic marching of feet through the years had worked grime irrevocably into the ceramic-tile floor. The kitchen had a stone sink that always seemed to be full of aluminum utensils and plastic plates, while large pots with chicken parts and peeled onions and potatoes bubbled on an adjacent gas ring. Marta's husband, Juan, worked for ETECSA, the state telephone company, but even that didn't qualify them for a new phone; like most Cubans, they made do with a rotary-dial dinosaur that crackled and fizzed like a bottle of soda. It rang constantly, but only infrequently delivered a voice at the other end. The television was more trustworthy and was never allowed to cool. I spent happy hours rocking in front of it.

Cuban programming struck me as intelligent and internationalist, with a heavy emphasis on science and culture, sports, Hispanic soaps, and foreign movies, reminding me of British television during my youth, before it became adulterated by MTV, moronic talk shows, and mindless violence. Fidel Castro was always popping up, however, filling the screen with his larger-than-life persona, doing good deeds and avuncularly exhorting his citizens to be good revolutionaries. He dominated the daily news, an adulatory piece of propaganda that always showed him in gilded light. And why not? At least he'd saved Cubans from Jerry Falwell and Jerry Springer.

My room had a dresser with a mirror, and night tables flanking a single bed upon whose sagging mattress and creaky springs I slept uncomfortably. An electric fan kept the air cool, aided by breezes through the jalousie windows. Cockroaches skulked in the recesses—I could see their antennae waving—and emerged to forage whenever I closed the door or turned out the light. The faucets in the bathroom rarely produced more than a trickle of water, always cold. I learned to take a shower whenever the water was flowing.

I knew that in time I would search for a better apartment.

"How was your journey?" Marta asked, setting a plate of food on the dining room table and beckoning me to eat. She liked to feed me—usually *pollo asado* (grilled chicken) with *moros y cristianos* (rice and black beans) and succulent fried plantains—but never asked for a dime on top of my 20-dollar daily rent. She was always apologizing that she couldn't offer me a better meal. "You've been gone a month. Tell me, how was Cuba?" she implored.

I began to recount the highlights of my trip as Marta watched me eat, her bulging eyes staring at me disconcertingly. One eye was slightly off-center and put me on edge. She was otherwise attractive, with a thick mane of hair, full and black despite the passage of time, though her chin and cheeks sagged under six decades of persistent gravitational pull. Fatty folds dangled like wattles under her arms.

We were interrupted by a knock at the door.

A young cubana entered—blonde and pretty with copper skin and bright hazel eyes—accompanied by a tall, well-groomed black man with sparkling teeth. Marta introduced the woman as Mavis, a neighbor, and the man as her boyfriend, José—a doctor, it turned out.

We sipped beer and exchanged small talk while the TV showed a documentary about the problems facing Latin America's indigenous communities in adjusting to the contemporary world. Mavis would have liked to see more lively programming. She complained about the government's attempts to suppress cable television beamed from across the Florida Straits. On my prior visits, Havana's skyline had been a Jacob's ladder of jury-rigged parabolic antennas—*parabólicas*—improvised from aluminum, tin cans, or even wire netting. They pointed at the Hotel Habana Libre, which was linked to a satellite and distributed U.S. television signals to other hotels. The government tolerated the parabólicas briefly during the hardest years of the Special Period, when tensions were running high. As things improved, the government coded the signals. Castro had recently declared the private dishes illegal and had given Havana residents 60 days to remove them.

"Why do they want to steal from us the pleasure of watching movies when they should be figuring out how to feed the people? Tell me!" bemoaned Mavis.

"They're too concerned with what we think," Marta replied with exasperation. "Who cares whether we have socialism or capitalism? As long as the system works."

José said nothing. He was the quietest Cuban I had ever met. He stared down at the empty fruit bowl and looked uncomfortable. A loyal *fidelista?*

Sensing the tension, Mavis leaned across the table and whispered in Marta's ear. The latter gave the former a quick, wide-eyed look.

"*Sí, mi amor,*" she replied, tilting her head over her shoulder. Marta's mouth curled in a loose carnal smile. José's dark eyes suddenly lighted with pleasure. His discomfort was no more than an urgent libido.

Mavis and José stood up and slipped into Marta and Juan's bedroom. The door swung closed, and Marta and I continued our conversation to a soundtrack of squeaking bed springs and unrestrained groans. We stepped onto the balcony, beyond earshot of the discomfiting symphony and its crescendo. The couple were illicit lovers seeking a place of coital convenience. It was a sign not only of Cubans' maturity in matters of sex but also the nation's acute housing shortage that you could simply ask a neighbor, *"Mind if we hop into your bed?"*

In the street below, a group of youths had gathered in the shadow of a tall jagüey tree. Beer and rum were being passed around, and loud voices rose to us on the steamy air, audible even above the blare of salsa music, the crashing of waves against the seawall, and the throaty wheezing of battered Buicks and overloaded buses rolling by.

"There are many problems with youth," said Marta, raising her clenched fists to demonstrate that the kids took to brawling. She touched her skin to indicate that it was *los negros*—the blacks—that she meant.

"They drink too much, then fight," she added. "They have no work. There is too much boredom."

It was the first time I had heard such negative comments about Cuba's blacks. I couldn't tell whether Marta's remarks were inspired by prejudice or were true. After all, she constantly had black friends flitting in and out, including a 13-year-old girl who arrived every afternoon and spent her time studying with her schoolbooks spread out on the dining room table.

I asked Marta what conditions had been like under Batista. She picked up my pen and toyed with it.

"If you wanted something, it was yours," she replied. "You could buy it. You could go anywhere without documents. There were no restrictions. Life was good. The stores were full." She drew her hand down her chin. "When *el barbudo* came from Mexico to the mountains, that's when our problems began. That's when Batista began *una fusilada*—the assassinations on the streets. That's when life went downhill."

Taking my elbow, Marta drew me inside and pointed at a faded black-and-white photo in a wooden frame. I recognized her and Juan. Marta was aglow in a sequined dress, her hair glossy and neatly coiffed. Juan was equally dashing in his crisp suit, clipped mustache, and glistening wavy hair. The couple beamed at the camera, happy with their rum and embrace.

"Look at it!" she exclaimed. "We had money before. It was taken at the Tropicana nightclub in 1959, the year the Revolution triumphed. We enjoyed life then. What do we have now? Nothing! There are no medicines. For Africa, yes," she added bitterly, "but we have nothing." Marta complained a lot about her aches and pains. She had recently been to see her doctor—an *"amigo muy íntimo,"* she called him, hinting that he was a lover—but he could do nothing for her.

"He couldn't even take my blood pressure. The machine was *rota*. Broken! Everything is broken in the hospitals."

Juan appeared, fresh from work.

"¿*Cómo anda?*" he asked, gripping my hand firmly and giving his usual greeting. *How goes it?*

He was a well-mannered, mustachioed, bespectacled man, swart and hairy and slightly bandy-legged. Unlike his wife, Juan felt uncomfortable expressing political opinions. He said little and spent most of his time under his car, chomping on a perennial cigar while he worked bare-chested, oil-stained, dispensing TLC and choice cuss words to keep the old Lada running.

I excused myself and picked up the phone to call Daisy's family, praying she hadn't left for Italy.

"Thank God you're still there," I replied, thrilled when Daisy answered through a fog of static. "I thought you'd left for Milan."

"*Cristóbal,* there are complications."

"What kind?"

"The government hasn't issued our exit permits."

"Why not?"

"My cousin had an argument with the woman who is handling our papers. Now she is causing problems."

I rode out to Cerro. Daisy greeted me eagerly, tempered by a hint of reserve. I stood in the open doorway, watching her tie up her hair and apply with consummate coquetry the toilette that would bring a bishop to his knees. She threw me an impish smile. White teeth, a slight gap between each, gleamed behind lips painted with lipstick, red as port wine, that I had brought as a gift. With her brown eyes, raven hair, and sable-colored skin, she was the essence of innocent beauty, a vision of heavenly youthfulness that gave me pleasurable sensations akin to the first joy of love.

Daisy wore a skimpy, curve-hugging black-and-white miniskirt that combined with her seductive mien to project the pure profligacy of her womanly youth. Standing five feet eight in her black high heels, she was finally ready for what would prove to be our last night together. My eyes traced the alluring curves that ended with round, sparkling eyes dancing in an oval face, bright and happy, full of sweetness. I was almost dumbstruck with bliss. It was difficult to accept that she was now married.

She created smoldering drama, setting off sparks as we walked down the street to where my motorcycle was parked under a streetlight.

"My nights are made longer when I think of you," Daisy crooned, gazing into my eyes across a table at El Aljibe. The restaurant, popular with Havana's elite, stood in the leafy Miramar district, a tony precinct full of grandiose mansions, many "donated" to the Revolution by wealthy owners long since departed.

To hear her speak thus stabbed at my heart. I tried not to let my discomfort turn to panic as Daisy told me that "to die without having come close to you is to die without having lived." I felt uncertain, torn with remorse, and overcome with the awareness of all she had tried to give me and all that I had refused to receive.

"Why you have fright, Cristóbal? Why did you frighten to marry me?"

I demurred and shrugged my shoulders, aware only that I was drowning in guilt. She had invested in me her hopes for a future beyond the decay of a dismal life. With Daisy I discerned so many of the problems faced by an older man enchanted by a younger woman. She was, quite simply, the sweetest person I had ever known.

"To think of you is all that I really need to enjoy life," she whispered, reaching out to stroke my face, hoping to soothe the pain. I felt that I had failed her miserably.

Well-dressed Cubans—Cubans of privilege, men mostly—stared at us. Government bigwigs and foreign businessmen, many of them carried portable phones and cosmopolitan airs. Most had slender cubanas draped on their arms: models from La Maison, an upscale boutique that hosts fashion shows. Daisy was the equal of any.

"Can we go dancing, Cristóbal?" Daisy asked.

"Of course. Where?"

"Club Habana. I like it there."

As we entered, a sultry cubana took hold of my arm and pleaded to be escorted in, "*por favor*," the 10-dollar cover charge beyond her means. She paid no heed to Daisy. *Two is better than one*, her eyes wickedly hinted. The disco was a zany, glittering, pulsating whirligig of neon and noise. Expensive, too. Havana's snazzier discos—most of them located at tourist hotels—are extortion machines catering to well-heeled foreigners. I forked out 30 dollars for a bottle of rum. On the dance floor, young women in minimal clothing writhed sensuously to *salsa caliente* while overweight, middle-aged Mexican men held them close to their sweaty bodies.

"They're disgusting," said Daisy uncharacteristically; she normally saw goodness in everyone. "I don't like Mexicans. They abuse us."

Back at my apartment, Daisy made love to me knowing it would be our last time. We loved remorselessly, tenderly as the sun's rays arced over the weary facades of Havana. Exhausted, Daisy finally turned on her side. I wrapped my arm around her and we slept past noon nestled like spoons.

I awoke to Marta's hammering on my door. Daisy's mother, Alicia, was on the phone, calling Daisy to say that the government had magically issued their exit permits. A date had been set for their departure. In two more weeks, mother and daughter would leave for Milan.

Daisy suggested we go for a swim.

She shook her head to find the BMW parked where I had left it the night before, tucked into a far corner of the open garage on the ground floor of my apartment block. Every night I locked the steering column, ran a steel cable and lock around the rear wheel and frame, placed a Kryptonite lock on the front wheel, then pulled the elasticized cover over the bike and secured it by looping a cable through the grommets and linking them with another lock.

"It not make difference," said Daisy, climbing up behind me. "I surprise every morning to see your *moto* still here."

Everyone I met in Havana warned me against thieves. That night I would dream that four men lifted up the motorcycle and carried it away.

We rode along the Malecón to the Hotel Nacional and laid our towels beside the pool. Daisy slipped into the rest room to change. She reappeared in a leopard-print *tanga*—a G-string bikini—and pumps. Heads turned as she langorously circled the pool, carrying herself in an upright manner that made her look taller. Graceful. Sleek. Arched back. Supple waist. Silky skin evocative of nocturnal passion. A black goddess.

We slipped into the pool and, as Daisy couldn't swim, splashed about in the shallows.

"Cristóbal," she said softly, "I have something to tell you."

"¿Qué, amor?" I replied.

"I cannot make love with you more."

She bit her lip, looking anxiously for my reaction.

"Yes, I know," I replied, drawing her to me and embracing her tightly in both arms.

"Oh, Cristóbal. I no think I see you again."

I raised my fingers to her mouth and touched the delicate edge of her agonized smile, traced the cherished details of her face, and grappled to combat the emotions that welled up inside.

"You are not a man who expresses his feelings, but I know you feel deeply."

I listened, saying nothing. The words were harder to get than the feeling.

"I'm sorry. I'm so terribly, terribly sorry. I failed you, Daisy."

Pathetically, that was all I could muster. Sadness overcame me, adding salt to the freshwater pool. Daisy dabbed at my tears and stroked my hair.

"How do you feel?" she asked as we strolled down Calle M toward the Malecón.

"Sad. Sad for myself, but happy for you. You made the right choice. All I want for you now is that you find happiness with your husband."

Our romance was over. When Daisy departed, Havana would lose part of its magic. I should have married her; that thought haunts me still.

We turned onto the Malecón and jumped up onto the seawall opposite the U.S. Interests Section at the bottom of Calle L. A Cuban policeman blew his whistle and moved us along—the better to avoid communing, I suppose, with CIA agents and low-profile diplomats serving Uncle Sam's whims.

Ciclotaxis—pedal-powered tricycle cabs—passed by carrying camera-toting tourists. Then a blonde in lime-green hot-pants and a blood-red halter top whizzed past, pulled along on in-line skates by a long-haired mutt. Was I in Santa Monica? Havana overflowed with such looking-glass episodes. The Malecón boulevard offered a microcosm of Havana life: elderly couples walking their dogs, shiftless *jineteros* and *jineteras* trolling for tourists, the young passing rum among friends, and scores of couples cuddling in every Kama Sutra position atop the weathered seawall. All through the night, lovers' murmurings mingled with the intoxicating crash and hiss of the waves.

"Silver lamé" was how composer Orlando de la Rosa characterized the seafront boulevard, which was designed in 1857 by Cuban engineer Francisco de Albear but laid out in 1902 by the U.S. governor, General Leonard Woods. The metaphor has stuck, even if today the boulevard is but a ghostly reminder of its former brilliance—what Martha Gellhorn, Hemingway's third wife, called "a 19th-century jewel and a joke." I gazed east along the Malecón twining toward the twin castles guarding the entrance to Havana harbor. Salt spray crashed against the rocky shore in great airy clouds, showering in rainbows the young bathers frolicking in the square baths known as the Elysian Fields. Hewn in the late 1800s from limestone rocks below the seawall, the baths originally segregated men, women, and Negroes into separate areas; with the Revolution, they became more democratic.

Seawater pooled darkly atop the road. A century of salt water had pitted the broad limestone walkway. The once-glorious three-story houses facing the ocean had proven no more capable of withstanding the corrosive assault. Those unprotected by seaworthy paint—the majority—were decrepit, held up by wooden scaffolding. Happily, restoration had begun on those whose painted facades— green trimmed with purple, pink with blue, yellow with orange—could be saved.

Daisy and I held hands and laughed at the absurdities and good times of our two years together.

"I remember the day we first met. *He soñado contigo,*" she said. *I had dreamed about you.* "It was as if I had been in a deep sleep and was awakened by the light of your two blue eyes," she continued, speaking in Spanish. "I feel so sad that I will no longer see the blue eyes in which I have so often lost myself. I do not need to close my eyes, I do not need the night to arrive, I do not need to look at your photos to remind me of you, because your memory lies within me. You were the air that gave me life."

"We were like children, weren't we?" I replied. "It was intoxicating."

After a short pause, she gazed into my eyes.

"Speak poetry to me, Cristóbal."

I searched for something appropriate but nothing would come. I felt inadequate, still grasping for words, like a newt out of water.

And so Daisy recited poetry to me.

"En amor y dulzura
serás mi sed
y el pozo de agua pura
donde beba hasta saciar mi sed."

In love and tenderness
You were my thirst
And the well of pure water
Where I drank until sated.

"You amaze me," I replied anemically. "Will you write to me from Italy?"

"I no think is possible, Cristóbal. My *esposo* is very jealous."

She smiled at me with her eyes and sparkling teeth and made me smile too.

A large black man passed, then turned to face us, square on. He was thirty-ish, about six feet tall, with a peculiarly square, oversize head, very flat on top, and a mouthful of misaligned yellow teeth.

"Hey, *chica!*" he called, pointing at Daisy. *"Negrita, ¿por qué estás con este hombre? ¡Este blanco es nada!"* Sister, why are you with this man? This whitey is nothing!

His steel-tipped barb stung. Was he *loco?* I thought so, and hoped that he would move on. Instead, he unleashed another tirade, this one in English.

"This blue-eyed devil is like all the others. He's interested only in dividing us, in stealing our women."

Holy shit! This guy is North American!

"Mira, chica," he persisted. *"¿Sabes quién es Louis Farrakhan?"* Listen, woman, do you know who Louis Farrakhan is?

Spittle flew as he continued his abuse for Daisy's benefit. I couldn't catch everything he said, but I got the gist: I represented a white pariah society acting in self-interest to divide black society, while Daisy was selling out her "brothers and sisters" by cavorting with the blue-eyed devil for money.

"You're a sad case, brother," I replied, tiring of his bullshit. "You need a psychiatrist."

"'A sad case'? The blue-eyed devil speaks."

The stranger switched back to Spanish, addressing his sickness to Daisy. She nodded meekly as he continued his pathetic bluster. Then I felt her wet hand trembling in mine. I had been lying back on the seawall, leaning into Daisy's lap. Now, sensing her fear, I shot up. Adrenaline coursed through my veins.

"Get the fuck out of here!"

He eased back a few yards but continued his crazy invective.

Furious, I jumped down from the wall.

"Two hundred pounds," he said, puffing himself up like a toad. "Two hundred pounds! See this?" He pointed at his chest with both hands.

"Two hundred pounds of *chorizo!*" I said, taking an unmistakable step forward.

He backed away, turned, crossed the Malecón, and disappeared.

Months later, back in California, I searched the Internet for some clue to this strange and disconcerting encounter. I found what I sought in a back issue of the *New York Times*. Farrakhan, leader of the Nation of Islam, had sent a team to Cuba, ostensibly to study the nation's health and education systems. I assumed our attacker was part of Farrakhan's entourage. If so, he was a pathetic ambassador.

I remembered Marta's comment, and my conversation with the old black man in Trinidad. I asked Daisy whether she had encountered racism.

"In my school," Daisy explained, "there was much racism with the blacks and with the poor people, and I was both—black and poor." Then, quickly dropping the subject, she urged, "Let's go now. That man scared me."

~

CHAPTER NINE

PIVOT POINT

I t began as a faint cough, a feeble hacking, a slight want of breath. I must be coming down with a cold, I thought, flippantly dismissing as trivial a disorder that would plague me for the rest of my journey. Twelve months would pass before I was fully cured.

Perhaps I wouldn't have felt so groggy if it hadn't been so damn hot—at least 90 degrees. I was riding in my tank top, mittened hands casually clutching the grips, my bare arms brown as cowhide. It felt fabulous to be riding again purely for the pleasure of being on the bike, to feel the sun and the rush of warm air on my skin, to hear the syncopated cadence of the opposed twin running sweetly. Refined. Powerful. Like a clenched fist of steel. My faithful motorcycle had its own identity. My alter ego. I stared down at it reverentially from the saddle. So beautiful I could take it to bed.

I thought of Daisy. Her lilting voice haunted my memory. Her scent seemed to come up to me from the moist, fragrant earth. I closed my eyes for a second, delirious with that musky odor in my head. Even with my eyes shut, her ethereal image was growing no fainter with distance. She was a half-glimpsed spirit in the gloom.

I watched the smooth, pothole-free Autopista whiz by in a blur. My riding skills had been honed to the degree that I knew my speed by feel. After 3,600 miles, the ride had attained its own modus vivendi, the intensity heightened by the thrill of discovery and the arousal of danger.

Six hours from Havana, I passed into Sancti Spíritus province; about 20 miles beyond, without warning, the concrete gave way to kitty litter. The rear tire squirmed and bucked, threatening to spill me. Not wanting to leave a trail of flesh and plastic bits on the hardtop, I coiled the power back and hung on grimly. The gravel causeway came to an abrupt end in the middle of nowhere. The collapse of the Soviet Union in 1991 had pulled the plug, and construction of the Autopista had been aborted. One moment a freeway, the next moment *nada*. Not even a sign to guide hapless tourists out of the boondocks and onto the Carretera Central—an ordinary two-lane highway that runs along the island's spine for more than 700 miles.

Ciego de Ávila, capital of its namesake, pancake-flat province, was forbiddingly forlorn, the kind of dreary town that turned guidebook research into drudge.

To catalogue towns I began at the central plaza, where I'd park the bike and shroud it with the nylon cover to keep inquisitive crowds away. Then I walked the grid of streets—the orderly Spanish laid out most Cuban towns in a rectilinear pattern—first one way, then returning parallel along the next, popping into hotels and restaurants and noting sites of interest, until I had walked all the streets. Next came the avenues, running crosswise, in order. Sweaty, wearying work in the insufferable heat of central Cuba. Especially in leather pants. I might just as well have worn a half-suit of armor.

Thoughtfully, the Cuban government had provided refreshment for the masses. On the northwest corner of Parque Martí I discovered La Casa del Agua La Palía, a watering hole—quite literally—where glasses of mineral water are offered free of charge to thirsty Avileños. The inside was cool and inviting. Two middle-aged males were chatting up the two barmaids. The women were in uniform: white, long-sleeved shirts buttoned at the front, black knee-length skirts, blue canvas plimsolls. The quartet stopped talking and stared me down as I entered.

My smile broke the tension.

"Not many tourists come by. You're the first in weeks," said the more matronly barmaid, offering me a tall glass of fresh-squeezed orange ladled from a metal barrel. I knocked it back and ordered a second. Thirty *centavos* each—two cents total at black-market rates.

One of the males, a swarthy man wearing a navy blue T-shirt and a camouflage cap curled up Aussie-style at the sides, asked me to take his photo. I liked

A reveler tosses a home-made firebomb during the *parranda*—a year-end fiesta that explodes in the otherwise peaceful town of Remedios.

Destination, Cuba: Dawn finds my 1,000cc BMW R100GS/Paris-Dakar motorcycle still lashed to the stern of the *Kalevala,* a 58-foot Finnish cruiser crossing from Key West to Havana.

ALL PHOTOS BY CHRISTOPHER P. BAKER

Striking a model's pose, Daisy Bartolomé shows off the grace and beauty that enraptured the author. Daisy planned on—and ultimately succeeded in—escaping her dismal life by marrying a foreigner.

Laden with fresh-cut tobacco, a worker harvests leaves that will be cured and rolled to make fine Cuban cigars.

Sheer-faced *mogotes* (freestanding limestone formations) stud the broad Valle de Viñales, where oxen have plowed the loamy, rust-red soils into an orderly quiltwork of *vegas* (tobacco fields).

Once thronged with traffic, Havana's Avenida de los Presidentes is relatively quiet these days. The boulevard anchors the Vedado district, where many mansions and high-rise apartments have gone to seed.

Beseeching a ride from a 1950s Yankee *cacharro,* a young habanera on Havana's Malecón—the seafront boulevard—resorts to Cuba's default mode of mass transportation.

A dachshund surveys cobbled streets that echo to the clip-clop of history in Trinidad's colonial quarter, which dates from the height of Cuba's sugar boom in the 18th and 19th centuries.

Street troubadors fill Trinidad with the haunting rhythms of *son*, a traditional country music that has resurged in tandem with the Buena Vista Social Club.

The smile of a young cubana in Trinidad's Plaza Mayor reflects the glow of a nation that cherishes its children and has achieved impressive breakthroughs in health and education.

A bike-top view of the dirt road linking Marea del Portillo with Chivirico, a wild stretch of south coast where the forested Sierra Maestra beetles down to the Caribbean.

Passengers overflow a flatbed *camión,* or truck, pressed into service as a bus. Outside Havana, most public transportation consists of such makeshift measures.

Dancers perform their nightly routine at Havana's Tropicana cabaret. This open-air extravaganza, dubbed "paradise under the stars," has operated continuously since New Year's Eve of 1939.

Outside the U.S. Interest Section in Havana in February 2000, Cuban youths show their support for Fidel Castro's demand that six-year-old Elián González be returned to Cuba.

his sly smile. He arranged his hair under his cap and adopted a proud posture leaning on the bar. Arms folded, hands tucked under his armpits, impish smile lighting up his face like a moonbeam.

Our conversation was just beginning to roll, bright Cuban smiles all around, when a third man entered, wearing mirrored glasses, a guayabera, and dark slacks. My companions went quiet. It's easy to spot a plainclothes policeman in Cuba.

The conversation briefly revived when a gorgeous, cream-colored '54 Chevrolet Bel-Air cruised to a stop outside; gussied up with sparkling chrome, it added intrigue to the otherwise morose central square. But the quartet seemed uneasy with the spook standing in the shadows, ears cocked like a dog, saying nothing, giving me a sullen once-over. He was there, I had no doubt, because of me.

I excused myself and exited into the halogen glare.

Leaving town, I saw a large billboard that read *"Sin comentario"*—literally, "No comment." It showed a dove carrying an olive branch and the Cuban flag in its beak; from the bird's behind, white guano dropped onto the words "HELMS BURTON," tagged with a *"Made in USA"* label.

I straddled the bike, engine idling, and fished out my camera. A *tráfico*—motorbike cop—pulled up alongside. A middle-aged chap. Mask of death on his face. He asked for my papers, which I kept in the safety box built into the gas tank. I switched off the ignition and began to unzip the tank back.

"No problema, señor! There's no need to go to that trouble," he said, smiling.

"Your helmet is pretty," he continued amiably.

He asked me where I came from and whistled when I told him.

"That's very far."

The fact that I am from California left him unfazed, except for the notion of distance.

Another cop pulled up, dismounted, and dropped onto his haunches to inspect my bike.

"¡Muy fuerte!"

"Yes, 1,000 ccs."

"Oyes, ¡un mulo! ¿Es muy rápida?"

"Not really. Maybe 100 miles an hour."

The cop whistled. *"Sí, ¡muy rápida!* Want to swap?"

He was riding a Jawa 350.

"Sure," I replied, "for *both* of your Jawas."

They laughed, saluted me, then puttered away, leaving a pall of blue smoke in their wake.

I completed my research and rode out of town, happy to have experienced another example of Cuban gentility.

I follow a well-paved road running south from Ciego de Ávila, expecting to find nothing of interest. But my provincial map shows a marina at Júcaro run by a Cuban agency called Puertosol, so I drop in for a visit.

The browbeaten fishing village exists on memories of better days. A hurricane blasted ashore here in 1932, and Júcaro looks like it has never recovered. I trace a rusted railway line down to the shore, where a timeworn wooden wharf supported by barnacle-encrusted pylons awaits its sure demise in the next storm. The track once brought sugar to Júcaro for loading, but the trade had been stolen by a modern loading facility a few miles farther west at Palo Alto.

A yacht tethered to the rotten wharf is flying the French tricolor. I hail the skipper.

"*Bonjour!*"

A balding head dappled with liver spots appears through the hatch.

"*Oui?*"

Aloof. I hear giggles below, and a solicitous voice—a *cubana*, by the sound of things—begging him to return. I gather that I have interrupted a rather important cross-cultural exchange.

"Can you tell me where the marina is?"

"Zis is it!"

Is he joking? It consists of the derelict wharf and a diesel pump. The Gaul must have been cursing his luck, but then again...the woman seems to be pulling on his leg, attempting to drag him below. He disappears and is greeted by a potpourri of squeals. *Two women!* Maybe more?

Retracing my path to the Carretera, I pass through Venezuela, comprising somber block-house apartments, salmon pink, rising over the cane fields. I see a photogenic scene. Lines of washing flapping in the wind. A *central* behind, belching out thick black smoke. The composition enhanced by a silver '59 Dodge with angel's wings for rear fins parked in front of a wall dominated by the words:

CON
FIDEL
REVOLUCIÓN

CDR—for *Comité de Defensa de la Revolución,* or the local neighborhood watch committee—is found on every city block in the nation.

I break out my Canon EOS and snap off a few frames.

A fellow in a green MININT uniform down the road leaps onto a bicycle and furiously pedals my way. His scornful look suggests trouble. Before I can stash the camera and roar away he is upon me, dropping his bicycle in the road and leaping before me with his flat palm signaling "Halt!"

"Why are you photographing the factory?" he snaps. "Are you working in Venezuela?"

"I liked the scenery. Especially the old yanqui car," I reply nonchalantly.

He is nearly apopletic, hopping about as if he might wet himself. "But you took a photograph of the factory!"

"It's a very nice factory, *señor.* Very impressive. A wonderful example of the accomplishments of socialism with which to impress the rest of the world," I obsequiously respond, appealing to his socialist pride.

Amazingly he thaws, then waves me away.

The ubiquity of petty control irks me. Little Communist Hitlers like this get my back up. I can't help feeling that way. I've always rebelled at authority—never a good move in a police state such as Cuba.

The heat has been building inexorably while the verdant landscapes have gradually withered to a featureless plain shaded by broad trees spreading their gnarled branches long and low to the ground; all that walks, crawls, or flies gathers in their cool shade. The rolling upland plain is the color of honey, daubed with the yellows and whites of wildflowers. It is starkly beautiful high country from which all of Cuba seems to explode into view. A Montana landscape with all the blue sky in the world overhead. Unlike any Cuba I have ever imagined.

I expect the Marlboro Man to come riding over the horizon, and he does.

Camagüey province is cattle country, with *vaqueros* (cowboys) adding an intriguing appeal to the landscape. The central plains are dominated by vast state-owned ranches—*ganaderías*—each named after a revolutionary hero or slogan, such as the Triunfo de la Revolución.

I pull up alongside a weathered fence and watch Cuban cowboys bringing in a herd of zebu cattle with floppy humps, nudging the cows along, keeping them in a loose line. The only sounds are the dull clip-clop of hooves and the slap of chaps against leather saddles and the whistling of the wind through the tall, rain-starved grasses.

And what a wind. It's a furnace blast tearing across the open plains, forcing me to bank against it, shouldering my torso half off the bike like a racer.

Then the road turns northeast and begins a long, gentle climb toward the province's eponymous capital city. The engine growls as it powers against the gravitational pull and the head wind. The gusts buffet the bike like an aircraft in turbulence. Searing spasms return in my shoulder muscles. By the time I reach Camagüey, my hands are trembling and my back has turned to concrete.

Cisne and Francisco Aguilar are delighted to see me.

"Muy religioso," Martha had said, making the sign of the cross to indicate that her cousin and her husband were devout Catholics. "I have called her. She would love for you to stay with her," she had added, scribbling her cousin's name and address on a piece of paper before wishing me *"¡Buen viaje!"*

I run the bike up a ramp that Francisco lays down from the street. Into the lounge it goes, a thick wad of cardboard under the engine to stop the oil from the leaking sump gasket staining the gleaming patterned-tile floor. Eclectic artwork festoons the walls of the hallway and lounge.

The Aguilars' home, in the heart of the 18th-century quarter, boasts a grand colonial frontage and an enviable location three blocks from Parque Agramonte, the main plaza. Their house seems exotically spacious, with two lounges, a dining room, and four bedrooms downstairs, and two bedrooms and a study upstairs, all overflowing with precious antiques: Crystal vases, marble busts, porcelain urns from Limoges, a genuine gilt Tiffany lamp, mahogany tables inlaid with mother-of-pearl, grandfather clocks chiming precisely. Everywhere I look there are clocks.

The couple is fastidious. Everything is arranged clinically at right angles, and the place sparkles as if a stiff breeze has come through and swept clear the dust. I have been transported into a middle-class home from the 1950s.

I feel quite grubby, out of place in my soiled leathers.

Cisne leads me through to my bedroom, where I sleep the next three nights on a priceless mahogany bed with a tall headboard carved with faux columns and a classical pediment and a centerpiece exquisitely adorned with whittled roses.

Francisco has the long, noble face of a thespian, dramatically wrinkled, with white hair slicked back in a sleek coiffure. It is the face of someone who feels sure of himself. A well-known doctor and medical professor, he studied at the University of Havana in the same years as Fidel (Castro had enrolled in law school in 1945, but plunged immediately into politics and did not graduate until September 1950).

I ask if they knew each other.

He laughs. "Everyone knew Fidel."

"Did you support him?" I inquire.

"We all supported him. Back then we all shared his vision."

Cisne serves us lobster and rice with boiled eggs in mayonnaise, then joins us at the polished mahogany dining table. Francisco says grace and I too, devout atheist, close my eyes out of respect for my hosts.

"Yes, we were revolutionaries, willing to sacrifice," says Cisne. "Most decent people were. Those first few years we were all full of idealism and hope."

Her husband nods in agreement.

"But we didn't fight for *this*," she adds bitterly, tilting her head back to indicate the state of affairs on the streets.

I am reminded of something Guillermo Cabrera Infante, former editor of the literary supplement *Lunes de Revolución* and a brilliant novelist, had written from exile in London:

"There were times that moved Cuba. A glorious time. Unfortunately, that golden age ended some time ago—the rest is propaganda."

I mention this. The couple respond that they are well aware of his writings, which are banned throughout Cuba.

"A brilliant author," says Francisco. "He was savaged, like all the rest."

I had recently read Cabrera Infante's *Mea Cuba*, an acerbic, wistful, brilliant set of essays in which the banished author pours out his bile at Castro, a lawyer-turned-revolutionary who at 32 came down from the Sierra Maestra and was considered a "younger, bearded version of Magwitch: a tall outlaw emerging from the fog of history to make Pips of us all." Like thousands of Cubans,

Cabrera Infante had supported Castro's revolution to topple Batista but soured when "the outlaw became a law unto himself." Many of Castro's revolutionary cohorts—even his heroic wartime *compadres*—were jailed or shot for treason when they protested being cuckolded into the Communist bed. In a way, Cabrera Infante had been fortunate: He simply became persona non grata, prompting him to quote the famous response by Lieutenant Lightoller, the only officer of the *Titanic* to escape with his life, when questioned by a stern judge as to why he had abandoned ship: "I didn't abandon my ship, your lordship. My ship abandoned me."

Abandoned. The word strikes a bitter chord with my hosts.

"Camagüey is not Fidel's favorite city," says Francisco. "The town has been neglected. He has turned his back on us."

"Why would he shun Camagüey?" I ask naively.

"Fidel got little support from the people of Camagüey. He has never forgiven. You'll see tomorrow," replies Francisco.

I had read that the city had a strong history of supporting the revolutionary cause. As far back as 1871, Samuel Hazard, traveling through Cuba, had noted, "This town has always been looked upon with suspicion by the authorities on account of the strong proclivities its people had for insurrection." True to form, the citizens of Camagüey had vigorously opposed the Machado and Batista regimes, and student and worker strikes had crippled the city (U.S. Marines occupied the city in 1917-23 to quell anti-government unrest). The citizens had also supported the army of Che Guevara and Camilo Cienfuegos when it entered the city in September 1958. But the Camagüeyans' notoriety for insurrection did not translate into strong support for *fidelismo*.

Before the Revolution, the province had been one of the most developed; after *el triunfo*, it continued to thrive under the efficient management of Huber Matos, the highly popular military commander of the Revolutionary Army in Camagüey, while the rest of Cuba slipped into economic confusion. Unbeknownst to Matos and most Cubans, Castro was operating a secret "parallel" government, brilliantly manipulating events and solidifying his power behind the scenes while paying lip service to the population's shared aspirations under the guise of establishing a pluralist democracy. (After Batista fled the country on December 31, 1958, a transitional moderate government was established, and recognized by Washington.)

In September 1959, Matos had urged Castro to convene a special meeting of the government to discuss growing "communist infiltration" within the army and INRA, the National Institute of Agrarian Reform that Castro had set up in May to subvert the established social order and secretly launch the *true* revolution. Matos, in command of the relatively wealthy and conservative heartland of Cuba, posed a serious threat. He and 15 fellow officers were swiftly arrested and jailed for sedition.

The affair soured many Camagüeyans, who expressed only lukewarm support for the radicalization of the revolution. Perhaps Fidel had felt scorned. Certainly local support for Matos would have caused Castro to harbor suspicions about the Camagüeyans' loyalty. For *el máximo* there is no middle ground. The man whose name means "faithful" is faithful only to those who are faithful to him.

"He even refuses to return to a place where he feels he's been slighted," says Francisco.

I take Cisne and Francisco at their word. Their candor is daunting.

We spend long hours talking. The couple speak rapidly in Spanish, spilling out emotional and often vitriolic portraits of Cuba. I catch only segments, but the nuance and the meaning are clear: With his obstinacy and his madcap schemes, Fidel has ruined the country.

"He has turned the country upside down," Francisco exclaims, gesticulating scornfully. "He ordered skilled workers, even the cleverest, to leave the factories and go work in the fields, while the farmers came to the cities to learn to be accountants and engineers. What did the urban workers know about farming? They didn't care. They had no inclination or ability. The farmers returned to the fields with skills they never used. You wouldn't believe the absurdities."

He leans forward, indignantly describing disasters that have been wrought on the country.

"And now look at us. How can I teach students who have no paper, no pens, *nada?* Even I have to scrounge to find workbooks. And who is there to teach these days, eh? The students no longer show up because they are working as *jineteros.*"

Francisco sinks back in his chair, deflated.

"They've no belief in the Revolution. They've lost faith," Cisne adds plaintively. "We had a magnificent future, but he has destroyed all our dreams. The youth are tired of this struggle. They're angry. We all are tired and angry. Who can blame us?"

"Come. I have something to show you," Francisco says, jumping up and guiding me upstairs to his office, where he proudly sweeps his arm along shelves containing rows of medical texts arranged neatly in glass-fronted mahogany cases. Most of the hardbound journals are in Spanish, but there are English-language editions, too, including *The American Journal of Medicine*. His subscription ended, I note, in August 1992.

"I had subscriptions to all the leading medical journals," Francisco proclaims. "Pah! Now I receive nothing."

I ask whether the state had supplied the journals.

"Some," he replies, "but most I subscribed to myself. Now I don't have the money. No one does. How can I teach when I am being left behind? Cuba is going nowhere medically."

It strikes me as a tragedy of historic proportions.

In 1978 Fidel predicted that Cuba would become the bulwark of Third World medicine, put a doctor on every block, become a world leader in medical research, and surpass the United States in certain health indices. In all four, he has been vindicated. According to Cuban government statistics, there were only 6,250 doctors in Cuba on the eve of the Revolution; in mid-1996 the country had more than 61,000—one for every 200 inhabitants, or twice as many as the United States. That year Cuba claimed an infant mortality rate of 8 per 1,000 births (compared with 7 for Great Britain, Canada, and the United States) and a life expectancy of 73.9 years (compared with 77 for Great Britain and 76 for the United States).

The prerevolutionary situation has been much debated. According to the *United Nations Statistical Yearbook*, for example, in 1957 Cuba ranked third in Latin America, behind only Uruguay and Argentina, in number of physicians and dentists per capita, with 128 physicians and dentists per 100,000 people; that equaled the Netherlands and surpassed the United Kingdom. Regardless, a near-100 percent immunization since 1959 has eradicated several contagious diseases, including malaria and diphtheria; the Pan American Health Organization declared Cuba the first polio-free country in the Americas; and Cuba has the world's highest measles-immunization rate, according to UNICEF, which puts Cuba four notches behind the United States in health indices but well ahead of all other developing nations.

A decade ago, Cuba also commanded the kind of technology that most poor nations could only dream about: ultrasound for obstetricians, CAT scans for radiologists, stacks of high-rise monitors in the suites for intensive care. *Science* magazine ranks the country's Ibero-Latin American Center for Nervous System Transplants and Regeneration as the world's best for the treatment of Parkinson's disease. Its Hospital Hermanos Ameijeiras "conducts research at the international cutting edge in the 38 specialties in which services are rendered." Interferons for AIDS treatments. A meningitis vaccine. A cure for vitiligo. Cuba developed and manufactures them all and has provided them free to all Cuban citizens.

All this was funded by the Soviet Union. Its collapse hit Cuba's admirable health system in the gut. The catastrophic blow was multiplied in 1992 when the U.S. Congress passed the Torricelli Act, barring shipments of food and medicine, previously exempt from the embargo, and prohibiting medical supplies and equipment manufactured in the U.S. or under U.S. patent from being sold to foreign companies for resale to Cuba. A fact-finding team from the American Public Health Association recently lambasted this American policy for exacerbating Cuba's medical crisis.

"Isn't the U.S. embargo to blame for Cuba's problems?" I ask.

"*El bloqueo* is morally repugnant," Francisco acknowledges. "It costs Cuba dearly. But *el sistema* is to blame. We are disgusted."

The litany of charges continues.

I think of my home country during the 1960s and 70s, when the socialist policies of the Labour government fostered mismanagement, waste, and a creeping anomie and sloth. I would never have admitted it at the time; I couldn't see it. I was a committed socialist myself back then. I mention this to Cisne and Francisco.

"You were fortunate that you were able to change direction," Francisco responds. "Other countries can correct their mistakes. But he is an obdurate man."

Cisne jumps in. "There is no one strong enough to oppose him. Only *el jefe* can be right. So many resources have been wasted, especially for the sake of the international proletariat," she sniffs with unconcealed bitterness.

"Do you know how many soldiers we sent to Angola?" asks Francisco. "Sixty thousand men. And 20,000 to Ethiopia. What a waste of our resources."

I reply that the CIA estimates the number of Cuban troops rotated through Angola was vastly higher than that (the official Cuban figure, quoted in *Granma International,* is 377,000).

"But didn't the Soviets foot the bill?" I ask.

""Ha!" the two laugh in unison. "Some, but not all," says Cisne.

"Life was good in the beginning," adds Francisco. "There was food on the table during the Brezhnev era. Brezhnev had a soft spot for Fidel. He had only to ask and Brezhnev gave. Two million here, three million there. The Soviets were a caretaker government. Now what do we have? Without dollars you do not eat."

"But what about your peso salary?"

"Bah! The peso is worthless coinage. It is robbery!" Francisco exclaims, eyes glaring. "The *mayimbes,* the privileged party members, eat well. They have food on their table. For the rest of Cuba life is a *lucha.*"

A lucha. A fight or struggle. The word is on every Cuban's lips.

I hear the lament again next day while walking through Plaza de las Trabajadores, an intimate triangular piazza whose heart encompasses a venerable ceiba—the tree that, according to Cuban legend, best comprehends human sorrow. An old man sitting on the steps of the Banco Nacional calls me over. He looks like a leprechaun with a hangover. He is unshaven, dark rings circle his eyes, and his convex forehead is a ski run sloping steeply down from an impossibly pointed bald peak.

He peppers me with questions. *Where are you from? Do you work here? What do you think of Cuba?*

I opt for a safe response. Tell him how much I love the people, the beauty of the countryside, how I am impressed by the Revolution's achievements.

"*¡Coño!* What do you know?" he replies caustically. "Life is a lucha! You have been here only a short time. You cannot see through *el manto.*"

El manto—literally, "the mantle"—is the Spanish term for a cloaked reality, a Machiavellian deception used in pursuit of a cause.

"What a revolution!" the old man continues, tilting his head forward and pointing the sharp crown toward a crone shuffling feebly across the square. "We are going nowhere...except back into the last century. We Cubans have nothing. Ha! Camagüeyans have even less!"

It is dangerous talk to be so incautiously tendered in public. I excuse myself and move off.

Camagüey strikes me as a stage for the sadness of the human condition. I see more wretched folk here than elsewhere on the island. Dirt-poor. Emaciated. Clothes in tatters. Discomforting enough to send me in search of a stiff Cuban coffee, which I find at a small *cafetería* on the northeast corner of Parque Agramonte. Here, I am reminded even more forcefully of Cuba's pain.

An old woman enters. Her skeletal frame is wrapped in wrinkled parchment corroded with festering sores. Her clothes are disintegrating around her. She holds in her upturned palm a few meager coins for a cup of coffee. It costs 90 centavos, but even this paltry sum—one cent at official exchange rates—is beyond her means. The young counter maid mocks her, then orders her out.

A more disconsolate scene I have never witnessed in Cuba. I look away, charity having failed me completely.

I stumble out into the square and the clutches of a bunch of off-duty soldiers dressed in army fatigues in disarray, swigging from bottles of rum. They are boisterous and bellicose. The air bristles with the angry static of impending violence. They egg me to take their photographs, but I decline gently and scurry away up Calle Independencia, losing myself among the youths crowding against the windows of dollar-only stores selling Western consumer goods. They stand entranced, staring wistfully, separated from their dreams by the glass reflecting their own destitution.

Camagüey, population 270,000, is Cuba's third largest city and one of its oldest, dating from 1515, with beautiful colonial plazas that have lent Camagüey its nickname, "City of Squares." Like that of most cities throughout Cuba, its heritage had been spared the wrecking ball—a silver lining to Camagüey's economic woes. Not a skyscraper in sight amid regal, once-glorious edifices crumbling onto the cobbles at their feet. Architectural restoration was under way, though, in plazas of tourist interest.

But where were the tourists? I hardly ever saw foreigners in Cuba's interior, and none that day as I explored.

My wanderings led me to Plaza de San Juan de Díos, an exquisite square, recently restored, drenched in late afternoon sunlight emboldening simple colonial facades painted in pastel hues. I checked out the former convent of San Juan de Dios (cream and green) and the birthplace (blue and white) of

Silvio Rodríguez, contemporary poet and songwriter, and a restaurant (pink and yellow) called Campana de Toledo. While crisscrossing the square, I noticed the warm, upturned face of a young *mulata* girl with tawny hair tied up by a pink ribbon sitting on the steps of the convent, smiling impishly with parted lips, her underlip glistening, her bold seal-pup eyes following my every move. She was enough, this limpid Lolita, to cast a spell over the Humbert Humbert within me. Smitten, I was powerless to prevent fawning compliments spilling from my lips as I knelt beside her.

Her name was Yudenia.

I begged a photo. She answered coyly, affirmative, in melodious notes like a bird. I snapped two shots, then moved off, scared by my own vividly erotic musings and by the dangerous knowledge that if I wished, I had only to ask and—hers eyes almost beseeched it—I could have her.

The Campana de Toledo specialized in *criollo* meals. I savored a corn-based stew called *ajiaco* while a gang of urchins peered in through the wide-open door, held up their palms, and called, "Hey, mister. Canadian? From Italy?" One kept repeating a mantra: "Friend, very nice."

The *custodio* attempted to shoo them away, but inevitably they returned to hang hungrily on the periphery like half-starved child-thieves from a Dickens novel.

A woman in her mid-20s appeared and, leaning against a wall across the street, fixed her eyes upon me as a cat upon a bird. Each time I looked up, she wiggled her eyebrows solicitously. Her pretty face could make no amends for a doughy body squeezed into turquoise Spandex shorts. She was joined by a slightly older man dressed in a scruffy, unbuttoned army jacket. He grinned obsequiously, waved at me as if I were a long-lost friend, and jumped up whenever I peered at him as if he had been goosed by an air hose. I ignored them both.

A tour bus pulled up in the square, and the entire cast of this street theater primed itself for a new assault.

There was Yudenia again, wheeling by on a bicycle. She stood on the pedals, displaying her small, agile rump and flashing me coquettish grins. She kept circling, like a carrot dangled in front of my nose. I paid my bill and headed west up Calle Raúl Lamar. The nymphet brushed past me; then, some 20 feet farther on, she leaped from her bicycle, bounded up steep whitewashed steps, and disappeared through an open doorway.

Her angelic visage appeared behind *rejas* and cast me an enigmatic smile. The sun shone sublimely on a face dusted rosy-gold. As I raised my camera she melted away, replaced by a woman staring perplexedly down at me through the half-shuttered window. Then the girl tantalizingly reappeared at her side. I beckoned her to the doorstep where I could photograph her awash in the roseate light. My presence stirred sounds of commotion inside the house. A young boy burst forth, wearing a baseball mitt on one hand and gripping the elastic band of his oversize shorts with the other. Two more youngsters popped into the light and looked at me, blinking, silent, jaws agape. The woman joined them.

"Are you Yudenia's mother?" I asked.

"I'm her sister."

"Where is Yudenia?"

"¡Mi madre!" the older sister squealed, fanning herself with the palm of her hand. "Come! Hurry!" she implored Yudenia, who emerged combing her hair, half-naked, a green fruit from the Garden of Eden. She sat on the steps, bronzed flesh all aflame, feigning indifference to my awkward attentions as I posed her and photographed under the scrutiny of *la familia*.

I asked her age.

"Fourteen," she replied proudly.

By now the mother and grandmother had appeared and looked on with obvious mirth at the palsied, agitated, flushed male.

"Fourteen? You're exquisite. I'll return in two years to claim you as my bride."

The grandmother laughed at the lunacy of lust. The older sister shrieked with delight and fanned herself again *"¡Ayee!* You have good luck," she said to her younger sibling. "I've prayed all my life that a foreigner would fall in love with me. And you, little precious, find a *norteamericano*, and a handsome one, too."

I imagined how differently the scene would have played out in the States. Her father would have punched me in the nose and called the police, but in Cuba I was considered a stroke of good fortune.

Yudenia wrote down her name and address. I promised to write.

Back at the Aguilars' that night, I regaled Cisne with the tale, deliberately garbling events—a tweak here, a nip there—to mask the deliciously perverse ruminations that had temporarily turned me into Nabokov's "Humbert the Hound, the sad-eyed degenerate cur."

"The family has broken down," said Cisne, sighing mightily, perhaps at the transparency of my subterfuge. "Before, young girls were protected by their elder brothers, aunts, and grandparents. Since 1959, the father is sent away to work, and the young boys and girls go to the country where they learn all kinds of promiscuities. Today our youth are taught that sexual relations are normal. The old constraints have broken down. Sex is everything.

"Be careful!" she warned later that evening as I ventured out in search of further adventure. "Trust no one. And beware the *muchachas!*"

Moonlight silvered sparsely lit streets full of the romance of history. In the dark, it was easy to imagine myself cast back 200 years. The hubbub of day had softened; friends talking over shots of *aguardiente* (cheap white rum)...hazy undertones of lovers tucked into recesses perfectly shadowed for secluded intimacy...soft notes of Spanish guitars...cafés murmuring with Afro-Caribbean melancholy. Women had pulled their *sillones*—rockers—onto the sidewalks in order to catch the breeze and share the day's gossip. The menfolk had dragged tables into the open streets and were playing dominoes, shirtless, beneath faint neon lamps. They smoked cigars. Sang idly. Laughed as couples took each other by the waist and danced to spicy *merengues* and *salsas.*

I cherished the Cuban instinct for gaiety, the fun-loving way they turned adversity on its ear.

I listened to an open-air concert on Calle República, bought an ice cream, and eventually settled at a moody demimonde saloon called El Cambio on the north side of Parque Agramonte. I sat on a high stool with my back against the bar and my elbows resting on the bartop and gazed out across the square toward the voluptuous cathedral with its tall belltower softly illumined within. An old Wurlitzer jukebox played a slow Latin tune.

The place was empty but for the barman and a woman with her face down on the bar and her hands knitted behind her head, which was rolling from side to side with the music. She was dressed in a blood-red camisole cut low at the bosom—a visibly heavy load—and her green floral skirt had ridden high up her ample bronze thighs. Her hair, cropped in a fashionable pageboy, was a deep chestnut that glowed like burnished copper in the wan light.

She looked up and managed a smile. Her deep hazel eyes gazed at me with all the lugubriousness of a bloodhound. She was sipping *aguardiente* and looked as lonely as any person I had ever known. Her eyes lit up when I sat down beside her.

We guessed each other's age. I thought she was 22; she was 19. She thought me 32. I thanked her, then guessed, correctly, that she was Galician. We talked about Celtic heritage. I drew a map in my notebook showing Galicia and the other Gallic parts of Europe. Then, tiring of the subject, she turned maudlin.

"There's nothing to do here," Sonia said despondently. "Life's a dead end. It's boring."

She wanted to be a model but thought that she would probably end up working in a *peluquería*, a beauty shop.

"What else can I do? There is no future here," she despaired.

Suddenly Sonia began to cry. I put my arm across her shoulder and tried to cheer her up.

Bobby Womack crooned on the jukebox.

A drunkard settled himself beside me, then collapsed backward from his stool and hit the floor with a dull, corpse-like thud. He laughed loudly while beer poured onto his belly from the bottle gripped tight in his hand.

Sonia's eyes sparkled at mine. She lifted my spectacles and stared intently, then leaned slowly forward with lips puckered. Her tongue prized my lips apart, gliding silkily over my teeth.

The drunk was peering over my shoulder. The hot breath in my ear was his. He smiled lasciviously, settled back onto his stool, and slapped his hand down on the bar.

"Why do you drink this?" I asked stupidly, pointing to the aguardiente. I had bolted three *tragos*, or shots, and each one tasted like sugared gasoline. Already I could feel the rum's heat in my belly and its cloudiness swirling inside my head.

"It makes me feel good," Sonia replied, knocking back another trago. "Life is shit. I feel...free."

We switched to dark, smooth, seven-year-old *añejo* rum. Sonia was now giggling between bouts of melancholy.

We navigated the darkness—stumbled is a better word—pausing occasionally to kiss before setting off again through the gloomy streets, I knew not where. I assumed she was leading me home, but it soon became clear to my fuddled brain that our perambulation was aimless. Eventually Sonia pulled me into a shadowy recess and pinned me against the wall. We were inside a small domestic courtyard, standing on an ungainly bed of rubble and coiled wires. I heard the laughter of passing people, then the sounds faded from focus.

Suddenly a lightbulb snapped on in the house across the way, bathing us in a boxed glare. Inside the house I could see a man in pajamas standing before a toilet, his head studiously bowed. Had he only looked up, he would have caught us in flagrante delicto not 10 feet away.

Sex is too beautiful an experience to ever be so dismal.

I crawled home and lay awake, tormented by sadness for Sonia and by what the future seemed to hold for that sweet 14-year-old girl named Yudenia. Was Sonia a harbinger of a life of unattainable dreams and unbearable sorrow? Melancholic thoughts swirled through my brain. The world spun, and I drifted off to sleep.

When I first conceived my motorcycle journey, I never imagined how my perceptions of this island would change. My conversations with Cisne and Francisco perplexed me; they turned my preconceptions on their head.

Cuba has always had a strong dairy industry, centered on Camagüey. Following the Revolution, Castro took a zealous interest in the field, especially in artificial insemination and the development of sturdier livestock. Castro's passion to play, in biographer Georgie Ann Geyer's words, "the Thai king as rainmaker" was so great that Fidel's friend Gabriel García Márquez once threatened to write a novel about him called *El Dictador de las Vacas—The Dictator of the Cows.* I had turned up dozens of glowing references to the success of Cuba's genetic breeding program and its homegrown F1 bovine strain—Canadian Holstein crossed with zebu from India—that yielded an admirable average of 6.1 kilograms of milk a day. Still, that was enough to supply only 30 percent of Cuba's needs; powdered milk from East Germany made up the shortfall. The Cuban dairy industry had also come to rely on imported feed grains. These disappeared, along with the powdered milk, with the collapse of the Soviet bloc, causing a catastrophic fall in milk production.

I asked Francisco how long he thought it would be before milk might again be found in the stores.

"Not while he's in power. He has ruined an industry," Francisco replied.

"But I thought that Castro was responsible for greatly improving milk production."

"Bah! Propaganda. Before the Revolution, we had fabulous ganaderías. Right here. Our dairy farms were among the best in the world. The government does not admit its mistakes," Francisco replied, drawing an imaginary zipper across his lips.

There were few coherent economic plans in the 1960s, just grandiose schemes that almost always ended in near ruin. Never able to accept his own mistakes, Castro refused to learn from the debacle. In a 1987 speech he said, "We must correct the errors we made in correcting our errors." Confusedly searching for "truly original socialism," Castro ordered abrupt reversals in direction. The capricious skipper tacked at whim.

Francisco and I were seated on bamboo and wicker rockers in a tiny patio to the side of the house, rocking gently in unison while Cisne tended her pristine herb garden.

"Our shops lacked nothing four decades ago," Francisco continued. "They were always full. There was a store down the street where you could buy whatever you wished. Life was good. It was easy. You could eat well for one peso."

"I thought that was also the case during the 1980s. Aren't the shortages only recent?"

"Pfff!" he exclaimed. "Every year since the Revolution there has been less and less until now there is nothing. Camagüeyans made all kinds of cheeses. They were *delicioso*. We have lost it all. The cheeses and the skills, too," he stammered, dramatically waving his hands.

"They talk of our excellent medicine. Bah! Go to the *farmacia*. Where are the medicines?"

"Surely this is only during the past few years, no?"

"Oh, it is far worse now, but it has been progressive for years. That is Communism. I can't understand the people here. They forget how good things were. We had medicines before. It's a disaster...an *infierno!*" he exclaimed.

A pig started squealing nearby.

"That, too, is Communism," he said, pointing his thumb over his shoulder at the neighbor's yard. "Everyone is raising pigs and chickens. No one has dollars with which to buy meat. It's true, no?"

"*Ssshh!*" Cisne implored him to lower his voice.

Many Cuban households now share living quarters with a pig, as depicted in the movie *Fresa y Chocolate*, where a pig is seen being pushed up the stairs of a tenement. But raising a pig inside is illegal, so many pigs are mute—they've had their vocal cords slit.

"We are sick of living like this, and tired of being afraid for what we say," Francisco continued. "Everyone is forced to break the law constantly to survive. Cubans live under enormous stress of being caught for the slightest transgression. Imagine, pigs—in the house! Now there is much salmonella."

Francisco leaned back and emitted a throaty guffaw at all the absurdities. "Even the food sold on the streets isn't clean. There's much illness. Women are dying because there are no medicines. *Nada. ¡No hay nada!* We have nothing!"

Francisco pointed toward the garage, where his gleaming Lada was parked. Like everything in the house, it was antiseptically clean.

"I worked hard, paid good money for that car," he said, thumbing imaginary banknotes into his palms. "It's mine, but if I need dollars I cannot sell it—only to the government. What will they give me? Worthless pesos. That is Communism. Who are they to say I cannot sell it to whoever wants to buy it?"

Francisco pulled the palm of his hand down his face. "The problem here is propaganda. It's a mask. The media is full of wonderful achievements. But life is not what it was. We lacked nothing. Our food was *maravillosa*. Cuba had great culture, too. The theaters were lively. And full." He paused while I scribbled down everything he had said. I told him to go on talking, assuring him that my pen could keep pace with his tongue.

"There were chefs here who could make anything," Francisco continued, growing more animated by the second. "There was a *negro* here in Camagüey who made desserts like you cannot imagine. Since the Revolution, it has all gone. I remember in 1955, a Frenchman in Havana, a very cultured man, who thought that the best dining in the world was in Cuba. Better than Paris. Imagine! Chinese. Portuguese. There were two Spaniards, too, in the old Hotel Havana in Camagüey who ran a fabulous restaurant. The waiters were like matadors."

Francisco leaped to his feet and flourished his napkin over his arm in a makeshift *muleta*, the red cape of the matador. The family maid—an elderly black woman named Anna—laughed out loud as Francisco, nobly erect, swirled his cape gamely as an imaginary bull thundered past.

"Even our education system was fabulous. It might not have served everyone, but even the poor could go to school, at least in the cities."

The statistics on education in Cuba have been much debated, reminding me of Brazilian economist Roberto Campos's remark that statistics are like bikinis: They show what's important but hide what's essential. According to Cuban government statistics, 43 percent of the population was illiterate on the eve of the Revolution, and half a million Cuban children went without school. The *UN Statistical Yearbook*, however, suggests that as many as 80 percent of the population was literate.

Whatever the truth, no one debates that from the very first days, the Castro government has fought a determined war on illiteracy. Today, according to UNICEF, the average Cuban receives nine years of schooling (compared with 9.6 for the United States and 1.2 for Haiti), and literacy has reached a remarkable 98.5 percent. Everywhere I traveled, smiling schoolchildren in uniform were, in James Michener's words, "the permanent face of the land." Castro deserves full credit for the extraordinary advances in education that the Revolution has bestowed upon Cuba. Once, when asked about the sister who turned her back on the Revolution, Fidel told Barbara Walters: "We have the same mother and father, but different ideas. I am a committed socialist. She is an enemy of socialism, and that is why she says [bad] things about me. But let me tell you, I have millions of brothers and sisters, and between us we have millions of children. We love these children." There is no doubt he is sincere.

Whom was I to believe?

"The School of Medicine at the University of Havana was without equal in the Americas!" Francisco boomed. He launched into a description of the school, with its glorious lecture theater and its marbled walls supported by Corinthian columns. The dissecting room had 60 stainless steel tables—here he swept his hands across an imaginary glistening surface—and stools, five per table, enough for 300 students. Francisco's face was full of pain.

"After the triumph of the Revolution I returned to the school. What did I find? The tables had been thrown into the streets! This glorious room—it was *bellísima!*—had been turned into a dormitory for revolutionaries." His voice rose to a crescendo. "It was the work of a *loco*...the work of a Caligula!"

Francisco's eyes bulged with the memory of the ignominy. He had turned purple with rage. His clenched fist slammed the air.

"¡Imagínese!"

I could see the hall clearly in my mind's eye, gleaming with marble, its dissecting apparati destroyed.

"Oh, such colleges we had. Unequaled in Latin America," he added dejectedly, shaking his bowed head.

Francisco composed himself, then disappeared and reemerged from his bedroom carrying his medical school yearbook, which he placed gently atop the dining room table. It was a leather-bound treasure, replete with black-and-white photos and advertisements touting the services of private doctors and clinics. There was the Laboratorio de Farmacología Experimental, and the film room, the library, the lecture room with seats steeply banked in curved rows like a Roman ampitheater, and the dissecting room with its 60 tables and its tanks for 70 cadavers. And there were the smiling students clad in their white gowns, dissecting corpses with clinical curiosity.

I thumbed through the book, enthralled. Francisco beamed proudly. I was stunned to see lots of black faces—middle-class mulattos—with clipped mustaches and slicked-back hair. And women, too, in high heels and hairdos tucked up in Betty Gable fashion, wielding scalpels over the cadavers.

"This surprises me," I said, pointing at the black faces. "How is it that so many students were black? I thought that the black population had no opportunities before the Revolution."

"Government lies!" Francisco replied. "We never had problems with racism." I wished he hadn't said that. It flew in the face of established fact.

What was indisputable was that I was staring down at a reality I had never imagined.

"Look," said Francisco, flipping to the back of the book. He ran his slender forefinger along the rows of photos showing each student smiling toward the camera. "Black...*Mestizo*...Mulata..." Every fourth or fifth student was either a person of color, female, or both.

I hadn't contemplated the idea of a Cuban black middle class. You never heard references to the middle class, period. As an entity, it had vanished from the land. Fidelismo was an agrarian-populist movement pitted against city-based middle-sector interests. It had warred against the old middle class and its bourgeois privilege, and destroyed them. But a black middle class? In that moment I realized how much prerevolutionary Cuba—at least in its urban component—must have resembled the United States in the days before its oppressed and powerless people shifted with the turmoil of the civil rights movement from "Negro" to "black." As Taylor Branch, author of the Pulitzer Prize-winning *Parting the Waters: America in the King Years 1954-63*, had written: "Truth requires a maximum effort to see through the eyes of strangers, foreigners, and enemies."

"Have care in the Oriente," said Cisne, blowing me a kiss. "They are not the same as Camagüeyans. And trust no one!"

"Write the truth, Cristóbal," Francisco implored, stabbing the air with his index finger. *"¡No mentiras!"*

As I motored away from Camagüey, Francisco's words echoed in my mind: "No lies!"

CHAPTER TEN

INTRIGUE IN BAYAMO

I spent the day roaming eastbound along the Carretera Central, making exploratory stabs at the sparsely populated south coast, where crocodiles slosh and gnash in swampy mangrove pools edging the dun-colored shore. Hovering on the hazy horizon out to sea and floating atop their own inverted mirage were scores of coral cays, cumulatively called the Jardines de la Reina (Garden of the Queen).

The countryside of Las Tunas province had a feeling of spaciousness that seemed to magnify the supercharged heat and barbarous wind. The stifling humidity didn't help. My head pounded inside my helmet. Catarrh raked my chest. I hiccuped tight little hacks as I rode, counting the miles by my coughs.

By midafternoon a turbulent front from the north had found its way to the island, and a watery gray ceiling of clouds cast a cold shadow over the plains. The earth seemed to breathe again, recovering from another day under the glare of the sun. I could almost hear it sigh with relief as a fine drizzle began to fall. I stopped and fished my leather jacket from the duffel bag.

The day wore on, weariness seeping into my arms and legs. I arrived at the Hotel Las Tunas feeling bushed. I shut the motor off and straddled the bike for what seemed like ages. No energy to move. In a daze, I listened to my cycle boots clomping across the lobby's linoleum floor; soon I was hauling my bags up concrete stairs to my room along hallways that smelled of harsh disinfectant.

Unloading the bike had become routine—a matter of minutes. But on this day no purgatory could have been more expatiating than unpacking those heavy bags. First came the large duffel, slung over my back like a corpse. Why had I packed so much? Next the two panniers—one containing my laptop computer (did I ever use it?) and research materials, the other crammed with plastic canisters of oil and spare parts for the bike. Then the expandable tank bag, which unzipped from its harness permanently strapped to the tank.

The elevator didn't work. The harsh rattle of my breath echoed in my ears as I repeatedly climbed the stairs, taking slow, plodding steps like a mountaineer on the final ascent of a summit. I stared at my ribs in the mirror, then sank onto the lumpy bed, malarial with misery.

In the restaurant, the air conditioning had been set at sub-zero. The menu was a wish list. I felt like I'd been placed on a starvation diet. Constantly ravenous, I could think of nothing but food. I bedded down early and slept fitfully while my empty stomach made strange rumblings, like bad plumbing.

Las Tunas is the small-time capital of a small-time province. Next morning I strolled around town, investigating the sites and making notes. The railway station lay farther out. My guidebook research included transportation facilities for each town, so I rode out that afternoon and parked the BMW where I could keep an eye on it while I jotted down the train timetable. Dozens of horse-drawn taxis—*coches*—stood in the tree-shaded plaza out front. In Cuba, nothing gets thrown away: not old cars, not old furniture, and certainly not old *volantas*—antique carriages with light bodies suspended as if in midair between enormous spoked wheels. Suspended, it seemed, like the country itself, in a strange kind of limbo, frozen between a romantic past and an uncertain future.

A friendly, rather tired-looking man about my age stepped up to the bike and began studying it intently. He was wiry but had a crushing handshake and a voluble tongue.

"It is very large. Very strong," he said, running his hands over the bike's haunches as if stroking a horse. "Bay...Em-ay...Doobla-vay." He pronounced the letters slowly, interpreting the BMW logo. "There is a similar *moto* in this town. Very old and very near."

He must mean a Ural.

"No, *señor*, it is a Bay Em-ay Doobla-vay. I will take you if you wish. Yes, it is the same make," he said, tracing his fingers around the edge of the blue-and-white logo on the gas tank. I was intrigued.

"Come!" I said, flipping down the rear pegs. He hopped aboard.

He guided me through unpaved, potholed back alleys and bade me pull up outside some tall metal gates. My passenger yelled, the gates swung open, and I was ushered into a small courtyard enclosed by high walls. It looked like a construction site. Stacks of ceramic tiles stood neatly amid large mounds of sand and heaps of concrete building blocks piled higgledy-piggledy. Luis Manuel Fernández, the owner, was adding an extension to the front of his house.

A motorbike stood in the center of the courtyard. Good Lord! It *was* a BMW.

The same year as Adolf Hitler, said 32-year-old Luis, a slender man with a thick crop of woolly black hair, a bushy mustache, a neatly clipped goatee, and a devilish grin. He looked more Mexican than Cuban. He was naked except for a pair of black sports shorts and flip-flops.

I guessed he meant that the bike had been built in the war years, but it looked younger, having been dolled up with a coat of cyan. Luis had bought it during a stint working in East Germany and shipped it to Cuba, he explained. He had added a racing fairing (with a shattered windshield), a tapered tail fender taken from a Czech-built MZ, and a huge, Teutonically rugged gas tank resembling a German Wehrmacht helmet. Luis had also welded on homemade aluminum footplates, one forming a handy support for a second battery that supplied power for the front lamp. The bike had 90,523 kilometers on the odometer.

I asked him what he did for spare parts, how he had kept it running all these years.

"*El cubano inventa, chico*," he replied, giving me a wink. Mostly he jury-rigs parts from Soviet Urals—or, failing that, any vehicle whose components can be tinkered with to fit.

I photographed Luis straddling the bike, gripping the handlebars like a racer, giving me that Cheshire-cat grin. He thanked me: "*Gracias, puro.*"

I wanted to ride it and asked Luis if he would fire it up, but the spark-plug leads lacked caps.

After loading the luggage, I check the bike. The oil level is fine, but I'm shocked to find the rear tire worn down on the left side. Must be because I've been traveling east, canted into the prevailing wind from the north.

No respite today. The cold front has arrived in earnest. I tool along, making miles. The moment I pass into Holguín province the road degenerates into a concrete conveyor belt of Swiss cheese, with holes big enough to bend a wheel. Then fat droplets begin drumming down from a sky as dark as *café cubano*, filling and obscuring the potholes. I groan and pull over to don my yellow rain slickers. As I zip up the jacket, a lightning bolt crashes down and thunder rumbles across the plains. I pass Cubans hunkered beneath tiny bus shelters.

Now it's really pelting down. I can barely see 30 feet ahead. The wind has picked up, too, adding to the gnawing chill. It tears and probes, gusting around me. *Keep your speed down.* I crouch behind the windshield and rest my chest on the tank bag. My sane half tells me to pull over, but some strange emotional inertia prevents me. I keep going, mile after miserable mile, the rain cascading down by the bucketful. I've switched on the heated grips to chase the chill from my fingers. In the far distance, off to the south, I see light at the end of the tunnel: The storm edge creates a remarkable scene, with clouds roiling in a tumbling slow motion of marmoreal colors—mauve, purple, and gold-tinged taupe—heralded by a fanfare of double rainbows that spell sunshine.

I skirt Holguín city and curl southwest, determined to outrun the storm, which soon dissipates to a steady drizzle. With the wind now behind me, I fairly fly across the floodplain of the Río Cauto, chasing chimerical rainbows down the glistening, ruler-straight highway. A warm, humid breeze swirls heavily under the clearing sky. I can see the Sierra Maestra hovering ghostly gray beyond. Then the sun burns through the mist like a great glaring headlamp, basking the rain-soaked flatlands in blazing light. Steam rises ethereally from the warming earth.

Beyond Cacocún the highway is lined with clusters of small thatched *bohíos*, each in its own little garden fenced by tightly packed cactus shaped like candelabra, neatly and lovingly trimmed. Topiary begins to appear, clipped into rondels and cones. For 20 miles or more, the mark of the scissor is on every bush. The *campesinos* hereabouts are fighting a friendly feud with their pruning shears.

José Martí's image hovers Christ-like over the *carretera*, his somber visage offering a martyred benediction as I pass into Granma province.

Granma tapers southwestward like an arrow tip piercing the Caribbean Sea, with the sharp point at Cabo Cruz. It is neatly divided into a great green wash of plain fanning out to the north and, to the south, a deep brooding mountain massif—the Sierra Maestra—running from Cabo Cruz to the city of Santiago de Cuba, 100 miles to the east. It is forbidding terrain. The mountains rise gradually, then plummet scarp-faced to the ruler-straight coast, with a narrow littoral at their base.

On the outskirts of Bayamo I tank up with gas, then use the compressed-air nozzle to blast a cloud of dust from my air cleaner. The bike has been breathing asthmatically. I check the oil. The dipstick comes up bone-dry. Once again, I'm lucky the engine hasn't seized up.

I haven't given much thought to breakdowns. The BMW's horizontally opposed twin-cylinder engine, dating to 1923, has been improved to peak efficiency over the decades. I'm banking on its renowned reliability to get me through. To be defeated by my own inabilities or—heaven forbid—an accident would be one thing; to be done in by a mechanical failure of my own making would be almost too much to bear.

I feel consumed by a gnawing foreboding.

The toilet seat is missing from my room in the Hotel Sierra Maestra, and the hot-water faucets don't work. Piped music is blaring in the lobby and through the corridors, so loud that it distorts the speakers. My head is throbbing. When I ask the receptionist if it can be turned down, I get a blank stare. At least the elegant restaurant looks hopeful. But that's too much to wish. The service is bad, as usual. Not rude—just slow and uncaring. And the fish that I order could pass for shoe leather. So could my *papas*, which are served hard and floating in grease. How can you screw up potato fries? My salad consists of sliced cabbage. It is one of the worst hotel meals I've had in Cuba. Even the *congrí*—beans and rice—is barely edible.

I send my fish back to the cobbler.

"It's like a *zapato*—a shoe!" I tell the waitress. She doesn't laugh.

"You don't want it?" She seems incredulous.

Groups of Cubans are sitting around in tank tops and shorts, inured to the chill. They are supping Hatuey beers and devouring the disagreeable food with gusto.

The supervisor arrives. I repeat my complaint. She shrugs her shoulders. Her indifference makes me mad.

"How is it possible to overcook fish like this? *It isn't beef!*" I yell. The Cuban diners look up from their plates. I wish to disturb them from their national doze by telling them some home truths. I have become an ugly American. My manners must appear atrocious.

"You don't want it?" the supervisor asks in disbelief, as if I am refusing prime sirloin. The fish has been grilled to a blackened crisp. It is curled up at the edges and defiantly resilient when I try to cut it. When I break through the surface, I get into a swordfight with the bones.

The supervisor frowns and walks away.

The sole dessert—*fruta bomba*—is canned. I order orange juice, which never arrives but appears on my bill. Francisco's words resound in my mind: Cuba is a culinary catastrophe!

Heads should have been rolling, but for fear of retribution Cubans never complain. I could send my food back night after night and know that nothing would change. No one is accountable.

I ask for a Hatuey, my favorite beer.

"¡No hay!" replies the waitress. She brings me a Cristal, a lighter brew. I notice that the Cubans are drinking Hatuey.

"Is Hatuey only for Cubans?"

"Cristal is better."

"But I prefer Hatuey."

"I think that Cristal is better quality," she replies.

Hello! Whose life is this?

Then the power goes out. I sit in the dark, cradling fulminations in my crossed arms.

I felt awful and retired to bed after my spectacular dinner. I dreamed of Daisy. Her tomboy smile. The curves of her breasts. The softly whispered words. I lay drifting and tortured, panting, fevered, clinging shallowly to a memory already fading to myth.

My phone rang. Groggy, I put the receiver to my ear and heard a mysterious voice ask if I would like to meet someone special.

"Excuse me?" I replied.

"I saw you in the park today, alone," said the stranger in Spanish. "I have a friend who wants to meet you. I will wait for you in the lobby."

I hung up, but the conspiratorial invitation had piqued my interest. Cuba is like that. You never want to sleep for fear of missing a vital experience. I never knew what adventure would strike me when I got up in the morning. Now here was a guy who had followed me three miles from Parque Céspedes to the hotel—I had walked—then waited until dark to determine my room and entice me with an offer of a nocturnal encounter. Cuba was laced with sharp edges and sinister shadows.

Since Camagüey, I had a new concern as well. Francisco and Cisne had put themselves at serious risk by entertaining me so openly and speaking with such candor. And it was all there in my notebooks. So too my own ruminations, less sanguine than I could ever have imagined. Paranoia was my constant companion. Protecting my notebooks became an obsession.

I wondered if the call was a ruse. *Maybe the stranger is trying to lure me from my room so that MININT agents can search it.* I hid my laptop bag containing my notebooks behind the shower curtain. Feeling like James Bond, I slipped into the hallway, pulled the door almost closed, then reached in through the narrow opening, unscrewed the top from a tiny bottle of cologne, and placed the bottle on the floor flush against the door, which I then closed. If someone entered my room in my absence, he or she would knock the bottle over and I would know.

I slipped past a crowd of Cubans watching television in the mezzanine lounge.

Who were those two men lingering in the lobby, scowling at me as I passed? I could feel their stares on the back of my neck.

The lobby was empty. I walked outside, looked around, saw no one. Then someone slipped unseen from the shadows and whispered in my ear, scaring the dickens out of me. Where had *he* come from? I didn't understand what he said, nor did I see what he looked like. He moved away swiftly and melded into the blackness.

My nerves were tingling. I felt as if I was living in a John le Carré novel.

I walked back inside. The two men were gone. Worried, I rushed upstairs to my room; the bottle of cologne was undisturbed, my notebooks secure in their bag behind the shower curtain.

Unable to relax, I returned to the lobby and ordered a shot of rum at the bar. I picked up where I had left off in Pico Iyer's *Cuba and the Night*, the story of an American photographer in Havana who gets drawn into a passionate affair with a vivacious young cubana under the watchful eyes of the secret police. Intoxicated with a fervid psychosis, I wallowed in Iyer's sinister and sobering plot.

Suddenly a shadow fell over the book.

I whirled around.

A tall black man stood over me. He was in his thirties, handsome, and neatly dressed in crisply pressed jeans and a white dress shirt.

"Excuse me for disturbing you. I think you are number 417, no?" he said arcanely, as if exchanging a secret code with a fellow spy. That was my room number.

"Perhaps," I replied cautiously. *Perhaps?* That sounded stupid.

"I called you," he said, lifting his hand as if to answer a phone. He asked if I wanted a *chica.* He revealed that she was his cousin. I wondered if whoever he had in mind knew that he wanted to pimp her.

I really wasn't interested in a girl. Physically I felt terrible. It was the intrigue of the exchange that stirred me.

"Depende," I said. *It depends.* "I am very fussy. She has to be extremely beautiful." I tried to make my voice sound indifferent in the hope that this might cool his heels. Fat chance. The women of Bayamo are said to be the prettiest in all Cuba; last century they had inspired "La Bayamesa," the national anthem and the most famous of all Cuban love songs.

"No problema," he replied. He smiled and strode out into the night.

I slipped from the bar, hurried back upstairs, and took the phone off the hook.

Bayamo, founded in 1513, is Cuba's third oldest settlement. During the late-19th century quest for independence from Spain, the city was the setting for some consequential events. Spanish colonial policy, applied throughout its empire, was based on exploitation, with power centralized in Madrid and politics practiced solely for the benefit of *peninsulares*—native-born Spaniards—who treated Cuba as a cash cow to milk. Cuban-born *criollos* resented the conceited and corrupt *peninsulares,* who disdained them and kept a monopolistic hold on the administration of Cuba. The criollo whites (most of whom carried some degree of black blood in their veins) considered themselves Cuban, not Spanish, and felt much like American colonials born in the mid-18th century had felt toward King George III and Great Britain.

Those were boom days for sugar in Cuba, and fortunes were being made. The criollo planters of southeastern Cuba, however, were isolated, relatively poor and struggling, unable to compete with modern plantation systems inaugurated elsewhere in Cuba. By the 19th century, talk of autonomy and emancipation were in the air, and Bayamo's bourgeoisie—influenced by the American War of Independence and the revolutionary fervor then sweeping Europe—were at the forefront of the swelling movement.

Alistair Cooke, in his BBC television series *Alistair Cooke's America*, had this to say: "In the weaning of colonies from mother countries there is usually a moment of organic change—an 'episode,' as the doctors call it, which is seen only later to have been decisive." Cuba's "episode" came in 1867, when the elite of Bayamo, led by a 48-year-old lawyer, planter, poet, and revolutionary named Carlos Manuel Céspedes, rose in revolt against the motherland following the coup that toppled Spain's Queen Isabella. On October 10, 1868, Céspedes freed the slaves on his estate at La Demajagua, near Manzanillo; then, in an oration known as the Grito de Yara, he declared an open revolt against Spain.

The rebellion spread quickly throughout Oriente. With a small force that included his liberated slaves, Céspedes marched on Bayamo and captured it from Spanish forces. Soon he had an army of 1,200 men at his command. The actions sparked the War of Independence that swept Oriente and central Cuba, ravaging the region for ten long years. In January 1869, as Céspedes' army was attacking Holguín, Spanish troops were at Bayamo's doorstep. The rebellious citizens burned their beloved city to the ground rather than cede it to Spanish troops. But internal dissent arose among the revolutionary leadership, and in 1873 Céspedes was removed from his position as President of the Republic in a meeting to which no one had bothered to invite him. He was cut down in a hail of bullets a year later, ambushed by the Spanish at San Lorenzo, where he had retreated to await a ship that would carry him to exile.

Remarkably, Céspedes' birthplace—a handsome two-story dwelling, now a museum, on the north side of Parque Céspedes—survived the conflagration that consumed much of Bayamo's historic core, which has been beautifully restored and preserved as a national monument. At the park's center was a granite column topped by a larger-than-life bronze statue of the Father of Our Country with carved motifs to each side depicting scenes from Céspedes' traumatic life. I sat among the townsfolk who had congregated to schmooze and flirt on marble-and-wrought-iron benches beneath trees whose leaves rustled with twittering birdsong.

Two old ladies, each with a walking cane, moved aside and held out their hands, beckoning me to sit down beside them. One of the women, a bespectacled, gray-haired *mulata*, offered to share her *buñuelo*—a deep-fried pastry made of flour and yucca root. So decent and considerate, like most Cubans. I looked into her eyes. They were vibrant, engaged.

Other than horse-drawn coches clopping by, the plaza was delightfully free of traffic, yet throbbing with traditional life. Men and women showed up to chat in the shade and play music while their laughing children chased each other in games of tag, played marbles atop the timeworn flagstones, and raced shoe-box-size carriages on tin wheels attached to broom handles.

Bayameses seemed the happiest of people, spiritually alive and at peace with themselves. I felt uptight and self-absorbed in comparison. Cubans, by their example, were showing me another way. Their heartrending warmth and disarming charm, their spirituality, their genteel expressions of human acceptance, their global innocence, their dignity and stylish forbearance, and—above all— their courage in the face of adversity made me feel ungracious.

"Cristóbal, you very serious," Daisy had told me. "You should smile more." She was unmoved by talk of my material accomplishments. Most Cubans were. They took pleasure in simple things, and they rarely complained. They were more concerned with *living* life, more concerned with sharing something with me than getting something from me.

"We may not have much," said the old mulata as we sat in the calming shade, "but we have the essentials. And, more importantly, we know how to enjoy life." We were sharing her *buñuelo* and my chocolate-chip cookies, which I had bought at a ServiCupet's dollar store.

I asked her to name Cuba's biggest problem.

"There is nothing wrong with our system, it is only the economy that needs fixing," she replied, parroting a phrase I heard often. "Things would not be so bad if the capitalists were not trying to starve us into submission. Your blockade causes much pain."

She laid her palm on my knee to let me know that she felt no malice toward me. Cubans didn't resent *los yanquis*. Only once, in all my visits to Cuba, had I come up against a hostile reaction based on where I came from.

"I'm English, by the way," I replied defensively.

"They should leave us alone," chimed in the second woman. She was white, with noble, angular Hispanic features and, in comical counterpoint, silver hair rolled up in plastic curlers. She was wearing a pale-blue Gucci T-shirt, plaid shorts, ankle socks, and sky-blue sandals.

From what I had witnessed, Castro retains the loyalty and affection of millions of Cubans, notably in the countryside. Urbanites, however, seemed lukewarm at best; most city folk I spoke to were tired of Fidel. But Bayamo seemed different: Fidel fever ran deep.

"We are proud of our revolution," said the mulata. "North Americans don't understand what the Revolution has meant to us. We owe all our accomplishments to Fidel. Life is a *lucha,* but hardship is nothing knew to us. I am black. I grew up poor."

"Cuba is not like Eastern Europe, you know," said the white, her voice soft and calm but full of pride. "We all participated in the Revolution and we gave ourselves willingly. The Soviets had nothing to do with it. Your government wants to dictate to us, but we don't want your system. We don't want to return to our bitter past."

CHAPTER ELEVEN

GETTING ORIENTED

Está jodido el coche!" The old man shrugged his shoulders.

The car was a cream-colored Chevrolet Styleline Deluxe, smooth and dentless, gleaming as brightly as the summer day in 1952 when it rolled out of its factory in Detroit. A yanqui anachronism. A grande dame with a potent, curvaceous solidity and a big, firm, well-rounded rear end like the *nalgas* of a robust *mulatta*.

I had been cruising along in a state of Zen-like meditation, absorbed by the scenery, enjoying the warm wind on my face, all alone with my thoughts, when I flew past this antediluvian automotive *abuelo*, dead as a dinosaur, stopped in the middle of the road in the middle of nowhere. I hadn't seen a vehicle—not a single car—for miles. Then this shapely Chevy staring me down with its acres of bechromed grillwork.

It wasn't the fact that the thing had broken down that caused me to turn around. Hell, broken-down cars were part of the Cuban reality. But this shining example had a come-hither allure that arrested me dead in my tracks. Time itself seemed to have stopped on the *carretera* midway between Bayamo and Veguitas. The Chevy bespoke a more elegant age, inviting me to peer in through the green-tinted windows and steep in pride-in-America sentimentality.

I hit the brakes, made a U-turn, and pulled up to those sumptuous *nalgas*. Faces pressed up against the back window. Then people began piling out. Four. Five. Six. All youths. I half-expected them to be wearing saddle shoes and Brylcreemed hair. The old man rolled down his window. I peered in. Perfectly preserved leather upholstery. Powerglide transmission. And—can you believe it?—air conditioning.

The grandpa's brown melon face lit up in a toothless grin.

"¿Qué pasa?" I asked the old man sitting in the soothing sanctuary of the backseat, out of the blistering heat. *What happened?*

"It's fucked!" the *viejo* repeated in fluent, lightly accented English. "It's fucked up. The driver has gone—God knows where."

He didn't have a clue what was wrong with the car. Nor, apparently, did the driver, who had vanished. The old man pointed across the empty fields to indicate the direction.

"Why didn't he walk along the road?"

"Who knows? This is Cuba. Who says things have to be done in a logical fashion? We've been here for hours."

The scorching wind was almost peeling the paint off the Chevy. I didn't envy him or the others.

"Sí hombre, ¡así vivimos!" the old man exclaimed, an incongruous smile on his lips. *Yes, hombre, this is how we live!* He began giggling like a laughing hyena.

In Cuba you had to laugh. If you didn't, the bizarre banalities would drive you crazy. I admired Cuban stoicism and felt a deep respect for the way the people faced their hardships with grace and style. They never seemed to lose their sense of humor.

The adolescents—five boys, one girl—had been ogling the motorcycle, but seeing me pull out my camera they began dancing around like a bunch of circus monkeys. Charles Atlas poses melded into cool-dude, hands-on-hips, rapper-in-da-hood poses and, settling down now for the group shot, nonchalant gangster postures leaning on the Chevy fenders. Cubans love being photographed, never more so than in front of a vintage *cacharro*.

I wished them good luck and remounted my bike.

The girl begged me—*"por favor, señor"*—to take her for *un vuelo*—a "flight"— down the road. Her name was Yudelmi; she was 15 and pretty in a homey, country-girl way. She was dressed in white moccasins, a turquoise halter top, and tight, pale-blue jeans rolled up to the shins.

"Of course," I replied. "But you realize if I take you for a ride, you might not return."

The old man cracked up. "Take her. The little bird now has wings."

Yudelmi smiled and jimmied herself between me and the duffel. I roared off, moving up rapidly through the gears with the tacho near the end of the dial, then eased off when the speedo read 80. She gasped. Her arms squeezed me tightly.

"You like it?"

"*Sí, sí...¡muchísimo!*"

Her brothers eagerly awaited their turns with beseeching faces. I gave the youngest a ride, then said that I needed to get going. Disappointment was written on their faces, another dream having passed the youths by.

At Yara I experienced one of those strange events that strike with a momentous gravity that can be judged only later. I'd noticed the front brake growing spongy during the past few days. At Yara the bike was reluctant to stop and the front disc screeched like a stuck pig.

Martin, my older brother, is a mechanical marvel. So is my father, and his dad before him. I am a mechanical moron. It didn't matter how much I studied the owner's manual, I didn't get it. Mechanics is no different from art or aesthetics. It's a talent, an appreciation. You're either blessed with what it takes, or you aren't. I can no more diagnose a worn valve guide or bent connecting rod than the average layman can diagnose Lou Gehrig's disease.

So here I am in Yara with the sun beating down, while curious onlookers gather to watch the foreigner in his sweltering leathers as he opens his Haynes *Owners' Workshop Manual* for BMW two-valve twins and spreads it on the ground.

I start with the easy stuff.

Check the brake fluid level. Looks fine. *Check the brake pads.* I read slowly, then follow the directions. Mechanics by numbers.

It looks like I'll have to remove the front brake calipers.

I unpack the bike to get to the tool kit beneath the seat. There must be 20 spectators by now, watching with solemn curiosity from a discreet distance of, oh, about six feet. No one says a word. I feel as if I'm on stage.

I unclip the plastic cover from the calipers, tap out the retaining pins, and remove the pads. *Blimey!* They're worn down to less than a hair's breadth. The gossamer of friction material is so thin that on one the base metal shows through. Fortunately I'm carrying spare pads.

Now the going gets tricky. I'm having trouble inserting the new pads. The caliper pistons refuse to move back into their bores. I defer to Haynes, which informs me that it "should be possible to do this with hand pressure only." I push. I lever. But the pistons refuse to budge.

The crowd has edged closer.

I study the text, trying not to appear as if I am floundering over such a simple mechanical task. I can't believe it. Sweat pours down my chest and spine.

Then a providential hand reaches down and takes the wrench from me. Without speaking, the stranger gently edges me aside, flips the covers off the bleed nipples and loosens them with a tweak of the wrench. Brake fluid begins to seep. Is *that* in the book? I read furiously. Haynes hasn't mentioned anything about loosening the nipples, but it does warn against seepage of brake fluid. The stranger has lodged my screwdriver inside the caliper assembly and is now putting his full weight into levering the pistons into their bores. I'm frightened he'll break something. I tap him on the shoulder to indicate caution.

"*¡Sí, sí, señor!*" he replies, loosening the nipples some more until the bloody dribble is a full-blown hemorrhage. His arm quakes from the strain of levering.

"*¡Cuidado!*" I scream. Be careful!

He fires me a look of utmost disdain.

The pistons ease back. He slides the new pads in, tightens the nipples, stands, and steps back into the crowd. I feel totally foolish.

"Thank you. I've never been a good mechanic," I say pathetically. He nods and shrugs his shoulders.

"You're a foreigner. In Cuba everyone must be a mechanic," he says, waving away my five-dollar bill.

I turned south and ran through impossibly green rice fields unfolding toward the Sierra Maestra, reflected in the dirty mirror of the Río Yara. From below, the mountains seemed like an impenetrable wall, gathering in serried ranges and forbidding valleys. Mulberry-colored plumes tipped the highest peaks. Ideal guerrilla territory.

At Bartolomé Masó the cement road began to climb, with the gradient soon so severe that tiny channels had been etched across the road at two-inch intervals for added traction. I dropped into second gear. The more I climbed, the more the road curved, winding in dizzying coils.

The climb spread the isle at my feet. Every other turn offered a heart-stopping drop-off, with spectacular vistas down through the steep, boulder-strewn ravines. I paused to breathe in the mountain air and listen to the agreeable silence, broken only by birdsong and the buzz of myriad insects. A few tiny *bohíos* perched on the slopes. Meager dwellings of adobe and thatch, most had coffee beans spread out to dry on small patches of hard-packed earth. There is electricity now, and telephones, and running water no longer consists of a boy with a bucket. Rural clinics and schools built during the past four decades have inestimably improved the lot of the local peasantry. But most of the hardy and humble mountain folk still get up at the crack of dawn to tend steep-pitched plots from which they eke out a subsistence living, as did their forebears. *Campesinos.* Living in a time warp. And enchanting for it.

A campesino passed by, leading a donkey saddled with well-worn wicker baskets laden with shiny red and green coffee beans. His face had an almost feminine delicacy beneath bronzed skin as hard-worn as his home-spun pants.

We greeted each other. His tight eyes regarded me quizzically. After a few pleasantries, he thawed enough for me to ask whether he sold what he grew.

"Only coffee. And peppers."

"What about marijuana?" I asked mischievously. "Is there much of that in the mountains?" Before the Revolution, it too had been an important cash crop hereabouts.

"We are only campesinos here," he replied elliptically.

When I asked if I could take his photo, he responded enthusiastically—"*¡Por favor!*"—and adopted a dignified pose, full of sunny pride. He thanked me before I could say the same, then invited me to visit his home, which he pointed out far down the hillside, tucked into an earthen yard edged by carefully tended crotons. I thanked him but asked, with all good intent, if I could perhaps visit on the way back down the hill. As it was, on my return journey I couldn't find the spot where we met. The world would be a better place if all men were as gracious.

Five miles south of a hamlet called Providencia, the road spiraled down dramatically to the Río Yara—I splashed across—and thence launched a first-gear assault so dauntingly sheer that I wished I'd brought crampons. The hairpin bends were enough to stump anything that didn't have hoofs. *Mi moto Fidel* was a mountain goat. I felt my heart beating faster. Incredibly, impossibly, those last hundred yards grew yet steeper. The gradient must have been 40 degrees. Thank God the smooth, big-bored Beemer was geared low and pumped out the oodles of low-rev torque that I needed, spilling me onto a ridge crest where the road stopped abruptly in a tiny turnout at the gateway to Parque Nacional Turquino. I pulled the bike onto the center stand and gasped at the superlative view back down the mountain. I was breathing deep, hearty breaths and grinning inanely, unable to imagine a more rhapsodic feeling.

It was hard to imagine, too, that four decades ago war was waged amid the sweet peace of these mountains. In 1956-59, this rugged region had served as the headquarters for Castro's Rebel Army. I had arrived at Alto del Naranjo and the trailhead to La Comandancia de la Plata, Castro's former guerrilla headquarters. A wooden sign pointed the way along a narrow, tortuous trail that led two miles to the camp, now a rustic shrine, with simple wooden structures concealed by thick branches deep in the fern-festooned forest. A second trail headed in the other direction to Pico Turquino; at 6,514 feet, it is Cuba's highest peak. I was tempted to ride to the top and claim my mark on Cuban history, a fanciful thought scuttled by the appearance of a *custodio*—a park guard—drawn from some hidden lair by the sound of the motorcycle. He seemed astonished that I had gotten this far without official permission. Apparently, a permit and guide are obligatory to travel beyond Santo Domingo, a village far below in the valley. He took me to task, then offered to guide me to La Plata, but warned that given the late hour, we would not return to Alto de Naranjo before dusk. The road down the mountain was not one I wished to ride in the dark.

"What about taking my motorcycle?"

My request to ride to La Plata elicited a scoff. He shook his head and replied that the track—tough clambering over rocks and mud—was beyond any moto.

I pressed the starter button. From the ridge crest the narrow road looked like the world's longest ski-jump. With bends. I took a deep breath as I stared down that hellish hill, then shook the brief terror from my head, put the bike in first, and eased out the clutch. Down I went with the throttle shut, using the engine for drag, my right hand and foot tight on the brakes and my ears popping from the loss in altitude. A shiver ran through me. To have tackled this mountain with worn brake pads would have been a certain invitation to suicide. No way could I have held the bike on that hill. I had been saved by a fortuitous fluke in Yara.

Someone quacks me.

After six weeks, I am weary of seeing the sign. Whenever I pass through a sleepy town, I feel as if I am passing a parade of geese. It's like watching a human wave move through the crowd in a football stadium. A rhythmic, predictable raising of the hands, then the calls begin: *"Lalooshendi!"*

"Quack, quack!" I reply as I zip past, making my own quacking motion. Sometimes I'll shout out, "Quack, quack!" too, lusciously. That only makes them quack more furiously. They take to screaming: *"¡La luz! ¡Lalooshendi!"*

This is fun. I enjoy their dumbfounded looks when I quack back. After a while, though, even that becomes boring. I try to ignore the gaggle, but in my morose state the quacking begins to grate.

Entering Bayamo, I see a hand rise.

"*Sí*, you idiot!" I mutter ungraciously.

Quack, quack!

"Turkey!"

Quack, quack!

"Quack, quack!" I reply.

Quack, quack, quack!

I keep going.

"¡La luz encendida!"

"To hell with *lalooshendi!*"

On the coastal plains south of Manzanillo, the sugarcane fields have been burnt for the *zafra*, the sugar harvest, and smoke-smudged field hands—*macheteros*—in tattered linens and sombreros of rough straw are slashing at the charred stalks with glinting, blunt-nosed machetes. Hot, dirty work. They look as if they themselves have been put to the torch. Black smoke rises in twirling tornadoes over the fields, eddying up from *centrales* that taint the idyll with the cloying stench of molasses.

Snowy egrets lift up like silken kites as I flash by.

In the somnolent sugar town of Media Luna, I pause at the simple green-and-white gingerbread house where revolutionary heroine Celia Sánchez was born on May 9, 1920. Sánchez, the "Most Beautiful Flower of the Revolution," was 30 years old when she met Fidel Castro for the first time on February 16, 1957—the beginning of a 33-year association during which she was the most important person in Castro's life. This intelligent and attractive woman, the daughter of a local doctor, set up and ran Castro's urban and peasant-based intelligence and supply networks under the noses of Batista's spies. She became Castro's secretary, compass, and lover. Later, Sánchez kept him in touch with the people, and was one of only a handful of people who could give him news and opinions he didn't want to hear. Her death to cancer in 1980 profoundly shook the Cuban leader and removed from his life the one person to whom he could let down his mask.

I am still coughing, but my tiredness has faded away. I feel deliriously light-hearted, enjoying the BMW's hypnotically steady harmonics as I cruise down the empty road with the mountains on one side and the sea on the other. All my senses are alive. I am riding with a heightened awareness, almost as if I'm floating, so attuned to the bike and my surroundings—the smells, the sun's rays, the warm wind caressing my skin—that I am not even thinking. Me and *mi moto* fused as one.

The road to Niquero is straight and fast, and I am cruising in a reverie when I spot a *tráfico* coming the other way.

He flashes his headlight.

I take it as a fraternal greeting—one motorcyclist to another. I flash my high beam.

He raises his hand like a duck's beak. *Quack, quack!*

Oh, that! The cop gets no response.

He is almost upon me, closing fast, and quacking furiously.

I quack back and permit myself a perverse smile. We're engaged in a motor-cycle joust with hand puppets in lieu of lances.

As we flash past each other he motions furiously for me to pull over. I glance down at my speedometer—55—and keep going.

I enjoy chatting with curious *tráficos*, but this day I prefer to be left alone. I glance in my mirror, see him turning around. *Damn it!* I pour on the gas.

I have about 500 yards on the cop, who is now flashing his headlight on and off, trying to arrest me by semaphore. He is hunched low like a possum, whipping his Jawa 350 as if this is the Isle of Man TT race. *Hmm, looks like he's gaining.* I tweak the throttle some more and take the bike above 60. This is more fun than I've had since that night with David and Roger in the Cabaret Parisienne. I'm laughing madly.

Oops! Now his blue light is flashing.

I ease back the throttle and pull over about a mile down the road.

"*¡Buenos días!*" I say as he leaps from his bike and storms toward me, his face snarling.

"Why didn't you stop?" he booms in Spanish. A gobbet of spittle hits my sunglasses. He's so mad he can barely breathe.

"I didn't see you?" I reply calmly.

He screams again. Same question. If he keeps this up, he'll give himself a thrombosis.

I remain composed. "I was doing nothing wrong," I say serenely.

"You have your headlight on. *Why?* Why do you have your light on?"

"It isn't possible to turn it...."

He interrupts me midstream, points at my headlamp and, still screaming, says that it is against the law.

"In California"—I stress the name lusciously—"the law says that motorcycles must have their headlights on at all times."

"This is Cuba!"

"Lighten up!" I reply, testing his English.

He is not amused.

"*¡Documentos!*"

I give him my international driving license and the *licencia* issued in Havana. He accuses me of speeding.

"*No es posible, señor,*" I respond, building up to the most glorious lie I have ever told. Remembering something I had learned in traffic court, I inform him that my speedometer has recently been calibrated by the

California Highway Patrol; I can therefore be certain, I explain, that I never exceeded the speed limit.

"Perhaps *your* speedometer needs calibrating," I suggest cheekily, easing myself from the saddle and leaning my bike on the side stand. "Your bike looks quite old. It's Czechoslovakian, isn't it?" I inquire, running my fingers across the cracked glass of the Jawa's instrument panel. You have to feel sorry for a traffic cop forced to chase a 58-horsepower BMW on a two-stroke motorcycle made in communist Europe.

"How fast does it go?" I continue, pondering whether this might put the air back in his deflated bubble, then realizing that I have delivered my *coup de grace.*

"Go!" he snarls, handing me my documents and raising a half-hearted salute that I shall treasure forever. I press the starter button and roar off, winding the twin up to 6,000 rpm on each shift and relishing pushing the tach needle up the dial.

South from Medea Luna, a warm wind gives a helping hand from behind. What a difference it makes not to have the headwinds wearing me down. But this southwestern corner of Cuba has its own microclimate in the rain shadow of the Sierra Maestra, and the heat is oppressive. The cylinder heat is cooking my ankles. I take off my shirt and ride bare-topped along a hard-top road that amazes me for being newly paved—a first for Cuba.

The Day-Glo cane fields have long since receded, replaced by thorn scrub, parched and withered, growing amid patches of bare earth glowing honey-brown in the afternoon light. Cacti push up from the alluvial plain that washes down to a mangrove-lined shore whose orange sands give the area its name: Las Coloradas. In the midst of drought the vegetation has exploded in vibrant colors, and the hot, heavy air is redolent with desert bouquets. I feel a sharp sting on my cheek. *Wasps!* I duck down behind the windshield to prevent protoplasm spattering on my glasses.

The road hugs the narrow coastal littoral that stairsteps up from the shore toward the Sierra Maestra in orderly terraces. Unawares—there is no sign to tell me—I enter Desembarco del Granma National Park, named for the spot where Fidel and Raúl Castro, Che Guevara, and some 80 other rebels came ashore on December 2, 1956, to launch the Cuban Revolution. Hallowed ground.

Castro and his revolutionaries had set out from Tuxpán, Mexico, shortly after midnight on November 25, 1956 for a hellish 1,235-mile crossing aboard the *Granma*, a vessel designed to carry 25 passengers. With a burden of 82 heavily armed men and supplies, the boat lurched laboriously toward Cuba in violent seas.

On November 30, the date scheduled for the landing, Celia Sánchez gathered five trucks and several dozen supporters at a Cuban beach called Playa Las Coloradas. They were to meet the rebels and transport them to Media Luna, where they would seize arms from Batista's troops and move into the Sierra Maestra. Unknown to Sánchez, however, an engine had failed and the boat was two days behind schedule. Castro ordered rationing; for the last two days, there was neither food nor water.

At dawn on December 2, the ship ran aground two miles south of the planned landing site amid an almost impenetrable mangrove swamp, where the revolutionaries instantly came under attack—from fierce mosquitoes. "This wasn't a landing," Guevara recalled, "it was a shipwreck." (When Sergei Yevtushenko asked Fidel to reenact the landing for the movie *Soy Cuba!*, Fidel told him to get an actor to do it. Once was enough.)

The exact spot where the *Granma* ran aground is a national monument.

I put the BMW on its stand and take a photograph of it next to a replica of the vessel resting on pedestals beneath a corrugated tin roof. Then I follow the cement pathway that leads through the hellish mangroves and disgorges me at the exact spot where the *Granma* came ashore. There is nothing to see, nothing to indicate that this wretched place was the pivotal point for Castro's long-dreamed revolution.

Famished mosquitoes whine in my ears. I retreat hastily to the safety of a concrete structure resembling a German bunker in Normandy. To one side is a small museum. Its sole exhibit is a map showing the route of the *desembarcaderos* and a larger-than-life black-and-white photograph of a youthful Fidel amid the mangroves. Attached, in large script, is a quote from Bertolt Brecht: "There are men who fight for a day, and they are good. There are others that fight a year, and they are better. There are some who fight many years, and they are very good. But there are those who fight all their life; they are the indispensable ones." It is a subtle piece of hero worship of the kind that *el jefe* favors.

It feels good to briefly get above the plains as I weave east through the foothills of the Sierra Maestra via cool vales of rust-red earth farmed in colorful counterpoint with a quiltwork of arable crops and tobacco. It is beautiful, and especially so toward the end of day, with the glinting light gilding the palms and flitting through the fronds. Beyond Sevilla the road swoops sharply down through a narrow ravine, spilling me onto the coastal plains along the southern base of the Sierra Maestra. On the long straight I move into top gear and open the throttle wide.

I tank up on gas at the fly-blown town of Pilón, where a thermometer under a shady eave reads 104 degrees. Farther east, the landscape changes abruptly. The mountains wring the rain from the clouds so that the narrow coastal plain is a virtual desert. I pass goats and hardy zebu cattle munching in stony pastures in the lee of penurious hills dotted with cactus.

North of the Sierra Maestra, the humid climate had acted as a mollifier for my chest. Now the dry heat is insufferable. I gasp asthmatically at the hot rushing air. Then I begin hacking up orange phlegm. *Blood!* I'm too fatigued to enjoy the scenery building to a stupendous climax.

With great relief I arrive at Villa Marea del Portillo, one of half a dozen resorts sprinkled along this remote shore. The hotel is enfolded by a vast bay that is a symphony in sand and stone—the turquoise waters of the bay a pretty aria and the mountains escalating to cloud-draped crescendos, with muscular flanks as monodies, thickly wooded and sheer.

I pull up unsteadily and cut the engine. As I step from the bike it begins to tilt. I'm so exhausted that I lack even the will to resist. I make a token effort and lean my featherweight body into the Beemer, but the Brobdingnag falls as if in a slow-motion movie. I turn off the fuel cocks and let the motorcycle lie there until the bell clerk arrives to help me haul it upright. Lethargically I carry my bags to my room, then collapse on the bed and find consolation in the view through the sliding plate-glass doors. Canadian package tourists from the snowy north are flopped grotesquely on the sand like beached belugas.

Fortunately, the resort—jointly operated by Commonwealth Hotels of Canada and the state tourism agency, Cubanacán—has a doctor on site. After a fitful snooze, I set out to find him.

Out by the pool, a Cuban band is putting its heart and soul into putting the northerners in a Cuban mood. But the audience hasn't thawed. I feel sorry for the performers.

"Going deep-sea fishing?" one of the Canadians asks, staring quizzically at my leather pants. I haven't found the energy to remove them. She is fiftyish and flabby, and dressed in a matching orange outfit: orange polka-dot skirt and orange pants to match her ginger hair tied in a ponytail with orange ribbons. Her face is orange, too, from a surfeit of sun. She looks like a carrot on its way to a Halloween ball. She tells me she's from Kent, England, but has lived in Toronto for the last 15 years. I tell her that I've lived in California for the same amount of time.

"Oh, I adore California. I was there quite recently...in Beverly Hills, of course. I dined at Spago. Thought I might see some movie stars." It had been *"terribly disappointing."* The only famous figure there had been Oscar Peterson, the jazz pianist. How "recently" was she there, I wonder?

"I ask you! I can see him any time in Toronto. He plays concerts there all the time," she adds disdainfully. "Oh, and Merv Griffin was there, and what's his name. Yul Brynner. No, not him. The other bald man. Telly Savalas."

She makes it sound as if she had somehow been duped, traveling to California to be rewarded with second-rate stars and dead jazz pianists.

"Did you ask for your money back?"

"When, dear?"

"At the restaurant. I would have asked for a rebate on my meal."

My humor flies over her head. She asks if I am writing a book. *Very perceptive.* I haven't hinted anything of the kind.

"Yes," I reply, "but don't hold your breath. I haven't finished my journey yet."

"I'll buy a copy. Give me your business card. I can fax you. We can fax each other. Are you on the Internet?" She doesn't strike me as the computer type. I say no.

"Dearie, you *really* must get on the Net."

She reminds of why I left England.

The young doctor and his nurse-wife live a world apart in a small one-room unit that doubles as a meager clinic, with their living quarters partitioned off by a curtain in a space not much bigger than the bathroom in my hotel guest room. The doctor's English is rudimentary and his examination more so. He asks a few questions, sticks a stethoscope to my chest, pulls open a drawer containing a meager stock of medicines, rummages uncertainly, decides upon a small packet containing four tablets of antibiotics, and writes out a receipt for 30 dollars.

In the frigid dining room, the Englishwoman is picking fussily from the dessert buffet. She returns to her seat bearing a plate piled with pastries and then gives a start.

"Oh, my God!" she exclaims, bringing her hand up to her chest. "I looked down and my plate was moving." The rest of the diners look up as she stares down aghast at her plate. At the buffet table, two hotel staff are fussing over the platter of pastries. One is flicking at the table with a cloth napkin. An elderly Canadian gent in a fading T-shirt that reads "Our Grandpa Ravishing Ray" is peering over their shoulders.

"What's that?" he asks, leaning closer. "Jesus! Ants!"

"*Ants!*" screams the ginger-haired lady. "Ugh, the thought turns my stomach." The fright starts her on a coughing fit.

"That does it," says a portly Canadian man, storming out of the dining room. "It's a good thing I'm already full," he adds. And indeed he is. I don't recall having seen more than half a dozen fat people in all of Cuba. There is more obesity in this one room than I have seen in the last two months.

I woke early, feeling listless with my room awash in tawny light. The sun glowed wanly, dusting in saffron the fine mist hovering over the water and bathing the tips of the mountains in bronze. The waters were still, and I had the strange sensation that at any moment a Viking ship might appear from the fog.

The taupe sand had the texture of potting soil and felt like wet mulch between my toes as I walked down to the water's edge, where the high tide was busy rearranging thick clumps of seaweed and tiny pebbles. Already, with the sun barely up, tiny beads of sweat glistened on my skin.

My map showed the route along the coast as a dirt track as far as Chivirico, a distance of about 80 miles. No villages were shown, or settlements of any kind. The hotel desk clerk thought a recent landslide had made the rough track impassable.

The enduro course began a few miles east of Marea del Portillo. The dirt road hugged the coast and I ran at the water's edge. The trail clawed its way over great headlands and hung suspended in air before cascading steeply to the next valley. Really wild country.

The slopes were littered with jagged scree the size of baseballs, shattered and flinty-sharp. Huge rocks scraped the underbelly. Fortunately the BMW's heavy-duty aluminum bash plate survived the direct hits and ensured I didn't crunch the sump. I stood on the foot pegs to let the bike buck beneath me, shift my weight, and heave on the bars to hoist the front wheel over the obstacles. It would help me leap off the bike, too, if I crashed.

The gnarly course grew steeper, wrinkling up into sharp curves. In places the angles seemed impossible, as if I were going straight up the mountain. But the Paris-Dakar seemed not to notice, pulling willingly, with plenty of torque. I kept the throttle open and powered uphill, bouncing madly, but with a light enough hand to stop the rear tire from spinning loose. I was glad for the bike's rugged brawn and superb balance. I praised the engineers of Munich. Surely these were the conditions they had in mind when they designed the Paris-Dakar to win the world's most arduous off-road race.

Proud thoughts flashed through my mind: *I really am in the middle of nowhere. There is nowhere I would rather be right now. And I wouldn't want to be here on anything but my BMW.*

Then, amazingly, I passed an old Chrysler New Yorker in cherry condition chugging uphill in the other direction, impervious to the mountain terrain. My jaw dropped. Suddenly, I felt less like a pioneer.

Uh-oh! There were the crabs again, more numerous than I'd seen before. The rough piste was crowded with crustaceans migrating en masse. Amazingly, the creatures were attempting to scale the bluffs that rose in places several hundred feet above the shore. Many had failed and succumbed to exhaustion. The track was a veritable potlatch of crabmeat for vultures that lifted off at my approach. Thousands of crabs lay dead from exertion or crushed by the bulldozers and trucks. Broken shells and sharp pincers threatened as much damage as the razor-sharp scree. This was no place for a puncture. Their live, ill-tempered brethren raised their claws defiantly as I passed.

I rode mile after mile without seeing a soul or a sign of habitation. Just the vultures picking at crustacean carcasses or swirling ominously overhead. The birds were unnervingly curious. A couple swept down before suddenly veering off within a few feet of my head.

Beyond the Río Macio, marking the boundary of Santiago de Cuba province, I picked up the concrete hard-top again. The scenery continued to stagger me.

Copper-colored cliffs loomed massively out of the sea. Cuba's highest peaks lay within fingertip distance, with the mountains dropping to the dancing blue waters. I passed beneath Pico Turquino, whose sharp peak lay within five miles of the shore.

The beauty of the looming mountains and the stark low-desert country and teal-blue sea began to rub off on me, and my illness was briefly forgotten. I took more photos than seemed reasonable for such inhospitable terrain.

My room in Santiago de Cuba's Hotel San Juan looked out over a pleasant park at the top of the steep knoll, about the size of a large tumulus, where on July 1, 1898, according to legend, a cavalry charge by Teddy Roosevelt's Rough Riders sealed the Spanish-American War—and Cuba's fate with it. Truth be told, Roosevelt never led a cavalry charge. In fact, cavalry weren't used during the campaign, and the battle was all but over by the time Roosevelt arrived. Victors don't just take the spoils—they also write the history books.

I sauntered over and studied the monuments. Cannon stood half screened by the overhanging foliage of a huge spreading ceiba. One memorial was dedicated to Cuban revolutionaries and—rather charitably, I thought—to "the generous American soldiers who sealed a covenant of liberty and fraternity between the two nations." From the Cuban viewpoint, Washington had stolen victory from their hands. The Spanish flag came down and in its place rose the Stars and Stripes, flying finally over coveted Cuba, ending one of the most foolishly run empires in the world. The Mambí—Cuba's mostly black independence fighters who had fought and sacrificed for half a century (they had even stormed the hill)—weren't invited to the surrender ceremony. The Cuban people have never forgotten the slight. Cuba ended the century as it had begun it—under foreign rule.

The maid had taken advantage of my brief absence to forage around my room with a broom. The sparkle in her eye as I entered said it all. She was pretty, and her body-hugging uniform suggested a figure that Michelangelo, had he been born in a less Rubenesque age, would have been hard put to equal. A woman I might have wished to invent. But she was real and proved it by pushing closed the door with a feigned sweep of the broom. An invitation? To what? To bed her? I couldn't imagine she'd risk losing her job by being caught with a guest. But that's what it looked like. She was staring at me now, the two of us caught in awkward silence. Caught in the uncertainty of how to proceed, I felt hesitation mixed with desire. Today, I told myself, I shall forsake passion and exercise a little restraint. She took the initiative and, plucking my notebook and pen from my hand, sat demurely on the bed and wrote her name and address, followed by the words: "Dedicated with all my heart and respect to a friend who knows my address and place of work, so that he'll never forget me. Chao. Sury."

All over Cuba, *chicas* would chat me up, then take my notebook and write how they would never forget me. I was the great white hope.

I explored Santiago while *jineteros* nipped at my heels. Jineteros make a living by seizing opportunities. Santiago was full of them. And the biggest opportunity seemed to be me.

It began at Bosque de los Héroes, a small monument of marble cubes arranged higgledy-piggledy and etched with the faces of homegrown revolutionary heroes on a knoll across the street from the Hotel Santiago. Behind the tableau a concrete pathway led uphill through a glade of bamboo whose wispy bowers created pools of sunlight and shade; it was only by sheer luck that in passing from the harsh light into deep shadow I avoided stepping in a large pile of feces coiled like a snake on the path. As my eyes adjusted, I saw half a dozen similar heaps, as dangerous underfoot as a pit full of serpents. Santiagueros were using the hallowed spot as a toilet.

A young black man followed me up the slope. *"¿Te gusta?* You like the *parque natural?"* he asked as I scribbled notes of disgust. I indulged him with a few moments of banter, then excused myself. He trotted after me.

"You want guide?"

"No, thanks."

"I'm good guide."

"Sorry, I don't need one."

"What wrong? You don't like Cubans?"

I replied that I loved Cubans. He persisted. I ignored him and kept walking. He dogged me step for step as I made for the Hotel Santiago.

"What wrong?" he repeated. "You don't like blacks? Are you racist?"

For God's sake!

"What is it about the word 'No' that you don't understand?" I said, exasperated. He looked puzzled.

"Give me one dollar," he replied imperiously.

"Bugger off!"

The Hotel Santiago seemed quite mind-altering after the drab hotels of the boondocks. Uncharacteristically avant-garde, the postmodernist hotel looked more Cubist than Cuban, an eclectic geometric jumble brazenly colored in trendy flavors: cherry red, banana yellow, gunmetal blue. Paul Klee might have concocted it from Lego bricks. A French tour group was checking in. Gallic accents echoed suavely in the glass-enclosed lobby. The restaurant prices befitted the Champs-Élysées.

I pushed past the jineteros loitering around the tour buses and, stepping onto Avenida las Américas, found myself caught up yet again in Cuba's neverending kaleidoscope of surreal vignettes.

This was *Día de la Defensa* Sunday, and the good citizens of Santiago had been marshaled to do their duty. I watched, mesmerized, through a chain-link fence as a balding, middle-aged man in an olive green uniform with red epaulets gave instructions to a dispassionate group who clearly thought they had better things to do on a Sunday afternoon.

A young woman fingered the trigger of what looked like a vintage Lee-Enfield rifle. She lay prone, resting on her elbows, her legs splayed and her behind round and tight inside pink spandex shorts. She cradled the rifle in her left hand and squinted against the harsh glare of the sun as she stared down the sights at a rusty steel cut-out GI Joe. She wriggled her hips and adjusted the symmetry of her arrangement on the hard ground.

She squeezed the trigger. *Click!*

To her left, an old maid with her hair coiled tightly in curlers beneath a red bandanna was teetering on one knee as she took potshots with an antique .22 rifle. *Click! Click!*

A few yards away, a septuagenarian in a pale yellow guayabera and neatly ironed brown slacks stood thigh-deep in a trench. He lobbed a large stone, and the makeshift grenade went arcing over the heads of his *compañeros* to explode on the disheveled lawn of the Instituto de Segunda Enseñanza (the Institute of Secondary Education).

Military training for citizens, Cuban style.

I hailed a *colectivo*—a peso taxi—lumbering down the street on well-worn, sagging tires. Amazingly the driver, a lanky fellow with a handsome bronze face and jade green eyes, pulled over (by law, *colectivos* aren't allowed to pick up foreigners) and in I hopped, sharing the back seat with an old Spanish woman and a young black boy. For 35 pesos, I got to cruise down the tree-shaded boulevard in a baby pink '55 Buick Roadmaster while the three of us slid around on the slick, vinyl-covered bench seat to the rhythm of the rumba on the radio.

The driver dropped me off near the Moncada Barracks, a vision of Beau Geste with its crenellated walls and turrets incongruous in the midst of a leafy suburb. The opening shots in Castro's revolution were fired here on July 26, 1953, when the hot-blooded 26-year-old lawyer and 79 lightly armed coconspirators dressed in Cuban Army uniforms stormed the barracks in a dawn raid meant to inspire a general uprising. The group struck during the height of Carnival celebrations, when Batista's troops were sure to be on leave or addled with rum. The attack began to go wrong almost immediately. The alarm was raised and the rebels were caught in a withering cross fire. Only eight rebels were killed in combat, but 61 others were captured and tortured to death. Gruesome photos of the tortured Fidelistas unleashed a wave of disgust and lent legitimacy to Castro's 26th of July Movement (M-26-7), the revolutionary group that evolved in subsequent years as the preeminent opposition body working to topple Batista.

Moncada was now a school: the Ciudad Escolar 26 de Julio. Schoolchildren wearing innocent smiles were streaming up and down the staircase. The facade was pitted with bullet holes (not the originals: Batista's troops filled those in, so Castro had the holes redone using photographs), and three of the rooms had metamorphosed as a museum full of blood-stained uniforms and other gory memorabilia from that fateful day.

The kids posed and smiled for my camera. Then one came tripping down the steps and stuck out his slender hand, palm upward.

"Friend. Give me one dollar!"

Santiago's old town tilted westward, flowing down to a large flask-shaped bay. I looked down the narrow streets upon the jaundiced roofs of the ancient quarter as if surveying a time-tempered chart. History echoed down the darkened streets. The dwellings were graced by fancy forged-iron railings, weathered timbers, shady hanging balconies, turned wooden *rejas*, Moorish balustrades, facades painted in faded tropical pastels, and cacti poking up through the rustic tiles—an Oriente superstition meant to ward off evil spirits. The morning sun sparkled on the waters of Santiago harbor. A nearly perfect Caribbean day.

The city streets were abuzz with Latin life. Lovers strolled hand in hand. Muted gossip drifted from doorways dizzy with the smells of Cuban cooking. Dogs lolled in the road with tongues extended from the heat, while around them couples danced overtly sexual *changüí* numbers and men, shirtless in the lurid heat, slapped dominoes on tables strategically placed in puddles of shade. The sounds of salsa music and laughter echoed above the wheezing and honking of weekend traffic, soaring above the syncopation of hoofbeats and Yankee cacharros.

I found my way to the Hotel Casa Grande. Dead beat, I plopped into a seat in the first-floor terrace bar overhanging Parque Céspedes, where an old man with a large cigar in his mouth was touting himself as a photo op to passing tourists. A Cuban photographer with a vintage box camera atop a tripod tried less successfully to do the same.

An old maid passed through the square, selling flower bouquets from tin buckets to kissing lovers. A slow breeze rustled the Royal palms—a benediction on this hot, humid day. I sipped from a bottle of mineral water with my feet up on the balustrade beneath Parisian-style awnings while a couple of attractive *mulatas* stared up at me with smiles of indefatigable optimism. I avoided their eyes and watched jineteros harry a phalanx of French tourists setting off on a walking tour.

Santiago, an industrial city, had taken it on the chin since the collapse of the Soviet Union. During my first visit to the city in 1994, jineteros had besieged me as if I had arrived bearing a sack of flour in the midst of famine. Two years later Santiago seemed infused with new vigor, but the hustlers were still in the wings, ready and more aggressive, eager to seize on any hapless tourist who stepped into the streets.

In all other regards, Santiago was grand.

Parque Céspedes emanated flavorful evocations of history. I heard the boot tread of Hernán Cortés and Diego Velásquez echoing across the square at the core of the city. Velásquez founded the city in 1514, named it the Cuban capital, and appointed Cortés as its first Capitán-General. Velásquez's beautifully maintained home still stands on the west side of the plaza. Moorish rejas and wooden shutters hung dark and heavy on its somber facade. On the north side of the square, the Ayuntamiento, the town hall, gleamed like dazzling snow in the sunshine. In my mind's eye, I saw Fidel stride onto the balcony and imagined I heard the reverberating strains of his voice, recalling the victory speech he gave here on January 2, 1959 following Batista's flight from Cuba. But it was only the throaty notes of a 1930 Phaeton convertible puttering past, adding another mantle to the multitextured layers of a *temps perdu*.

The car pulled up catercorner to the hotel. The owner, a white-haired chap named Jorge, gives city tours to *turistas*. I took a five-dollar jaunt for the fun of it while my chauffeur chattered away like a parrot. Jorge loved the girls. That was the highlight, old Jorge interrupting his own monologues to honk at the pretty chicas, smiling as they waved back and blew saucy kisses.

Santiago de Cuba, home of rum and revolution, had a beguilingly enigmatic appeal wholly unique on the island. I thought it more "Caribbean" than other cities, more African. The faces were mostly black, and the people seemed more infused with a tropical lassitude. During the course of three centuries, Santiago's relative isolation from Havana and its proximity to Jamaica and Santo Domingo (Haiti) had fostered close links with both islands, and thousands of English- and French-speaking immigrants, black and white alike, had arrived to stitch their customs into the cultural quilt of the city. Even the traditional clapboard houses hinted at a Caribbean potpourri, as did the lilting tongue of the Santigueros and their exciting music.

Cuba's second city lacked Havana's grandiloquence but simmered with sentimental allure. I liked its exoticism.

I was wearing a T-shirt showing stenciled photographs of Bill Clinton and Fidel Castro dressed in baseball gear, and a picture of a baseball diamond emblazoned with the slogan, "TIME TO PLAY BALL WITH CUBA." Many young Cubans wore clothing depicting Che, yet cartoons of Fidel were nonexistent— too risky. As I retraced my steps to my hotel, passers-by pointed at my chest. Wide-eyed with incredulity, they stopped me and peppered me with good-natured questions.

Do most North Americans support the blockade? The Cold War is over; why does Senator Helms want to add to our misery? Doesn't President Clinton understand that you must open the doors and windows if you want to have light in the house?

It was the same all over the island. Cubans I had met moments before embraced me, called me "amigo," and invited me into their homes, welcoming me openly, generously offering *cerdo asado* (roast pork), rice and black beans, cheap rum and beer. On this day it happened again. Cubans whose names I never learned urged me to join their *cumbancha*, the local word for a street party. A portable radio was cranked up until I thought the beer bottles would get up and dance. Friends and neighbors arrived, took my hand, and kissed my cheeks, like a diplomat. I was pulled bodily into the street and found myself, despite my lassitude, caught up in the Latin rhythms, whirling and swaying.

I didn't know how to repay my hosts. I offered money, which they refused. I was welcomed and feted from human goodness with no expectation of return.

"Of course not. Giving is in our blood," Daisy had responded when I asked her why hard-up Cubans refused offers of payment in exchange for their hospitality.

"Is *that* a product of the Revolution?"

"Perhaps. But when the stomach is empty, the heart becomes full," she had replied philosophically.

In Cuba, "miser" is the worst possible insult. Cubans treated one another as if they belonged to one big, relaxed, open-armed family. They treated me the same way.

With many expressions of goodwill, we parted.

I longed to be back on the bike, so the next day I rode out to Dos Ríos, the holy site about 70 miles northeast of Santiago de Cuba where José Martí, the most revered figure in Cuban history, gave his life for the cause of Cuban independence. En route I paused at El Cobre, a copper-mining town dominated by its red-domed basilica that is a Cuban Lourdes, on the eastern flanks of the Sierra Maestra. I pulled up in the parking lot at the rear of the church. Before I had time to dismount, a pack of young touts rushed forward and thrust pieces of glittering metal under my nose. Iron pyrites—fool's gold—culled from the residue of the nearby mine.

"*¡Es real!*" they intoned, taking me for a fool. "Gold, mister. Only five dollar!"

West of Baire, the carretera began a long, steady downhill sweep onto the floodplain of the Río Cauto. Straight as a plumb line and not a vehicle in sight—sublime! I was traveling light, without side panniers or baggage. I twisted the throttle and opened the bike up to 80, sending tingles through the grips and blurring the image in the mirror. I reveled in the engine's growl and the sensation of hauling ass down Cuba's main highway with a great yawning grin on my face and a bandanna around my head like a revolutionary.

A Brahma bull in the road jarred me out of my reverie. He stared me down, his head low as I approached. I dropped down into fourth, third, and then second, cautious now, nerves tingling, seeing the horns pointing my way. As he and I came eye to eye, I cranked the throttle and flew up through the gears, spinning the bull around in the road like a dog chasing its tail.

I took the Beemer back up to 70 and had settled into a state of bliss when two figures appeared in the distance. A couple of cyclists—a man and a woman—were freewheeling downhill with their backs to me. I was closing fast, the land whizzing by in a blur. The woman began edging toward the center marking. I slowed and, almost upon her now, tweaked the throttle to accelerate past with my fingers covering the front brake lever just in case. At that moment the man glanced over his shoulder and screamed. The girl panicked and swerved broadside into my path.

I saw her look of terror and heard her pitiful shriek—"*Eeeyaah!*"—as I flew past. Then...*BANG!* Her front wheel had clipped me. Fortunately, the BMW didn't waver. I didn't feel a thing, but when I looked in the mirror, she was down. I braked and watched as the man helped the woman to her feet. She was crying but unscathed. The front wheel of her bike drooped, flop-eared.

Where had she hit me? I couldn't find any marks on the bike.

Her partner approached cautiously, then saluted. He was trembling.

"*¿Todo bien?*" I asked. Everything okay?

"*Sí, sí,*" he replied, smiling meekly and motioning me to leave. He stuck out his hand for me to shake. "*Todo bien, señor. Go!*"

I roared away overwhelmed with relief.

Before the Special Period, few Cubans had ever ridden a bike. Sandra Levinson once told me that when she brought her bicycle to Havana in 1972, her neighbors had laughed. "Why should we ride bicycles? They're for underdeveloped countries. Cubans, or at least habaneros, considered themselves First World citizens," said Sandra. And Maurice Halperin, formerly a professor at the University of Havana and the author of *Return to Havana,* couldn't recall "seeing a single adult Cuban on a bicycle in Havana during the entire period of my residence in the city from 1962 to 1968."

In November 1990, with the meltdown of the Soviet bloc well under way and transportation at a virtual standstill, Castro had announced sweeping energy-saving measures, including the "widespread substitution of... hundreds of thousands of bicycles [to replace] gasoline-consuming vehicles." Castro described the program of bicycle importation, domestic production, and mass distribution as a "militant and defensive campaign." The policy was symbolized during the 1991 May Day parade, when armed forces rode through the Plaza de la Revolución on Chinese-made bicycles. By the end of 1991, 530,000 single-gear, hard-to-pump Chinese pachyderms were in use on the streets of Havana. Within two years, that number quadrupled. "The comprehensiveness and speed of implementation of this program is unprecedented in the history of transportation," said a 1994 World Bank report, which noted that about two million bicycles (one for every five Cuban citizens) were then in use island-wide.

Unfortunately, few Cubans knew how to ride their new bikes. Cyclists rode the wrong way down major boulevards, which they traversed willy-nilly. The brakes on the Chinese-made models barely worked, and few bikes had reflectors or lights. Inevitably, during those early days, hospital emergency rooms were flooded with accident victims.

In 1995 I had interviewed Gina Rey, a chief planner with the Group for the Integral Development of the Capital, for a story I was writing about the "bicycle revolution" for *Américas,* the magazine of the Organization of American States. Rey confirmed that there had been turmoil on the streets. She and her team were challenged to reorganize Havana's transportation network. A four-year plan was initiated. Many streets in Old Havana were closed to motorized traffic. Bicycle lanes were created. The city government initiated classes in bicycle etiquette. They also kept citizens informed about planned bike paths, impending cycling rules, and new traffic regulations. "The accident rate dropped quickly once we were able to implement our program," said Rey.

But that was Havana. In the boondocks, Cuban cyclists continued to display a kamikaze disdain for motorized traffic.

Farther down the road, I pass a billboard that reads: "THE BICYCLE IS THE VEHICLE MOST INVOLVED IN ACCIDENTS."

Northeast of Jiguaní the vast, barren pan of white earth conjured up the drought-ridden African Sahel. I wouldn't have been surprised if a herd of wildebeest had thundered across the dusty furnace. Tough zebu cattle with rippling muscles and reflective white hides foraged the plain, while rust-colored goats nibbled at the scrubby roadside margins. A scouring wind tore across the prairie, slapping me broadside. I leaned into the gusts and ran against the wind with the throttle opened up and the bike canted like a gyroscope.

At Dos Ríos the road opened out into a vast parking lot large enough to land a jumbo jet and dominated on one side by a massive billboard showing Mambí guerrillas in action. A brightly gleaming obelisk marked the site where Martí fell. From a distance it seemed hewn from marble, but following the narrow path that led to it through a prim garden shaded by tousled palms, I arrived at its base to discover that it had been cast from concrete crudely splashed with white paint. A bronze plaque merely recorded that Martí *"Died at this place on 19 May 1895."* He deserved more.

Revolutionary literature gives Martí—apostle, poet, and freedom fighter—the role of a hero who died fighting the enemy on the battlefield. In fact, he committed sacrificial suicide to save the land he loved. After 16 years of exile in the United States, Martí returned to Cuba on April 11, 1895, accompanied by General Máximo Gómez, and linked up with Antonio Maceo and his army of 6,000 Mambís. On May 19 the nationalist troops exchanged shots with a small Spanish column at Dos Ríos. Martí, as the nationalist leader, was a civilian among soldiers. Gómez therefore ordered Martí and his bodyguard to place themselves at the rear. Instead, Martí sought romantic death on the battlefield and rushed forward to meet it, whipping his horse headlong down the riverbank with his bodyguard in pursuit. Martí was shot through the neck almost instantly, and he fell from his horse without ever drawing his gun.

Says Guillermo Cabrera Infante: "There was in Martí an eagerness for immolation that was actually a will to martyrdom....But why complain that Martí should not have died? Martí has not died. He is alive in his living prose."

I returned to Santiago de Cuba over a massif called Loma del Yarey. The road snaked steeply uphill, offering all-round views over the sprawling steppes with the mauve mass of the Sierra Maestra looming through a heat-induced fog. Looking down upon this austere landscape—shimmering and phantasmagoric in its infinity—conjured up images of the wanderings of the demented Don Quixote across stark La Mancha.

I was brought back to earth at the Villa el Yarey, a rustic hotel and restaurant of log and thatch with an enviable, breezy location atop the massif. A busload of German tourists were having lunch on the patio. They were pink-faced, flushed from the heat. Their tour bus—a gleaming Mercedes Benz— had its air conditioning running, and the thrum of its engine fractured the beatific hush.

I parked the bike beneath a gnarled *majagua* tree from which filamental mosses dangled like miniature fishermen's nets. I found a seat in the sun, away from the group. Two Germans walked over to inspect my BMW. One returned for his camera, shot some frames, then came over to question me. He was well over six feet tall, well-muscled, with close-cropped blond hair and cold blue eyes.

"You are from California, I sink? Ze moto is yours? No problems to bring it here?"

Apparently this was going to be an interrogation. He stood over me with the sun behind him. All I could see was his silhouette haloed in blinding light.

"It is good, no? Ze roads, they haf no cars," he continued.

"Very good," I replied, answering sparingly. Nonetheless, I invited him to be seated.

"No sanks," he answered. Then, "I too haf a motorbike. I made once a grand trip through all of Africa wiz my moto."

We chatted about our respective journeys. I warmed to him even though he remained aloof, never smiling, robotically asking questions.

"Ze BMW is ze best zer is for zis kind of trip, no? You must not worry about any mechanical problems, I sink?" I said I sunk not; *mi moto fidel* was treating me well.

"And ze police, zay are friendly?"

Their bus drew up. The sweating Germans clambered aboard. Then, thankfully, they were gone. I was left alone with the twittering of songbirds and the rustle of the breeze through the branches.

~

CHAPTER TWELVE

GUANTÁNAMO

G uantánamo. The name reverberates around the world. Everyone knows it as a U.S. naval base and a humiliating thorn in the side of Castro's Cuba. Actually, Guantánamo is a Cuban city (population 180,000) 82 miles east of Santiago de Cuba; it sits at the head of a deep bay from which the city and the U.S. base take their names.

The city sprawls across a barren plain ringed by mountains. Carlo Gébler, in *Driving Through Cuba*, thought it "a depressed city of miserable, low houses and railway marshaling yards filled with decrepit railway stock." Beyond the historic core, Guantánamo was utterly soulless. The city had mushroomed during the past four decades, acquiring dozens of grotesque government buildings and vast acreages of cheap housing that had been thrown together with cement blocks and bricks. The broad roads were paved but potholed, littered with stones and piles of refuse, lacking trees, grass, or gardens, and crisscrossed by telegraph wires and clotheslines sagging under the weight of laundry. The city outskirts resembled a Mexican shanty.

Guantánamo is an army town. Military figures with briefcases tucked under their arms strolled through the streets in short-sleeve, mustard-colored uniforms. I passed a platoon of women in full battle gear marching in quick time down Avenida 5 del Prado. They were toting AK-47s and looked deadly serious but broke into smiles as I cut the motor and watched them file by, reminding me of something Tom Miller had written: "They all wore earrings, flowers in their hair, and wide smiles. Cuba has a lovely army."

I pulled into the huge concrete Plaza de la Revolución, boasting a monument to Cuba's war heroes and a dynamic frieze honoring Karl Marx and Friedrich Engels. Nearby, a large billboard extolled the virtues of martyrdom: "TO DIE FOR THE FATHERLAND IS TO LIVE FOREVER." Another read: "NO, NEVER! WE SHALL NOT VACILLATE, RUN AWAY FROM OUR PRINCIPLES, OR RETREAT. SOCIALISM OR DEATH!"

These patriotic murals were part of the Cuban landscape. Heroic allusion was everywhere. Che Guevara kept popping up in the most unlikely places. The standardized image—the famous shot by Korda of Che, the "Heroic Guerrilla," wearing his trademark black beret with five-point revolutionary star—marches symbolically across the walls of Cuba, sometimes as elegantly as Korda's original and often as boisterously vulgar as a piece of pop art.

Exhausted, I pulled up outside the Hotel Guantánamo. The doorman stood with his arms folded and watched me unload my baggage and haul it up the stairs into the lobby. He had the face of a puffer fish, with large ears sticking out to each side and a short, upturned nose oddly creased down the center.

"Hello. I think you are American," he said in a voice that sounded like a bow being drawn across a taut wire. "Am I correct? There is no need to speak Spanish. You can speak to me in English. I speak it fluently," he added.

What a supercilious prig. I disliked him immediately. His near-perfect English surprised me.

The desk clerk was a timid young woman who addressed me in Spanish. The doorman translated her words into English.

"It's okay, I speak Spanish," I replied, turning back to the clerk. I secured a room for two nights, then asked the woman if it was possible to arrange a trip to the *zona militar* at Caimanera, a small town and Cuban military post south of Guantánamo. From there I hoped to look over the U.S. naval base, which Castro has called "a dagger plunged in the heart of Cuban soil."

"Not possible," replied the doorman. "You cannot go!" he added gruffly, as if he was trying to dissuade me from trying.

I told him I knew people who had been.

"Who do you know?" he asked haughtily, poking his piggy snout where it didn't belong. I couldn't imagine the doorman of Claridge's talking to guests this way. I felt like hitting him.

"One of my friends—an author—has been there. And I've read in guidebooks that it can be arranged."

"They are wrong. *You cannot go!*"

That afternoon I had sidetracked to Caimanera in hopes of serendipitously slipping through without a permit. A policeman at the military checkpoint had turned me back, instructing me to report to the MININT office in Guantánamo.

I stretched the truth for the hell of it: "The guard at the border post at Caimanera also told me it was possible. He would know."

The runt glowered. "It is impossible to go there. There is no way." He seemed determined to thwart me. I figured he was employed by MININT. Either that or he was a *jala leva*...a *guataca*...a *canchanchán*. Cubans have dozens of words for a bum-boy—that is, someone who rides the coattails of a person in power or advances himself by being a brownnose for the police.

I turned to the desk clerk. "It's possible to visit Caimanera with a group from this hotel, is it not?"

"*Sí, yo lo creo,*" she replied. Yes, I think so.

"Speak to him in English," the doorman said sharply. He had a hard, narrow look on his face

I continued in Spanish. "I can go, then, if I arrange it through this hotel?"

The clerk looked at the doorman uncertainly.

"Do you have other people?" he replied, giving me a cold stare.

"No!" I answered. "How about a group of one?"

"One is not a group." My joke was above him.

Fortunately, Pedro Hope, the hotel manager, was more amiable. He was tall and stocky, and his lips were permanently parted in a congenial grin. Muscles bulged against his crisply pressed dress shirt.

"Call me Peter," he said in effortless English. Peter grasped my hand firmly and pumped it vigorously.

I told him that I was writing a guidebook.

"Excellent! You want to visit Caimanera? There should be no problem. Actually, you're in luck. I want to introduce you to Señor Grizzle, our regional manager," he said, beckoning me to sit in a soft leather chair by the door. Peter disappeared and returned moments later accompanied by Ibrahim Grizzle Duarte, the *jefe* in charge of Islazul hotels throughout Guantánamo province.

Peter explained that I was a writer. Grizzle's lips pursed doubtfully. He looked at me long and hard, as if trying to determine if my journalistic credentials were a cover. Perhaps he thought I was a CIA spy. "I remember on various occasions the CIA tried to infiltrate our ranks with people who posed as journalists," Fidel told television producers Kirby Jones and Frank Mankiewicz when in 1974. "And we always knew right away who they really were. You see, journalists are particular kinds of people. They always ask hundreds of different questions. They are very inquisitive. That is their job....But a phony journalist—a CIA agent posing as a journalist—never asked questions the way an authentic reporter would. They couldn't play the role. A real journalist could be a CIA agent, but a CIA agent can never realistically appear to be a journalist."

Sensing Grizzle's caution, I pulled out a copy of my *Costa Rica Handbook*, showed him the page with my photo and bio, and launched into an enthusiastic explanation of my mission to write a similar guidebook to Cuba. Grizzle thumbed through the book, then asked if a government agency had given me official permission to undertake my research. I replied that Publicitur was my sponsor, carefully neglecting to tell him that I had severed my ties with the state tourism agency.

"How can I help you?"

"I want to visit Caimanera."

"It is good that you are traveling with permission," Grizzle replied. "It is difficult for foreign tourists to visit Caimanera—for now, at least. We are planning to offer group package excursions from here. The price is already fixed. We'll have extras, such as lunch on the beach and a visit to the *mirador*," he continued, growing animated. "There are many things to see in this area. We're planning a map showing all the sites and excursions that we hope to introduce." Grizzle pointed to a corner of the lobby. "It will go there."

Boom days were planned for Guantánamo. The U.S. naval facility was to be turned into a tourist attraction. I liked the notion of a war base-cum-Disneyland. I made hurried notes, barely able to keep up as he talked proudly of these and other plans for the city.

And my visit to Caimanera? Could he suggest how I might do this?

"No problem," said Grizzle. "I'm meeting tomorrow with the chief of MININT—he's a friend. I'll arrange it for you; call me tomorrow afternoon."

He scribbled his telephone and fax numbers in my notebook.

I was buoyant.

When I called Grizzle the next day, however, he curtly told me, "It is impossible." His voice had changed. He seemed cool. His friend the jefe, he said, had gone out of town, and no one else could authorize a permit. It sounded like an excuse. Grizzle hung up. I should have known.

Getting this close without seeing the U.S. base seemed like touring Agra without visiting the Taj Mahal. I was leaving town the next day and felt desperate for a permit. Against my better judgment, I decided to ride down to the MININT office on Calle José Martí to try for myself.

The agent on duty smiled as I outlined my request.

"I'm sorry, *señor*," he replied, conjuring a pained look of regret. "You need authorization from Havana. Only the Ministerio de Relaciones Exteriores can issue an authorization."

"But I'm leaving for Baracoa tomorrow and I won't be back this way. Isn't it possible to expedite this?" I thought I'd stretch the truth: "I'm being sponsored by your government."

"*No es posible.*"

"But I've already been cleared by Raúl Colominas at MINREX."

Jesus! What am I saying? I had cut my ties with Colominas and Juan Pardo, Publicitur's press executive, and had avoided further contact with government agencies. Why on Earth am I reopening that Pandora's box?

"I'm sorry," the agent replied solicitously, tilting his head in a suggestion of "If only there was a way."

I placed on his desk a letter from Medea Benjamin, the director of Global Exchange, a San Francisco-based nonprofit organization at the forefront of efforts to end the U.S. embargo. The left-leaning organization had recently initiated a "Freedom to Travel Campaign" that was gaining notoriety across North America. Benjamin had also authored two books sympathetic to the Revolution, and her name was well respected among Cuban authorities, including Fidel, with whom she was friendly. I had recently done some writing for the organization, and Benjamin had obligingly written a letter of recommendation praising the value of the work I had done and requesting assistance on my behalf from any Cuban authority to whom I might present it.

A broad smile spread across the agent's face. His eyes mellowed. The letter seemed to have cracked the ice.

He gave me a slight nod, turned to a rusted metal file cabinet, pulled open a drawer, and extracted a small yellow card. *A permit?* He asked me to fill in my pertinent details, including my father's and mother's names and the reason for my visit, to which he added a few vital stats gleaned from my passport. He then turned and slipped the card back into his files.

"Aren't you issuing me a permit?" I inquired naively.

"No. That is impossible," he replied.

The crafty bugger had duped me.

"You can see the military base from the mountainside on the road to Baracoa," he said coolly, his duty performed.

Of course I wouldn't be allowed to visit. Cuba was still on high alert following the Brothers to the Rescue downings. Naturally the government would be interested in checking out anyone asking to see Caimanera during these tension-filled times.

I sulked by the hotel swimming pool and watched a woman and a young boy splashing about in the shallow end about 12 feet away. She was very dark and comely, with a taut, solid body. The boy was paler and terribly thin.

Soon enough the woman emerged, burnished like well-polished ebony in the late afternoon sunlight. My libido stirred. She sidled past, swaying undulantly to accentuate her remarkable figure, which she displayed in a turquoise bikini small enough to fit in a matchbox.

"*¡Hola! Eres hermosísima!*" I said, intercepting her as she flowed past like some exotic denizen from a sultan's harem. "Hi! You're beautiful!"

I said it thus, without flinching, nonchalant in the certitude of lust.

"*¡Gracias!*" she replied, taking a calm step toward me. Her innocent curiosity gave me a playful feeling of superiority.

"What's your name?" I asked, reaching out for her hand.

The important details emerged quickly. Her name was Milagros, she lived in Havana, she was visiting her family in town, and, better yet, she was staying in the hotel. She told me her room number. I suggested we meet later that evening. She was unsure; she had family obligations. Determined, I slipped a note under her door asking her to come to my room at nine o'clock.

Peter invited me to dine with him in the hotel restaurant. It was full of local Cubans. I wasn't surprised. Scarcity had made them indifferent to standards. I spent that afternoon and the following day walking through town. Few of the restaurants had anything to eat, and many had nothing—not even a *boca-dito*. The Restaurant Oriental had seemed the most promising. The menu listed pork, chicken, fish, and *papas fritas*. I ordered the chicken. The waitress took the menu and wrote *"No"* next to it. I ordered the fish. She wrote *"No."* I asked for the *papas fritas*. She pointed at the menu; someone had already written *"No"* there. How on Earth did *guantanameros* survive? They struck me as the most resourceful people in the world. The hotel restaurant was the best thing in town.

A trio of troubadors moved among the tables.

Like many educated Cubans, Peter had turned from academia to tourism to earn precious dollars. "I was for 15 years a professor of social linguistics," he told me over a tomato-and-cucumber salad. "I'm hoping to complete my doctorate on English Creole culture."

"Is that where you learned to speak English?"

"No. Many *guantanameros* speak English," he replied. "Much of the population has Jamaican blood. We're called *ingleses*—Englishmen."

Several thousand Jamaican laborers had been hired in the 1920s to work in the sugar fields of Guantánamo province. Others came from Barbados, Saint Kitts, or other English-speaking islands. Many stayed.

"We're very proud of our heritage," Peter continued. "There is even an institution here where we work to keep alive not only our English language, but also other aspects of our cultural heritage. It has a library of books in English. You should visit the British West Indian Welfare Center, on Serafin Sánchez. I will take you!" he beamed.

I asked him what he thought about the inequities wrought by tourism. The disparity had created an inverted society in which bellhops and *jineteras* make far more money than surgeons and college professors. I remarked that tourism seemed to me like a Faustian bargain.

Peter qualified my observation: "We have special events here at the hotel for the poor and the handicapped. The disco is free, for example. And we often rent the Casa de los Sueños at a nominal rate to Cubans for birthdays and special occasions. We call it a humanistic approach to tourism." The casa was a beautiful protocol villa—one rented out to dignitaries and tourists—that Peter had shown me earlier that day.

The troubadors came over and asked if I wanted to hear a song. I requested *Guantanamera*, Cuba's unofficial folk anthem. I tipped them a dollar apiece.

As our talk turned to Cuba's economic problems, Peter observed that "We need to develop an entrepreneurial mind." With his firm grip on capitalist principles of marketing, Peter struck me as unusually savvy. He was one of the bright hopes for Cuba's future. With people like him, Cuba would survive any challenge.

As we talked, I noticed an elegant cubana at an adjacent table. The woman was giving me the eye. She had noble, olive-skinned, Spanish features: fiery cobalt eyes and a tumbling mass of glossy raven hair cascading over her shoulders. She was wearing a teal-blue cocktail dress and a simple bead necklace. Two young children, a boy and a girl, well turned out and well behaved, sat facing her. I smiled. The woman looked down.

We repeated this minuet several times. Each time I looked her way, the woman was eyeing me. Finally she bestowed on me a coquettish smile, which her daughter noticed. The girl turned to see me smiling, then peered up again at her mother; recognizing her simpering glow, the girl looked back at me, raised her eyebrows, and gave me her own knowing smile.

The family departed. Peter and I lingered over our meal, but when we left, the young boy was standing alone in the hallway. He stepped in front of me and looked up with pleading eyes.

"You like my mother?" he asked in Spanish.

"Well, er, yes. Why?"

"She is waiting for you downstairs. At the bar beside the pool. Will you come?"

"Oh! I'm not sure I can," I replied, thinking of Milagros. "I will try."

"She will wait," replied the boy.

Cuba never failed to amaze me. I tasted the poison of the male predicament: the choice between women.

I returned to my room, turned on the TV, and waited for the phone to ring. Nine o'clock came and went. Then—a faint knock at the door. Milagros had been trying to call me.

"Why didn't you answer?"

"My phone never rang."

"But I called you and I heard ringing."

I picked up the phone. The line was dead. Cuba's telephone system was a joke.

We sat at the hotel's dreary and dimly lit upstairs bar, which was paneled with wood veneer. It had frosted windows the color of stale nicotine to match the nicotine-stained ceiling. The bartender and a Cuban couple were engrossed in watching television. There were no other patrons.

Milagros was 24 years old. She was a schoolteacher, quoted Hemingway, Carpentier, and Neruda, dreamed of working for the United Nations, and had a dead-on fashion sense. Her jeans had been spray-painted on. She wore a bright orange tank top, crocheted in a see-through trellised pattern, and no bra.

Milagros was eager to learn about life outside Cuba, and her first questions betrayed a certain naiveté: "Is it true that your streets are full of beggars?"

I admitted that capitalist nations have much homelessness, but I also painted a broader perspective, explaining about Social Security and welfare. She was surprised to learn that the U.S. government paid unemployment benefits, and Medicaid for indigents. When I told her that Canada and most nations in Western Europe had socialized medicine, she exclaimed: *"¡Muy interesante!*

"What about education? You pay for that, don't you?"

"No, education is mandatory and free. The government pays. Private schooling is optional."

"What about universities?"

"It depends. American universities are pretty darn expensive, but most communities in cities have inexpensive college systems, and there are countless other educational outlets for adults. In England and most European countries the government pays, at least for most costs."

This was a surprise to Milagros. I was confounding everything she had learned.

"I'm tired of teaching about the Revolution," she said. Then: "Are you married?"

I thought of the words to a song popular at the time in Cuban discos, in which a top Cuban band had advised Cuban women to find a *"papirriqui con guaniquiqui"*—a sugar daddy.

Our conversation veered toward the purpose of our being together.

"What do Cuban men think when they see a foreigner taking their sisters or cousins to a hotel room?" I asked.

"They smile. They understand. Where can a Cuban boyfriend take me on a Saturday night?" she replied. "And who knows, maybe they hope for a chance to hang on our coattails."

"Aren't they jealous?"

"Perhaps. But they have their own girlfriends. Some have foreign women."

I told Milagros that I had several female friends—middle-class women in their 30s—who made pilgrimages to Cuba for love. I had asked one, a Jamaican, what it was about Cuban men that Jamaican men failed to supply. "Jamaican men is chest beaters, mon!" she had replied, pounding her chest like a male gorilla. "Dey insecure. Dem philosophy is, 'Beat it down and mash it up.' In Cuba, de men know how to romance a woman. I feel loved."

Milagros laughed. "It's true. We Cubans respect each other in lovemaking. Pleasing your partner is an obligation. We see sex as a positive, essential aspect of adulthood. We're sexually liberal, maybe because the church is not so influential here. We got rid of the stigmas. It's fun to dance and drink and have sex. So what if it's with a foreigner?"

Sex had become the substitute for hope in hopeless Cuba. If Cuban girls liked the look of a man, foreign or otherwise, they had no qualms about getting it on and having a little enjoyment. With luck, a foreigner would be a generous sort and might treat them to a meal or a new pair of jeans. If not, at least they were happy simply to have fun. Color meant nothing. I'd seen dozens of interracial relationships.

Cuban women also genuinely seemed to cherish the affections of men twice their age. "Why do Cuban women prefer older men?" I had once asked Daisy.

"They treat us with more consideration," she had replied. "And they're better lovers."

Milagros and I stared into each other's eyes, saying nothing, then sneaked away.

The Cuban government has strictures against Cuban women entering hotel lobbies alone, and the staff of tourist hotels is on guard to keep Cubans from slipping upstairs with foreign guests. But this was an Islazul hotel, used primarily by Cubans—and, occasionally, by foreigners. We went straight to my room.

Afterward, we lay together, she gripping my backside while I grazed on her neck and ear and thought of the other woman and her two children still waiting, perhaps, by the pool, still hoping, like Mr. Micawber, for something to show up.

East of Guantánamo the next morning, I passed another billboard showing a dove representing Cuba defecating on a pile of bricks that spelled the words:

HELMS-
BURTON

I snapped some photos, then continued east past little coves as private as my innermost thoughts. The coast was magnificent and the road more so. Deserted. Well-paved. Delivering views over lonesome beaches and jade-colored waters.

At Cojababo, a side road led me down to the shore. Schoolchildren on a field trip were splashing about in the shallows of a vacation camp called Campismo Playita Cojababo. Their joyous laughter mingled with the *Ssshhh* of the surf washing over cold, pewter-gray pebbles. Cabins the size of large dog kennels nestled beneath shade trees. I wouldn't have been surprised to see English day-trippers sunning themselves on the porches of shallys—the wooden huts the size of garden sheds that line England's working-class beaches.

I kept going, crested a headland, and swooped down to another beach encusped by scrub-covered pincers. I wrestled the bike onto its center stand, stripped off my shirt, and settled down on the shore where José Martí had landed in a rowboat on the stormy 11th of April, 1895, accompanied by General Máx-imo Gómez and four other prominent patriot exiles. There wasn't even a plaque to mark the site where Cuba's national hero first kissed the soil he hadn't stepped on for 16 years.

I sat with my leather-clad knees up to my chest and stared out at the cinere-ous sea. My mind flashed on a larger-than-life photograph of Fidel gazing out to sea at Cojababo that I had seen in the Martí Museum in Havana; it had been taken one year before, to the day, on the centenary of Martí's landing. I was sit-ting on the exact spot where Fidel had stood exactly one year before.

Images of the billboard I had passed earlier that afternoon shadowed my thoughts. The dove had carried an olive branch in its beak. It didn't make sense. The Clinton administration, expounding a more moderate approach to Havana, seemed to be easing toward some sort of tit-for-tat rapprochement with Castro. If Castro genuinely wanted to end the embargo and establish nor-mal relations with the United States, as he claimed, why invite a new chill by shooting down two civilian planes on the run-up to a presidential election? The incident had virtually guaranteed that the Helms-Burton Bill would be signed into law.

The whole affair troubled me. I sank into deep rumination and skipped pebbles out to sea. Martí's words seemed to roll ashore with the waves: "It is my duty...to prevent, through the independence of Cuba, the USA from spreading over the West Indies and falling with added weight upon other lands of Our America. All I have done up to now and shall do hereafter is to that end." Where had I heard those words before? Then I recalled what Fidel Castro had written in a private letter to Celia Sánchez on June 5, 1958, during the war in the Sierra Maestra: "When this war has ended, a much bigger and greater war will start for me, a war I shall launch against them. I realized this will be my true destiny." He, too, meant the United States.

I imagined I saw Fidel standing before me, shaking hands with Martí's ghost as if he was seizing a baton. Of course—that was it! Fidel had cast himself as Martí's heir; he didn't *want* normal relations with Washington.

Then, as "sudden as a shout and as definite, and a thousand times more bright," in the words of poet Thomas Merton, my mind revealed a realization so profound that I felt like an atheist who has just seen a vision of God. Fidel had shot down the two planes *on purpose*, knowing that an international incident with Cuba during the Florida primaries would send Congress into an anti-Castro frenzy. He had done it knowing that it would guarantee passage of the Helms-Burton bill.

My vision struck me like a thunderclap.

I couldn't blame Castro for wanting to hold the U.S. at arm's length. In many ways, his country was better off for it. But my revelation exploded my long-held belief in the leftist myth of Castro as abused innocent. His denunciations of an admittedly repugnant embargo were false. Castro secretly conspired to maintain the blockade. The protracted war was his, birthed and sustained by what biographer Georgie Anne Geyer called his "profound, implacable...largely disguised hatred for the United States," a passion boldly stated in 1988, when Castro had told NBC correspondent Maria Shriver, "We are left with the honor of being one of the few adversaries of the United States." If Castro had so desired, relations would have a chance to improve. He could ease up on his own people, allowing individuals greater control of their lives and their destiny. But the Rabelaisian schemer had lived his entire life obsessed by a malarial psychosis that, says Geyer, "sees everywhere a pervasive sense of threat from the overpowering presence of the *americanos.*"

El jefe was full of hot air. Contriving deceits and distortions, forever percolating formulas for battling his nemesis, he thrived on contradiction and paradox like a character from the novels of Gabriel García Márquez.

Since Camagüey I had inched day by day toward a profoundly distressing conclusion. Now I suddenly acknowledged what had at last become clear: I've had the wool pulled over my eyes. Not just me had he fooled—Castro had hoodwinked the Cuban people, and they were suffering mightily for his proud obsession. The general in his labyrinth.

The realization transformed my outlook on Castro and contemporary Cuba. Not immediately, but fundamentally, in a most profound way. I felt confused, angry. Emotions ricocheted inside my fevered mind. It was Castro's Machiavellianism, his mendacity, that irked me. His brilliant masking of truth. What had Francisco called it? The mantle? Words from Guillermo Cabrera Infante's *Mea Cuba* came to mind: "Fidel Castro's real genius lies in the arts of deception and while the world plays bridge by the book, he plays poker, bluffing and holding his cards close to his olive-green chest."

My epiphany left me with one less hope to cling to.

"The State Department figured that out some time ago," Wayne Smith, former head of the U.S. Interest Section, replied three weeks later. I had just finished explaining the left hook that hit me at Cojababo. Smith, author of *Closest of Enemies* and *Portrait of Cuba,* had served with the Department of State for 25 years and had been appointed Washington's top Cuba diplomat by President Jimmy Carter.

Smith and I sat facing each other in Sandra Levinson's home in Havana, surrounded by potted plants and Cuban artwork. A warm breeze blew in off the Straits of Florida and eddied in through the louvered glass windows.

"You're kidding! Then why doesn't Washington change its policy?" I asked.

"Neither side wants to," Smith responded. "The Reagan administration had placed four conditions for improved relations with Cuba," he explained: a halt to Cuban support of revolution in Central America; withdrawal of Cuban troops from Angola; a reduction of ties with the Soviet Union; and improved human rights.

"Cuba met all these conditions," Smith continued, "but we kept moving the goalposts. It was impossible for Castro to meet our conditions. Washington wasn't serious. When Cuba met the new conditions, Bush moved the goalposts again."

The saw cut both ways. Washington, for example, had extended an olive branch to Castro in 1975, when Secretary of State Henry Kissinger let Cuba know that the Ford administration was considering lifting sanctions and was willing to negotiate the fate of Guantanamo naval base. Extensive secret negotiations were initiated and, reported Tad Szulc, "the United States joined a majority of OAS members at a conference in San José, Costa Rica, to abolish the collective embargo." To prove its good faith, on August 19, 1975, the State Department rescinded the 12-year-old restriction that had kept U.S. companies in foreign countries from doing business with Cuba.

Just as things looked hopeful, however, Castro massively escalated Cuba's military presence in Angola to aid the Marxist MPLA fighting against U.S.-backed FNLA and UNITA forces. He also called a Puerto Rican Solidarity Conference to urge Puerto Rico's independence, "knowing perfectly well," claims Szulc, "that it was an issue calculated to provoke United States anger."

The opportunity was lost. President Carter's initiatives for a more open policy—he lifted travel restrictions on U.S. citizens, for example—also swiftly dissolved when Castro concocted the Mariel boatlift; this "gesture of supreme personal rage," as Szulc has defined it, was Castro's response to Carter's promise that the U.S. would welcome Cuban political refugees with "open arms." Even President Bill Clinton's early behind-the-scenes efforts to thaw relations with Castro had been nixed when Castro created the *balsero* crisis. The buzz among Cuba watchers had been that Clinton was angling to lift the embargo in his second term. Instead, the fallout from the Brothers to the Rescue debacle led to Clinton's signing the Helms-Burton bill, which cemented the embargo in place.

A conspiracy theorist could not have dreamed up a better plot. I felt breathless from shock.

A flurry of realizations crystallized on the beach at Cojababo, breaking through the barrier of my prior perceptions. Castro has said that he will never relinquish power while Washington remains hostile. He has cast himself as a giant-killer in the tradition of José Martí, who wrote: "My slingshot is the sling of David." Having draped himself with Martí's mantle, Castro needs an antagonistic Washington so that he can fulfill the role of Cuba's savior.

His trump card is Cuban nationalist sentiment. Clinton's saber rattling in the wake of the shooting in February 1996 allowed Castro to revive flagging anti-Yankeeism and consolidate his tenure at home by jailing dissidents in the face of renewed U.S. aggression. Passage of the Helms-Burton bill had taken things one step further: The law had been condemned by everyone from the Pope to the Organization of American States. Every time I watched the evening news on Cuban TV or picked up a copy of *Granma,* the lead story gloated that U.S. allies had overwhelmingly taken Cuba's side. To Cubans, the law—publicized all over Cuba—reeked of Yankee imperialism. It also threatened to worsen their hardships. Understandably, it united Cubans behind the Castro government as nothing else had done in years.

It was difficult to keep my mind on the road as I roared up La Farola, the highway sometimes called "Cuba's roller coaster," winding up and over the Sierra del Purisal extending like a dragon's spine to the easternmost tip of Cuba. The road twisted up through the valley of the Yumurí and Ojo rivers, whose banks were lined with palms like Moroccan oases. Above, steepled cliffs soared skyward like the great buttresses of a medieval cathedral. Squinting upward, I could make out the hairline road and bridges suspended magically upon the mountainside. La Farola struck me as a marvelous piece of engineering.

There are times when it is wonderful to be utterly alone amid a wild landscape. This was such a time. The noise of the bike seemed like an invasion of the mountain serenity, so I pulled over, cut the engine, and savored the scene—the air fresh and clear and scented by pines, the sky deep blue and cloudless, the sunlight combing down through the treetops, playing mercurially upon the jagged green-draped peaks, highlighting distant waterfalls that glittered like quicksilver ribbons.

The only sound was the wind in the pines. I put my feet up on the hand grips, leaned back into my luggage, and fell asleep beneath the warm caress of the late-afternoon sun.

CHAPTER THIRTEEN

THE INTERROGATION

Baracoa was as haunting in its fantastical unfamiliarity as it was enchanting in its beauty.

The town's setting seemed fitting for a Hollywood epic. Baracoa spread-eagled below a dramatic flat-topped formation—El Yunque (the Anvil)—that floated mysteriously above the surrounding hills, forming a great amphitheater flowing down to the Bahía de Miel (Bay of Honey).

I discovered Baracoa's beauty at dawn. A fitful, asthmatic slumber had led me to rise before sunup. I rubbed the sleep from my eyes and stepped onto the veranda outside my room at the Hotel El Castillo, which occupies a former fortress—Castillo Seburuco—constructed in the 1730s atop a promontory that separates the bay from the roiling ocean and offers a bird's-eye view over town. The scent of a recent shower hung in the air. Baracoa basked in a felicitous silence. Below, tiny red-roofed wooden houses were cloaked in shadow. Dawning sunlight glittered upon the waters, and a rubicund radiance mantled the mountain meniscus. El Yunque glowed like hot coals. I leaned against the porch rail and watched sun-reddened mists pour down from the jagged palisade.

As the sun rose above the horizon, it ignited the rusting fishing boats and tinged the spindly palm tops with saffron. Burning sunlight splashed the rooftops with methyl violet and fiery vermilion, and for a moment it seemed as if the Lilliputian town was ablaze. Then the tropical sun shot skyward and the sublime conflagration was extinguished with magical swiftness, leaving only a chimerical memory of the evanescent enchantment of Baracoa at dawn.

I set out with pen, notebook, and camera to rummage the dusty streets. They were lined with humble wooden edifices fronted by eaves supported by creaking timber frames. Baracoa—the oldest colonial city in the Americas—was feeling its age.

The town was the first of seven *villas* founded by Diego Velásquez de Cuellar, the first governor of Cuba. Looking quite dapper in his plumed hat and velvet cloak tufted with gold, Velásquez had arrived in 1511 and established La Villa de Nuestra Señora de la Asunción; from there he set out to conquer the rest of Cuba. The indigenous Taino population resisted the strange Europeans who came dressed in leathers and metal helmets and breast plates. The Spaniards, for their part, were not on a holy mission: They quested for silver and gold. Bartolomé de las Casas, a Jesuit priest who accompanied Velásquez, recorded a typical encounter in his *History of the Indies*:

> "The Indians came to meete us, and to receive us with victuals, and delicate cheere…the Devill put himselfe into the Spaniards, to put them all to the edge of the sword in my presence, without any cause whatsoever, more than three thousand soules, which were set before us, men, women and children. I saw there so great cruelties, that never any man living either have or shall see the like."

Cuba's peaceable Taíno population did its best to resist the cutthroat proselytizers. The ill-fated resistance was led by Hatuey, an Indian *cacique* (chieftain) who had fought the Spanish on neighboring Hispaniola and fled to Cuba after his people were subjugated and enslaved. It was a hopeless cause. Hatuey, was captured and put to the stake. As the flames crackled around Hatuey's feet, he was asked if he would like to be baptized so that he might go to heaven. Hatuey asked whether the Spanish went to heaven when they died. When Father Juan de Tesín replied "Yes," Hatuey replied that he did not want to go where there were such cruel and wicked people as the Christians. The Spaniards had just provided Cuba with its first martyr to independence.

The citizens of Baracoa had honored the Indian hero with a bust that rested upon a whitewashed concrete pedestal in a corner of Plaza Independencia—a compact, triangular park colloquially called by its old name, Plaza Cacique Hatuey. A row of checkered plastic sheets atop aluminum trays had been laid out in the cool shade of lofty coconut palms to serve as chessboards, and six steel-tubed folding chairs were set out along one side. Six youths, all boys, occupied the seats. They played the black pieces. A handsome adolescent with a thick crop of black hair moved from table to table, working the white pieces. He wore navy blue sneakers, black jeans, and a yellow T-shirt. Twelve-year-old Andrés Pierra is a local hero hailed as the next José Raúl Capablanca, the Cuban-born chess player who reigned as world champion from 1921 to 1927 and spawned Cubans' abiding passion for chess.

In every town I visited I saw Cuban males, young and old, playing chess. Cuba was a nation of thinkers.

I sat on a bench and scribbled some notes.

"Pardóneme, señor."

I looked up into the square face of a woman with light bronze skin and wide, angular cheekbones bespeaking Indian blood. Baracoa was made up of a polyglot mixture of people; if ever a pot had melted, it was Cuba. She asked anemically if I could spare my pen for her son. "My boy has nothing to write with."

I was about to gladly hand over my pen when out of the blue a midget ran up and swiped the woman in the belly—more to my astonishment, I think, than hers. He stood there, grinning inanely, an easy target. She slugged him hard on the side of his head with her fist. He collapsed against a tree and remained there, hurling insults at the amused onlookers. Minutes later I passed a tall, slender black man with a large nose—Cesár Paumier Frómeta—striding along the Malecón, leading by a thin leash a small pig tiptoeing on dainty trotters.

Baracoa resembled a real-life Macondo, the setting for Gabriel García Márquez's novel *One Hundred Years of Solitude*, in which José Arcadio Buendía and his wife, Ursula, flee their native village to escape death and the fate of intermarriage that will end up producing a child with a pig's tail. Although José and Ursula establish Macondo, they carry within themselves the seeds of that which they seek to elude. At times, Cuba seemed like a magical realm where the borders between reality and fantasy intertwine. Perhaps Compañero Frómeta was really José Arcadio Buendía, and perhaps his pig Catalina was...Perhaps the sun was addling my brain.

Isolation breeds individuality. Historically, Baracoa's inauspicious geographical circumstance had done little to favor the settlement. Because Velásquez's Spanish *villa* was remote and cut off by rugged mountains from the rest of Cuba, in 1517 Santiago—with its vastly superior harbor—was proclaimed the new capital. For four centuries, Baracoa stumbled along on smuggling and a meager cocoa trade (the mountainous terrain kept the land from being planted in precious sugar). On the eve of the Revolution, the town still languished in limbo, with no road or rail link to the rest of Cuba.

After Castro came to power, Baracoa's status changed significantly. Doctors and nurses arrived along with teachers sent to staff the health clinics, schools, cultural institutions, and sports centers that the town had long been denied. Finally, in 1964, a long-touted highway—La Farola—was built over the mountains, linking Baracoa with Santiago de Cuba.

I watched youngsters bounding along the parapet of the tiny Matachín fortress, dragging homemade kites behind them. Cyclists teetered en masse through the dusty streets, many with passengers, even whole families, hanging precariously onto *parrillas*—jury-rigged luggage racks—and *tetos*, or rear-hub extenders. The bikes' chirping warning bells lent the town the air of a tropical aviary.

By noon, Baracoa sizzled in fatty heat. Walking the streets was exhausting, so I cooled off in the hotel pool. A group of *norteamericanos* was supping Hatuey beers beneath poolside umbrellas. They were voluble, New Yorkers mostly, writers and photographers on assignment to research a special issue of *Colors*, a cutting-edge magazine published by the United Colors of Benetton clothing company. "To find out what life in a small Cuban town is like," said photographer Marirosa Toscani Ballo.

I relaxed on a lounge chair and watched Marirosa arrange a handmade coffeemaker for a still-life photo. She snapped away—click, whirr...click, whirr—while the hotel maid poured water from a tin kettle.

I tried some small talk, but my heart wasn't in it. After two months in Cuba, I realized that I didn't miss contact with the United States. Or with Americans.

Baracoa is acclaimed for its regional cuisine, with coconut as the staple—something I hadn't experienced anywhere else in Cuba. Come to think of it, I hadn't seen many coconut palms on my journey either; the Royal palm, which produces datelike seeds, not nuts, dominates the Cuban landscape. Around Baracoa, however, the coconut palm—the Jamaican Tall that has enchanted tourists to the Caribbean for years—was truly the tree of life. I had snacked on sweet tidbits from streetside stalls: *pudin de boniato* (made from sugar, coconut milk, and sweet potato), sold for one peso; *yemitas* (sweet balls made with chocolate, coconut, and sugar); and delicious *turrón de coco*, a baked bar of grated coconut mixed with milk and sugar.

Baracoa therefore seemed like the place for a zesty meal. The menu in the hotel restaurant looked hopeful. I asked for the seafood dish prepared in coconut sauce, with annatto seeds, coriander, onion, hot pepper, oregano, and salt.

"*¡No hay!*" replied the waitress.

I tried a couple more options, but they too were inexplicably not to be had. Fortunately, the chicken casserole was available—a first for Cuba.

After an interminable wait, the waitress delivered a fried chicken leg and fries. My jaw dropped. "Excuse me. I ordered the casserole."

She stared at me quizzically. "*Sí, señor. Casserole,*" she replied, deadpan.

"But this is *pollo frito*."

"*Sí, señor.*"

Naively, I sent it back to the kitchen. The waitress returned moments later, bearing my chicken exactly as before—except for three pieces of sliced garlic sitting on top. There seemed no point in pursuing the issue.

Baracoa is delightful in the evening, when the midday heat is spent and the air more congenial for strolling the streets. I joined the local perambulation and was drawn to the Plaza José Martí, where the amiable townsfolk had assembled to watch TV alfresco. They were sitting on folding chairs arrayed in neat rows facing the television that by day is kept locked inside its case atop a stand. Virtually every household in Cuba owned a television. What were they doing here?

"*¡Los apogones!*" I was told. Electricity blackouts. They hit Baracoa nightly, drawing to the plaza the residents of whichever quarter had been assigned that evening's four-hour blackout.

Cubans, like everyone else, enjoy a good soap. That night they were watching *Te Odio, Mi Amor*, an immensely popular Brazilian soap opera. Faces silvered by the flickering light of the TV stared up in rapture.

My travels took me out to Punta de Maisí, the easternmost tip of Cuba. I followed the coast road east, past coves lined with silvery beaches and slender coconut palms tilting over the shore. Waves blasted rocky headlands. The scenery was greener than any I'd seen in Cuba. This is the island's rainy corner. Year-round, moist northeast trade winds meet the Sierra Cristal mountains and...bingo! The land seemed swollen like a bullfrog's neck with lush vegetation.

At Yumurí, 20 kilometers east of town, the road dropped to a delta where the wide Yumurí River breaks out of a deep canyon and pours into the sea. The wooden bridge had recently been washed away in a storm, and villagers were being ferried across the rushing water in small rowboats cobbled together from polystyrene and driftwood.

Three youths ran up and urged me to ride across the boulder-strewn river mouth where it met the hissing breakers of the Atlantic. I balked.

"Yes, yes! No problem. We will lift you," they intoned, eager to earn a few dollars hauling the BMW across the narrow causeway between river and sea. I studied the chances. I didn't fancy getting the bike soaked with salt water. Finally, cowardice got the upper hand and I took a backcountry route over the mountains.

The level road, designed to shake the fillings from my teeth, soon deteriorated into a track riddled with cavities and steeper than a dentist's bill. I was forced to forget the view and concentrate on the riding. Impossibly, the enduro trail then turned into a muddy stairway that my bike could negotiate only with wheezing difficulty. Thankful for first gear to fall back on, I coaxed the Beemer up and over the mountain; beyond a hamlet called Veguita Amarilla, I looked down over a canyon that seemed to descend into the Stone Age.

"Yikes!" I exclaimed, sounding like a character from a Walt Disney cartoon. I had spent the last two months perfecting my riding technique over terrain that would have challenged a mountain goat, but this was a whole new level.

Recent rains had gnawed at the mountainside, and a landslide had washed away the track ahead. The scree-littered scarp had settled at its angle of repose—the maximum angle at which loose material, such as a sandpile, stabilizes. Running perpendicular to the slope would be tricky, and I feared that the weight of the motorbike would trigger an avalanche, but I had come too far to turn back.

Feeling adventurous, I let out the clutch and trickled the bike down the steep slope with my feet out to prevent a spill. Scree fell away and the rear tire spun and squirmed, kicking up clouds of dust. Pebbles pinged off the crash pan like bullets. My ears popped with the fall in altitude.

The Paris-Dakar took the trail like an ibex. It seemed so incredibly light and responsive, as if the bike itself were in charge. *Mi moto Fidel* never failed to impress me with its handling.

Beyond the village of La Máquina, I looked down from the edge of the escarpment upon a vast coastal plain spread out like a Spanish *mantilla*. The journey over the mountains had taken almost two hours. The light was already failing as I descended a coral-strewn terrace bristling with thornbush and cactus, and pulled up where the trail fizzled out beside a lonesome *faro* (lighthouse) at Punta de Maisí, Cuba's easternmost land's end, experiencing sunset 40 minutes before it occurred in Havana.

April 20 dawned sharp as a needle. The scent of a nocturnal shower hung in the cool morning air, which sizzled with the wingbeats of dragonflies. Hummingbirds zipped back and forth, a cameo of iridescence against liquid green fronds and emerald sky.

I loaded up the bike, checked the oil levels, and set off for Holguín province. One hour west of Baracoa the landscape took a torrid turn, palm-clad plains and escarpments giving way to parched hills and golden savannas that rolled out to meet them. Beyond soared mountains the color of heated chrome.

These mountains, the Cuchillas de Moa, are a godsend for Cuba, fraught as they are with precious metals—cobalt, manganese, nickel—whose extraction forms the linchpin of the local economy, generating almost one quarter of the island's export earnings.

I pulled up before a massive ore-processing plant called Empresa Comandante Ernesto Che Guevara, guarded by a statue of the namesake hero towering astride the gates, cast in concrete on the scale of the Colossus of Rhodes. I whipped out my camera and, with the engine still running, snapped a few shots of tall smokestacks belching out vaporous plumes in a bouquet of bilious colors. Downwind a fog of metallic dust scoured my nostrils and ripped like talons at the back of my throat. I twisted the throttle and ran through the pall with my eyes squeezed tight. The powder rained down on the town of Moa, blanketing everything with a fine wash of rust-red dust. The rivers that ran to the sea flowed like the gutters of an abattoir. Leaking pipes hissed and bubbled, disgorging who knows what noxious stews.

U.S. mining corporations established the first mining ventures here during the 1930s. One, the Nicaro nickel mine, had been owned by the U.S. government. When relations between Havana and Washington turned rancorous, the operations were nationalized. Soviet money financed future expansion. The environment had been hammered and sickled into a grotesque gangue pitted with pestilential lagoons. Gnarled, splintered trees added to the dramatic effect, as if I had ridden into the aftermath of a World War I bombardment.

I traveled the low road of Cuba's fouled shore and tried not to notice the children swimming in the sickly soup that passed for the sea.

Cuba's landscapes are kaleidoscopic. Farther west I find myself back amid lime-green cane fields dusted by delicate white blossoms and speckled with the shade of Royal palms like shining sentinels made from petrified light. Familiar icons of this lovely country.

Cuba shimmers in the sun, a dream world between hallucination and reality. By midday a heat-induced delirium whirls around my brain. My body has been beaten with baseball bats, my right lung dissolved by mustard gas. My breath comes in harsh gasps as I ride, coughing up blood. Comatose in the saddle, I struggle to maintain my morale.

Holguín province is a blur.

I pass a junction marked for Birán. Here Fidel Castro Ruz was born on August 13, 1926 at Finca Manacas in a two-story house on wooden pilings with a cattle barn beneath. Fidel was the fifth of nine children of Ángel Castro y Argiz. His mother was the family housemaid, Lina Ruz González, whom Ángel married after divorcing his wife. Fidel's father had emigrated from Galicia in Spain as an impoverished 13-year-old, and he became modestly wealthy leasing land from the United Fruit Company to grow sugarcane to supply to their mills. Eventually his property expanded to a 26,000-acre domain that included a sawmill and a small nickel mine as well.

Fidel enjoyed a happy and privileged childhood, including an old-fashioned Jesuit education, though he lived modestly amid humble peasants and knew how atrociously the U.S.-owned *latifundio* treated local workers. Castro's boyhood impressions of destitution had a profound influence on him; there is no doubt that his empathy and concern for the underprivileged owes much to his youth. He works hard to downplay his social advantage, however, stressing with some validity the simplicity of his background. The early records of his family life are sketchy, and *el comandante* likes to keep it that way.

Whatever the reason, Castro's birthplace is not promoted. Nor is it marked on my maps. In my oneiric stupor, the name Birán fails to register. I keep going and eventually pull up outside the Hotel Guardalavaca.

Guardalavaca is a pocket-size resort, albeit Cuba's second largest. I count five hotels, a fistful of anemic restaurants, a couple of artisans' stores, a disco, two car rental agencies, a grocery, and a white-hot blazing beach on which Cubans and foreigners mingle. Having heard a lot of hype about Guardalavaca, I figured there'd be more. After a brief exploration I collapse, exhausted, in the scant shade of a thatched umbrella and savor the feel of the sand between my toes. The sun glancing off water the color of seedless grapes makes me squint. I watch the tricolor sails of windsurfers skim across the pellucid sea.

The tourists have a volleyball game going with the Cubans, and they are getting trounced. Their flaccid, pink-skinned, oil-basted bodies cause tremors as they splatter on the sand in futile attempts to reach perfectly placed spikes to the line. They smell of coconut suntan oil.

A Cuban picks up a guitar and strums a tune. Someone else joins in on an hourglass *batá* drum, and another with the *claves,* causing still others in swimwear to jump up and come together. They dance to the infectious rhythms, showing everyone else how to have a good time.

A svelte, cocoa-black girl sashaying along the beach in a string bikini tenders me a sibilant hiss and a ready smile suggestive of possible love beneath the palms.

I hear a long, involuntary sound like air escaping from a pinched balloon. An appreciative sigh from a lobster-red fellow lounging nearby.

"Prime, eh mate?" he calls in a thick London brogue. A bronze-skinned, blond-haired *cubana* laid out alongside him stabs him with the little paper umbrella from her flame-orange cocktail, then wiggles her body in a provocative reminder that she is his *chica.*

"Bloody brilliant! Beats Clacton, eh?" he cackles, referring to a tacky sea-side resort beloved of the English working class. He sounds like he's chewing on whelks. "Down't wonnit?" he adds, when I decline to acknowledge the black girl's advances. "Where you fwom then?"

This is not a conversation I wish to be drawn into. I join the Cuban children splashing about in the sun-warmed salt water. This would be paradise if only I weren't so ill.

The hotel's bland buffet dinner confirms the staggering monotony of state-proffered cuisine. I don't get it: How can every kitchen in Cuba produce such uniformly poor results? Like Cubans, I can't get my mind off thoughts of food. I'm going crazy. Visions of sushi and salmon and the pungent aromas of pad thai and curried lamb swirl around in my tandooried mind. Later I learn that Havana's bureaucrats dictated restaurant menus years ago, even stipulating how each dish should be prepared. Every restaurant kitchen in Cuba received a directive to be posted. Decades later the commandments were still there, with predictable results.

I am, to say the least, feeling less than charitable toward Cuba. I sink into a bitter mood in which all I can discern are imperfections, decay, and dishevel-ment. Bad food and dolorous decor. Peeling paint, plastic furniture, faded linoleum, worn shag carpeting—bland, bland, bland! Socialist utopia looks dis-mal. I notice only the stench of socialist decomposition hanging over the streets like Banquo's ghost. My fever is sapping not only my strength but my objectiv-ity, clouding my view of this enchantingly beautiful land.

Or is it?

Nothing has seemed the same since my shocking revelation at Cojababo. I feel betrayed. I hear Francisco's accusatory voice in my ears: *"¡Caimán!"* The Cuban word for crocodile, colloquially used to describe a cunning, deceitful per-son. The hiatus in my heart has flooded with contempt and cynicism, curdling my affection for this haunted land and its leader.

I flop by the pool and fill my notebooks with swarming *recherches visuelles*, let-ting my acerbic imagination run unchecked in a rage of flamboyant revenge. My caustic comments twist Cuba's misfortunes into Machiavellian misadventures, depicting Fidel Castro as a genius of the surreal and the hallucinatory scope of his dreams as chimerical as the long-legged elephants in a Dali painting. By the time I've poured out my bile, my notebooks are hot enough to burst into flames.

Depression engulfs me. There's a vacuity in my soul. I feel like I'm becoming ungrounded, that I've lost my foundation.

I decide to call Sheri Powers, my best friend and attorney in California. The hotel receptionist puts me through on her telephone in an office the size of a jail cell.

"Hi, honey!" Sheri exclaims, sounding delighted to hear from me. "How's it going?"

"I'm so-so," I reply over the fizzling static. "This journey has turned into an ordeal." The receptionist leans back in her chair and begins preening her fingernails.

"Oh, no! How come?" says Sheri.

"I'm weary. I'm having a change of heart. Cuba no longer looks so rosy."

"Why? What's wrong?"

"For one thing, the food is atrocious. I've lost so much weight I look like a bloody scarecrow. Plus, I'm sick and the doctors don't have a goddamn clue."

Sheri's reassuring voice and my own inflamed emotions make me incautious. I launch misanthropically into a litany of the nation's failings.

"Wow!" she responds. "It sounds like you're ready to come home."

"Yeah! I feel like I'm trapped in a screwed-up time warp where nothing works."

A thirty-something man in neat-pressed denim jeans and polished dress shoes peers at me from behind a copy of *Granma*.

I slept soundly and greeted the next day in strong spirits. Cuba's New Man. My conversation with Sheri had exorcised my mordant musings. The day had broken gin-clear, with a rich, pearly quality to the morning sky. Plump clouds scudded across the horizon, mutating into huge pillowy towers above the lapis lazuli Atlantic. Guardalavaca registered more impressively. I set out for the provincial capital of Holguín humming lines from a popular Cuban love song: *"Bésame...Bésame mucho!"*

Bright-red crotons flamed alongside route 6-241 as I climbed gently inland, the road rising mile after mile as steady as a line in a logarithmic equation. As I crested the hill, two *tráficos* on Moto Guzzis streaked past in a blur, roaring toward Guardalavaca. My sixth sense stirred. I glanced in my mirror and saw them brake sharply and turn, blue lights flashing. A siren pierced the stillness:

"*Whee-whee! Wheee-wheee!*" I pulled over and cut the engine. One cop pulled up sharply, crosswise in front of me. The other pulled in behind, tire to tire. Checkmate. They were stern-faced, filled with police purpose.

"*¡Documentos!*"

No salute? That was a first—and it meant business. I handed over the vehicle registration license issued to me by MININT in Havana.

"*¡Pasaporte y permiso!*"

I unzipped the tank bag, flipped it up, unlocked the safety box built into the gas tank, and fished out my passport and international driver's license. The cop walked over to his bike, turned on his radio microphone, and began reading details of my documents over a flurry of static.

I'd been anticipating this moment. It seemed remarkable that I had ridden more than 5,000 miles through Cuba without being questioned by police. Juan Pardo had warned me that I wouldn't be able to travel through Cuba alone without being monitored. I guessed that someone—probably the guy with the shiny shoes—had reported my choleric conversation with Sheri to MININT, the agency that oversees state security. Cuban authorities do not look favorably upon foreigners making inflammatory comments. Given 30-odd years of efforts by the U.S. government to destabilize the Castro regime, who can blame them?

I thought of my notebooks, brimming with bilious comments. The gravity of my situation was clear.

"You must wait here," said the policeman.

I asked why.

"*Compañeros* are coming from Holguín," he replied. He unzipped his black leather jacket and slipped my documents into an inside pocket. Then he lit a cigarette for his partner and a second for himself, and together they studied the BMW in silence from beneath the shade of a nearby tree. I lay back in the saddle and watched buzzards gliding on thermals.

Twenty minutes later, a Prussian-blue Lada pulled up. Cracked windshield. Rusty fenders. It looked ready for the knacker's yard. Two MININT agents stepped out. One was short, stocky, and well muscled, with close-cropped hair. He was dressed neatly in a pale blue guayabera worn Cuban fashion outside his chestnut-colored pants, and he had a calm, confident air. The other was a weasly fellow of medium height, with a hollow chest and narrow, childlike hips accentuated by a form-fitting white shirt tucked inside tight black trousers. He had a stoat's spiteful face and a ferret's furtiveness. He studied me from behind Ray-Ban sunglasses.

The cop handed my papers to the shorter agent, who scrutinized them, then ran his gray-blue eyes over me. A blue-and-white police car also arrived, and into it the agent inserted himself, settling into the passenger seat to initiate a lengthy dialogue on the radio that seemed to involve the particulars of my passport and papers. Minutes ticked by with the thrumming of bees and the steady cadence of cicadas harmonizing with the crackle and buzz of the radio.

Three French tourists drew up in a rented Peugeot 205 and asked me if I needed help. The weasel stepped between us and shooed them away. As they drove off, a woman peered back through the rear window, looking concerned for my welfare. By contrast, I felt curiously serene and confident; in a perverse way, I was actually enjoying the adventure. Anxiety had been edged out by a sense of inevitable absolution and the intrigue of wanting to discover the denouement.

"*Señor*, please follow us," said the shorter agent, emerging from the car. He directed the *tráficos* to ride alongside. I fired up the boiler and dropped into first gear. One of the cops held his index finger erect to my face and spat out a command: "*¡Despacio!*" Slowly! He indicated a limit of 40 kilometers per hour, then slid his finger across his throat in case I had missed the point. The Lada led the parade with me behind, sandwiched between the two moto cops. The police car brought up the rear.

We cruised along like a presidential motorcade all the way to Holguín, where we pulled up outside MININT regional headquarters—a small, nondescript building on Avenida Francisco Frexes. I was led into a windowless anterior room. A fan stirred the thick air, and an air-conditioning unit hummed a shrill drone as droplets of condensation fell rhythmically into a puddle on the tile floor: Plop!...plop!...plop! The only decoration was a faded photo of Fidel, hung on a mildewed wall the color of verdigris.

"Forgive me," said the shorter agent in Spanish, seating himself behind a large gray metal desk. "This is very unusual, you understand. Tourists are not normally questioned in this way." He beckoned me to be seated. "I hope you don't mind if I ask a few questions?"

A young woman entered and sat down behind an adjacent desk. She had remnants of cherry-red polish on her long feline nails, which clacked on the keys of an old Royal typewriter. The keys fell with a dull *thwump* on a sheet of coarse brown paper.

The questioning began matter-of-factly. "What is your name? What is your country? Where do you live now? For how many years have you lived in the United States?" Then, leaning forward, he asked weightily, "And what do you do for a living?" The agent smiled slightly to put me at ease.

Journalists are a suspect breed in the eyes of Cuban authorities. Those wishing to visit Cuba are required to obtain a special visa in advance from a Cuban consulate; once they arrive, they face the likelihood of constant surveillance. Not wishing to compromise my freedom, I had cut all ties with Publicitur and other Cuban agencies. I had entered on a simple tourist visa and at all costs wished to avoid implicating myself as a journalist. On the line asking me to define my profession, I had written "Consultant"—a suitably malleable occupation—but I sensed that my inquisitor knew the true answer. MININT, which oversees all aspects of state security, had had two years to collate a file on me following my early contacts with Raúl Colominas of MINREX, Juan Pardo of Publicitur, and others. Details from my dossier had most likely been faxed here from MININT headquarters in Havana. For all I knew, they were recording details of my journey through Cuba.

"I work for myself as a *consultante de turismo*," I replied, believing it best to stay close to the truth.

"What is a *consultante de turismo?*" the agent asked, not missing a beat. His look flashed from smiling to serious.

"Well," I answered, "I consult and teach about travel, and occasionally I write about it, too."

"Then you are a journalist."

It sounded like an accusation, not a question.

"No, I am a consultant. But sometimes I am asked to write."

"What do you write?"

"Mostly promotional profiles for the travel industry."

"Do you operate tours?"

It was an astute question. I had once owned my own tour company and had dissolved it only recently. I told him the truth. He asked for the name of my business. I told him, but I sensed that he already knew.

The security agent turned his attention to the BMW.

"How did you bring it to Cuba?" he queried. Here was my opportunity to establish my support for socialist Cuba. I described my connections to BASTA!, an organization sympathetic to Castro's Cuba, and explained that I had crossed on a boat bringing humanitarian aid. I also pointed out that I had donated my time and energies on behalf of Global Exchange and other nongovernmental organizations in the United States working to end the embargo.

"Do you have the addresses of these organizations?" he asked skeptically.

"Wait a minute!" I replied, asking permission to retrieve the letter I was carrying from Medea Benajmin, director of Global Exchange. He studied it, then passed it to the other agent, who had been sitting behind me, drilling a chill stare into the back of my neck. The weasel began copying the letter in longhand. I let him finish while the questioning continued, then nonchalantly pointed at the photocopied sheet I had handed him: "You can keep it."

His purple eyes tightened, sinister as a snake's.

The interrogator smiled. He was warming, but still he probed.

"Where did you stay last night? At what time did you leave the hotel? What route did you take? Are you going to stay in Holguín? At what hotel?"

He leaned forward again. "Forgive me for all these questions, but we have to check. It is highly unusual to see a foreigner on a moto. There are many foreigners, but few receive this type of questioning."

"Entiendo, no me molesta," I replied. It was okay, I understood.

"Cuba has many enemies," the MININT agent explained.

I agreed. "You must be very cautious."

Finally, after more than an hour, he got up to leave. My hopes that the interrogation was over, however, were dashed when the weasel took his place. Our eyes met. He stared, unblinking, for 20 or 30 seconds. I held his gaze the entire time.

"How did you like Guardalavaca?" he asked, breaking the frosty silence. I told him I found it quite beautiful.

He glowered, then leaned forward. His halitosis crinkled my nostrils.

"Is this your first visit to Cuba?"

I said simply, without embellishment, that I had visited the year before.

"And how do you like Cuba?" he probed, hinting tangibly that the feelings I had expressed to Sheri had not been private.

"It's a splendid place," I replied, digging deep into my well of attachment.

"And what do you *think* about Cuba?" he asked, digging deeper himself.

〜

CHAPTER FOURTEEN

DIAMOND-DUST BEACHES

T he encounter in Holguín sobered me. I decided that I needed to slow
down instead of galloping through the country like some sort of
mechanical centaur. My political disenchantment was making me aloof and
inaccessible to the Cuban people. I had begun seeing them from an emotional
distance, seeing Cuba through Western capitalist eyes.

I was feeling maudlin, insensate to the enchantment around me and
overflowing with the flakiness and fluff of the Me Decade I carried within.
Baker, you bloody narcissist! Wasn't that what this journey was all about,
anyway—a search for a masculine model on which to bolster my own sense
of self?

Feverish, I slumped in the saddle and let my melancholic mind trawl up memories of cherished moments with Daisy. I rode with her angelic image in front
of me, floating in a heat mirage at an intangible distance. I tried to scrutinize
her features, break her beauty down into parts. I felt happy that I still had her
with me, inside.

I reached out my left hand, grasping for a morsel of discarded affection. In
my mind's eye our hands touched and I saw her tender, dreamy look. I tried to
speak but my voice broke, so I took a deep breath and tried again. All I heard
was my plaintive cries and the rippling of the tires on the asphalt.

The road ran past thick mangrove tangles growing in brackish backwaters that smelled like ripe Brie. Side roads probed the spartan landscape, spilling me now and then onto white sand beaches where the tracks petered out by the shore. I passed the rotting carcasses of abandoned rail carriages and bulldozers rusting in the sun and salt air.

I'd done enough touring to know that roads marked on Cuban maps were often no more than a cartographer's whim. Some of the squiggles matched the real world; the squiggle to Playa Uvero did not. Beyond Gibara the road whittled down to packed chip rock, then sand churned into a bone-jarring washboard designed to rearrange my kidneys. It was a bad sign, but I kept going.

I passed a lighthouse at Caletones, where the track really began to get gnarly and the mangroves closed in. As long as I wasn't carried off into the mangroves by the mosquitoes, I reckoned I could get through. A mile or so farther on at the very end of the trail, engulfed by stagnant swamps, ankle deep in gloppy mud resembling sewage, I discovered that my back tire had picked up a six-inch nail buried deep between the treads about an inch left of center. I groaned, then wrestled the bike around and managed to get back to dry land while I still had some air in the tire. I unloaded all the heavy gear and put the bike on the center stand. Sweat dripped off my eyebrows and into my eyes, drawing a squadron of buzzing flies. Mosquitoes whined in my ears. I yanked out the nail with my pliers, unzipped my emergency tire repair kit, reamed the hole, cemented and inserted a rubber plug, and cut the excess away with my Swiss Army knife. Then I pulled out a screw-in canister of carbon dioxide designed to screw into the valve and—hey presto!—inflated the tubeless tire.

I took a recuperative dip in the ocean and savored the tug of the cool white surf, then fired up and ran south on the main road for Las Tunas, keeping the speed down to 50 in case the plug blew. When my journey came to an end one month and 2,000 miles later, I was still riding on that plug.

I found myself once more at the Hotel Las Tunas, where I awoke fatigued and famished after a night spent coughing up a wild lynx in my chest.

"Sorry, señor, there is no fruit juice," said the waitress. "How about butter?" I asked, pointing at the rock-hard bread. "No hay," she replied. Nor was there ham for my tortilla. Things are really bad when there is no ham in Cuba. But there were plenty of flies buzzing about, as there had been one month prior. That made sense: Flies feast on famine.

Next day, in Santa Lucía, I splurged on a room at the Golden Tulip Caracol, a modern two-story hotel operated jointly by Cubanacán and the Netherlands' Golden Tulip International. My air-conditioned suite was a bargain at 45 dollars and boasted a separate bedroom and lounge with cool tile floors, a TV showing CNN and HBO, and a view beyond the swimming pool to white sand silvering the shore like Cuban sugar.

I set out to research Cuba's third largest resort, which ran the length of a single road unspooling beside a 12-mile beach. Santa Lucía had been popular with Cuban vacationers until the Special Period put a serious dent in their budget. Tourist literature now hyped it to foreigners as a "sophisticated resort," but the raptures were a decade too soon. I counted five hotels and a fistful of restaurants scattered like far-flung planets in a vast void of flat grassland backed by a salt-crusted meringue. Still, there was scuba diving and sportfishing and horseback rides to keep guests amused, and bicycles and mopeds could be rented. A complex of prefab concrete boxes, three stories high, provided housing for Cuban workers, many who derived added income from renting rooms to out-of-town girls seeking a good time in the arms of Dutch, German, or Italian men.

Bronchitis bedeviled me. I was hacking miserably, short of breath, fevered, my energy spent, done in by heat exhaustion. I collapsed on the bed, sank into a fitful slumber, and awoke next morning swimming in sweat. A heat-induced lassitude overcame me each afternoon, compounding my month-old malaise.

Santa Lucía had a Clínica Internacional catering to tourists. The doctor, a tall mulatto, didn't even take my temperature or blood pressure. He let me offer my own diagnosis, then stuck his stethoscope to my chest and said nothing. Instead of asking questions, he looked perplexed.

"I'd appreciate it if you could take an X ray," I said. "Just to be sure I don't have pneumonia."

"I don't think that will be necessary."

"Yes, but I'd prefer one just to make sure. I'm willing to pay."

He stared down at the floor. "I'm sorry, *Señor* Baker," he replied after a long silence. "Our X ray machine isn't working."

The doctor rummaged through his meager drug supply and handed me three tiny tablets wrapped in silver foil stamped with the words *"CIPRO. Hecho en Mexico.*" I referred to my booklet, *A Comprehensive Guide to Wilderness & Travel Medicine*, which listed Ciprofloxacin as a cure for pneumonia. The booklet also recommended a dosage of 500 milligrams, taken twice daily for a week. My three tablets wouldn't go far.

I asked if the doctor had more.

He grimaced, then shook his head. "Unfortunately, that is all I have."

I felt his pain.

Even before the Special Period, Cuba's vaunted health system faced severe shortages. Since 1991, its plight has become perilous. That year 70 percent of U.S. subsidiary-company trade with Cuba—about $800 million—was in food and medicines (Cuba relied on the U.S. for the majority of its medicines). In 1992, believing that Castro was on the ropes, the U.S. Congress hit Cuba below the belt by passing the so-called Cuban Democracy Act, sponsored by Rep. Robert Torricelli (D-NJ), which banned all trade in food and medicines except humanitarian aid. It struck me as an act of utter spitefulness, heartless and immoral in the extreme. By barring such trade, the embargo has forced Cuba to import medicines and medical supplies from elsewhere at vastly inflated prices. Not content with its own turpitude, Congress—egged on by right-wing Cuban-Americans—also forced third-country companies to seek the U.S. Commerce Department's permission to export to Cuba any medical equipment or supplies manufactured in the U.S. or under U.S. patent. The Commerce Department then routinely denied such requests.

As a result, dissemination of medicines had plummeted. Doctors were writing prescriptions that pharmacies could no longer fill. Cuba's home-grown pharmaceutical industry—a world-class operation that had produced cures for meningitis and vitiligo—was exporting most of its products to raise funds to buy desperately needed oil and other essentials. Critical medicines were in such short supply that doctors had resorted to herbal remedies; hospitals, finding themselves without anesthetics, were forced to turn to acupuncture. Operating theaters and hospital wards went without soaps, antibiotics, antibacterial medicines, and disinfectants. And materials for diagnostic tests had virtually disappeared. An exemplary health system that had been able to guarantee every Cuban citizen free and accessible care could now guarantee nothing. It was Uncle Sam's shame, and it made me angry.

Whatever medicines were available, I knew, were going to foreign visitors.

"The mangrove roots were showing plainly now and the key looked as though it were on stilts," wrote Ernest Hemingway as his moody protagonist Thomas Hudson approached Cayo Guillermo in *Islands in the Stream*. Then he saw a flight of flamingos coming from the left. They were skimming the water, lovely to see in the sunlight.

I could see them now, too, as I roared toward a large, low-lying cay—Cayo Sabinal—attached to the mainland by a hairbreadth isthmus. The road of hard-packed coral seemed to float above the waters of Laguna de los Flamencoes, a precious mirror reflecting the gawky flamingos tiptoeing around in hot pink. They looked like feathered roses atop carnation stems, quite at odds with their blue surroundings.

I grabbed my camera, dismounted, and sat the bike at idle, then scrambled down the bank. Stepping onto the gelatinous mud was an error; I was up to my calves before the third stride. The flock retreated en masse. One step too far and the birds were off, webbed feet stamping the water surface to foam as their flame-pink wings beat for lift in their ungainly takeoff. Several hundred blushing birds suddenly poured into the blue bowl of sky like a great cloud at sunset. With reaching head and neck and trailing legs outstretched, they circled and came to rest where they started.

Cayo Sabinal is the easternmost of the Cayería del Norte, a seagirt wilderness of sandy coral islands that crouch five to 15 miles offshore in a great line that parallels the coast for almost 300 miles. Few among the 400 or so are inhabited or even accessible. Together they are among the least disturbed of Cuba's terrains—sun-bleached coral jewels in a sapphire sea. The cays are encircled by reefs, edged by mangroves, and smothered by scrub with thorn-clad stems; casuarinas, a hardy Australian pine, push up between saucerlike pools filled with a fetid broth, yellow and salty white.

I passed a few *bohíos* belonging to charcoal burners, soot-stained *carbonero*. These isolated, hospitable people eke out an austere livelihood axing mangroves, accepting the country on its own terms. They pointed the way to Playa Los Pinos. Tough going in the soft sand. I needed Michelin "Desert" tires. I couldn't afford to lower the tire pressure; heaven knows when I'd find more air. So I stood on the foot pegs and cranked the throttle to give the bike some oomph and ran in third gear with the power on, letting the engine's torque do the work.

Playa Los Pinos was the most beautiful beach I had ever seen. When I took off my sunglasses, I was blinded by the glittering glare of the sun on the sand dissolving into a lagoon of startling hues. Pale green were the shallows. Aqua and azure and then sapphire was the sea farther out. Far off, the Gulf Stream gleamed deep indigo. A few stilt-legged waders patrolled the shoreline with their heads tilted forward, long beaks jabbing at the sand, while a lone frigate bird with scimitar wings and forked tail hung in the sky. The silence was absolute, save for the muffled drone of the surf breaking on the outer reef. Then a stingray leaped clear of the water and fell back with a slap that echoed across the lagoon.

There were no jet skis, no catamarans or Sunfish, no waterskiing—nothing but frost-white sand and coral reef and turquoise ocean stretching off into the hazy beyond. I was seeing Cuba through the eyes of a conquistador. The Cuban government, however, is savvy to the archipelago's untainted allure. Cuba's master plan for tourism development has slated Sabinal to receive 12,000 hotel rooms.

My only option was a homespun cabana made of palm trunks and mangrove roots, with thatch for a roof. Robinson Crusoe would have been proud. It had a rough-hewn bed, a side table with low-watt lamp, a cement floor, and a simple bathroom with a cold-water shower. My folksy home was one of five such cabanas attached to a bucolic beach bar with chairs of sunbaked cowhide and walls of woven palm festooned with fishing nets and grinning shark jaws. There were no other guests, bestowing a wonderful silence. For 25 dollars I got breakfast and dinner included.

Francisco, the old Cuban caretaker, took a simple pleasure in keeping the place spick-and-span. Kind and friendly, full of integrity, he spoke sparingly and smiled willingly. I enjoyed his presence.

I hauled my bags to my hut, stripped off my leather pants, showered and put on shorts, then settled beneath the shady thatch by the bar. Magically, on cue, a rowboat pulled up and a tall, well-muscled young man dressed in swimming trunks jumped out and held up the lunch menu: a huge lobster in one hand and a large incarnadine snapper in the other.

Far out in the limpid shallows, two white males were wading with some *negritas*. Later, I watched them splash ashore and settle themselves on the sand. One of the women held in her hand a bright pink conch shell that accessorized her bright pink bikini. I thought her exquisite. She looked like a mermaid that had washed up from the waves, sleek and fish-like.

"Excuse me," I said boldly. "Your colors are fabulous. I'd like to photograph you, with your permission." She beamed, then looked beseechingly at the man.

"I suppose so," the Italian replied glumly on her behalf. She lay willingly as I requested against the white sand at the water's edge and arranged herself in a sexy pose, her breasts jutting forward and her back arched.

"*Basta!*" the Italian exclaimed excitedly, putting an end to things after I had shot only two frames. "*Enough!*"

I wandered down the beach and lay on my back with my eyes closed and savored the salty air, feeling drunk on the radiant sunshine. Minutes later the second girl sashayed past, splashing along in the ripples. I heard her shout to her friend and laugh. She advanced toward me until I could feel the cool of her shadow cross my skin. I peered upward, squinting against the harsh light, and admired her long foreshortened legs still glistening from the sea. She introduced herself as Diana. Her friend's name was Luzel.

"You're alone?" she asked matter-of-factly in Spanish.

"Yes."

"Why no *chica?*"

I explained that I was just passing through.

"Are you staying here?"

I told her I was.

"There are chicas in Santa Lucia," she added, as if a man without a woman was no man at all.

"I think your male friend is watching." The Italian was staring down the beach toward us, his furrowed brow shadowed in the harsh sunlight.

"You have beautiful eyes," Diana said. With that she turned tail and sauntered off, as sensuous and sinuous as Sonia Braga. I lay back and let my imagination conjure a perfect fantasy with this saucy *señora*. It was the elderly Italians, however, whose fantasies were being fulfilled. It seems they had rented a bohío for "short time." The males disappeared and reappeared with each of the women in turn until all four permutations—and, presumably, all four libidos—had been sated.

"*Señor... ¡ciao!*" Diana called, waving gaily much later as the foursome walked to their car and departed.

I got up and continued strolling. The beach was firm underfoot, and as I walked the silky sand seemed to coruscate, like sparkling diamonds washed ashore from a Spanish treasure ship. Two soldiers passed, hauling a large piece of driftwood between them. One, slender and a deep chestnut color, was dressed in a camouflage jacket, shorts, and designer sandals. The other, a tall, sunbaked black man, wore deep green battle dress, much faded and greatly torn. Each had an AK-47 assault rifle slung across his back. We nodded to each other in passing.

The two soldiers returned at dusk and sat at the bar. I offered fraternal greetings: *"¡Buenas noches!"* They raised their heads in acknowledgment, but neither said a word. I asked them whether their rifles were Russian. The short one merely nodded. The darker of the two said nothing, but stared me down and drove me off with his piercing gaze. I walked a short way down the beach and sat on the soft sand and listened to the drowsy monotone of the surf breaking on the distant reef. The warm breeze had shifted and was now blowing offshore, bringing toward me the voices at the bar. The soldiers were asking questions about the foreign motorcyclist.

I was as curious about the soldiers as they were about me, and after a sufficient time I returned to the bar and stood the aloof duo drinks.

"Compañeros. May I buy each of you a *mojito?"*

The dutiful guardsmen could not be tempted. Instead, they promptly paid for their drinks and departed, as if I bore the plague. A short time later the tall one reappeared and hovered in the shadows, whispering conspiratorially in Francisco's ear.

Francisco was not at all garrulous. As I tucked into my dinner, however, he broke his long silence. "Have you been long in Cuba?" he asked. It was the first question he had asked me all day, and I felt sure that the soldiers had put him up to it.

"How do you feel about Cuba?" he added, straining to appear nonchalant.

I felt a sinister déjà vu. Indubitably, MININT was still at work: My passage through Cuba was being tracked. On my blazing red-and-white behemoth, I might as well have been riding through Cuba with a herald of angels.

That evening, Francisco's assistant—a young, rake-thin chap named Tony— slipped me a scrap of paper tightly folded like a piece of origami to the size of a postage stamp. I unfolded it and read the hastily scribbled words: "Secret. Please not say anything about nobody. Write me after June 11." It was from Luzel. She had added her home address in Santiago de Cuba. Like Daisy, she was hedging her bets.

That night, with the sky undimmed by city lights, I sat for a while on the still-warm sand and watched the northern constellations wheel west. The blue-black sky was plump with stars, and the lagoon shimmered like silk in the moonlight, so clear and calm that the reflection of the winking stars kissed the glassy waters. Waves whispered as they broke on the distant reef. Eventually a light wind that smelled of the open sea picked up, rustling the palms. The sigh of the breeze between the slats of the walls was the sweetest lullaby. Lying beneath a well-worn cotton sheet and ruminating on the encounter with the soldiers and Francisco's transparent questioning, I drifted off to sleep.

I had parked the bike where I could see it, stripped off my leathers, and in my underwear waded out through the knee-deep shallows until I finally reached the reef and discovered a world more beautiful than a casket of gems beneath the crystal surface. Looking back to shore, I could see the land as Ernest Hemingway saw it when sailing with the sun at his back, advancing with an alert eye through a canal heading for a line of dark green cays rising out of the water until he was close enough to see their sandy beaches. It was here, at Puerto Coco, that Thomas Hudson set foot on the sands seeking traces of German sailors in *Islands in the Stream*.

The novel wasn't all make-believe. In May 1942, Hemingway showed up at the U.S. embassy in Havana with a proposal to retrofit his beloved sportfish-ing boat, the *Pilar*, as a Q-boat, equipping it with .50-caliber machine guns, other armaments, and a trained crew led by himself. The boat would navigate the cays off the north coast of Cuba, ostensibly collecting specimens on behalf of the American Museum of Natural History but in fact prowling for German U-boats, which Hemingway intended to engage. The author was "quite pre-pared to sacrifice his beloved vessel in exchange for the capture or sinking of an enemy submarine," reported Hemingway's biographer, Carlos Baker. The Chief of Naval Intelligence for Central America, Colonel John W. Thomason, Jr., was a friend of Hemingway's, and he pulled strings to get the plan approved.

The vessel was camouflaged and duly set out for the cays. Gregorio Fuentes—who from 1938 until the writer's death was Hemingway's skipper aboard the *Pilar*—went along and served as the model for Antonio in *Islands in the Stream*. They patrolled for two years. Several times they located and reported the presence of German submarines that the U.S. Navy or Army Air

Corps was later able to sink. Only once, off Cayo Mégano, did Hemingway come close to his dream: A U-boat suddenly surfaced while the *Pilar* was at anchor. Unfortunately, it dipped back below the surface and disappeared before Hemingway could get close.

Cayo Coco's colors were prime, like a Hockney painting pulsating in the dazzling Caribbean light. I had reached the remote coral isle via a *pedraplen*— a 17-mile-long, man-made tombolo unspooling across the mirrored waters of Bahía de Perros. It was built in 1988 of solid landfill without thought to sluices, so the roadway had dammed the currents, raising the salinity of the waters; as an inevitable consequence, the ecology was beginning to suffer. The flamingo population had been in decline for a decade.

The security checkpoint guarding the entrance to the *pedraplen* looked like an aircraft control tower. Minutes ticked by as a MININT agent in blue uniform scrutinized my documents. I could see him talking into a speaker behind the plate glass window, relaying details of my passport to headquarters. Eventually the agent emerged and brusquely asked for my driver's license and *chapa*. Another 10 minutes passed before my documents were returned and I was waved on. I was beginning to feel that I was being tailed.

My suspicion faded away with the exhilaration of chasing a heat haze down the unceasing drag strip. Well paved, sticky with melted tar, the road stretched 10 miles like a laser beam, then began to snake through the tiny cays that precede Cayo Coco, winding and looping past a morass of mangrove marshes studded with briny pools filled with a scum of pea green and jade. I savored the beauty of the stark landscape, riding now for its own sake, enjoying the calm and the silence as the harsh glare of midday gave way to a soft amber light. I was slicing and swooshing, doing the twisty two-lane tango, pressing down with my hand in the direction of the curves and pressing my opposite knee to the tank to aid in carving the turns—real racer stuff. Then I scraped the bottom of the crash bar on the tarmac. Then my knee scuffed the ground, and the bike yawled from the luggage throwing the ergonomics out of kilter. Whoa! I eased up. The bike was too heavily laden for this Kenny Roberts stuff. One mistake and I would end up in a fetid platter of caustic marzipan.

The road leaped a cobbled humpback bridge and deposited me at the entrance to the Hotel Tryp, a joint Spanish-Cuban venture with a hangar-sized lobby held aloft by wide-girthed timber beams. Tourists dressed in homely Hawaiian shirts and enough Tommy Hilfiger to make me gag looked askance as I clomped across the luminous marble floor in my boots. I was wearing a sweat-stained tank top and mud-spattered leather pants, and my hair was matted and dusty from a long day on the road.

"How will you pay, sir?" asked the pretty receptionist in a stylish uniform, unruffled by my ragamuffin appearance.

"Credit card."

"¿Estados Unidos?" she asked, noting the tie pin of the Stars and Stripes over-laying the Cuban flag that I wore on my suspenders.

"No, I'm English," I responded, handing her my passport and a credit card issued by a British bank.

"Perfecto, señor. Would you prefer oceanfront or pool view?" She scanned her computer screen. Moments later she handed me a computer-coded plastic card key. "Have a nice stay, Señor Baker."

Two bellboys hurried forward to help haul my bags to my room. I could have been checking into the Sheraton Resort in Cancún. Cuba was learning.

Cuba's future is written in Cayo Coco's frosted sands. The cay is slated for major development, with a projected investment of $1.6 billion and at least 12 hotels due to rise along a whiter-than-white beach that seemed to unfurl for-ever. The Tryp has lassoed the Caribbean's trend for all-inclusive resorts: cash-free, self-contained properties where guests never have to dip into their wallets once inside the door, and even the booze is "on the house." The hotel boasts a whopping 1,000 rooms and a casual sophistication unlike anything I'd experienced thus far in Cuba. My airy room was done up in trendy tropical papaya, peach melba, and verdigris. It boasted a soft-cushioned sofa, a well-stocked mini-bar, CNN and HBO on the Sony TV, and a sleek marble bath-room with a wall-to-wall mirror, heaps of snow-white fluffy towels, and enough makeup space for a troupe of showgirls. I eased into a mood of recuperative indulgence by soaking up to my neck in the tub.

I was lured back into the bronze light of late afternoon by screams echoing from the large, amoeba-shaped pool: noisy revelers enjoying a boisterous volleyball game. Lively Latin rhythms ricocheted from the swim-up bar, where Canadian guests were slapping palms in high fives and breaking into loud peals of laughter. A lithe, café au lait cubana stood hip-deep in the shallow end, her body pressed up against a graying European male twice her age.

Coiling pathways spilled me onto the beach, where bathers—predominantly French and Argentinian—soaked up the sun's dying rays and windsurfers scudded across a chlorophyll sea. The beach service outlet offered snorkeling, scuba diving, and massage.

Soon I'm lying facedown beneath the cool penumbra of a thatch lean-to. Shafts of sunlight play through the leaves, creating the sensation of being showered with petals. The only sounds are the rustling of palm fronds and the easy voice of the masseuse, a buxom bundle of joviality who croons softly as her fingers and the therapeutic salt-laden breeze go to work. "Fidel will be here next week," she says languidly as I slip into peaceful oblivion.

For all this I pay 89 dollars a night, meals included—a bargain, though even here the cuisine is somewhat wanting. That's way too expensive for Cubans, even if they were officially permitted to stay here, which they are not. The European and the cubana, I imagine, must be married. The government has a schizoid attitude toward the mingling of Cubans and tourists, resulting in accusations of apartheid against its own citizens.

As it happens, there's a *campismo* for Cubans nearby. Next day I ride out to see it and am amazed to find the holiday camp bubbling with Cuban workers from the resort in swimwear, conjuring tropical excitement out of thin air. The place looks utterly joyless, almost vulgar in its austere construction, and, in these bleak times, quite threadbare and enfeebled. Weeds sprout from the cracked floor of the empty swimming pool. But what do the Cubans care? Their pleasures are simple: vivacious music, cheap rum, and sex. It pleases me to find them eliciting simple pleasure, swigging *tragos* of cheap aguardiente, dancing hip-swiveling, groin-to-groin boogies to the pulsing beat of the sun.

And they have the beach. And the transparent waters.

I'm running now. Driving hard. Feeling Havana pull me on like a magnet.

Off to the right, coral islands slide by. Clouds float like lily petals atop the glazed waters and the distant cays levitate above a silvered mirage. To the left, sugarcane fades to citrus and back again. Concrete carbuncles rise over the fields: three-story shoe-box apartments for rural workers interspersed at such regular intervals that I count the miles by these scars on the lyrical landscape. The population keeps changing, too—white to black and back again. I hadn't noticed these little pockets before.

An MZ motorcycle appears in my mirror. The young male rider in full face helmet is scrunched down low over the tank, his feet folded up on the engine crash bar and his throttle hand egging the machine on for all it is worth. His passenger is hanging off the rear seat, one hand holding the fender tight, the other hooked around a large pig flopped across the saddle. The rider flaunts a grin as he passes. For the first time in Cuba, I am being overtaken by other vehicles. I let him go—can't risk the plug in the rear tire blowing out at high speed. Although I've ridden almost 6,000 miles, my tires seem hardly worn down at all. And the plug is holding up nicely, though mysteriously the tire has developed a hard ridge left of center. I wonder if it has something to do with the puncture.

I thrum along at a steady 55 miles per hour, canted against the hot wind whipping across the coastal plain. Still, I am hurrying now, wanting to get the research over with, hungry to get back to Havana before my permit expires, eager to soothe the physical pain. In a bid to rack up some miles, I push on against my better judgment toward a calamitous sky. Then rain begins to fall and I find myself riding through a deluge. The road is full of unseen potholes; the headlamp is virtually useless in the half-light. I slow to 20, soaked and cold and miserable inside my rainproofs.

Bedraggled, I check into Los Caneyes resort, strip off my leathers, and flop back exhausted with my legs spread apart and my feet framing a Russian TV at the foot of the sagging bed. A snow blizzard flurries across the screen. Tele Rebelde, the state-run television station, is broadcasting a performance by Cuban piano impresario Frank Fernández of Rachmaninoff's second piano concerto live from Havana's Teatro Nacional, buoying my spirits. The classical concert is followed by a documentary about how the human body regulates temperature. I could be watching BBC2 or PBS. Between shows, advertisements exhort the citizenry to work hard; another ad calls for everyone's participation in the May Day Parade. Then a young couple appear and enter a family planning clinic hand in hand. A doctor dispenses advice along with a packet of condoms, and a message flashes on the screen: *El aborto no es un método anticonceptivo.* All nations should have such intelligent programming.

"In all the beaches in Cuba the sand was made of grated silver," says a character in Robert Fernández's *Raining Backwards*, "though in Varadero it was also mixed with diamond dust." I couldn't argue. The 12-mile-long swath of white radiance is Cuba's lambent lodestone—ground zero in the tourism explosion that threatens to topple the tattered revolution more effectively than four decades of U.S. embargo.

Varadero has been Cuba's trendiest beach town for more than a century. In the 1870s, residents of the inland town of Cárdenas built summer homes and, later, boardinghouses for vacationers fleeing the torrid heat of Havana. During ensuing decades, the village evolved into a full-fledged resort town. In 1926, U.S. industrialist Irénée Du Pont bought most of the peninsula beyond the town and built a large estate, complete with a golf course, called Xanadu. Du Pont drew other wealthy *norteamericanos* in his wake; having reputedly paid four centavos a square meter for his land, he profited handsomely by selling off parcels at 120 pesos a meter. Al Capone bought a house here, as did dictator Fulgencio Batista. Varadero gradually metamorphosed from a barren waste into a Miami in miniature, with exclusive neighborhoods and grandiose villas commanding private sections of beach.

During the 1950s, yanqui corporations put up ritzy hotels with casinos run by mobsters and high-class hookers on hand for the rich habaneros and Hollywood idols who flocked to sun and sin and indulge in white lines in view of the longest white line of all. On the eve of the Revolution, most of the beachfront was in private hands; villagers living within sight of the powdery sands, it is claimed, could do no more than stare wistfully. After the Revolution, the beach was declared public property and the proletariat were finally able to feel the diamond dust between their toes. So says the official version.

Twenty bucks bought me a private room on Calle 27. It was small but well built and airy, and its kitchenette and spacious shower with modern plumbing delivered a rare Cuban commodity: piping-hot water. The owner, an upbeat young chap named Tito Hernández García, had even welded together a cage of iron rods, into which the Beemer fit snugly. My circumstances could hardly have been better. The beach was just two blocks away.

Varadero's prize beach coats the north shore of a slender 20-mile peninsula protruding east like a crooked finger into Bahía de Cárdenas. The town lies at the western end of the island-peninsula; it is separated from the mainland by a man-made lagoon, and from all Cuba by a metal drawbridge with a MININT checkpoint whose diligent personnel guard against infiltration, ensuring that only foreign tourists and Cuban residents with permits gain access to Cuba's cut-rate Cancún.

"Many of us are fearful of returning home," a *jinetera* named Barbara told me. "It's so difficult now to get back into Varadero."

I had ventured out this evening to discover what changes had befallen Varadero since my last visit nine months before. A nocturnal deluge drove me to seek the shelter of the canvas cover of an open-air bar full of young Germans, most of them boorish lager louts with young cubanas by their sides. Surplus jineteras hovered expectantly in the wings, sharing Coca-Colas that they passed around in a typically Cuban spirit of égalité. I was happy to be alone, nursing a Tecate beer and recording the scene, when suddenly a lanky, light-skinned *mulata* launched herself at me and curled her arm around mine. I tried to escape, but she gripped my arm like a vise.

"The police! It's very dangerous!" Barbara cried in Spanish. I thought she was trying out a desperate pickup line. I'd noticed her a few minutes before, soliciting a German who had rudely shoved her away; her aggressive approach tempted me to be almost as callous.

"*¡Abrásame!*" she pleaded desperately. "Hug me!"

I saw why. Two plainclothes policemen were muscling their way through the crowd, asking the unescorted females for identification. I watched aghast as five young women were manhandled from the bar and onto the sidewalk. A dark blue van pulled up and the women were pushed curtly into the windowless rear. The policemen climbed in behind them, the door slammed shut, and the van sped off.

"What will happen to them?" I asked my pushy companion.

"They'll probably spend a night in jail, then be taken to the bus station and sent back to their homes in the country."

The government had initiated a crackdown. "*Es serio,*" said Barbara.

I wasn't surprised. A crackdown seemed long overdue. "It is not legal in our country to practice prostitution," Fidel Castro told a delegation from *Time* magazine in February 1995, "nor are we going to legalize it. Nor are we thinking in terms of turning it into a freelance occupation to solve unemployment problems. We are not going to repress it either," he added disingenuously, for even then it had seemed impossible that the government would tolerate a situation spiraling out of control. Varadero had become the Caribbean's hot new sex resort. Four-fifths of its visitors, I estimated, were single men who had heard that Cuba's hot spot was a beachside *bayú* (cheap brothel) full of lithe, olive-skinned girls with ready smiles for a stranger. By day, sultry cubanas sashayed down the beach in neon swimwear, pursing their lips and swiveling their hips for whichever male caught their eye. Come nightfall, Varadero was languid and sensual, with residual heat and the smell of night blooms in the air; along dim-lit Avenida Primera, perfumed young women in high heels and tight spandex called out to unaccompanied males.

As I strolled past the Hotel Cuatro Palmas, built around Fulgencio Batista's former summer house, a lively wisp of a girl grabbed my hand and asked if I would buy her a drink. Her face was cute as a button, her body brown and supple.

"I'm Viviana. You like me?" the young beauty crooned, rubbing her body up against me. She looked 16.

"It's nothing personal," I replied, "but I prefer my own company."

"What's wrong? You don't like me?"

"Listen, you're very pretty, but I want to be alone. Okay?"

"You want *sexo*? Nothing more," she answered matter-of-factly, dismaying me with her stark proposition. "Only 20 dollars," she added, smiling gaily. Twenty dollars was 400 pesos—more than a month's wage for the average Cuban. Professional child prostitution was rearing its ugly head. One night at the Hotel Riviera in 1995, I had answered a knock on my door at four a.m. A young chica, perhaps 15, stood at the door. She said she was lonely and would like to spend some time with me. I said no and closed the door. Through the fish-eye peephole I watched her knock on the door across the hall. She was checking the rooms at random, hoping to find a lonely foreigner. The blossoming of jineteras is the result of Cuba's poverty. But this? I was saddened. Cuba's remarkable society was on its way to becoming as spiritually impoverished as it is materially poor.

I asked Viviana her age.

"Nineteen" she replied. I raised my eyebrows. She shrugged. "Sixteen. *¡No es un problema!*" she answered blithely.

I thought of a line from Rudyard Kipling: "The wildest dreams of Waterloo are commonplace in Kathmandu."

Why hadn't the government responded sooner?

"They were fearful of jeopardizing the tourist flow," replied Michael Crocker, a savvy young Canadian I bumped into the next day in the lobby of the Hotel Villa Caribe. Michael runs the Cuba programs for a Toronto-based travel company.

"How do you think the government managed to kick-start tourism?" he continued. "They promoted Cuba as a sexual paradise."

One of Castro's first moves in 1959 had been to close the *bayús* and strip clubs. This, together with reeducation programs for prostitutes, had resulted in Cuba's ostensibly becoming the first society on Earth to eradicate prostitution. The government had railed against bourgeois decadence ever since. Castro, like a latter-day Prometheus, had striven to create a nobler human who could walk tall, full of dignity. Michael's premise sounded farfetched. I told him so.

"Come on," Michael responded in a nasally Canadian brogue. "Imagine. Your entire economy crashes, you're desperate for dollars, and tourism is about the only way you can get them. But you've gotta get the tourists...and quick, eh? How do you do it? You can get the Canadians with cheap package deals, but that's a limited market. And the Yanks can't come, eh? So you've gotta chase the Europeans. It takes time to build up a tourist market, eh? But you can do it overnight if you're selling sex. Guys will come. It doesn't matter if it's a war zone."

I remained skeptical.

"Look at Thailand," Michael persisted, waving his Romeo y Julieta expansively. "Their economy went to hell in a breadbasket after the Vietnam war ended and the GIs went home. Suddenly they had God knows how many unemployed prostitutes. And they had those beaches, eh? It didn't take them long to see two and two. Here you've got the beaches and women, not prostitutes, eh, but everyday women who'll fuck a lamppost if it moves, and every second one is hankering to get a hold of a foreigner." On that I had to agree.

In fact, the world's oldest trade reappeared within a few years of the Revolution. Fred Ward recorded in 1977 how "a few girls have been appearing once again in the evenings, looking for dates, and willing to trade their favors for goods rather than money." Straight-up prostitution was replaced by a more esoteric form that Ward thought "almost more a comment on rationing than on morals." Sex is sought out in a country short of almost everything else. The state's inability to provide for Cubans' material needs combined with a general postrevolutionary promiscuity so that "prostitution" had come back stronger than ever. But different. Educated, morally upright Cuban girls were looking for affairs—*luchando un yuma*—that in the worst of circumstances can earn them in one night the equivalent in *fula* (dollars) of one month's salary in worthless pesos.

I thought of Daisy. And Theresa. And Milagros. And all the others. Strong, sexually aware sirens, regarding sex without shame, reveling in flaunting their bodies not as a hedge against hunger but as a free expression of sensuality inherent in the Cuban sense of a liberated self.

"The government here was pretty keyed in," Michael continued. "They treated the Cubans' libertine view toward sex as an asset."

I thought about it overnight and awoke to the thought that Michael's argument seemed plausible. Since Cojababo, such a notion no longer appeared quite so fanciful. Castro, one of the most principled men on earth, could also be one of the least. "The revolution's ideological principles were bent every which way in the bid for new tourist dollars," claimed Andres Oppenheimer in his scathing book, *Castro's Final Hour.* "Castro's diatribes against bourgeois decadence were quickly forgotten, as the cash-starved government invited *Playboy* magazine—long prohibited in Cuba—to produce a ten-page girls-of-Cuba pictorial photographed in various Cuban tourist resorts. A simultaneous Cuban government ad campaign featured tourist posters showing bikini-clad Cuban women under the title, 'Cuba. Come and be tempted.'" More recent tourist literature downplayed the sultry cubana theme in favor of families and cavorting couples. The crisis was over. The government had tacked to the mainstream.

Since my last visit 12 months before, a ban had come into effect prohibiting Cubans from entering tourist hotels, and *casas particulares*—private rooms—were springing up like mushrooms on a damp log. The owners were cashing in on illicit carnal commerce. Varadero was in the midst of a building boom. Piles of sand and concrete blocks lay beside half-finished extensions framed by scaffolding.

Almost three-quarters of the island's hotel rooms face onto Cuba's most famous beach. I counted more than 30 hotels in the span of three miles. The gaps were being filled in. A few miles farther east, at a haughty distance, rose the deluxe mega-resorts run by Spain's Sol Meliá, Jamaica's SuperClubs, and Club Med. I rode out to see them. Every mile brought a coterie of cranes rising over yet one more fledgling hotel. The Cuban government's tourism master plan slates 23,000 hotel rooms for Varadero—about as many as in all of Jamaica. Even the Campamento Internaciónal de Pioneros, the youth camp where Daisy and her schoolmates had spent their summers, was being conjured into a high-class hotel.

Back at Tito's, I stowed the bike in its cage and strolled down to the beach. A blood-red Porsche Carrera with Swiss diplomatic insignia roared past. Another of the bizarre incongruities that bombarded me every day.

"*Ssst...Ssssst!*"

It was Barbara, strutting along Avenida Primera, rising from her high-heeled shoes like a long flower stalk. She was dressed, barely, in white hot pants and a turquoise halter top, exposing her navel. Her skin was the color and smoothness of toffee. She seemed taller, prettier than the night before as she sidled toward me.

"Where are you going?" she asked.

"The beach."

"Oh good! Come!" she replied ecstatically, seizing my hand and leading the way.

She knelt on the sand beside me and flung back the braided hair that twirled down over her shoulders, revealing five golden rings in each ear. Barbara was studying chemistry at the Universidad de las Villas in Santa Clara, but the Special Period had dealt a heavy blow to the school, and she had joined the exodus of students whose anomie of arrested ambition led them to seek employment in the tourism industry. Or, failing that—and this she thought the ultimate prize—a *papirriqui con guaniquiqui*. A sugar daddy with dollars.

"Have you had many chicas?" she asked after she had folded up my T-shirt and laid it under my head for a pillow.

"Er, no," I replied. "And you, have you had many men?"

"No," she answered, counting on her fingers. "Only three in the past two weeks. *Italianos.*" Most of the other beachgoers at this western, budget end of Varadero were Germans. The Italians preferred a ritzier section farther east. To my right, two topless blondes reclined against backpacks on the equally blond beach, reading novels in German, while their Cuban boyfriends lay on their backs on the sand. The women looked 30-something, the men 10 years younger. Gigolos trading on their good looks, they were lean yet well muscled, with pitch-black skin and sun-bleached dreadlocks. It seemed odd to see Rastafarians in Cuba.

A Honda ATV roared past, kicking up sand. The rider was selling soda pop and ice cream from an icebox strapped to the rear. Hawkers trailed behind, selling papayas and fresh-baked snacks, peanuts in paper cones, and *pipas*, coconuts full of refreshing water. Pelicans flew by, dipping low in unison. Far out, the waves were a thick Prussian blue, choppy and capped. I could have been enjoying a pleasant day on the Costa Brava.

Barbara ran her fingers over my four-day-old stubble. "I'd like to shave you. I've never shaved a man," she said. Not having a razor at hand, I fished around in my rucksack for my Swiss Army knife, then lay back and enjoyed the intimacy of her hands tending lightly upon my face as she clipped my mustache with the scissors of my pocket-sized prodigy. When she had finished, she leaned closer and puckered her lipsticked lips. Our first kiss was announced by the audible contact of teeth.

CHAPTER FIFTEEN

∾

HAVANA HOME

found a new home in the heart of Vedado, Havana's middle-class
business district. My apartment was to the rear of a ground-floor unit
beautifully maintained by live-in owners Jorge Coalla Potts and his wife, Marisol.
It was a good size—about 15 feet square—with a cool tile floor underfoot and
a lofty ceiling with a fan that stirred the hot air of the city in May. Black and jade
tiles lined the cavernous bathroom.

Jorge kept the louvered windows firmly battened down. I opened them
every morning before I went out, but when I returned the slats had been shuttered again.

"Why do you keep closing my louvers?" I asked Jorge one day.

"¡Robos!"

How on Earth could anyone steal from my room through barred windows
seven feet off the ground?

"They can throw in a fishing line with a hook," Jorge explained, prompting
me to hang my clothes in the closet thereafter; I didn't want a sneak thief to
get my fly on his hook. Petty theft had reached a pandemic in Havana. Lord
knows the Cubans were full of integrity, but otherwise honest people will do
unprincipled things in times of desperate shortage.

Jorge was a stocky, caramel-colored mulatto with a craggy face, thick eyebrows, and wide, stubby fingers and thumbs. The name Potts came from his

maternal grandmother, an Englishwoman who had married a Cuban, but Marisol—a redhead of Galician extraction—was the one with the porcelain skin. The couple slept in an adjacent room with Jessica, their six-year-old daughter, snuggled between them. Jorge kept his bedroom door ajar; if he ever had a problem with the various *chicas* who passed down the hallway to and from my room, he never said so.

The L-shaped living room was airy and sparsely furnished with four *sillones* (rockers), an antique mahogany dining table, a taupe sofa by the door, and a profusion of potted plants that Jorge watered daily. Louvered windows ran the length of the side wall, but these, too, were kept shuttered to guard against thieves; by filtering out the harsh sunlight, they also helped to keep the house cool. A larger window faced the street, and I took great pleasure in leaning on the windowsill or sitting in a rocker, sipping a demitasse of Marisol's thick, sweet, Cuban coffee—appropriately called an *infusión* on menus, for it has the kick of a cocaine injection—and staring out through the protective bars, watching pretty *habaneras* pass by.

The driveway sloped down to a basement garage where the bike could be securely parked behind gates. Best of all, my apartment was close to Parque Coppelia, the ice-cream citadel at the top of La Rampa that the government had built in 1966 as the world's largest ice-cream emporium; it served an estimated 30,000 people each day.

I donned my jeans, stuffed my notebook in my back pocket, and set out on a pilgrimage.

A young boy trailed me down Calle 23, reproachfully droning, "Dollar...dollar," while outside the Hotel Habana Libre *jineteras* attempted to catch my eye with sibilant hisses. Most wore lurid makeup and flouncy miniskirts or body-fitting Lycra. *Jineteros* whispered beneath their breath, "Hey, friend...taxi?" and "Want a pretty chica?" I felt like Wormold, the English vacuum-cleaner salesman, walking the streets of Havana during the heyday of sin:

> At every corner there were men who called "Taxi" at him as though he were a stranger, and all down the Paseo, at intervals of a few yards, the pimps accosted him automatically without any real hope. "Can I be of service, sir?" "I know all the pretty girls?" "You desire a beautiful women?" "Postcards?" "You want to see a dirty movie."

A rumbling behemoth of a bus rolled to a stop, and a jostling horde of habaneros pitched forward in a mad melee to board the already overcrowded contraption. The puce warehouse on wheels resembled a bactrian camel, "humped" at either end and sagging in the middle. Introduced only recently, these giant buses were designed to save the day during the gasoline crisis, when Cuban engineers had added bodies to articulated flatbeds pulled by International and Mack trucks, creating a *supertrenbus*, nicknamed a *camello*, that weighed more than 20 tons and could carry 200 people. They were usually stuffed with passengers far exceeding their capacity; the true number could never be counted.

Havana sizzled and the entire city had descended on Coppelia, seeking relief. A strange concrete structure loomed over Coppelia park, resembling a flying saucer mounted on spidery legs. It sheltered a marble-topped diner-bar where Cubans seated on tall bar stools slurped ice cream from stainless steel bowls. A series of circular rooms was arranged overhead like a four-leaf clover, offering views over three open-air sections where *helados* could be enjoyed beneath the dappled shade of jagüey trees. Each section had its own *cola* (line) proportional in length to the strength of the sun. Even on temperate days, the colas snaked out of the park and onto nearby streets.

Cuba's rich diversity could be found standing in line at Coppelia on a sultry Havana afternoon.

Determining the last person in line—*el último*—is not easy. That's because Cuban lines are never static. While some habaneros wander off to sit in the shade, others disappear from view altogether, creating the impression of having given up. Invariably they reappear at the critical moment, and the cola coalesces in perfect order through some unfathomable and puissant osmosis.

I joined a cola and asked for *"¿el último?"* A statuesque, middle-aged black woman turned and answered through smiling lips. Her eyes sparkled warmly. The early evening light slanted full upon her skin, gilding her face like an eggplant. She exuded an extraordinary combination of strength and grace and was unlike any Cuban woman I had ever seen.

I introduced myself. Lydia held an important post in a government agency. On her way home from work, she had stopped by Coppelia on a whim. We made small talk while the cola moved forward at a pace barely discernible from rigor mortis: We crept forward a yard, halted, then edged forward again before abruptly stopping once more. At this rate, we'd be served around midnight. Just when I was about to give up, the line surged forward. A young waitress in a red tartan miniskirt showed us to a table with two other diners. At the world's most democratic ice-cream parlor, all the tables are communal.

Before the Revolution, Cuba relied on its northern neighbor for much of its helado supply, and Howard Johnson's 28 flavors were the brand of choice. Fidel, however, vowing to eclipse the Yanks, had come up with flavors that Ben and Jerry's has surely never heard of. In 1996, after five years of the Special Period, Coppelia could manage only one flavor a day. Today's flavor of the day was vanilla. I ordered an *ensalada*—five scoops—for four pesos (15 cents).

"What were conditions like before the Special Period, Lydia?"

"*Oh, Cristóbal.* Coppelia served many flavors of ice cream. Marañon. Guanábana. Zapote."

"And what about cheeses? Were there many flavors?" I remembered what Francisco had told me in Camagüey.

"Oh, yes," she replied. "There were many types. Until the year 1990. Everything changed with that year. We wanted for nothing before then."

Nearby, cheery habaneros poured out of the Yara Theater, where Tomás Gutiérrez Alea's *Fresa y Chocolate* was playing.

"It's a magnificent movie," said Lydia. "I always cry."

"How many times have you seen it?"

"Five—no, six—times."

When released in 1994, Gutiérrez's trenchant classic was in such demand that it caused near riots at cinemas throughout Cuba. The poignant and provocative movie, set in Havana during the repressive heyday of 1979, explores the nettlesome friendship between a flagrant homosexual and a macho Party member. It reflects the producer's abiding questioning of the Revolution, to which he nonetheless remained loyal.

Sandra Levinson had introduced me to Gutiérrez in October 1995. Daisy and I had then briefly taken a room with the internationally acclaimed producer and his charming actress-wife, Mirta Ibarra, at their simple apartment full of fine abstract paintings on Calle 0 in Miramar. I had known Gutiérrez too briefly to call him Titón, as friends nicknamed him. My first sight of the formidable intellectual—enfeebled by lung cancer and lying on his old-fashioned wrought-iron bed—had filled me with a sense of trespass; this was magnified by my host's chill stares through the open bedroom door and the yapping of his white poodle, Gordo. Gutiérrez said not a word as he watched me pass down the hallway. I made a deferential retreat and, much to my later regret, kept myself to my room in dalliance with Daisy.

Gutiérrez had died on April 16, 1996. Two weeks had passed since his death, which still weighed heavily upon habaneros, to whom he was a cultural hero. I asked Lydia if his works were critiques of the Revolution. She hesitated.

"No doubt. But they are also part of the revolutionary tradition," she replied, weighing her words carefully. "Our experiment is an evolutionary process. There have been mistakes, often quite painful, but that is true of every society and system. We are still searching for a more perfect way. We debate and criticize. Titón was in the vanguard. He spoke for all Cubans. Yes, his films are criticisms of the Revolution as far as they contribute to the ongoing dialectic as to how the Revolution should evolve."

Cubans often spoke in such terms, displaying an intellectual voracity that made me feel shallow by comparison. Habaneros flaunted their appreciation for culture. For all their dearth of literature, they were among the most erudite people in the world.

Gutiérrez's work was frequently misinterpreted outside Cuba. Much to his own dismay, the critical, parodic nature of his films led to his being branded an arch anti-Castroite. The extraordinary subtlety of films such as his 1968 classic, *Memories of Underdevelopment*—a study of a bourgeois intellectual adrift in the new Cuba—proved too sophisticated for Cold War mentalities to the north; U.S. propagandists seized upon his works in ways he never intended. Gutiérrez's faith in the Revolution, however, never faltered. Like Fidel, he clung to the thread of his dream as the health of his country declined.

Coppelia had figured in *Fresa y Chocolate*, a movie based on Senel Paz's short story "The Woods, the Wolf, and the New Man" and named for the scene at Coppelia in which Diego, the homosexual, orders strawberry ice cream, much to the consternation of David, the loyal *fidelista*: "Although there was choco-late that day, he had ordered strawberry. Perverse." I had heard that Cuban males, concerned with their macho image, had taken a cue from the movie and now avoided ordering *fresa*.

"Is that true?" I asked Lydia.

She laughed and looked around. "I don't see anyone eating fresa."

"That's because they're serving only vanilla today."

She smiled, flaunting white teeth, slightly crooked at the front.

Birdsong rained down from the treetops. A girl in a black halter top and yellow hot pants whisked by on roller skates. Nearby, schoolchildren in uniform engaged in teenage foreplay, kissing and fondling in public without any sense of self-conscious shame. More mature lovers sauntered through the park hand in hand.

My mood was upbeat. I was seeing the goodness in Cuba again.

It was a lovely day in Havana.

I loved the city for its demimonde, for its tawdry, ethereal moods. I loved its flirty *mulatas* adding peppery flavors to the frisson of the forbidden. I loved its colonial facades wearing away all around me like garish old whores, and its high-finned, chrome-spangled Detroit dowagers rumbling along the Malecón, conjuring images of men in Panama hats and white linen suits. I loved its stage-set exoticism like a palimpsest written upon and imperfectly erased time and again. I loved walking the streets, rarely took taxis, wanting to feel the city's soul through my feet.

I let the bike rest for a while, then gave the Paris-Dakar its first scrubbing in more than a month and decided to ride out to the suburb of San Francisco de Paula, nine miles southeast of Havana, where Ernest Hemingway's house is preserved just the way the esteemed writer left it. I'd been in Havana a week and had recently met a young woman named Juanita, whose muscular legs—tanned and well honed—had caught my attention, inspiring me to offer an invitation to sample a ride on my sturdy steed. I called her.

"Want to go for a ride?"

"Where to?"

"San Francisco de Paula. Museo Hemingway," I replied.

"*Oh, sí!* I've never been."

"Good, I'll pick you up. Where do you live?"

Juanita hesitated before reluctantly giving her address. She asked me to park around the corner, out of sight of her house. I met her at the gas station outside the entrance to the Tropicana nightclub, in the Marianao district five miles southwest of Vedado.

"Why didn't you want me to come to your house?" I asked Juanita as she put her hands on my shoulders and hoisted herself onto the rear saddle.

"Oh, nothing."

"No. Why?" I probed, looking over my shoulder to find her giving me a hawkish look. After a pregnant silence she responded: "I work for a government department. We're forbidden to mingle with foreigners. I don't want the CDR spies to see me." After another pause she added, ominously: "It's dangerous. But you're an experiment."

An experiment? I guessed I'd picked up a loyal *comunista*.

The Vía Blanca, the main arterial highway that loops south around the harbor front and leads to San Francisco de Paula, was pocked with potholes large enough to swallow Cuba's fat homebred cattle. Fortunately, the BMW's long-travel suspension soaked up the worst. In places the hardtop gave out, replaced by gravel. Railway tracks crisscrossed the old concrete two-laner at acute angles. Russian trucks belching out black smoke ran nose to tail, playing Dodg'em with decrepit buses. They gave me no quarter. I hated the Vía Blanca.

I was upon it now, Hemingway's 20-acre hilltop estate, its gateway framed by bougainvillea, with the well-varnished cabin cruiser—the *Pilar*—poised loftily beneath a wooden pavilion on the former tennis court shaded by bamboo and Royal palms. Mango trees and sumptuous jacarandas lined the driveway leading up to the gleaming white house. It was as I remembered it when I had last visited in February 1995 with Daisy and Ralph Martell, a free-spirited, 69-year-old New Yorker and cubaphile I had met at the Havana Jazz Festival.

In 1939 Hemingway's third wife, Martha Gellhorn, was struck by Finca Vigía ("Lookout Farm"), a one-story Spanish-colonial house boasting a wonderful view of Havana. They rented it for 100 dollars a month. When his first royalty check from *For Whom the Bell Tolls* arrived in 1940, Hemingway bought the house for $18,500. Hemingway loved Cuba and lived here for the better part of 20 years. Spain, the green hills of Africa, were nowhere near as beguiling.

Hemingway's presence seems to haunt the large, simple home. Juanita and I were not allowed in. No one is. Reasonably so, I thought, for every room can be viewed through the wide-open windows, reducing the temptation to pilfer priceless trinkets. Two years after Hemingway died in 1961, someone offered

$80,000 for his famous Royal typewriter, set on a shelf beside his workroom desk. I bought it for $7, inscribed in gray on a T-shirt that reads "MUSEO ERNESTO HEMINGWAY, FINCA VIGIA, CUBA."

"No photos!" a female guard commanded as I prepared to steal a quick snap of Papa's bedroom. Through the large windows I could see trophies, firearms, bottles of spirits, old issues of *The Field, Spectator,* and *Sports Afield* strewn about, and scores of books arranged neatly but without concern for authors or subjects, the way he supposedly liked it. The dining room table was set with cut crystal, as if guests were expected.

Here Hemingway wrote *Islands in the Stream, Across the River and into the Trees, A Moveable Feast,* and *The Old Man and the Sea,* his simple and profound novel that won him the Pulitzer Prize, and later the Nobel, for Literature. The four-story tower next to the house was built at his fourth wife's prompting so that he could write unmolested. We were alone, a guard and I; hinting that I wished a quick snapshot, a small token changed hands. I, too, shot a lion, though Hemingway had already bagged the beast on safari and turned it into a rug. Papa disliked the tower and continued writing amid the comings and goings of the house, surrounded by papers, shirtless, in Bermuda shorts, with any of 60 cats at his feet as he stood barefoot on the hide of a small kudu.

It was eerie being followed by countless eyes—those of the guides (one per room) and those of the beasts that had found themselves in the cross hairs of Hemingway's scope. "Don't know how a writer could write surrounded by so many dead animals," Graham Greene commented when he visited in 1959. "Taxidermy everywhere, buffalo heads, antlers, such carnage." There were bulls, too. Everywhere bulls, including paintings by Moro and Klee, photographs and posters of bullfighting scenes, and a chalk plate of a bull's head, a gift from Picasso.

Hemingway had berthed the *Pilar* at Cojímar, a fishing village about 10 miles north of San Francisco de Paula. Gregorio Fuentes, the now ancient skipper, still lived there. I wanted to meet him. In 1993, Castro had named the creaking seaman a national treasure, bestowing upon him a color TV and double pension and free meals at La Terraza, the shoreline bar-restaurant that Hemingway had made notorious in *The Old Man and the Sea* and *Islands in the Stream.*

Juanita said she was hungry. I suggested we appease our hunger with fisherman's soup and paella at Cojímar's famous restaurant; because it accepts only dollars today, the place gets few locals, but travelers come from far and wide to hear Fuentes recount his adventures.

Our timing was off. Fuentes wasn't there, so Juanita and I toasted the old man's good health with a turquoise cocktail, a "Coctel Fuentes," named after Cojímar's best-known icon.

A stiff wind was whipping up whitecaps and fluttering the Cuban flag above the pocket-size fortress that guards the cove's entrance. Small fishing craft were returning to Cojímar through the chop. The locals were holding a fishing tournament and had gathered in a compact *plazuela* ringed by gas lamps, metal grills, and shade trees. Scratchy salsa music drifted over the scene from a decades-old record player, drawing the locals to dance on the cracked concrete square.

I spotted Cojímar's premier tourist attraction sitting in a chair in the cool shade of a jagüey tree. He was dressed in a short-sleeved ocher dress shirt buttoned to the neck. The shirt had a small motif of a marlin and the words "Brian's Shop" sewn above the breast pocket. For shade he wore a sun-faded navy-blue baseball cap that read "Sloppy Joe's, Key West." He sat alone, expressionless, in a metal folding chair. An aluminum crutch lay across his lap. I approached and asked about his health.

"Poor," Fuentes replied, looking me straight in the eye. "And I can't get the medicines I need because of your goddamn blockade. When you go home, tell that president of yours that his blockade has done enough harm."

"I'm afraid I don't have much influence."

"So much for your democracy."

Gregorio Fuentes was 15 months short of his 100th birthday. He had met Hemingway in 1931 on Tortuga, in the Bahamas, where the two men had sheltered their vessels from a storm. Four years later, Hemingway hired Fuentes as his skipper; later still, he supposedly used him as his model for Santiago, the proud old fisherman cursed by *salao*—the worst form of bad luck—in *The Old Man and the Sea*. Virtually inseparable, the two men shared many adventures in Cuba and farther afield.

"I still feel the pain of his absence," Fuentes told me, speaking through rheumy eyes misty with memory.

I saw the old man now, "thin and gaunt with deep wrinkles in the back of his neck. The brown blotches of the benevolent skin cancer the sun brings from its reflections on the tropic sea were on his cheeks....Everything about him was old except his eyes and they were the same color as the sea and were cheerful and undefeated."

Fuentes was helped to his feet and presented to the crowd, which applauded the venerable homegrown hero. The old man lifted his crutch in salute. He hobbled forward, steadied at the elbows by friends. The prize fish had been strapped aloft by their tails in the plaza. Blood pooled on the mossy cement. The winners were announced, and three sun-bronzed skippers shuffled forward self-consciously, looking down at their feet from embarrassment. They were followed by three young girls in red gym suits and white leggings, who caught the nervous contagion and giggled as they marched across the plaza bearing the prizes on trays.

As soon as the prize-giving ended, the music cranked up again and couples swarmed into the square and got back to dancing. They slithered around each other like electric eels performing a display of choreographed public concupiscence, pursuing their passions freely in the fresh afternoon air.

We rode back to Vedado and spent the late afternoon hours making love. Juanita loved well and industriously, perhaps because she took no other pleasure from life, and her sad face eventually drove me away.

"Let's go see a movie," she said, stirring briefly. Cine Riviera was showing an adaptation of *Of Love and Shadows*, Isabel Allende's tragic tale of two people prepared to risk everything for the sake of justice and truth amid the terror and violence of General Augusto Pinochet's Chile, a country of arbitrary arrests, sudden disappearances, and summary executions.

Afterward, back in bed, I asked Juanita if she saw any parallels to contemporary Cuba. Her raven hair was cut page-boy fashion, and I was entranced by the way she constantly blew the fringe out of her eyes. Now she blew upward in a puff of disdain and shot me an angry look for good measure.

"It's not like that here. In Batista's day, yes. But not now."

I told her that I had recently witnessed a disturbing "disappearance" in Miramar, when an unmarked van had screeched to a halt and a young man walking a few yards ahead of me had been hustled inside by four men.

"I don't believe you," she replied, raising her head off my shoulder. Perspiration glistened on her tobacco-colored skin.

Something about Juanita made me uneasy. Seeking to get to the root of things, I asked her point-blank what she thought of Fidel.

"He's a good man," she replied as we lay naked together on the bed and let the downdraft of the ceiling fan cool the sweat on our bodies. She had been fearful to date me and still seemed nervous. My questions began to unnerve her.

"Do you think the government knows I'm here, in this house?"

"Most likely."

"Do you think they know that you're here with me?"

"*Sí,*" she replied, turning her face away from me slightly and piercing me sideways with her cold eyes.

"How?"

She shrugged, then pursed her lips and let out another puff of air. "The government knows you are here and where you go. Cristóbal, I don't want to talk of this."

I wasn't sure I could trust her. Still, I confided in her perhaps more than was prudent, saying that I was unsure of how many dark Cuban realities to reveal in my guidebook. I told her about Francisco's admonition to tell the truth: "*¡No mentiras!*"

"*¡No!*" she exclaimed.

Juanita grew agitated as I told her of the restrictions that I felt MINREX and Publicitur had tried to place on my travel.

"What kind of restrictions?"

"They wanted me to be accompanied. I think to keep tabs on me. After all, I'm a journalist."

"*¡Ay, madre de Dios!*" she exclaimed. "You will make my life a misery."

Her fears sparked my own paranoia. Perhaps she's a Mata Hari. Why not? G2, Cuba's KGB, often used shapely agents. "If you belong to G2 and are young and female and beautiful you can become a delectable detector of enemies of the party," wrote Guillermo Cabrera Infante. "You see, they can perform cover and uncover jobs."

Cubans were always warning me to be careful: "Anyone can be an informer," "Don't talk to strangers," and my favorite, "Beware the HPs," for *hijos de putas* (literally, "sons of whores"), one of many names used for informers or people in cahoots with the government.

Next day I introduced Juanita to a trusted friend, a woman whose opinions I valued. After Juanita departed, my friend raised her forefinger and tapped the end of her nose.

"What does that mean?" I asked.

"She's an *embori ciciñanga*."

"What's that?"

"Untrustworthy. A fidelista."

"How do you know?"

"I can tell."

Juanita called me daily, but I kept her at arm's length. Her presence made me nervous. I wondered if I was being followed on the streets. Sometimes I peered at the reflections in storefront windows, trying to identify anyone who might be tailing me. Finally, I became paranoid that MININT agents might search my room and seize my notebooks, so I hid them. Whatever else happened, I couldn't afford to lose those.

At the Customs headquarters, Carlitos is telling me I must return to Marina Hemingway to renew my *chapa*. I ask why.

"You arrived by sea."

"But in April you reissued my chapa directly. Here."

"Listen, hombre. You must return to the marina."

"But last time I went to the marina first and the *aduana* sent me to you."

Carlitos is adamant. He rolls his eyes effetely and rolls his broom-brush mustache into pointy tips with his thumb and forefinger, then extends one arm, palm upward, toward the door. Discussion over. So I ride the 10 miles to Marina Hemingway, where the Customs office is closed, and grow indignant at being drawn into a bureaucratic runaround.

My tourist visa will also expire in two days, and since the marina has an immigration office, I plan to kill two birds with one stone. Alas, I've already been in the country 60 days—the legal limit for foreign visitors. Journalists are granted a three-month sojourn, but I am traveling on a tourist visa and am reluctant to play the journalist gambit, preferring to remain incognito. I am fooling myself. I don't need Juanita to tell me that MININT is keeping tabs on my presence.

I ask for another 30 days, *"por favor."* The immigration officer curtly tells me that it isn't possible: "No more!"

"But I'm here with my motorcycle."

"You have to leave."

"But I have no way of leaving the country."

He shrugs. "Sixty days is the limit."

"*Con respeto, señor.* How can I leave? There are no boats scheduled to depart."

I point at a chart on the wall that lists the vessels currently docked and their scheduled dates of departure. He locks me in his steely stare.

"Sixty days!"

It's useless to argue. Still, I'm confident that things will work out in my favor, so I make a tactical retreat to Los Caneyes Bar at the tip of one of the marina's two-mile-long *intercanales*. Four middle-aged yanqui seamen are sipping bottles of Heineken in the company of four bikini-clad teenage chicas hoping for positions as captain's mates.

I nurse a Hatuey beer until the Customs officials arrive.

One of the skippers also needs an extension for his chapa. He's blown the engine on his Indian motorcycle and wants to store it at the marina.

"I've been told that foreigners who fail to secure the correct paperwork have had their motorcycles confiscated," he tells the sour-faced Customs official. "I need to know it ain't so." I, too, have heard the same thing but keep mum.

"Who?" the official replies indignantly. "Tell me who?" He wants proof, but when the American can't provide names, the official denounces it all as imperialist lies. "It isn't true," he says. Then, inevitably: "Only one." Apparently, some cheeky yanqui had been cruising around Havana for two years without a chapa. "Finally we had to take his *moto*. We warned him."

Luckily I receive a *prorróga*—an extension for my motorcycle—good through June 6; I return to the immigration office brandishing my little yellow *licencia de chapa* in my hand. The immigration officer inspects the booklet, sighs deeply, and returns it dismissively.

"Sixty days!"

"But if it's 60 days, how come the Customs official gave me another 30?"

He glowers. I can see his tormented mind working overtime, searching like one of the barristers in Charles Dickens's *Bleak House*, "mistily engaged in one of the 10,000 stages of an endless cause, tripping one another up on slippery precedents, groping knee-deep in technicalities." Then, with an excruciating slowness indistinguishable from rigor mortis, he writes out a visa extension.

"Thirty days only!" he booms, bringing down his rubber stamp like a gavel. "No more!"

All I need now is to find a skipper willing to run me and the bike back to the States. There are only four U.S. vessels berthed, far fewer than when I arrived.

I do the rounds of the vessels but no one is willing to take me, so I post a note letting incoming skippers know I need a ride. When no one replies, I call Rolf Runerberg.

"You know I haf married my Cuban girlfriend," he says, sounding pleased to hear from me. "She cannot leave Cuba yet, so I must make a journey back. There is much paperwork. I zink I shall be zer in two veeks."

Lydia called. She was on her way to Coppelia after work. Would I like to join her? I dug about in my duffel and dragged out my black dress pants. They looked as if they'd been trampled by wildebeest. I put them on anyway and donned my best shirt.

Lydia pulled up in a new Nissan Sentra, a sign that she held an important position. I opened her door, noting how she had hoisted her skirt up her thigh and took no concern in exposing the tops of her stockings as she turned toward me, legs apart. She pulled on high heels. I took her hand and helped her step from the car. She was wearing a blood-red executive suit. We looked quite the pair among the other Cubans in their tank tops, Lycra body suits, and *guayaberas*.

Later, I leaned forward into the car. Lydia's eyes were black spots dancing with desire and intrigue. I mouthed the words "I want to kiss you!" and leaned forward until she could feel my moist breath on her carmine lips. To my dismay, Lydia pulled back and let her gaze wander momentarily before flashing me a wide-eyed look. She breathed deeply, saying nothing. She bit her lower lip but her gaze was steady, and I could see that I had stirred her desire.

"I have to be careful," she whispered.

"How so?"

"Government employees are forbidden to have relations with foreigners."

I awoke with Lydia on my mind. There she remained throughout the torrid day, luring me back to Coppelia, as if the ice cream could chill the desire building inside me.

One day I rode out to Playas del Este and spent an idle hour settled on the warm white sand watching the all-black women's national volleyball team drilling under the blitz of the sun. One side of four women practiced serving and blocking; the other four executed the classic return. Every 20 minutes or so, they switched sides and roles. They served rifle-shot into a stiff onshore breeze, but every delivery was a blazing bullet straight to the heart. Then came the forearm block. The ball spiraled upward and came down, miraculously placed, for the lobbed setup and the leaping blast over the net. They were wearing bikini briefs and T-shirts or blouses tied in knots at the waist. Even in sports you couldn't take the sexuality out of Cuban women.

I'd drawn the bike up the beach, twisting the throttle so that the rear wheel dug in. The Paris-Dakar was a dose of eye candy. One of the team members came over. She towered over me as she asked me to chauffeur her home. Damaris lived in one of Centro Habana's *solares*—communities of humble, unsanitary dwellings crowded within patios hidden from view of the street. She shared the slum home with her mother and older brother and an ugly black mutt that Damaris adored. The tiny lounge contained an aged refrigerator, a single cupboard, a Formica table, and two upright chairs. Damaris's mother cooked on a one-burner kerosene stove, using water drawn from a communal standpipe. Makeshift cardboard partitions divided the single bedroom into three tiny cubicles.

"I wanted to be a *bailarina*," Damaris told me as we dined on baked chicken at El Aljibe.

"Why didn't you?"

"The school doesn't accept blacks," she replied, speaking of the Ballet Nacional de Cuba. I never confirmed it, though later when I asked a friend if that was true, she replied: "Yes, everyone knows Alicia Alonso prefers a whites-only company."

"Do you want to leave Cuba?" I asked Damaris.

"No! I love it here. I love Cuba," she replied, wrapping up half her dinner to take home to her mother and brother.

Damaris admired Fidel. Believed in the Revolution. Atheistic, she led a purely spiritual way of life, full of dignity and compassion and kindness, making do with so little with graciousness. Like Daisy, she never stopped smiling. Reminders that the principles of the Revolution are still alive in the younger generation. Cubans like Damaris made me take stock of my yo-yo emotions. As Ralph Waldo Emerson had put it, one's "opinion of the world is also a confession of character." I bought Damaris a pair of Nike trainers for the pleasure of the smile it produced.

Another day an elderly man approached me and initiated a conversation that repeated itself in various guises. He was leading by a frayed nylon string a young English boxer, a breed popular among dog-loving habaneros. I reached forward to stroke the puppy. It nibbled at my laces, then splayed its legs and peed on my sneakers.

"¡Cojones! He has respect for no one," the man cried, his false seriousness unable to cover his laughter. He sat beside me, then picked up the dog, cradled it in his lap, and began stroking it tenderly. The man's name was Pedro. He had a wide, friendly face crosshatched by creases, a thick mustache, and drooping, lugubrious eyelids. He was wearing a white guayabera and a white baseball cap with the words "DO IT BETTER." Pedro puffed on a fat cigar, rolling it around in his mouth with his callused fingers. Every now and again he extracted the stogie and admired it.

"The way to smoke a cigar is to imagine you're making love to a woman," he said, admiring the *puro* again, running his eyes along it before bringing it gently back to his puckered lips.

Pedro asked me what I thought of the situation in Cuba. I played safe and replied that my impressions were in flux. Feeling uncertain about speaking frankly, I intended to say no more. Those willing to take part in political discussions usually broached the topic themselves.

"The system of government is a *gran mafioso*," Pedro stated in a plangent whisper. "Remember the Stalinist system in the Soviet Union? The system here is the same. Remember *socialismo nacionalista* in Germany? If you thought differently from the government, you were in trouble." He looked pointedly at the young adults sauntering past. "People won't talk about our problems. They're afraid to open their mouths. Look at them, walking as if they've been castrated. ¡Jacas!"

Pedro seemed candid and fearless. It was incautious talk, and I was unused to hearing it proffered so freely in public. I said so. He stood and brushed the dust from the seat of his pants. Pedro suggested we take a walk. We strolled down streets lined by laurel trees. A bicycle puttered past, driven by a chainsaw engine rigged to the frame. Then a Cadillac Fleetwood rattled by, trailing balloons behind. A young girl was leaning out of the window. She waved. I waved back.

"Fiesta de quince," said Pedro, speaking of the traditional celebration to honor a Cuban girl's 15th birthday. The day marks the *quinceañera's* coming of age; though it is a direct legacy of a more conservative Spanish heritage, in today's more liberal Cuba it is also the day on which she may openly begin her sexual life without family recrimination. Except her wedding day, there is no more important date in the life of a Cuban female; parents often save money for the affair for years. An entire team may be involved: a hairdresser; a dressmaker hired to produce a knock-'em-dead Scarlett O'Hara outfit; a photographer; and a chauffeur to drive the American classic that is de rigueur for conveying the young woman and her friends to her party.

We passed a policeman, black, 20-something. Leaning against a wall, arms folded, one leg cocked, foot flat against the wall. I felt his eyes on my back.

"There's great repression here," Pedro continued once we were out of earshot. "It isn't possible to walk down the street without the police interfering. They check our documents. If you live in one area and are walking in another, they want to know why. Just a few years ago if you and I were seen talking like this, it would have meant...." He stopped in mid-sentence and drew a finger across his neck. We walked in silence for a while. Pedro seemed to be seething.

I had talked to dozens of habaneros, heard their sorry tales of stifling and repugnant restrictions.

We passed a 1957 Dodge Coronet with four flat tires, stuffed full of mangoes. I asked him how he made a living.

"Chapista," he replied. A panel beater. *"Trabajo particular.* Private work. Come, I'll show you."

We arrived at his home in a leafy suburb of Vedado. It was a middle-class house with a column-lined veranda made mournful by its deteriorated state, almost to the point of dilapidation, a sad situation it shared with neighboring homes. Pedro led me down the driveway, unlocked a large, rusty padlock, and swung open the gate of a great iron cage built onto the side of the house. A Lada was revealed under a large plastic sheet. The interior had been gutted.

"The original floor rusted away, so I've welded a new one onto the frame. I beat it by hand from sheet metal. The customer is coming to pick up the car later today."

"Good business?"

"Listen, hombre. The government forbids me to employ any workers, but I do so illegally. I have too much work to handle alone. They take 500 pesos monthly in taxes, regardless of how much or how little I make. They're trying to squeeze *trabajadores particulares* out of business."

Blue smoke spiraled up from the end of Pedro's half-smoked cigar.

One thing perplexed me. Who owned the scores of new Japanese cars with private license plates I'd seen driving around Havana? Did Lydia own her new Nissan Sentra?

Pedro explained. "Most belong to Cubalse [the state agency responsible for buying foreign products], which distributes them to other government corporations. They then grant them to privileged workers. Very few are owned by individuals. Only certain artists and sports stars are permitted to own their own."

Pedro's wife, Anna, joined us. She was a slender, sallow-skinned woman with a frail voice and dark eyes set in cavernous sockets the color of kohl. Her hair was rolled up in coiled sheets of paper.

"Pedro was a good driver," said Anna. "Then his car was stolen."

"Who stole it?" I asked.

Pedro laughed. "The government!"

Apparently it had disappeared off the street—stolen, thought Pedro, by government agents during the days when Cubalse was selling prime Yankee autos to international buyers as precious antiques.

"We're sick of him!" said Anna.

"What will happen after...." I stroked my chin, not finishing the sentence.

"When he dies, they can put him in the Plaza de la Revolución or anywhere else they choose. Anywhere except *Ciudad Santa,*" Anna replied.

"*¿Ciudad Santa?*" I asked.

"Jerusalem."

"Why not there?"

"Because we don't want another resurrection!"

"Listen," said Pedro, turning serious. "Raúl will attempt to rule by force. But he lacks his brother's intelligence. No one likes him."

"Do you think there'll be violence after Fidel dies?" I asked.

"*¡Claro!*" exclaimed Pedro.

"Shh!" said Anna, putting her finger to her lips.

"Between who?"

"*La policía,*" Pedro replied, lowering his voice and turning his back to the street. Habaneros criticizing their government often turned their backs to the streets so that tattletales couldn't lip-read their traitorous truths.

"The people will be out in the streets demanding a change," Pedro continued, "and the fidelistas will attempt to suppress it."

It sounded like a recipe for a repeat of Tiananmen Square.

"Not many people are committed communists," Pedro added, "but there are lots of loyal fidelistas. They're brainwashed. He has the ability to make people believe whatever he wants them to. I try not to listen."

Pedro put his hands over his ears.

"Believe me, *muchacho,* he can talk you into anything. *Anything,*" he said, pulling one hand down his chin and mimicking the voice of Fidel: "'Let me fuck you in the ass, compañero!'" Pedro stood up and put his hands protectively around his butt. His voice shifted an octave: "'Listen, papá, I'm not gay.'" He mouthed silently like a goldfish gasping for air, miming Fidel's yakety-yak. Pedro began to unbuckle his belt, pretended to whip off his pants, then bent over. "'Oh, okay, in that case, comandante!'"

When I started this journey, I was a Castrophile with a soft spot for the Revolution. Only two years had passed since my first visit, yet it was as if I were traveling through a different world. Cuba hadn't changed, just my perception of it. I had seen Cuba along a distorted parallax. My new thinking, however, felt like lese majesty. I made a halfhearted stab at defending Castro's achievements in culture, education, and health.

"You don't understand, Cristóbal," replied Pedro. "It is easy to be a socialist when you live in the United States. You can believe in the dream without having to exist in this nightmare."

Pedro was right. It was a fantastic place to visit. I longed to live in Havana. But Castro's Cuba has no place for free-willed loners like me.

Rolf had finally arrived. I rode out to Marina Hemingway.

The *Kalevala* was a mess, her deck littered with beer cans, used plastic cups, and uncoiled ropes like long strands of spaghetti underfoot.

Rolf had jumped ship and headed off for Las Tunas with his young Cuban wife, leaving his vessel in the custody of a fiftyish fellow named Willy who resembled a second-rate crook. He was short and wiry, and his thinning gray hair—disheveled and lightly brilliantined—resembled a windswept toupee. Willy wore a light-blue guayabera draped Cuban fashion outside denim jeans. A cigarette hung limply on his lower lip.

Willy wasn't sure when Rolf would return, so I visited the marina daily. Trying to get through on the phone was an exercise in futility and frustration. Willy always poured me a large tumbler of rum and begged me to linger and chat. He was a talkative fellow; in fact, he couldn't keep his mouth shut, and he kept his tongue lubricated with Mayabe beer and Habana Club rum.

"I've been bringing stuff into Cuba for years," he blurted out that first day as I sat in the captain's chair. "Cigarettes. Whiskey. Stuff like that."

I took notes as we talked. My scribbling seemed to draw Willy out further, luring him into bold indiscretions. I almost choked on the tidbits he told me. "I've got a company in the Bahamas," he continued. "Keep it strictly offshore." He pulled a business card from his top pocket and handed it to me.

I didn't need to ask questions. I couldn't get a word in edgewise. Willy the Weasel was ahead of me, anticipating my queries before I knew they were there.

"The U.S. Treasury tried to indict me," he went on, "but I hired a famous drug attorney. He got in their face. Uncle Sam dropped the charges."

Willy didn't know me from Adam. I could have been a CIA or DEA agent. Whenever pregnant silence descended, Willy delivered another gem.

"You've got to have protection if you want to operate in Cuba. I work with a colonel who oils the wheels for me. Opens doors." Willy named him. I wrote it down. We'll call him Nestor.

"I pay Nestor and a second employee 600 dollars a month, plus Nestor receives a 50 percent cut from each deal." Willy paused while I wrote. Nice courtesy. "You've gotta be careful, though. Cubans can't handle money," he explained, speaking of a second employee. "If I gave him his cash, he'd spend it on a new color television and a flashy car. I have to pay him a bit at a time. The rest I keep in a trust account. I show him his monthly statements so he knows how much he's earned. Nestor's more circumspect."

Willy topped up his tumbler with *añejo* rum. I declined, told him I had to get going.

"Hey, come over for dinner tomorrow night. Nestor will be here with his wife."

Coppelia had become part of my daily routine. I was a creature of habit, always choosing a seat downstairs at the counter, but one Saturday for a change I joined the cola for an outdoor section where the late afternoon sunlight filtered down subaqueously through the trees. The line curled out of the park and along Calle 21. I had become inured to the colas' interminably slow progress, but that day I was still in the spot where I started after 20 minutes. What on Earth was going on? I strolled to the head of the line. The section was empty, but the neighboring sections were full of happy customers spooning ice cream with gusto. I asked the couple at the head of the line if this section was closed.

"*Sí*," the woman replied.

"All day long?"

"*Sí, compañero.*"

Then why was she standing in line? "Is it closed every Saturday?" I inquired.

"Only on Mondays," she replied.

Five waitresses were seated at one of the tables, gossiping, oblivious to our welfare. I leaned over the gate.

"Excuse me. I'm sorry to bother you. Is this section open?"

"Yes," one of the quintet answered.

"Then how come there's no one sitting down? All the other sections are open."

"*Horita mismo*," she replied, looking away. Horita mismo—literally, "any moment now"—is the Cuban equivalent of Mexico's *mañana*. Cubans have learned to shrug and put up with bureaucratic indifference. I hadn't been in Cuba long enough.

"How long is horita mismo?" I might as well have asked her when she expected Fidel to retire.

"*¡Horita mismo!*" she replied, as if I were the village idiot.

"How many minutes?"

"*¡Pronto!*"

The other patrons gawked, mixing astonishment with their amusement. I persisted. "Yes, but how many minutes exactly?"

"Ten minutes!" she shot back.

"Thank you!" I looked at my watch and walked back to my place in line. Ten minutes came and went. The cola didn't move. We stood in line like torpid reptiles warming their blood in the sun. I thought about joining another line, but then…surely, any minute now! I breathed deeply and tried patience. The inertia tired me out.

Another 10 minutes passed. The waitresses were still gabbing merrily. I pushed open the gate and entered the hallowed sanctum.

"Excuse me, but there are 200 people waiting in line." The uninterested quintet looked up and said nothing.

"Do you have ice cream?"

"*Sí!*"

"Then what's the problem?"

"*El helado está demasiado duro.*" I couldn't believe my ears. How could the ice cream be too hard? I'd been waiting in line for 40 minutes. I swept my arms over the other sections. "What are the other patrons eating?" The waitresses shrugged and turned away.

"What did they say?" Cubans asked as I rejoined the line.

"The ice cream is too hard!"

They raised their eyebrows in disgust, too afraid to take on the lie. Making sense of this island was an exercise in madness. At times I thought I was posing in front of a fun-house mirror.

"Where are you from?" someone asked.

"Could this happen in England?" asked another.

"It's better not to fight the system," said a third.

"You're a foreigner," added a fourth. "For you to protest isn't a problem, but we have no rights. If I'd made the same scene and protested this disgrace, I might spend six months in jail."

Interminable minutes passed. Some of the other patrons wandered off and returned with snacks. I grew increasingly agitated. After 10 more minutes, I could contain my frustration no longer. I stormed into the serving station. Six large tubs of vanilla ice cream were set on the counter, so I marched up to them and plunged my forefinger into one of the tubs. *Soft!* I knew it!

"Who is in charge here?" I demanded. The staff glowered. No one spoke. "Doesn't anyone here have responsibility?" One of the girls pointed out a man in a navy blue shirt. I called him over. He consulted the waitresses, then repeated what they had told me.

"The ice cream is too hard."

"That's ridiculous," I replied. "It's soft. Look!" I showed him the incriminating hole I had made.

He sighed and walked away. Disgruntled Cubans were now pressing at the gate and voicing their disgust. Patrons in other sections looked up from their bowls. Then a uniformed *custodio* ushered us all back into line. The line stayed frozen in place.

I began to hatch a plot for a charge up the hill. We would seat ourselves and start banging our spoons: *"¡Helado! ¡Helado!"* I was preparing to do just that when the line magically began to move.

As I reached the gate, the custodio put his palm up to my face: "Full!"

I saw vacant seats. I pushed past him.

The waitresses ignored me until finally one asked if I had pesos. I replied that I did.

"You're a tourist?"

"Not exactly."

"¿Un residente?"

"Yes, I'm a resident."

She wanted proof.

I came clean: "Okay, I'm a tourist."

"In that case I can't serve you," she replied, "You have to buy your ice cream over there, at the hotel, in dollars." She pointed to the Hotel Habana Libre.

"But I eat here every day. Over there." I pointed at the counter. "I've been coming for almost a month and have never been refused before."

She rolled her eyes and asked the others at my table for their orders, so I tried being nice. Turned humble. Told her that I'd been standing in line almost an hour. She said nothing and merely pointed at the hotel. Ubiquitous and elusive forces opposed my every step, making a Pilgrim's Progress out of a weirdly illogical sequence of simple events.

Steamed, I began scribbling notes. That seemed to unnerve her. She rushed off to consult with the manager and returned. *"No problema, señor,"* she said contemptuously, and took my order.

I devoured the ice cream almost as soon as she brought it and asked for a second bowl.

"That's not possible."

"Why not?" I always had two bowls, which was not unusual. Most Cubans ate two or three bowlfuls at a sitting.

She struggled for a moment, the silence pregnant as she sifted through her mind for an answer. "The ice cream is too hard," she replied, whisking away my bowl while the last scoopful was still cold in my mouth.

Rolf had returned and was ready to sail: "The day after tomorrow, vee go!"

I spent the day packing, calling friends, and trying to think of any outstanding research I had forgotten. I had visited the museums and castles, eaten at most of the major restaurants, and checked out all the tourist sites and hotels. The only place I hadn't checked out was the new show at Tropicana, Havana's most spectacular nightclub. It seemed a fitting finale.

Neither the Revolution nor the recent economic crisis has ruffled the feathers of the "paradise under the stars," which opened on New Year's Eve 1939 in the district of Marianao in an open-air theater in the gardens of the former residence of the U.S. ambassador. The Tropicana featured effusive tropical foliage as part of its setting. International celebrities such as Nat "King" Cole, Josephine Baker, and Carmen Miranda headlined the shows, drawing the Havana elite. The show was so popular that a 50-passenger "Tropicana Special" flew nightly from Miami for an evening of entertainment that ended in the nightclub's casino, which offered a daily $10,000 bingo jackpot—and, on Sundays, a free raffle giveaway of a new automobile.

In the late 1950s, the club was owned by Martín Fox, who held a legal monopoly on the installation and maintenance of slot machines—*máquinas traganikeles*—in Havana. Managing the casino was Mob associate Lefty Clark. Martín was a friend of mobster boss Santo Traficante, whose lawyer, Frank Ragano, visited Havana in 1958 and was treated to a tour of the sex scene. Martín gave him a choice seat for a special performance. The night's theme was "Miss Universe." Martín offered Ragano any girl he desired.

"Take your pick," he told Ragano, "You want two girls? Three girls? Anything you want!"

Figuring that "Miss Cuba" would be the obvious winner and therefore the most beautiful, Ragano chose her sight unseen. Sure enough, after the show Miss Cuba was shown to his table. Martín then arranged for them to go to the Hotel Comodoro, where entertainers performed live lesbian acts and had sex with members of the audience.

Havana was that kind of place. Sex was "the great Havana subject," wrote

Graham Greene in *Our Man in Havana.* "The sexual exchange was not only the chief commerce of the city, but the whole *raison d'être* of a man's life. One sold sex or one bought it—immaterial which, but it was never given away."

Then as now, the key attraction was the sensual mulata parade featuring the most beautiful women in Cuba. Talent scouts scoured the country for the most exquisite models and dancers, and held beauty contests to lure women from working-class neighborhoods with the promise of a gilded future, including the chance to become arm candy for moneyed bigwigs. Tropicana's performers—more than 200 of them—are still handpicked from the crème de la crème of Cuba's beauties, dancers, and singers.

I bought a ticket for $50 and rode out helmetless and dressed in denims. The lush entrance grounds resembled the fictional jungles of Tarzan, with the subaqueous greens lit from below by colored lights as if for a *son-et-lumière.* A doorman in a tuxedo led me into the amphitheater and seated me on one of the aisles. The chairs and tables were arrayed in great half-moons looking down on a circular stage beneath the stars. Backing the stage was a trellis in a 3-D geometric design; it was festooned with golden-hued lights like a Christmas tree and spanned by twin staircases with neon-lit glass steps that reached into the treetops, connected by boardwalks. A huge sign flashed between the trees:

TROPICANA 1996

1939

The music began. A troupe of near-naked showgirls in silver thigh-high boots appeared at the back of the auditorium and paraded down the aisles wearing glowing chandeliers atop their heads. They wore see-through fishnet body suits dripping with silver baubles that dangled like still-wet tiny fishes, and they strutted down the aisle like sex washing up from the sea.

The rest of the show comprised a medley of flamboyant cabaret routines highlighted by a never-ending parade of stupendous mulatas sashaying and shaking in sequined bikinis, ruffled frills, sensational headdresses, and feathers more ostentatious than peacocks. They appeared like creatures in a Rousseau painting, mahogany and ebony of skin, bedecked in audacious plumage the color of vermilion lipstick and emerald like the green flash of sunset at sea. Others, equally exotically plumed, were as variegated in turquoise and teals as the Caribbean, and they flashed absinthe to magenta and yellow and back to iridescent green like birds of paradise shaking their bodies in a mating routine.

Ninety minutes into the show, Cuba's state mulatas came down from the stage and streamed up the aisles. Suddenly, standing in front of me was *my* Miss Cuba, shaking like Jell-O and smiling down at me like an angel almost within fingertip reach. The woman was exquisite, but her serene smile told me that her beauty ran more than skin deep. Our eyes met and I registered a mutual fancy as she cast a spell on me with a lingering and tender *ojito,* such as Daisy had given me in the plaza two years before. I leaped into the aisle and snapped a quick photo.

As suddenly as she had appeared, Miss Cuba sashayed back down the aisle trailing her streamer tail behind, and the entire Tropicana troupe joined her on stage in a final explosive finale like a kaleidoscope spinning out of control. Then the parade flounced up the neon-lit staircase and disappeared. The lights went up, the crowd filtered out, and I was left alone in the auditorium—alone with my simmering ambition to meet my Miss Cuba.

I sat in the dark, contriving to make tangible my delicious desire. A waitress approached and asked if I was sitting in the gloom for a reason.

"I want to meet one of the dancers."

She lit up. Inside every Cuban is a romantic eager to help guide Cupid's arrow.

I tried to describe the object of my interest, tried to separate her out among the denizens of this exotic harem, but she ended up sounding like all the others. The waitress rushed off and returned minutes later leading a tall, leggy woman svelte of waist and with a drop-dead gorgeous face. My jaw fell. She was wearing a body-clinging ice-blue silk shirt and spray-painted jeans that stopped short of her ankles, which tapered down to pointy high heels. But this was no booby prize.

"Hello," she said, flashing a broad, glinting smile. "I'm Olga." She was buoyant and seemed delighted that I had beckoned her so.

"I'm Cristóbal," I replied. "I'm pleased to meet you....But you're not the one."

She should have slapped me. Instead, she raised her shoulders and sauntered off whither she came. The waitress looked crestfallen. Determined to try again, she rushed away. I thought to call after her, *"Bring back Olga!"* Agonizing minutes passed before the waitress returned empty-handed, looking more disconsolate even than I.

"They've all left."

"How so?"

"The dancers have all gone home on the Tropicana bus." Then, "You didn't like her?"

She must have thought me a loony.

I wrote a note on a napkin asking my Miss Cuba for a date. The waitress promised to deliver it the following evening.

And bless her heart, she was true to her word.

The streets were stark and deserted. Havana had a funereal, dead-of-night quality. I rode home through the one o'clock gloom, squinting to see the potholes ahead in the eerie glow of phosphorescent street lamps while the BMW's halogen high beam burned a long hole in the hazy night. I lay awake, fantasizing that in Miss Cuba I might find my next Daisy.

That night I hatched a plan to return to the Tropicana during the dance rehearsals next day; using my journalistic credentials, I would gain entry and introduce myself to Miss Cuba. That's what I did, taking a taxi with a tropical rain sheeting down.

"The dancers have the day off," said the young woman sitting behind a steel-legged table in the ticket booth. "It's a national holiday."

I quickly hatched plan B: "Do you have a public relations manager?"

"Yes. Juan Caballo. He should be here shortly."

I killed time chatting inside the ticket booth while the tropical rain beat unrelentingly on the tin roof. But Caballo never showed, so I wrote him a note requesting his help in researching a magazine story on Tropicana. An investment for the future.

I decided to return to Tropicana that night, my last. After three months in Cuba, my cash reserves were dangerously low, and I was in no shape to fork out another $50 for the show. I settled on an audacious plan.

I timed my arrival for the final act, intent on pushing past the doorman as the dancers streamed up the aisle. The music was reaching its climax as I stepped from the taxi. I hurried toward the door. Suddenly, someone reached out from behind and grabbed my arm, stopping me dead in my tracks.

"Cristóbal!"

It was the girl from the ticket booth. She introduced a slender fellow of medium height, about my age. Juan Caballo, the public relations director, lit up. He shook my hand, then put his arm around my shoulder and ushered me into his office. My desire to write a story had enthused him. Caballo promised his full support. I grew agitated as he bantered on, making small talk. I looked at my watch. Two minutes before eleven o'clock. Jesus! The show was about to end.

"There's one other thing," I sputtered, feeling desperate. "I'm here tonight to meet one of the showgirls. I think she likes me as much as I like her. I want to meet her before the show is over."

"Why didn't you say so?" Caballo replied. *¡"Venga!"* He jumped up, grabbed my arm, and rushed me into the auditorium. The dancers were already swanning up the aisle. There wasn't a moment to lose. I rushed forward and stopped in front of the woman of my dreams.

I spoke. *"Eres hermosísima. Te espero afuera."* Five words—nothing more. "You're beautiful. I'll wait for you outside."

She smiled a big, wide smile and told me where she would meet me. Then, still shimmying her ruffled behind, she turned and disappeared back down the aisle. The next dancer leaned over and asked, "Why not me?"

Miss Cuba appeared, dressed all in white. She hurried toward me wraith-like in the dark, the moonlight shining full upon her white turban, blouse, shawl, and calf-length skirt that billowed around her sleek legs, now adorned in white stockings. Copper and bronze amulets glinted upon her arms, and she wore many necklaces—*collares*—of colorful beads. Marleni—for that was her name— was a *santera*, a follower of the *Santería* religion; dressed thus, I knew that she lived at this moment in a high state of grace.

"Hola, Cristóbal" she said, her big brown eyes beaming widely, her whole pretty face lit up with a sublime mixture of innocence and joy. Our smiles ricocheted.

She took my hand, and I sensed once again the simplicity with which in Cuba desire can strike flaming miracles from charming scenes of tropical naiveté.

Marleni was an *iyawó*—an initiate or "bride" of the *Orishas*, the spiritual emissaries of Olorún (God) in the traditional Yoruba religion of modern-day Nigeria and Benin. In the New World, West African slaves hid their religion behind a facade of Catholicism, with various saints representing the Orishas. A follower of *Santería* may choose at any stage in life to undertake an elaborate initiation that will tear the follower away from her old life and set her feet on *La Regla de Ocha*—the Way of the Orishas. During this time, she will be possessed by, and under the care of, a specific Orisha who will guide her to a deeper, richer life for the rest of her time in this world.

The rites of *Santería* are complex. They include having to dress solely in white and stay indoors at night for a year, though exceptions are allowed for employment. An iyawó may not touch anyone or permit herself to be touched, except by the most intimate family members—or, this being Cuba, by lovers. In taking my hand, Marleni had disclosed that we were already intimates.

We hailed an illegal taxi—a '53 Ford with blackened windows—tucked ourselves in the back seat, and rode hand in hand back to Vedado through dimly lit streets. On a dark, narrow lane off Infanta, a policeman suddenly leaped into our path and frantically waved down the jalopy. A man lay bleeding in the street, he explained to the driver. The policeman wanted to bundle him into the car and commandeer it for a trip to the hospital.

"¡Ay, mi Dios!" Marleni exclaimed. She leaned forward and spoke through the driver's window: *"¡Estoy de santera. No se puede!"*

The policeman, a young black man, looked aghast, then waved us on and ran off to look for another car.

"What did you tell him?" I asked, astounded.

"I am not myself," she replied. "I am Santa Teresita, the *patrón de los muertes.*" The patron saint of the dead. "If he had put that man in the car, I might have killed him."

I felt a chill run down my spine, and pondered what my last few hours in Cuba had in store.

I do the rounds of Cuban friends, say farewells, load up the BMW with bags, press the starter button, and set off for Marina Hemingway with a warm rain drumming on my helmet. The water glistens on the Malecón unspooling ahead of me like Orlando de la Rosa's sensuous thread of "silver lamé." I arrive at the marina already homesick at the thought of departing Havana.

The Customs officer is all business. He never smiles as he rummages through my belongings and records with perplexing exactitude details of everything I have purchased.

He studies the panniers. "What's in those?"

"Spare parts, tools—that sort of thing."

"Where's your computer?"

He has me turn on my laptop and show him my files.

"I never used it," I say, displaying the dates listed in my C: drive directory.

What a waste. I've carried the damn thing around Cuba, shaken the guts out of it on terrible roads clocking more than 7,000 miles.

If he discovers my notebooks, I'll surely lose them. So I've hidden them, taped to the underside of the saddle. I'm prepared to leave my BMW behind in a worst-case scenario, but my notebooks I must never surrender. Beads of sweat seep down the inside of my arms as he approaches and inspects *mi moto Fidel*.

"Your chapa!"

"My chapa?"

"*Sí.*"

"Can't I keep it as a souvenir?"

"Your chapa, please."

The Customs officer tells me I'm free to leave. My relief is enormous, as if I've been issued a reprieve on the gallows.

I clean the engine with solvent, then ride the BMW up the *Kalevala's* gangplank. Rolf and a Cuban mechanic lift the front end to clear the handlebars over the rail while I feather the clutch and inch the behemoth between the narrow gateway with a hairbreadth to spare on each side.

Finally we're ready to sail. Rolf fires up the two General Electric diesels, maneuvers the *Kalevala* into the channel, and points her prow toward the marina exit. I feel shadowed by sorrow as we slip down-channel, my three-month journey now at an end. I think of my notebooks taped under the saddle and laugh aloud at the absurdity of my paranoia. Maybe Juan Pardo had been serious about having a person with me each day to *help* me. The government certainly hadn't placed any obstacles in my way.

I'm walking on cloud nine from a sense of accomplishment. Not just the smug self-absorption of having ridden more than 7,000 miles through Cuba, but the acknowledgment that I have researched my guidebook diligently. I feel elated knowing that my notebooks are finally safe. To have had them confiscated, or stolen, would have been too much to bear. Relieved, I retrieve the nine notebooks, arrange them in chronological order, secure them with a large rubber band, then wrap them in a plastic bag. This I seal and tuck beneath my clothes in the base of my duffel, which I place below behind a chair in the main cabin. Back on deck, I down a cuba libre and breathe in deeply, savoring the briny air and the sight of the aquamarine sea.

Rolf draws up to the immigration office by the marina entrance, where final clearance is given. Two officials in faded olive uniforms come aboard and seat themselves in the shade. Willy becomes obsequious, offering each a beer and cigarettes. "Keep the packet," he says, handing over his Marlboros. Willy's tongue never ceases. He can't let up for a moment, barraging the matter-of-fact Cubans with abject banter. Eventually they tire, stamp our papers, and leave.

"Vee go now," says Rolf, motioning for one of the officials to slip the ropes that tether us to the jetty. But the official denies us departure. I notice armed soldiers. The uniformed officials seem to be waiting for someone. We grow fidgety. Two hours slip by. Eventually three uniformed MININT officers arrive and briskly step aboard, followed by two poker-faced men in plain clothes. The duo wear Rolex watches and Ray Ban sunglasses—well-known symbols of counterintelligence.

"I've never seen these spicks come on board before," Willy whispers. "Nor that." He points at a young cocker spaniel. The dog seems more interested in investigating puppyish things such as Willy's loose shoelaces than in sniffing around for contraband or Cuban stowaways. We go below and watch the officers search desultorily through cupboards and drawers while the cocker spaniel capers among the clothing strewn about Rolf's cabin.

The Cubans file aloft. Rolf follows, leaving Willy and me alone with a MININT officer and one of the Tweedledee spooks. They have saved me for last.

"Which are your bags?" asks the MININT officer, a tall, clean-shaven black man with close-cropped hair and handsome features. He has piercing eyes in an intelligent-looking, coconut-shaped face, and he speaks in Spanish. I point to my bags.

"¡Por favor!" He motions for me to place them in the center of the room. Then he unzips my computer bag. "Why the computer?"

I ad-lib an answer about needing e-mail to stay in touch with friends back in the United States. The computer—a Toshiba L1000—is a DOS-system dinosaur and isn't configured to provide e-mail access. I'm praying he doesn't ask for a demonstration.

Next, the MININT officer turns to the duffel and rifles through it with a diligence that suggests he knows exactly what he is seeking. He finds it, wrapped in the plastic bag at the base of my duffel. I feel my toes curl involuntarily. I am panicked. I pray that the counterintelligence agent hasn't noticed my reaction.

He stands over me, instilling a kind of low-grade fear as he stares down from behind his dark glasses.

I look up at Willy. He's gone pale with the realization that his corrupt enterprise is about to be blown.

"It's hot in here," Willy gasps feebly. "I think I'll go up top."

"What's wrong?" the officer asks, shifting to clear, well-crafted English. "You frightened of something?" Shifting from friendly to officious and mean. Silence envelops the room until Willy manages to sputter, "No, no. I'm hot, that's all."

"What are these?" the officer asks as he pulls off the rubber band and begins thumbing through the top notebook.

"My diaries."

"What about?"

"My experiences."

"What do you do with them? Are you a journalist?"

"No," I reply, struggling to stay cool. "I'm a consultant of tourism."

"Why do you need to record your experiences?"

"I teach about destinations around the world. Notes help my recall and assist in planning my lectures."

"Do you write?"

"I write personal journals about my travels."

The officer scrutinizes my notes with an eagle eye. I feel that he is fully aware of my enterprise and has been sent to ascertain what my notebooks contain. He's here to determine whether to confiscate them or not. I flash on my interview with Francisco and hear and see in my mind's eye the clatter of boots on the cobbles and the officious knock of the secret police at his door. I see my own ruminations on the mad Machiavellianism of contemporary Cuba and sense the bile beginning to rise in my stomach. If he sees my comments on Fidel, it is over. My books will be confiscated and all my research—my entire journey—will have been in vain.

I can hardly believe my reality. It's as if I'm looking at a wildly spinning world through a fishbowl. I stand up, lean over his shoulder, skim for a positive line, and start reading aloud: "Nueva Gerona is surrounded by attractive mountains." He waves me aside, closes the book, then opens the second and chooses at random. He, too, begins reading aloud. Thankfully I've arranged my notebooks in chronological order. My early impressions are mostly laudatory.

"You write positive things about Cuba?"

"Yes, I like Cuba very much!"

He stares me straight in the eye, then turns to the third notebook, again pausing at random to read.

"What do you think about Cuba?" he asks, echoing the question asked a month prior in Holguín. I tell him how much I respect the Revolution.

"You write anything bad about Cuba?"

"I love Cuba!"

He fingers the fourth notebook—the one containing Francisco's impassioned comments, which sparked my epiphany and an outpouring of more perilous notes. I feel my heart race and my temples thump from the blood pulsing through my veins.

The MININT officer begins to read, then miraculously changes his mind. He closes the book, stacks the notepads in chronological order, secures them with the rubber band, and hands them back to me. He nods to the agent, who disappears up the stairs into the soft evening sunlight. The officer follows.

As he touches the stair rail, he peers over his shoulder and remarks, "You can write a good book about Cuba. *¡Buen viaje!*"

EPILOGUE

~

M y Cuba guidebook was published in November 1997, fulfilling a four-year labor. In April 1999, I returned to spend six weeks in Havana. As always, it was both uplifting and unsettling—Cuba sweet and sour.

The city had changed, its louche aspect much diminished. The restoration of Habana Vieja had expanded considerably, even extending along the Malecón, and scores of heretofore decrepit colonial structures gleamed afresh like confections in stone. Derelict hotels were being restored in the historic quarter, and several deluxe hotels and an international trade center were under construction in Miramar. Even condominiums—starting price $67,000, with payment up front—were for sale to foreigners

To ease Havana's traffic nightmare, modern buses had been imported from Europe. Tourism was booming, hotel rooms were booked solid, and dozens of dollars-only stores had opened citywide, selling Western goods from toothpaste to Nikes. More Cubans had finagled access to dollars through the tourist economy, aided in early 1999 when President Clinton eased the trade embargo to permit more cash to be sent to Cuban individuals and nongovernmental organizations (Castro called the move a "fraud").

The peso stores, however, were as threadbare as they had been three years earlier. Cubans who had only pesos to live on were in a dire state, and many habaneros had resorted to begging. Despite all this, materially things had improved substantially (I even saw overweight Cubans for the first time). I was surprised, therefore, when first one, then several Cuban acquaintances told me: "Things are much worse." Even habaneros with regular access to dollars talked of Castro and the current situation with a disdain as vehement as I had ever heard. Cubans' marginal material improvements belied a deep-rooted, melancholic malaise as Cubans bristled at ever increasing proscriptions.

In January 1999, Castro had announced legislation—the Law for the Protection of Cuba's National Independence and Economy—that created a new counterrevolutionary felony: "supporting" hostile U.S. policies. Anyone providing information to foreigners—notably foreign media—faced a 30-year sentence. To get the point across, in March of 1999 four prominent dissidents—the Group of Four—received harsh sentences, while a prominent doctor was jailed for admitting an outbreak of dengue fever. The sentences signaled a crackdown throughout Cuba, prompting the United Nations Human Rights Committee to place Cuba on its list of worst offenders. More so, however, the policy was "a battle against disorder, crime, disrespect for authority, illegal business and lack of social control." In the three years since my motorcycle journey, serious crime and *jineterismo* had risen dramatically, and Havana had even developed an incipient drug problem, with cocaine and crack being sold on the street and at discos. When two jineteras died of cocaine overdoses in December 1998, Havana's discos and bars were closed down. The following month, several thousand black-bereted police from an elite National Brigade were deployed on street corners throughout the city. Thousands of young men and women were arrested, accused of prostitution, pimping, or *peligrosidad,* which makes a crime of *appearing* to perform a misdeed. The police were stationed on street corners 24 hours a day, reducing crime virtually overnight. It was eerie walking streets where I was rarely beyond view of the police.

Most of the self-employed, evident everywhere in 1996 and getting on well outside the state-controlled sector, had been driven out of business. Private restaurants—*paladares*—were being squeezed, too; their numbers had been vastly curtailed. Even small-scale foreign entrepreneurs were being pushed out; like *gusanos* in the early 1960s, some reportedly had to leave their assets behind as "donations to the Revolution."

"Things are much worse now, and they get worse every day," I was told by Martin Kaupp, a German who has lived in Havana since 1994. "Many of my friends have bailed out of their businesses and left. There are more problems now. You see the police? I don't even take my girlfriend out now anymore. They molest us."

Emboldened by the country's modest economic recovery, the Cuban government was also reneging on contracts with major foreign partners, many of whom were giving up. It was also becoming greedy. Without free-market competition to regulate prices, the regime was using its monopoly to gouge tourists. Hotels had doubled their prices, and many were now vastly overpriced by international comparison. The same went for state-run restaurants, where food quality had hardly improved. Tourist charges were being levied on the most marginal items. Staffers at car-rental outlets were scamming renters as a matter of course. Low-level corruption among government officials was becoming more obvious. And I witnessed the first worrisome signs of a local Mafia presence, hinted at when I was shaken down at the Habana Club—the hip new nightclub in Vedado that had just opened as a clever takeoff on the Hard Rock Café.

In Europe, the Kosovo crisis had erupted, and NATO forces from the U.S. and 16 European nations were bombing Yugoslavia. Cuban news reports were full of denunciations of the "U.S. genocidal war," portrayed as "imperialist savagery." The stories focused on what Cuban propaganda organs called "U.S. messianism" and a military operation directed "almost exclusively toward civilian targets." No mention was made of Slobodan Milosevic's brutal genocide against Kosovo Albanians, which had brought about the tragic war. Instead, the Balkan thug was portrayed as a victim of imperialist aggression and slander.

My Cuban friends scoffed when, on May 1, I attended the May Day Parade. Ostensibly a spontaneous demonstration of revolutionary loyalty, it appeared carefully choreographed: Several hundred thousand Cubans marched past carrying placards denouncing NATO's bombing campaign while stooges used the loudspeakers to whip up the crowd with chants of *"¡Viva Fidel!"* I stood in the press arena barely 30 feet from the glum-faced Cuban leader as he responded with saintly gestures, like Napoleon in George Orwell's *Animal Farm*, "majestically upright, casting haughty glances from side to side."

Then, on May 7, 1999—the day I flew back to Miami—the U.S. Attorney's Office filed charges against Cuba's intelligence agency for carrying out Operation *Scorpion*, a plan that had led to the downing of the two Brothers to the Rescue planes in February 1996. A Miami grand jury indicted the head of Cuba's Directorate of Intelligence and 13 other defendants, charging that the intelligence agency had actively worked to provoke a violent incident with the Brothers organization through its agents in Miami. The FBI had arrested several Cuban agents, and they had spilled the beans on Castro's plot. I felt vindicated in my revelations on the beach at Cojababo. Castro, a half-mad Don Quixote, *had* contrived the shoot-downs to secure passage of the Helms-Burton bill.

At year's end I returned to Cuba, arriving during yet another surreal moment in Cuban history. Two weeks earlier, a five-year-old Cuban boy, Elián González, had been found bobbing in an inner tube after his mother and 10 other people drowned when their boat sank during an escape bid for Florida. The Immigration and Naturalization Service (INS), after declaring its intent to return the boy to his father in Cuba, had granted temporary custody of Elián to rabidly anti-Castroite relatives, who then refused to hand the boy over. Instead, they filed a petition seeking political asylum for the young child, unwittingly playing directly into Castro's crusade against Uncle Sam and cynically turning the issue into the latest round in the last and longest-running battle of the Cold War. Castro—who treats Cuban-American emotions as a fulcrum on which to lever Washington's Cuba policy—ordered "Free Elián" protests, vowing that demonstrations would last "10 years, if necessary." Meanwhile, the case began a convoluted course through the Florida courts.

Daily, throughout the country, I witnessed rallies in support of Elián, whom the besotted Cuban exiles—Castro called them the "Miami Mafia"—were showering with gifts, turning him into "a poster boy for the American way of life," thought one reporter. The story monopolized Cuba's airwaves and journals, which broadcast only dour footage of Elián in Florida. His impish face was posted in every storefront, on every lamppost, and every second billboard across Cuba. Schoolchildren paraded on stage wearing cardboard handcuffs. Then everyone began wearing T-shirts (distributed en masse throughout the country) bearing Elián's downturned face, shown imprisoned behind metaphorical bars.

I attended the Havana rallies, immersing myself in a sea of chanting, flag-waving Cubans. Some teenagers sang a muffled version of the protest chant "Elián, our friend! Cuba is with you!", turning it into "Elián, our friend! Take us with you!" While CNN newscasts (available in tourist hotels) aired bloated reports about spontaneous passions in Havana, trucks with loudspeakers cruised the streets, summoning loyalists to the demonstrations.

Schoolchildren and workers were bused in for these almost festive occasions. Overnight, bulldozers appeared and began tearing up the grassy knolls in front of the U.S. Interests Section to make way for a new plaza—Plaza de la Dignidad—to accommodate the masses brought in to taunt Uncle Sam. I watched round-the-clock work crews give Potemkin makeovers to the crumbling facades of apartment blocks in view of the TV cameras. The neighbors got no such treatment.

Cuba was split down the middle. Most Cubans I spoke to were eager to hear my impressions, aware that perhaps they weren't being permitted to learn the whole story. Few Cubans knew, for example, that Lincoln Diaz-Balart—Castro's nemesis and the Florida Republican congressman championing the crusade to grant Elián U.S. citizenship—was Castro's former nephew-in-law. For Fidel, the battle over Elián was a family feud that had trawled up a vignette fit for a Hollywood movie.

In 1954, Castro's estranged wife, Mirta Díaz-Balart, had left for the United States, taking *their* five-year-old son with her. The courts, seeing Fidel as a radical revolutionary serving jail time, awarded custody of the son to the mother. Fidel, enraged by the thought of Fidelito being raised in Miami by a family he despised and who despised him, had refused to acknowledge the verdict: "One day I'll get my son and my honor back," he wrote to his sister, "even if the earth should be destroyed in the process....I am prepared to reenact the Hundred Years War. And I'll win it."

In October 1956, Fidel persuaded Mirta to let the boy visit him in Mexico on his word "as a gentleman" that Fidelito would be returned after two weeks. Instead, the boy was secreted away, and Mirta had to enlist the help of the Mexican police to win him back; some reports suggest she hired kidnappers, who seized the boy while he was being taken for a stroll in Mexico City's Chapultepec Park. Mirta then married a Cuban diplomat; after a year in New York, she returned with the boy to her new home in Havana. In due course, Fidel took power and Cuba turned Communist; Mirta fled the island for Spain in 1964, but Fidel would not let her take her son with her. Fidelito—who briefly headed Cuba's nuclear program before being demoted—lives to this day in Havana.

The congruities with the Elián epic loomed larger than life.

By the time I returned to the States in February 2000, most Cubans I spoke to had tired of the saga, which had become a 24/7 part of their lives. Castro, who believes that children belong to the state and routinely prevents the children of Cuban exiles from joining their parents abroad, continued to use the Elián debacle to prod Cuban passions. In May, once again in Havana, I found the public spirit buoyed as Fidel traded his black boots for white tennis shoes, grasped a red-white-and-blue Cuban flag, and led marchers at the May Day Parade on a sweaty two-mile hike to the Plaza de la Dignidad. On April 22, INS agents had recovered Elián at gunpoint and reunited him with his father, Juan Miguel, whom Castro had permitted to leave Cuba for the occasion. Juan Miguel confounded right-wing pundits by refusing to seek asylum; he even turned down their $2 million offer to stay.

No wonder. He had witnessed mob rule, intimidation, and an arrogant disregard for the law by a Cuban exile community that had become spoiled by a warped sense of self-importance and an overindulged taste of the good life. I couldn't blame Juan Miguel for wishing to trade the corruption, crime, and crass consumerism of Miami for a more nurturing upbringing in a more peaceful and respectful community.

As the case wound its way through U.S. courts, an entourage of Elián's school pals arrived along with their teachers. Elián appeared on Cuban TV dressed in his Cuban school uniform, shown being educated—"indoctrinated in Communism" was the right-wing verbiage—in a secure compound in Washington, D.C. The U.S. public overwhelmingly approved. The Cuban Americans had been publicly humiliated. That they had misspent their moral and political capital was signaled in May, when Jesse Helms dropped his ironclad opposition to a congressional bill permitting food and medical sales to Cuba.

Political pundits in the United States hailed the affair as a harbinger of more amicable relations with Cuba. I saw things differently. Fidel had just spent $2 million to build a high-tech concrete stage—the José Martí Anti-Imperialist Platform—in front of the U.S. Interests Section in Havana's Plaza de la Dignidad, where a statue of the nationalist hero now held in his arms a bronze effigy of young Elián. The stage looked like it had been built for the long haul. "This is just the beginning," said Fidel the day after the Miami raid reunited Elián with his father. "There are many more issues."

David had no plans for making up with Goliath.

I hankered for the wind in my hair as I circumnavigated the island again, this time by car. The "Che song" played over and over on the tape deck, haunting me throughout my journey:

*"Aquí se queda la clara,
entrañable transparencia
de tu querida presencia,
Comandante Che Guevara"*

*Here Lies the clear
deep purity
of your beloved presence,
Comandante, Che Guevara*

Traveling by car revealed that Cuba's transportation situation remained dire. The roadsides were littered with people waving frantically, flourishing peso notes, begging rides. Rare were the miles driven without the company of Cubans I had picked up on the road. Many graciously invited me into their homes—hovels, many of them, hidden to the rear of more substantial houses facing the streets. I witnessed dwellings made of packing cases, tin, and cardboard, and urban apartments no less dour.

"I don't want you to see inside my house," a dancer named Rosa told me as we climbed the dangerously unstable stairs to her cement-and-brick home in Holguín. "It's black!" *Black?* Rosa hesitated, then pushed hard on the door. The bare walls of her dingy living room were filthy with soot from the smoke of wood pyres she was forced to burn on the floor of what passed for a kitchen—hardly bigger than a telephone booth—bereft of a stove. The next day I bought her a three-ring gas burner (a shoddy affair manufactured in Canada and assembled in Cuba) and two cans of watery Cuban paint at dollar-goods stores. She jumped for joy—quite literally—her eyes almost popping out of her head at such fortune.

I had cruised through the island on my motorcycle without realizing how much real poverty still exists in Cuba. It was hard to keep my balance. Poverty? I had seen enough of the hard-core version in Jamaica, Sudan, and India—and read enough about its appalling equivalent in prerevolutionary Cuba—to realize how much Cuba's remarkable revolution had achieved. Nonetheless, I was sobered.

Socialist stalwarts living in dismaying conditions saw their own lives different than I. "I'm not interested in material things. The spiritual is more important," said Abundio, a revolutionary war hero (he showed me his bullet wounds earned in the Sierra Maestra) whose home I shared one night in Remedios. Mosquitoes hung in great clouds in the squalid kitchen and bathroom. "You are not a friend, you are a brother," said Abundio, hugging me with genuine affection as I departed. It was a reminder that life can appear richer when you have fewer things— a reminder of what it was I so loved and admired about Castro's Cuba.

Abundio was in the minority. Most Cubans decried what they saw as Castro's determination to thwart their economic advancement. During months of crisscrossing Cuba in 1996, I had heard the same frustrations voiced with stoical fatalism. Four years later, despite the dollars-only stores that had mushroomed throughout the isle, they were expressed with impatience and anger.

"*¡Jaca!* We're all *jacados!*" exclaimed Ramón. Castrated. "There's no opposition here because people are too busy resolving their problems and meeting their daily needs," continued the short, middle-aged habanero. "Look around you. See these houses? Can you imagine what these streets looked like 40 years ago? This was a prosperous city. A middle-class city. We vacationed in New York. Shopped in Miami. He's destroyed the middle class and the city, too. You think he wants me to succeed?"

I felt conspicuously guilty, like a bourgeois cruising through a country that has despoiled its own.

"Listen," Ramón continued, echoing sentiments that still rebounded up and down Cuba's streets. "The government isn't serious about improving our lives. It's content with leaving things the way they are. When people concentrate so entirely on solving their problems, it's impossible for an organized opposition to form. He's not going to permit any openings. Not for us," he said, touching his elbow to indicate *duro* (misery). Ramón drew his hands together, fingertip to fingertip, forming a perfect circle. "Look at the Soviet Union. Gorbachev permitted a little liberty," he said, separating his thumbs a fraction, "and *poof!*" Ramón's hands flew apart. "Here there is absolute control. The system is perfect."

Ramón looked nervously over his shoulder.

"He's *loco*," he added. "Power is an aphrodisiac for him. *Está pajando.* He's jerking off. That's all that matters to him. *Es su problema católico-sexual,*" he replied, using the Cuban equivalent for a hang-up.

On earlier visits to Cuba, I had felt sublime elation the entire time I was there. Havana still satisfied my soul, but this time around the island seemed to have lost much of its magic. At first I thought I was becoming blasé about its unique enchantments, its genuine uplifting achievements. Then I realized I had seen through *el manto*—the mystical, otherworldly enigmas, the deception that Castro uses in pursuit of his cause. Having figured out the *rompecabezas*, I now felt like Mark Twain, for whom the Mississippi River lost its captivation once he acquired the knowledge needed to pilot his way through its shoals.

It wasn't simply a matter of Castro's niggardly-altruistic duality, or the oppressive limitations on an individual's freedom to live the life he or she chose. For all the wonderful care it provided for the aged and the indigent, the Cuban state was also robbing its own—requiring, for example, that Cuba's foreign hotel partners pay the government $450 monthly for each Cuban worker, who saw none of it; instead, they received worthless pesos from the state. I met a model who received five bottles of rum in lieu of a monthly salary, and a destitute elderly couple forced to sell the family gold and silver to the Cuban government for a fraction of its true worth. Another friend, refusing the state's paltry offer for a treasured family heirloom worth many thousands, had been threatened with its confiscation; the work of art, claimed the corrupt city official, belonged to Cuba's patrimony. Some Cubans saw these indignities as necessary sacrifices on behalf of the Revolution. Most expressed deepening bitterness; their idealism seemed betrayed by power, corruption, and lies.

The counterpoints struck me more forcefully than three years prior. Tourists in flashy rental cars—I drove a 1999 Audi A4—zipped past ox carts and creaky yanqui *cacharros* trundling along rural roads formerly devoid of traffic. A national bus service—Víazul—had inaugurated service, guaranteeing tourists with dollars prompt service islandwide aboard gleaming new Volvo buses. Cuba's first championship golf course had opened, and more were being built.

Dozens of deluxe resort hotels had sprung up along the north coast. Run on an all-inclusive basis, they catered to package-vacation tourists who had virtually no contact with Cubans. Varadero and Cayo Coco remained off limits to island residents. Even the beach at the Bay of Pigs was now restricted to foreigners, as were the stunning beaches of Cayo Largo, which operated as a nudist resort.

The antiseptic resorts were boring, and the Cuban government's suppression of sexual relations between Cubans and foreigners made them more so. The once-prevalent Italian males had forsaken Varadero and Playas del Este, where *casas particulares* had been banned and zealous police were a ubiquitous presence. Elsewhere private room rentals had boomed, though the government had begun to regulate the comings and goings of guests, and MININT officials actively policed for transgressions. Everywhere Cuban women, deprived of the yeast of their buoyant hopes, were scared to be seen with foreign boyfriends. "We can't even walk through the square hand in hand," I was told by a ginger-topped Englishman whose forays to visit his long-term girlfriend in Santa Clara were now sadly curtailed. "The police harass us. We just sit on the wall by the railway station." In Cienfuegos, even Cuban males hesitated to engage me in public.

One night in Trinidad I listened to traditional music in the Casa de la Trova while working the scene with my camera. A Cuban couple—man and wife—asked me to snap a memento, then scribbled their names and address so I could mail them the photo. Two pretty females did the same. I paid my bill and moved on. Realizing I had left something behind, I returned. To my horror, two secret-police agents were pulling the foursome out of the audience. I hung back in the shadows, unsure whether to intervene. A white Lada pulled up in the cobbled plaza; the four innocents were pushed inside and whisked away for interrogation. Next day, I was tailed as I walked through the streets.

Cuba, police state, was more apparent.

The vast majority of Cubans clung to their dignity and generosity, found pleasure in unlikely outlets, and enjoyed happy times with their families undeterred by—or perhaps because of—their spartan living conditions and a government that continued to control all but the most intimate aspects of people's lives. Still, twice Cuban youths gave me the finger as I drove past, suggesting a budding resentment toward tourists. The government was losing the battle for the minds of Cuba's exemplary youth—losing it not to ideology, but to the lure of Nikes, Calvin Klein, and music videos. "We used to live in a glass bowl, sanitary and pure," said Castro. "And now we're surrounded by viruses, the bacteria of alienation and egoism that the capitalist system creates."

Osmany Cienfuegos had fallen from grace, it was said, for his part in a sex-tour scandal. Don Pedro had died, and his *bohío* had been expanded and turned into a charmless motel. Punta Maisí had been declared a military zone and was now off limits. Signs had gone up prohibiting photography of the devastated land around Moa. And the fabulous piste east of Marea del Portillo had been paved.

Thankfully, Cayo Sabinal remained as lonesome and lovely as I remembered, but Trinidad—where my landlady Isabel had recently been fined $1,500 for the most spurious and inconsequential infraction—was now crawling with tourists. So too Santiago, magnetically beset by Italian males like iron filings; though the jineteros were much diminished, their female counterparts still operated here, uniquely, with cautious yet unrestrained freedom.

In Holguín, I rented a 1920 Baldwin antique steam train and careered ahead of it in my Audi to photograph it as it thundered, puffing mightily, down the narrow tracks.

In Remedios, I dodged rockets and spiraling pinwheels in the mayhem of the year-end *parranda*, in which macho, rum-sozzled males from the two sides of town battled it out with homemade fireworks and mortars.

And I finally made it to Finca Manacas, at Birán, where Fidel Castro was born on August 13, 1926 in a handsome two-story home tucked within a copse and looking west over a serene lake surrounded by pasture and canefields. "The house was made of wood," Castro told Brazilian theologian Frey Beto in *Fidel: My Early Years*, giving the impression of a primitive property. "No mortar, cement or bricks." In truth, it's a surprisingly substantial house: the home of a well-to-do rural patriarch. Barbed wire surrounded the unmarked *finca*, and the gates were padlocked. By pulling aside a gate some distance away, however, I reached a good vantage point in the midst of a cattle pasture; there, with the aid of a telephoto lens, I snapped a few shots of Fidel's birthplace gilded in late afternoon light before slamming the car in reverse and roaring off.

Back in Havana, I met with Philip Agee, the ex-CIA agent who had exposed purported CIA operatives and catalogued a litany of CIA misdeeds in his 1975 book *Inside the Company: CIA Diary*. Accused of jeopardizing national security, Agee had fled the States and resurfaced in Hamburg. He had recently settled in Havana. U.S. intelligence officials charge that Agee has been on the payroll of Cuban intelligence since the early 1970s—a claim supported, apparently, by a senior Cuban intelligence officer who defected in 1992.

We talked in his apartment-office in an exhausted high rise on Calle E, in Vedado. Agee's spacious abode had been remodeled and fitted out with modern accoutrements, including banks of computer terminals. He had just launched a website—the first U.S.-owned business in Cuba in 40 years, he claimed—in partnership with the state tourism body, Cubatur, aimed at American travelers wishing to visit Cuba.

Agee, a slight, chain-smoking figure, seemed to cling uncertainly to the leftist argot he had adopted after he soured on his homeland. He appeared naive, out of touch with the street.

"Why do foreign journalists keep reporting about drugs in Havana?" he demanded. "Have you ever been asked if you wanted to buy drugs?"

"Yes," I replied. "Several times."

I couldn't quite figure him out. He asked about my involvement with the Cuban government and briefly came alive when I let word slip about my interactions with MININT officers. "Who?" he asked, leaning forward with his hands cupped behind his ears. I nearly had to shout when repeating my reference. As I rose from his black leather sofa and departed, I wondered if our conversation had been recorded.

Meanwhile, my friend David married a Cuban woman he had met during his visit to Havana; they are now the happy parents of a baby girl.

Rolf sent a newspaper clipping: The *Kalevala* had sunk on a crossing to Cuba, and Rolf and an unlucky passenger had barely survived after clinging to life jackets for more than 24 hours.

Lydia and I met again at Coppelia, which had created a charmless dollars-only section for Westerners charging a dollar per scoop.

Yudenia, who had stirred the Humbert Humbert within me, wrote several times asking for money and repeating that she was waiting for me to return and marry her; we finally met again in Camagüey, but there was nothing more than hot air in our fantasies.

Daisy finally wrote me from Italy. Despite difficulties with her in-laws, she seemed happy in her new life. She was training to be a counselor for geriatrics and the disabled. She signed off: "Your friend, always."

ACKNOWLEDGMENTS

Around the time I completed the first draft of *Mi Moto Fidel,* the National Geographic Society announced the launch of its Adventure Press imprint. When editor Elizabeth Newhouse attended one of my presentations on Cuba in Washington, D.C., the die was cast. I am therefore first and foremost indebted to Newhouse and to the staff of the National Geographic Society, including designers Suez Kehl and Melissa Farris, all of whom worked with exemplary speed and professionalism. The opportunity to feature some of my color photography was a cherished bonus, and thanks for that go to National Geographic illustration editors Annie Belt and John Agnone. Special thanks also to John Paine for a matchless edit, and to Tim Barrall for his outstanding cover.

I am also obliged to Tom Miller, author of *Trading with the Enemy: A Yankee Travels Through Castro's Cuba,* who lent valued advice and support and became a friend along the way.

I am especially grateful to Sandra Levinson of the Center for Cuban Studies in New York and Medea Benjamin of Global Exchange in San Francisco, who were extremely helpful in providing valuable perspectives and introductions in Cuba.

My gratitude also goes to my special friends Jim and Ginny Craven, Roger Oyama, Sheri Powers, and David Wardle, as well as to Melissa Daar, Gail Dolbin, Court Fisher, Vicente Franco, David Garten, Adolf Hungry Wolf, Jane Jordan Brown, Michael Krinsky, Adam Kufeld, Claes Eric Jarneberg, Marael Johnson, Ciaran McGowan, Vinnie Mandzak, Ralph Martell, Skip Mascorro, Chris Mattison, Abe Moore, Doug Scott, Ted Simon, Wayne Smith, Veronica Stoddart, Nancy Stout, Ben Treuhaft, John Young, and all my other friends and acquaintances who lent their encouragement and support.

In Cuba, I am indebted to Juan Carlos Aguilar Caballo, Yudenia Beltrán Torres, Damaris Bencomo Nay, Cisne Calixto García, Lester Campa, Jorge Coalla Potts and his family, Manuel Estefanía Seaone, Raúl Durruthy, Tomás

Gutiérrez Alea, Pedro Hope, Marta Ibarra, Dulce María, Yanet Morales Martínez, Lourdes Mulhen Duarte, Juana Reyes Sánchez, Marta Rojas, and to numerous others who, whether mentioned in this book or otherwise, deserve credit. Alas, many must remain anonymous. I also acknowledge Osmany Cienfuegos, former Minister of Tourism, Raúl Colominas of MINREX, and Juan Pardo of Publicitur, for their stated willingness to support my journey.

An especially deep and affectionate thank you goes to Daisy Frometa Bartolomé and her mother, Alicia, and to Mercedes Martínez Crespo. Words cannot express the appreciation I feel for their love and support.

My deepest gratitude goes to the many Cubans who contributed in their own unique ways to assisting my journey; aided in sparking the insights described in this book; helped in the discovery of myself; and inspired awe for their lessons in generosity, courtesy, and human acceptance.

Certain readers may be angered by my political take on Cuba or by my sexual indulgences. To the latter charge, I make no apologies: I was a single male on a motorcycle, loose on a libertine isle. To the former, I sincerely regret any offense caused by my commentary or analysis. My intent was merely to report as accurately and honestly as possible on an extremely complex and controversial country, and to do so in a respectful and sensitive manner. I had no political agenda. Instead, I have striven to express some painful truths, balancing them with praise for a system and a political leader whose many accomplishments are exemplary and profound.

ABOUT THE AUTHOR

⁓

Christopher P. Baker is the author of *Cuba* and *Costa Rica* in the National Geographic Traveler guidebook series, as well as acclaimed guides to Cuba, Havana, Costa Rica, Jamaica, and the Bahamas. A four-time winner of the Lowell Thomas Travel Journalism Award, Baker has contributed to such periodicals as *National Geographic Traveler*, *Newsweek*, *Islands*, *Elle*, and the *Los Angeles Times*. Born and raised in Yorkshire, England, he now lives and rides in Oakland, California.